The Censorial System of Ming China

Stanford Studies in the Civilizations of Eastern Asia

Editors

Arthur F. Wright   Thomas C. Smith
John D. Goheen   Mary Clabaugh Wright
Robert H. Brower

Charles O. Hucker

The Censorial System of Ming China

Stanford University Press, Stanford, California 1966

Stanford University Press
Stanford, California
© 1966 by the Board of Trustees of the
Leland Stanford Junior University
Printed in the United States of America
L.C. 66-10916

Preface

My reasons for undertaking this work are for the most part suggested in the beginning pages of Chapter 1. Since it has been done single-handedly, I accept full responsibility for the way it has been done. However, I am indebted to E. A. Kracke, Jr., of the University of Chicago, for guidance in early stages of the work; and I am grateful for my wife's forbearance as the work stretched out over more than a decade. I also owe something to all those colleagues in the Chinese studies field who have so persistently inquired, after accepting my congratulations on *their* publications, "And how is *your* book coming?" Such reminders must be what preface-writers usually refer to as "the constant encouragement of my professional colleagues." Without them I confess I might not have found the will to persevere in the work despite all sorts of distractions, and I suppose I can now be grateful for them.

C. O. H.

January 1966

Contents

viii

Contents

Major Epochs of Chinese History

1766? – 1122?	SHANG DYNASTY
1122? – 256	CHOU DYNASTY [Feudalism; major philosophical systems]
221 – 207	CH'IN DYNASTY [Legalist dominated; emergence of centralized state]
202 – A.D. 9	FORMER HAN DYNASTY [Imperial Confucianism; emergence of scholar-bureaucracy]

A.D.

25 – 220	LATER HAN DYNASTY
220 – 589	Era of political division
581 – 618	SUI DYNASTY [Political reunification]
618 – 907	T'ANG DYNASTY [Ascendancy of civil-service bureaucrats]
960 – 1279	SUNG DYNASTY
1260 – 1368	YÜAN DYNASTY [Mongol dominance]
1368 – 1644	MING DYNASTY
1644 – 1912	CH'ING DYNASTY [Manchu dominance]

Chapter one

The Censorial Heritage in China

INTRODUCTION

This book attempts to explain the nature and workings of an important part of the governmental system of Imperial China, one that had its beginnings in the third century before Christ and survived until our own century. I hope to contribute substantially to the general effort of Chinese studies specialists to understand the traditional governmental system as a whole and to grasp its relevance to both traditional and modern Chinese history. I also hope that my work will hold some interest for all scholars concerned with organization theory, administrative theory, decision-making processes, comparative government, and political theory in general.

My subject is that complex amalgam of formal institutions and functional procedures which Western observers of China call "censorship," and which I shall most commonly refer to as "the censorial system." The system involves what modern political scientists call "control"; and it almost equally suggests such familiar terms as "inspection," "surveillance," "supervision," "censure," and "discipline." Westerners have derived the term "censorship" from a misleading analogy with the censors of republican Rome. One could just as misleadingly point out resemblances between the Chinese censors and the ephors of ancient Sparta, the missi dominici of Charlemagne, the fiscals of Frederick the Great and Peter the Great, the inspectors-general of Napoleon, the ombudsmen of modern Sweden, or even the party commissars of some modern totalitarian states.

In the contemporary United States, many intragovernmental controls have elements in common with China's censorial system. These include the controls that Congress exercises over the executive branch through impeachments, resolutions, and the activities of investigating committees; the work of the Federal Bureau of Investigation; the Bureau of the Budget's fiscal controls and the work of public accountants; the specialized supervisory functions of such agencies as the Army Inspector General's Department; review of judicial decisions by appellate courts; and the locally exercised rights of recall and referendum. The main similar control outside the government is public opinion focused on government affairs through the press, public demonstrations, political strikes, organized pressure lobbies, and letters from individual citizens to their representatives in government. But making too much of such similarities would be as misleading as the use of the term "censorship" itself.

In general terms, censorship in Imperial China was a formal, systematic institutionalization within the government of three principal functions or roles: (1) the maintenance of surveillance over all governmental activities from outside the normal hierarchy of administrative responsibility; (2) the consequent impeachment, censure, or punishment of civil officials, military officers, and other governmental personnel for violations of prescribed or customary norms of conduct, private as well as public; and (3) the initiation or transmission of recommendations, and in some instances the direct issuance of orders, that current governmental policies, practices, or personnel be changed, the recommendations often including direct or indirect remonstrances about the conduct and decisions of the ruler himself. The system comprised several types and levels of specialized censorial agencies, each staffed with members of the regularly recruited civil officialdom on short-tenure appointments between assignments to other types of governmental work. The ultimate purpose of all their activities was, in the Chinese phrase, "to rectify administration."

In other words, the censorial system was an elaborately organized and highly systemized effort by the government to police itself. It was intended to discover all violations of public policy, administrative regulations, and operational orders; thereby to purge the government of incompetence and malfeasance; and consequently to help maintain a governmental tone that accorded as closely as possible with the Chinese ideal. The system was considered an essential buttress in the structure that Westerners like to call "the Confucian state system."

Virtually every Western observer or historian of traditional China has taken note of the censorial system and its importance in state affairs. The great Jesuit Matteo Ricci (1552–1610), the first modern European to live in and write extensively about China, called the

Chinese censorial officials "keepers of the public conscience" who "inform the King as often as they see fit of any infraction of the law in any part of the entire kingdom." He added with admiration, "they do their duty so thoroughly that they are a source of wonder to outsiders and a good example for imitation. Neither King nor magistrates can escape their courage and frankness, and . . . they will never desist from their admonitions and criticism until some remedy has been applied to the public evil against which they are inveighing."[1] The modern historian K. S. Latourette, judging that "in spite of its defects the [Chinese] political structure which so largely disappeared in the first three decades of the twentieth century was among the most remarkable and successful ever devised by man," has emphasized that the censorial system was "uniquely characteristic of China."[2] One contemporary authority on the history of the traditional Chinese state, E. A. Kracke, Jr., has suggested that "the longevity of China's political system must be credited in significant degree to the power and vigilance of the Censorate."[3] Among the Chinese themselves, the long prevailing attitude toward the censorial system is well represented in a comment by the great emperor Ming T'ai-tsu (reigned 1368–98): "There are three supreme national institutions. The Secretariat is in general control of administrative matters, the Military Command is in charge of the armies, and the Censorate is in charge of surveillance. The dynastic principles all depend upon these, and the Censorate's surveillance duties are of most particular importance."[4]

It is not surprising, therefore, that modern Chinese and foreign scholars alike have attempted general histories of the traditional censorial system.[5] All they have been able to do, however, is provide superficial chronicles of changes in the system's organizational structure. In large part this is because, for the earlier periods of Chinese history, source materials that could contribute to more meaningful analyses of actual censorial operations do not exist, and for the later periods they are too voluminous to be manageable in their totality. Concentrating on seemingly more manageable single-dynasty eras, the Chinese scholars Yü Teng and T'ang Chi-ho have studied, respectively, the censorial systems of the Ming (1368–1644) and Ch'ing (1644–1912) dynasties;[6] and the Western-trained Chinese scholars Edgar Cha Tang (in the United States) and Li Hsiung-fei (in France) have both produced dissertations on the censorial system of the Ch'ing dynasty.[7] But even the single-dynasty scope of their efforts has proved unmanageable. They have successfully summarized regulations concerning structural organization, personnel procedures, and prescribed functions of the censorial system; but in attempting to analyze actual operations of the system they have had to rely on secondary materials that are much too general and random in their selections of data to provide a basis for reliable evaluations.[8] The European scholar Eugene Feifel, without presuming to grapple with the censorial system as a whole, has provided a useful study of the censorial career of Po Chü-i, a famous poet-official of the T'ang dynasty (618–907), including full translations of some of his memorials to the throne.[9] But such work is necessarily too particular to be used as a basis for any general evaluation of the system.

In short, existing studies of the Chinese censorial system are inadequate. They do not answer questions modern scholars ask about the system, nor do they resolve the conflicting common interpretations of it, which range from extravagant claims that it was by nature a democratic restraint upon the ruler's despotic inclinations to equally extravagant denunciations of the system as a ruler's tool for terrorizing his servants and subjects. The present work is intended to help clarify the situation.

What is attempted here is another single-dynasty study, focusing on the Ming period (1368–1644). It differs from prior attempts of this sort in several ways. Although it incorporates thorough descriptions of the organizational structure and the prescribed duties of the censorial agencies and officials, it gives primary emphasis to what censorial officials actually did in practice, seen in relation to the total governmental and historical context in which they found themselves. Furthermore, an effort is made to take full account of all kinds of censorial activities, not merely of those that were dramatic enough or curious enough to be selected for attention in secondary compilations. It is this effort to be comprehensive that has prompted me to focus on the Ming dynasty, since that is the earliest dynasty for which we still have a complete day-by-day court chronicle of the sort called *Shih-lu* or "True Records," the most inclusive of all compilations of political documents in the Chinese tradition. At the same time, the effort to take into account all types of censorial activities in relation to their institutional and political context has required use of some systematic sampling procedure. Coverage of the whole Ming period in depth would demand a lifetime of work, and in any event the volume of data it would accumulate might well prove too great for manageable analysis. To come to grips with the routine details of Ming censorial operations, the study therefore focuses on two short, contrasting periods in the dynasty: (1) the decade 1424–34, encompassing the reigns of Jen-tsung and Hsüan-tsung, a notable early Ming era of peace and governmental stability; and (2) the seven-year period 1620–27, the reign of Hsi-tsung, a late Ming era of great political turbulence. Thus, descriptions of the structural arrangements, personnel regulations, and prescribed duties of the censorial agencies relate to the whole 277-year expanse of the Ming dynasty. But detailed analyses of what censorial officials actually did, which illustrate and give life to the all-Ming generalizations, are derived only from the two periods 1424–34 and 1620–27.

I cannot claim that the two eras chosen for analysis are in any sense typical of the whole Ming dynasty, though they may well be, respectively, the best of times and the worst of times as regards the functioning of the Ming governmental system. Similarly, I cannot suggest that the Ming dynasty as a whole is in any sense typical of the long history of the traditional Chinese state, though it is a dynasty in which the censorial system undoubtedly reached a high point of organizational complexity and political prominence. What I offer, therefore, is a case study of the censorial system in only one stage of its long history, with analyses of samplings of the relevant data. A comprehensive analytical history of the system unfortunately must await the preliminary production of many more comparable case studies.

The Ming censorial agencies and activities discussed in detail in the succeeding chapters cannot be understood in isolation. They had both ideological and institutional roots stretching back to antiquity. To be fully understood and appreciated, therefore, the practice of censorship in Ming times must be seen in the context of China's long censorial heritage, from which Ming censorial officials drew their inspirations and precedents and in reference to which they were judged by their contemporaries.

THE IDEOLOGICAL BASIS OF CENSORSHIP

Part of the distinctive Chinese style or mode of life is a penchant for self-evaluation, a compulsion to examine, rationalize, and justify one's actions. Both of the indigenous systems of thought that have principally shaped and reflected China's national character, Confucianism and Taoism, have stressed the reflective aspect of the good life, and Confucius himself is reported to have stated its main principle: "If a man does not continually ask himself 'What am I to do about this, what am I to do about this?' there is no possibility of my doing anything about him."[10] Even today the Chinese habitually speak in a kind of rationalizing, dialectical monologue: "I do not want to sell the pig today. Why do I not want to sell the pig today? Because today," etc. It is therefore not out of character for the Chinese to develop a highly institutionalized form of governmental self-evaluation.

Sanctions for the two most prominent modes of censorial action, impeachment and remonstrance, are specifically to be found in the two ancient schools of thought that most directly influenced the traditional governmental system.[11] Individualistic, anti-authoritarian Taoism is not one of these. One is of course Confucianism, the heavily moralistic code of "the gentleman," with a pre-eminent emphasis on paternalism in government and other forms of social duty. The other is Legalism, a Machiavellian code for working bureaucrats which is dedicated to the welfare of the state rather than to the state-promoted welfare of the people. Both the early Confucians and the early Legalists advocated criticism in government, and a well-established right to criticize was essential to censorial impeachment and remonstrance.

It is clearly Legalism rather than Confucianism that sanctions the censorial function of impeachment. Confucius and his followers trusted to the virtuous example of the ruler to maintain morality and morale in the administration, and they seemed to feel that once a good man had been put in office he should suffer no constraints other than those imposed by his own conscience. Moreover, the Confucians did not condone informers. "The gentleman," in Confucius's definition, "calls attention to the good points in others; he does not call attention to their defects. The small man does just the reverse of this."[12] And Confucius' great early follower Mencius had plain contempt for informers: "What future misery have they and ought they to endure," he exclaimed, "who talk of what is not good in others!"[13] The Legalists, on the other hand, trusted neither the ruler's example nor the individual conscience. They trusted only to codified laws and regulations, enforced by ruthless surveillance on the part of state-rewarded informers. The great thirteenth-century Mongol emperor Kublai Khan once said of his three top-level governmental organs in China that "the Secretariat is my left hand, the Bureau of Military Affairs is my right hand, and the Censorate is the means for my keeping both hands healthy."[14] This is precisely the essentially Legalist concept that sanctioned censorial impeachment throughout Chinese history. It naturally appealed to many efficiency-minded rulers and ministers.

Remonstrance, on the other hand, finds its clearest sanction in classical Confucian doctrines. Pre-Confucian records abound in examples of ministers who doggedly remonstrated with rulers, often at great cost to themselves. The early Confucian thinkers, always interested in imposing their own notions of good government on the rulers of their time, modeled themselves after these ministers. Confucius often rebuked the powerful to their faces, and Mencius frequently said such bold things that rulers "changed countenance" or hastily changed the subject. Through their own conduct Confucius and Mencius thus became examples to be emulated by later remonstrators. Moreover, their expressed principles made remonstrance more a loyal duty than a right. When asked by a disciple how a prince should be served, Confucius said, "Do not deceive him, but when necessary withstand him to his face."[15] He is also reported to have said that "for one whose place is near the throne, not to remonstrate is to hold his office idly for the sake of gain."[16] Even parents, to whom a good Confucian owed supreme loyalty, were not to be exempted from remonstrance. We are told that when a disciple asked if filial piety meant for the son to obey his father's orders Confucius cried out, "How can you say this! How can you say this! . . . When confronted with unrighteousness, the son cannot but remonstrate with his father and the minister cannot but remonstrate with his ruler. Therefore, when confronted with unrighteousness, remonstrate against it! How could merely obeying the father's orders be considered filial piety?"[17] So strong was the Confucian insistence on remonstrance that Chinese rulers throughout history actually called upon their officials to remonstrate with them, and did so consistently. The Legalist view of kingship, on the other hand, had no place for the moralistic criticism of rulers that classical Confucianism advocates, though the early Legalist thinkers did warn rulers about the dangers of not heeding advice, and instructed officials in the art of "persuading" rulers without threat to themselves.[18]

Confucius and Mencius, and the early Legalist thinkers as well, lived in a time when China was divided among competing feudal lords. When their remonstrances were ignored, or when they felt that the moral Way did not prevail, Confucius and Mencius were free to leave one lord's court and wander to another in search of a more congenial atmosphere. In the last centuries of the feudal age, the competition between regional states was so keen that a renowned adviser could get a hearing and a substantial emolument almost anywhere, and this circumstance naturally emboldened such men as Mencius to speak very frankly to their temporary patrons, in a spirit of independence and detachment. However, after China was brought under one rule in the third century B.C., the adviser found himself in a much less enviable position. He might remonstrate, and if his remonstrances went unheeded or if his principles were consistently compromised he might indeed withdraw from service. But there was no escaping the state; there was only one governmental structure. The adviser had the choice of giving loyal service to a ruler whom he might not trust, or of abandoning entirely the sense of political responsibility that is imbedded in the whole Confucian ideology.

Faced with this choice, some frustrated Confucians did abandon bureaucratic careers in favor of the anchorite self-cultivation that had always been advocated by China's anti-government Taoist thinkers.[19] Other Confucians resolutely upheld the traditional ideal of political service by remonstrating fearlessly, at the risk of disgrace and perhaps death for themselves and their families. The typical Confucian adviser of imperial times, however, was neither a do-or-die moralist nor a resigned hermit, but a practicing bureaucrat. By being prudently subservient to his ruler in much the way Legalism had prescribed, he kept himself alive and prospering, and hence able to provide the filial service to his parents that classical Confucianism demanded. Nevertheless, his subservience was so modified by moralistic considerations that he was hardly an ideal Legalist minister and at times brought disgrace and hardship upon his family, contravening a basic Confucian principle.

All these considerations were never far from the conscious thoughts of Chinese officials of Ming times. All officials, in the course of their administrative routines, regularly evaluated their subordinates and remonstrated with their superiors. In reference to matters within his administrative jurisdiction, any official might submit to the throne impeachments of his associates or policy recommendations; and the highest-ranking officials naturally advised and remonstrated with emperors about governmental affairs of every sort. For that matter, even a common citizen could feel free in Ming times to submit directly to the throne a denunciation of any official or a complaint or recommendation about any policy, if he could convincingly demonstrate that the matter in hand significantly affected the national interest. And anyone among the educated classes might be just as zealous as any censorial official in bombarding the throne with memorials in defense of the Confucian heritage.

The censorial agencies, in other words, did not monopolize control techniques in the Ming governmental system, and a study of their activities cannot exhaust all the control possibilities that existed in the system. But the censorial agencies specialized in control techniques as no other agencies did. Whereas other officials might exercise the right of criticism and might even feel a moral obligation to criticize, the censorial officials alone had the prescribed legal duty of criticizing. It is this institutionalization of control techniques outside regular administrative channels that gives the Chinese censorial system its special character and made censorial officials the particularly designated, self-conscious "avenues of criticism."

THE INSTITUTIONALIZATION OF CENSORSHIP

Three kinds of agencies constituted the specialized censorial hierarchy in Ming times: a Chief Surveillance Office or Censorate proper, based at the national capital; thirteen Provincial Surveillance Offices, one in each province of the empire; and a cluster of six coordinate Offices of Scrutiny, based, like the Censorate, at the national capital. Using the traditional techniques of surveillance officials (*ch'a-kuan*, those who investigate and impeach) and speaking officials (*yen-kuan*, those who counsel and remonstrate), they covered the whole governmental establishment with a net of remarkably systematic controls.

Each agency had a prescribed sphere of jurisdiction and a prescribed functional specialty. The metropolitan Censorate, which had the broadest scope of activity, maintained empire-wide surveillance over all government operations, and its officials, who were both surveillance and speaking officials, submitted both impeachments and recommendations. Provincial Surveillance Offices maintained similar, but more intensive, surveillance over governmental operations within their respective provinces. Their officials characteristically submitted impeachments but not recommendations. The Offices of Scrutiny characteristically restricted their activities to the capital. Their personnel specially scrutinized and controlled the documents sent to and from the throne, and though they were principally speaking officials, they also submitted both impeachments and recommendations, as did members of the Censorate.*

Each of these censorial agencies was heir to a long institutional

---

* Throughout this book the term "censor" is used only in reference to officials of the Censorate. "Surveillance officials" includes both censors and officials of such agencies as the Ming Provincial Surveillance Offices. "Speaking officials" includes supervising secretaries of the Ming Offices of Scrutiny and all their prototypes, such as remonstrators, reminders, omissioners, etc. "Censorial officials" includes both surveillance officials and speaking officials, not censors alone, just as the term "censorial system" refers to all surveillance and remonstrance activities and not to the Censorate alone.

past, and the techniques that each used were in large part justified by precedent.[20]

Institutional Background of the Ming Censorate

The institutional character of government in China's earliest antiquity is still very poorly understood, so that an attempt to trace any censorial agency back to its ultimate origins would be futile. But it is noteworthy, perhaps, that the title *yü-shih,* traditionally used to identify surveillance officials of the Censorate proper, probably had longer continuous use as a ministerial title than any other in any language. The term appears as a title in oracle-bone inscriptions of the Shang dynasty (1766?–1122? B.C.) and was used thereafter until A.D. 1912.[21] The basic element, *shih,* was originally the Shang term for a tally-holding archery scorekeeper, and from an early time it undoubtedly had the sense of "recorder" that was its standard meaning throughout imperial times.[22] The modifying element, *yü,* can apparently also be understood in its later sense of "royal" or "imperial." During the Chou dynasty (1122?–256 B.C.) the title "royal recorder" was one of several in use ("grand recorder," "junior recorder," "inner recorder," "outer recorder," etc.) for feudal-age officials who hereditarily performed semireligious functions at court and evolved before the third century B.C. into choniclers of court events.[23] Although the term *yü-shih* has been called one of several "authentic titles for historians among the oracle-bone inscriptions,"[24] and although the Chou dynasty *shih* in general has been typified as a "stern recorder of the ruler's deeds and censor of his actions,"[25] we in fact have very little information about the functions with which the terms were associated in either Shang or Chou times, and there is certainly no evidence that the office of any *shih* at these times represented an institutionalization of specialized censorial techniques.

Institutionalized censorship appeared, concurrently with other lasting characteristics of the imperial state system, when one regional state destroyed the decentralized feudal system in 221 B.C. and established the centralized, bureaucratic Ch'in dynasty (221–207 B.C.). Then, as later, the state administrative staff consisted basically of two personnel services, a civil service and a military service; both were made up of what might be called "commissioned officers" appointed by and responsible to the emperor, who were assisted by "noncommissioned" functionaries recruited in less formal ways and having much less status and authority. During the centuries following the Ch'in, the civil service and the military service came to be more and more clearly differentiated, and long before Ming times the separate services had become thoroughly bureaucratized, with their own distinctive standards of appointment, promotion, and so on. Beginning in Former Han times (202 B.C.–A.D. 9), and to a notable extent in the T'ang dynasty (618–907), heredity as a qualification for office was de-emphasized and the principle of regular selection for office on the basis of merit was introduced, especially in the civil service; so that long before Ming times, public, competitive, written examinations based on the classical Confucian philosophical and historical literature had become the predominant means of recruitment into the civil service, and the civil service had become an almost autonomous, largely self-perpetuating and self-regulating power bloc in the Chinese state system. Moreover, so great was its prestige (largely derived from the general prestige of learning) that before 1368 the civil service had eclipsed the military service in administrative importance. Though dynasty after dynasty naturally depended in the last resort on military strength, China had long accepted what we know as the principle of civilian supremacy over the military. Censorial officials from the beginning were integral members of the civil service and thus shared in that service's steadily increasing bureaucratization and prestige.

From Ch'in times on, imperially appointed officials of both services were in unchallenged control of all governmental functions throughout the empire, from local district magistracies and military commanderies up to the various departments and bureaus of the central government. In both civil and military hierarchies, as China's population grew and government became more sophisticated and complex, the basic units of administration gradually became more numerous and their geographical jurisdictions more restricted. There was an inevitable need for supervisory coordination at an intermediate level between the local districts and the central government, and as early as Han times proto-provincial establishments began to appear. In T'ang (618–907) and Sung (960–1279) times the local districts were subordinated to supervisory prefectures, which were themselves placed under circuit commissions or intendancies. From there it was but a step into the full-scale provincial order of the last dynasties. From their beginning right down to the end of the empire, these intermediary agencies consistently had a censorial or quasi-censorial quality and status.

Likewise, from Ch'in times on, the structure of the central government, though it grew and changed through the dynasties, fell into a stable general pattern that emphasized the censorial functions. The top echelon of the government, directly under the emperor, was always tripartite, including a supreme military establishment, a supreme general-administration establishment, and what we call the Censorate, usually bearing the literal designation Tribunal of Censors (*yü-shih t'ai*). Thus the Han governmental hierarchy was headed by a triumvirate called "the three dukes": a grand marshal, a grand councilor, and a censor-in-chief (*yü-shih ta-fu*). In T'ang and Sung times, the top general-administration establishment previously represented by the Han grand councilor became a several-man grand council, supervising three great administrative organs called the Secretariat, the Chancellery, and the Department of State Affairs; but the Censorate retained its old parallel, autonomous status. By these times, it also had spawned subdivisions: a Court of General Affairs (*t'ai-yüan*) staffed by associate censors (*shih yü-shih*), a Court of Palace Affairs (*tien-yüan*) staffed by palace censors (*tien-chung shih yü-shih*), and a Court of Surveillance (*ch'a-yüan*) staffed by investigating censors (*chien-ch'a yü-shih*). Overall supervision remained in the hands of a censor-in-chief, now usually assisted by two vice censors-in-chief.

Since the Censorate was expected to extend its surveillance over officials throughout the empire, its personnel from the outset were regularly deputed to make inspection tours of areas remote from the capital. Ch'in censors were thus sent out as investigators (*chien-ch'a shih*) to watch over and report on the conduct of local administrators. Such censors-on-commission in Han times, known collectively by the awesome designation "straight-pointing commissioners" (*chih-chih shih*), apparently exercised considerable authority and enjoyed great prestige. In Han times there was also a special corps of circuit inspectors (*tz'u-shih*), who stayed on relatively long-term duty in the local areas supervising work of the regional authorities but were accountable to the Censorate's chief executive. Thereafter, through the T'ang period, censors customarily divided their time between service in the capital and inspection tours in the provinces. And regularly commissioned circuit inspectors of T'ang times (*hsün-an yü-shih,* suggesting "reconnoitering censors") probably spread a finer net of direct Censorate surveillance over the whole empire than had ever existed previously.

One striking facet of the Censorate's early history is an attempt by censors in Sung times to encroach upon the prerogative of remonstrance, which had always been the specialty of the separate "speaking officials." Since its beginning the Censorate's officials had no special right to offer remonstrances or policy recommendations.[26] But early in the Sung period special "speaking censors" (*yen-shih yü-shih*, "censors who speak out about affairs") were established in the Censorate.[27] For a time newly appointed censors were even punished if they failed to submit important policy criticisms within a short time following appointment.[28] But this first Censorate invasion of the remonstrators' preserve was short-lived. In 1084 the offices of speaking censors disappeared and the Censorate's right of remonstrance was apparently no longer recognized. In 1103 the situation was clarified in an imperial edict defining the proper roles of censors and remonstrators:

> The duty of remonstrators is to repair omissions. Whenever the government omits or neglects what is proper, they are entirely permitted to discuss the matters in memorials. . . . If those employed are not the proper men and if in the conduct of affairs there are violations of propriety, they are entirely permitted to submit exhortations so as to make rectifications. The duty of Censorate officials, on the other hand, is to denounce faults and correct errors. Whenever officials are dilatory or offensive, they are entirely permitted to impeach them. . . . If there are failures to observe the law . . . or other matters that ought to be denounced, they are entirely permitted to submit denunciations so as to make rectifications.[29]

Thus the traditional distinctions between "surveillance officials" and "speaking officials" were restored. But a precedent had been established which was to lead to the coalescence of surveillance and remonstrance in the operations of the Ming Censorate.

Institutional Background of the Ming Provincial Surveillance Offices

The Provincial Surveillance Offices of the Ming era grew out of a different institutional tradition than did the Censorate itself, one dating back only into T'ang times; and these agencies from the beginning had a somewhat different character and status than did the Censorate's touring representatives.

With the possible exception of the Han circuit inspectors (*tz'u-shih*), all the early surveillance officials in the regional and local areas were delegates from the metropolitan Censorate. That is, they were temporary visitors in the provinces rather than members of the regular hierarchy of provincial authorities. Moreover, they were characteristically low in the scale of civil service ranks. In Han times, when ranks were scaled in terms of bushels of annual salary grain, even the circuit inspectors had the relatively low rank of 600 bushels, whereas the regional prefects over whom they maintained surveillance had the high rank of 2,000 bushels. After three years of satisfactory service a circuit inspector might be promoted to a prefectship, but while he was a circuit inspector he did not enjoy exalted rank. Similarly, in T'ang times the investigating censors who were commissioned to duty as circuit inspectors had the low rank of 8b on an 18-point scale running from 1a down to 9b, whereas the regional authorities whom they inspected ranked as high as 2b. The inspectors, therefore, were not only outsiders without status in the regular provincial establishments; they were decidedly inferior in rank to many of those whom they inspected.

A prototype of the Ming Provincial Surveillance Offices was introduced in T'ang times with the establishment of permanent surveillance commissioners (*an-ch'a shih,* later called *ts'ai-fang shih* and finally *kuan-ch'a shih*) in each of more than 20 circuits into which the empire was divided.[30] These imperial commissioners were originally delegated by the central government, and they always had titular status in one of the central government agencies; but after 711 they became permanent regular members of the local government establishment, which the Censorate's own inspectors never were. They were no longer outsiders, visitors from metropolitan organs. Moreover, they characteristically had rank in the fifth or higher civil service grades. Unlike the Censorate's inspectors, they therefore resembled administrative superiors in the local government hierarchy, and the surveillance they provided could be more routine and more pervasive.

The Sung dynasty distributed local surveillance responsibilities among several kinds of circuit intendants: fiscal intendants, judicial intendants, military intendants, and intendants of transport and monopolies.[31] Each of these had a limited functional as well as a fixed territorial jurisdiction. Though no one of these intendancies can be singled out as the direct ancestor of the Ming Provincial Surveillance Offices, all seem to have had some censorial as well as administrative functions, and judicial intendants in particular had a mixed role.[32] In any event, the Sung circuit intendants were clearly administrative superiors in the regional hierarchy, more so than even the T'ang surveillance commissioners had been, and they were also more numerous, so that their surveillance net was spread still more finely over the empire.

On the other hand, the multiplication of regional-level surveillance organs was accompanied by a corresponding decrease of direct Censorate surveillance. The Sung Censorate had no counterpart of the T'ang circuit inspectors. Early in the period the Censorate did include positions of touring commissioners (*hsün-shih*), held by nominal palace censors; but there were only two such positions, and even these were abolished in the 1080's. Moreover, only capital offices were within the surveillance jurisdiction of investigating censors. In fact, the sphere of this surveillance jurisdiction was made specific following a censor's plea that the Censorate should be allowed to investigate the functioning of the capital agencies as thoroughly as affairs of the prefectures were investigated by the circuit intendants.

For a very brief time the Sung Censorate's surveillance jurisdiction was indeed extended beyond the capital area. In 1080, after investigating censors had been organized into functionally differentiated Surveillance Sections (*ch'a-an*), a vice censor-in-chief complained that the various circuit intendants were not properly carrying out their duties. He said:

By law, the Censorate should investigate violations and dilatoriness on the part of all officials. If this law is clarified to provide for surveillance of the various circuit intendants, there will be advantages, and the matter is not impracticable. The Surveillance Section for Revenues might maintain surveillance over the fiscal intendants, and the Surveillance Section for Justice might maintain surveillance over the judicial intendants. If this were done, then the inner and outer officials would all diligently perform their duties, and the imperial laws and edicts would not be ignored.[33]

His proposal was accepted. Very soon thereafter the Censorate further requested that several other "outer" or provincial agencies, all apparently of a specialized economic nature, also be assigned to the jurisdiction of the Surveillance Sections. There is no indication that the request was approved.[34] In any event, late in 1082 the emperor changed his mind about the extension of censors' surveillance jurisdiction and proclaimed:

The censors' investigations of official matters in the capital are very numerous. In addition, they have been directed to maintain surveillance over the provinces. Can they possibly manage such duties? Actually, in the light of established custom, this is improper. Censors' surveillance over the various circuit intendants should be terminated. . . . Let it be so ordered.[35]

During a two-year period, then, investigating censors were expected to extend their jurisdiction beyond the capital area, but the situation was clearly exceptional.

Nevertheless, the whole empire was theoretically within the impeachment jurisdiction of the Censorate: Sung censors were repeatedly exhorted to denounce any wayward officials, in or outside the capital, and whenever capital officials returned from tours in the provinces censors were assigned to interrogate them about the conduct of all local authorities with whom they had come into contact, with the aim of submitting impeachments.[36] But there was no really practicable arrangement for extending the Sung Censorate's direct surveillance over the whole empire, as there had been in prior periods.

In Sung times, in other words, censorial surveillance over the officialdom in its totality was not subject to centralized control and direction. Surveillance functions were decentralized, so that the Censorate kept watch over the capital officials and the circuit intendants separately kept watch over the provincial officials. Except during the brief period from 1080 to 1082, the circuit intendants were not subject to any direct investigation by the Censorate, and they were never in any sense provincial representatives of the Censorate. There was no organizational link between the censors and intendants, even of a nominal sort.

This decentralization of censorial surveillance in Sung times reversed a trend that can be clearly seen in earlier periods. The local investigators of Ch'in times and the "straight-pointing commissioners" of Han times were actual members of the Censorate staff, temporarily detached but not separated. The Han circuit inspectors were of a somewhat different character, not being considered quite censors-on-commission; but they were nevertheless under the administrative control of the Censorate's chief executive.

In T'ang times, whereas circuit inspectors were agents of the metropolitan Censorate, the surveillance commissioners were not. But they were frequently given nominal concurrent titles as censors-in-chief or vice censors-in-chief, and in official parlance they were collectively spoken of as an "Outer Censorate" (*wai-t'ai*). In contrast to the Sung situation, therefore, it seems to have been recognized through T'ang times that disciplinary surveillance over the officialdom as a whole was the proper business of the metropolitan Censorate and should—albeit nominally in some instances—be coordinated under its direction.

The Sung dynasty's questioning of the practice of centralizing all censorial surveillance under the direction of the metropolitan Censorate provided a precedent for the gradual movement of the Ming Provincial Surveillance Offices out of the Censorate's orbit and even to a substantial degree out of the censorial sphere, which will be discussed later.

Institutional Background of the Ming Offices of Scrutiny

The function of remonstrance, by its nature, did not lend itself to routinization and institutionalization as well as did the surveillance function. Moreover, the censorial control exercised by the speaking officials was basically different from, though supplementary to, the control over implementation of policy and over bureaucratic conduct that was the special responsibility of the surveillance officials. The job of speaking officials approximated control of policy making. Consequently, they were somewhat like personal attendants of the emperor, and their offices evolved in early times without any relation to the surveillance organs.[37] Through the early centuries of the empire, also, their prestige tended to be greater than that of the surveillance officials.

Traditionally, there were two primary kinds of speaking officials: supervising secretaries (*chi-shih-chung*) ancestral to the personnel of the Ming dynasty's Offices of Scrutiny, and a separate body of remonstrators (collectively called *chien-kuan*). Both kinds of officials originated with the Ch'in dynasty in the third century B.C. At that time and thereafter for many centuries, however, the titles of supervising secretaries and remonstrators were all used only for honorific purposes. They were conferred on dignitaries of the central government in addition to their regular titles, in recognition of their being suitable companions and mentors for the emperor. The honorific status involved no duties other than attending and giving counsel to the emperor when called upon. The fact that the title *chi-shih-chung* literally denotes "palace attendant" emphasizes the functional limitations of these offices.

By the seventh and eighth centuries, in the T'ang era, the speaking offices had become regular components of the civil service bureaucracy like the surveillance offices, and a degree of specialization had appeared among them. All were now subordinate offices in the two great counsel-giving departments of the central government, the Chancellery and the Secretariat. There were 32 remonstrators of various kinds, divided equally between these two departments: 8 grand remonstrators (*chien-i ta-fu*), 12 omissioners (*pu-ch'üeh*, literally those who "fill in gaps"), and 12 reminders (*shih-i*, literally those who "pick up what is forgotten"). All had very similar prescribed duties—to attend the emperor and proffer counsel and admonitions. They thus exercised the speaking officials' traditional control over formulation of policy, and they were held in notably greater public esteem than were officials of the Censorate and other surveillance organs. The great T'ang bureaucrat-poets Po Chü-i and Tu Fu both had distinguished careers in such offices.[38]

Supervising secretaries, on the other hand, had evolved into a new type of censorial official by T'ang times. There were four in the Chancellery (called *chi-shih-chung*) and six more in the Secretariat (called *chung-shu she-jen* or "palace drafters"), and they had the clerkly control over documents sent to and from the throne that was their principal responsibility later, in the Ming era. This control seems to have been directed primarily toward rectifying the form of government documents. However, since the supervising secretaries could also criticize the substance of governmental policies and operations, they did not entirely lose their original role as counselors and admonishers.[39]

It was not until the Sung dynasty (960–1279) that both kinds of speaking officials, now wholly bureaucratized, escaped from their subordinate positions within the Chancellery and Secretariat and gained organizational autonomy similar to that long enjoyed by the Censorate. In Sung times, remonstrators were organized independently in a Bureau of Remonstrance (*chien-yüan*), and supervising secretaries staffed six separate, independent bureaus (*fang*) that were forerunners of the autonomous Offices of Scrutiny of Ming times. Their new organizational status seems to have given the speaking officials even greater prestige and a more influential political role than they had previously enjoyed.[40]

Meantime, however, the speaking officials had undergone several transmutations that subtly altered their role in government. During Han times and the centuries that immediately followed, when the titles of speaking officials were used to augment the dignity of eminent personages, the practice of remonstrance reflected the fact that great semifeudal families still retained a measure of political power that derived from their own independent status rather than from imperial favor. Remonstrators and supervising secretaries, as clansmen of the emperor or spokesmen of great families, were in a position to deal with the emperor almost as equals, and no emperor could lightly ignore their counsel. One might almost consider them a council of peers whose advice and admonitions rested upon a sharing of interests and viewpoints with the ruler. The emperor might dominate them, but he could not contemn or patronize them.

This relationship changed, however, when by T'ang times the speaking officials became regularly established officials of the Chancellery and Secretariat and the officialdom as a whole came to be dominated by civil-service bureaucrats instead of representatives of great families. The government became more autocratic, and a gulf opened between the emperor and his remonstrators, who were now more employees than colleagues. The force of tradition may have lent remonstrance continuing influence, but the transition had necessarily affected both remonstrators, who had to remonstrate with a more self-conscious aggressiveness, and emperors, who had to prepare to see hostility in remonstrance more often than sympathy.

A second transmutation came with the change of status that supervising secretaries experienced in T'ang times. They were still considered speaking officials, but they now found themselves assigned to routine document-control processes, and their absorption in this routine inevitably distracted them somewhat from their ancient role as counselors and remonstrators. Moreover, it tended to draw them into surveillance operations directed against the officialdom. In their document-control activities (*feng-po*, literally "blocking and annulling") T'ang supervising secretaries examined all edicts and decrees being prepared and were able to veto and return for revision whatever they considered unsuitable. Thus their censorial sphere was transferred from policy formulation to policy promulgation. They no longer were intimate attendants in the palace household, and they no longer participated in policy deliberations at the highest level. In addition, they inspected, corrected, and amended memorials and reports from government agencies before they were submitted to the emperor. They also collaborated with censors in considering complaints of official injustices and recommending rectifications. They were now, in short, post facto critics of governmental operations, barely a step removed from the status of surveillance officials.[41]

The organizational autonomy that both remonstrators and supervising secretaries achieved in Sung times seems to have brought about yet another transmutation. The modern historian Ch'ien Mu has suggested that organizational autonomy seriously impaired the proper exercise of the remonstrance function. So long as they were subordinates of the ranking grand councilors or prime ministers, Ch'ien argues, the speaking officials could concentrate on criticizing the emperor because it was in the prime minister's interest for them to do so. Inasmuch as it was their acknowledged duty to remonstrate, the prime minister could use them with impunity to offer criticisms that he might be embarrassed to offer himself. Thus, whereas the independent censors as the "ears and eyes of the emperor" harassed the bureaucratic administration, the speaking officials harassed the emperor as the "lips and tongues of the prime minister" and provided in some measure a check on absolutist inclinations. But when remonstrators gained Censorate-like autonomy, they likewise became direct agents of the emperor and thus aimed their remonstrances at the prime minister rather than at the throne. In this way the prime min-

isters, harassed by both censors and speaking officials busily trying to
live up to their prestigious titles, increasingly found their powers
frustrated and steadily lost prestige; whereas the emperors, having
escaped from the nuisance of institutionalized harassment of this sort,
became increasingly absolutist.[42]

Conclusive judgments on such matters necessarily must await thorough studies of the actual workings of surveillance and remonstrance
in early times; but it is possible to believe that through the Sung
period, while censorial surveillance was becoming a more pervasive
control over bureaucratic performance of duty, censorial remonstrance was steadily becoming a less effective check against despotism.

Functional Aspects of the Censorial Tradition

As regards the functioning of the system, the censorial tradition included four notable elements:

First of all, in comparison to other agencies the censorial agencies
functioned autonomously and enjoyed high prestige.* The Censorate
throughout its history, and the speaking officials beginning in the
Sung period, were not subordinate to any other governmental organs.
That is, they had direct access to the throne, which guaranteed that
they could not be prevented from memorializing by any line administrative officials of either the civil service or the military service. This
was a valuable asset when the censorial officials undertook to impeach
or censure powerful personages or to denounce policies supported by
court favorites. They were, of course, vulnerable to retaliation. They
themselves could be impeached by non-censorial officials for abusing
their privileges. Moreover, since censorial personnel did not constitute a separate personnel corps and were subject to normal promotion and demotion procedures of the general civil service, their enemies in other agencies eventually had some opportunities to harm or

---

* It would be wrong to suggest that the Censorate or any other censorial agencies
or officials enjoyed genuine independence of the throne. The imperial Chinese
state system did not provide for modern, Western-style separation of powers. All
legitimate power derived from the emperor, who as Son of Heaven assumed for
himself the sole right to make any final governmental decision, however petty.
Although at times, as in the T'ang dynasty, orders from the throne were not considered binding unless countersigned by designated members of the officialdom,
and although in general practice high-ranking officials by their erudition and expertise often cowed emperors into tolerating their usurpations of imperial prerogatives, no official really had any powers that were not explicitly or implicitly delegated from and subject to withdrawal by the emperor. Like all other officials,
therefore, the censorial officials had to rely upon their powers of persuasion in
dealing with the throne.

even wreck careers of individual censorial officials. But the censorial agencies could not easily be wholly silenced or otherwise intimidated.

There were two major justifications for this censorial autonomy. As the early Legalist thinkers clearly foresaw, it was essential from the emperor's point of view that "avenues of criticism" be kept open to ensure that information provided by the line administrative officials was reliable and thus to prevent the ruler's being made the dupe of any one minister or clique.[43] Secondly, the people seem to have trusted the censorial officials to transmit their grievances about local conditions and local authorities to the throne. The non-censorial officials seem to have been the only group that might have been glad to see censorial powers circumscribed. But in fact it was the officials who complained most loudly at attempts to tamper with the "avenues of criticism." For from a very early time the censorial agencies seem to have gained the reputation of being fearless defenders of the unwritten constitution upon which the state system and the Chinese way of life were based. In consequence, there was no other group in the officialdom that had comparable prestige. One great statesman of the Sung dynasty reported that in the eleventh century the prestige of the Censorate and the Bureau of Remonstrance was so great that people ridiculed the grand councilors for being merely their errand-boys.[44]

The second noteworthy element in the function of the censorial system is the degree of independence enjoyed by almost every censorial official. This freedom of action derived from the traditional right of an individual to submit memorials directly to the throne, without consulting with his administrative superiors. How early this tradition emerged is not clear, but it was an established aspect of censorship by the early years of the T'ang era. We know this because the privilege was dramatically withdrawn from Censorate personnel in the year 726. Thereafter censors were required to submit impeachments "through channels"—that is, in consultation with both the vice censor-in-chief and the censor-in-chief. Moreover, their impeachments passed through routine document-control processes in the Chancellery and Secretariat. The imposition of such "clearance" requirements naturally caused a severe drop in the status and prestige of censors.[45] And it was not until the eleventh century, under the Sung dynasty, that the restrictions were removed.[46] Thereafter censors' impeachments went directly to the throne as in the years before 726. I know of no evidence that the right of speaking officials to memorialize directly was ever tampered with in comparable fashion.

The individual censor's independence of action also derived in part from a traditional right to impeach an official on hearsay evidence. Impeachments of this sort began with the conventional phrase, *feng-wen* ("I have heard a rumor that").[47] This privilege, which somewhat offset the perennial natural limitations on direct surveillance and the narrower limitations imposed in Sung times, was particularly valued because it enabled censors to conceal and protect their sources of information.[48]

But censorial independence was not unlimited. The censorial officials of various sorts did belong to agencies, and these agencies had internal hierarchical structures. For example, the censor-in-chief was recognized as the administrative superior of all personnel in the Censorate. He therefore exercised certain controls over the censors. He assigned them to specific tasks, sent them out on or nominated them for commissions as touring inspectors in the provinces, and gave them periodic merit ratings which influenced their subsequent careers. In other words, censors as individuals were subject to some centralized direction and control within the Censorate itself. Presumably there was similar intra-agency control over speaking officials as well, but the available evidence suggests that such constraints were substantially fewer than the controls over surveillance officials.

In general, the censorial agencies were not accustomed to function as collegial bodies, collectively responsible for their impeaching and counseling activities. The censorial official was expected to be independently responsible for what he said—a circumstance that contributed to the high prestige of his position, whatever its salary and rank. One consequence of this, however, was that the censorial official could be punished for speaking out in ways that displeased his ruler. Though it was popularly considered a serious breach of propriety for a ruler to punish a censorial critic, no censorial official had personal immunity.[49]

The third notable element in the functioning of the censorial apparatus is that censorial officials had relatively low rank and were characteristically young. Notable exceptions were the aristocratic remonstrators and counselors of earliest imperial times and the senior officials—the executive officers so to speak—of the various censorial agencies. Such exceptions notwithstanding, none of the censorial agencies was thought of as a body of elder statesmen, with the wisdom of long experience, who might most naturally have been relied upon for astute criticism of governmental operations. The reasons for this are not difficult to perceive, especially in the case of surveillance officials. For one thing, only a relatively young man could have the physical capacity for grueling inspection tours under variable travel conditions. More important, a relatively inexperienced man could be expected to take a more aggressive and idealistic approach to his surveillance duties. He would not be resigned to bureaucratic incompetence and corruption, and he would not yet be bound by compromising political ties. It might have been hoped that, being at the mere threshold of a bureaucratic career, he would have little to lose by being brash and much to gain by acquiring a reputation as a fearless critic.

The T'ang poet-official Po Chü-i once submitted a memorial realistically explaining the low rank (and, by implication, the relative youth) of speaking officials. In the following translation, the term "censor" actually refers to the speaking-official post called *shih-i* or "reminder," which Po himself held at the time. He wrote:

There are good reasons why these censors are very carefully chosen and why their rank is very low. It is natural for one who holds a high rank to value his rank (above principles); it is natural for one in an exalted position to love his position (above principles). If a man values his rank (above principles), he is likely to compromise and keep silent. If he loves his position (above principles), he is likely to overlook mistakes and fail to remonstrate. This is necessarily so in the nature of things.

When the office of the imperial censor was established it was assigned a low rank so that it would not be valued and loved (above principles). The reason why these officials are chosen very carefully is to insure that they are men who never forget their obligation to the emperor and to their own conscience. Only when a censor does not have a position which he overvalues, only when he is a man who never forgets his obligation toward the emperor, will he not fail to correct mistakes when any occur, nor to remonstrate when the law has been violated. He will note the wise and the foolish measures of the Court and point out what is good and what is bad in the empire. This was the original purpose for which the State established the office of the shih i.[50]

Fourth and last, censorial officials, though specialized in censorial functions, commonly performed some non-censorial functions as well. I have already noted that surveillance officials early showed inclinations to intrude into the realm of the speaking officials and that by T'ang times some speaking officials had been assigned tasks similar to those performed by surveillance officials. Multifunctionalism, however, was far more general than this. As early as Han times, there was a tendency to use surveillance officials in particular for non-censorial work.

The censor was in essence a critic. One might suppose that to guarantee effective surveillance, he should not have been given magisterial

responsibilities, lest by becoming an active participant in administration he might lose the detachment and objectivity that were vital
to his role as critic. But this ideal was not attained.

Dilution of censorial objectivity is most observable in the sphere of
judicial administration. All Chinese magistrates traditionally combined the functions of prosecutors and judges. Historically, the Chinese have not prized the judicial detachment that has been so important a part of the Western tradition, and it has not seemed incongru-
ous to them that an official whose principal duty was to impeach
might at times be called upon to judge. The nature and extent of
early censorial participation in judicial processes has not yet been
thoroughly studied. It is clear that censors often served as appellate
judges rather than judges of original jurisdiction; but from Han
times through Sung times they did serve in judicial capacities of a
sort that unquestionably impaired their detachment as critics of government. The Censorate came to be known as a judicial tribunal as
well as an organ of surveillance.

Surveillance officials also acquired non-censorial responsibilities in
other areas. The surveillance commissioners of T'ang times and the
circuit intendants of Sung times had mixed censorial and magisterial
powers, and the mixing could only have served to dilute their surveillance effectiveness. Moreover, members of the Censorate itself were
regularly assigned to special duties that distracted them from their
proper surveillance pursuits. Even in Han times censors were often
employed as envoys to tributary principalities, as the arrangers of
important funerals, as leaders of bandit-catching expeditions, and in
other capacities that were more directive than censorial.[51] These practices were perpetuated under subsequent dynasties.

The Sung rulers seem to have recognized at least some of the incon-
gruities of this tradition, for they tried to restrict censors to the exercise of impeachment powers. In 1080 the Censorate requested the
right to specify punishments or other rectifications when offenses were
not important enough to merit impeachment. This request was vigorously denied, and soon thereafter the Censorate was sharply reminded that its role was impeachment, not magisterial action of any
sort.[52] In Sung times, too, not all censors always had the right even
to submit impeachments: under the early Sung emperors, investigating censors were charged only with discovering discrepancies, while
impeachment of the persons at fault was the prerogative of the palace
censors and the executive officers of the Censorate. This rule was not
rescinded until 1085, and even then the old restrictions seem to have

retained some customary force, for the right of investigating censors to submit impeachments had to be reiterated in 1164.[53]

THE YÜAN DYNASTY CENSORIAL SYSTEM

The Ming censorial system was shaped in many ways by precedents found in the long and complex tradition that has been discussed above, but its most immediate model was the censorial system of the intervening Yüan dynasty (1260–1368). Invading Mongols founded the dynasty and inaugurated a governmental regime based superficially upon the T'ang and Sung tradition. But it was unprecedented and innovative in many respects, and especially in its ruthless authoritarianism.

By rearranging structural elements inherited from the T'ang and Sung dynasties, the Mongol rulers created a highly centralized and intricately articulated government with a three-way division of responsibilities.[54] They did away with the old Chancellery and Department of State Affairs, but retained the Secretariat as a general organ of civil administration. Its officials served as an advisory council for the emperor (the senior member being grand councilor or prime minister) and directed detailed administrative operations through six subordinate Ministries of a type now customary—Ministries of Personnel, of Revenue, of Rites, of War, of Justice, and of Works. There was also a Bureau of Military Affairs, which had general charge of military plans, preparations, and operations; and a Censorate still called the Tribunal of Censors, which exercised general impeachment control over all government personnel, civil and military.

The Mongols divided their Chinese empire geographically into prefectures and counties but superimposed on them a new unit of local coordination called a route (*lu*). At fullest development there were 185 routes. But channels of administrative accountability did not lead directly from the routes to the Secretariat in the central government; there were two levels of intermediate supervisory agencies. (See the accompanying chart of Yüan administrative and censorial structure.) The lower level consisted of 60 agencies of eight different designations but collectively called Pacification Commissions, each having a territorial jurisdiction called a region (*ch'u* or *tao*). The Pacification Commissions supervised the subordinate routes, but only those in the immediate vicinity of the capital reported in turn to the metropolitan Secretariat. Eleven branch Secretariats were gradually established for the administrative supervision of other areas. The resulting 12 sections supervised by the various Yüan Secretariats are commonly called provinces, and they began the development of China's modern provinces. The branch Secretariats were equal in rank to the metropolitan Secretariat, but in practice they were clearly subordinate to it, as administrative links between it and the Pacification Commissions distant from the capital.

In a similar structural alignment, surveillance organs were established on three levels, culminating in the metropolitan Censorate.[55] The Censorate was established in 1268 "to investigate the morality of all officials and the advantages and disadvantages of government policies." As in earlier times, it was divided into three staffs. The administrative staff included 2 censors-in-chief, 2 vice censors-in-chief, 2 associate censors, and 2 secretarial censors. There was also a Court of Palace Affairs consisting of only 2 palace censors and a Court of Surveillance consisting of 32 investigating censors.

The Censorate had its own widespread network of subsidiary units, through which it subjected all local government units to its surveillance. For censorial purposes the empire was divided into three large jurisdictions, covered by the metropolitan Censorate and two branch Censorates (*hsing yü-shih t'ai*). Similar to the case of the various Secretariats, the branch Censorates were equal in rank to the metro-

Basic Structure of Yüan Administrative and Censorial Systems

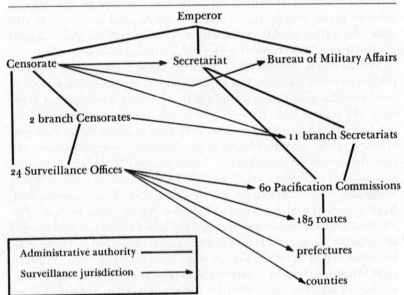

politan Censorate but in practice were subordinate to it. The metropolitan and branch Censorates, furthermore, directly supervised the
operations of a varying number of lower-level Surveillance Offices
(*t'i-hsing an-ch'a ssu*; after 1291 called *su-cheng lien-fang ssu*). At the
most, there were 24 of these, each assigned to a territorial jurisdiction
called a circuit (*tao*). Each such jurisdiction might include several of
the regions governed by Pacification Commissions, just as each jurisdiction of a branch Censorate encompassed several of the provinces
governed by branch Secretariats.

All these censorial agencies combined to maintain surveillance over
court routine, general administrative activities, the military establishment, and legal processes. Their officials periodically inspected the
records of all government agencies; they accepted and investigated
complaints about injustices; and at all three levels of jurisdiction,
they went out annually or semiannually to make systematic and thorough tours of inspection. The metropolitan and branch Censorates
concentrated their attention on the various Secretariats, whereas the
Surveillance Offices covered the Pacification Commissions and their
subordinate routes, prefectures, and counties.[56] The Yüan censorial
system was consequently far more pervasive than any preceding one,
and its degree of tightly knit centralization was never exceeded in
China's censorial history, before or after the Yüan period. The Mongols' surveillance apparatus can be reckoned as one of the institutional marvels of Chinese history.

Finally, in Yüan times surveillance officials were explicitly endowed
with magisterial powers. Often even an individual censor was expected to punish as well as to discover offenders. An official of a Surveillance Office was empowered to punish functionaries who were
not of the nine civil-service ranks, and those officials of the lowest
ranks (6 to 9) whom he found guilty of lesser crimes. At least after
1301, however, he could do so only after joint deliberation of all the
officials of his particular Surveillance Office. Cases involving officials
of ranks 6 to 9 who had committed crimes punishable by dismissal
from the service had to be referred to the Censorate for action, and
apparently the most serious cases had to be referred to the throne for
final disposition. All cases involving officials of ranks 1 to 5 still had
to be referred to the throne.[57] These restrictions merely serve to emphasize the important fact that in Yüan times surveillance officials
had ceased to be mere critics of the government.

While the surveillance organs were being developed to this degree
of extension and centralization, the remonstrance tradition was al-

most being extinguished in its organizational aspect. A few omissioners and supervising secretaries were retained in the Yüan governmental structure, but they were assigned to keeping a register of
memorials submitted to the throne by the various government agencies. In addition, after 1278 they were charged with maintaining a
diary of imperial activities. Neither duty burdened the nominal
speaking officials with any prescribed censorial responsibilities.[58]

However, the remonstrance tradition was not wholly obliterated,
since it gradually passed from the erstwhile speaking officials to members of the Censorate. Moreover, in a revival of the abortive Sung
trend already noted, the Mongols called on censors in particular to
criticize the formulation as well as the implementation of policy. Kublai Khan made the final coalescence of surveillance and speaking
functions explicit: "The duty of Censorate officials is to speak out
straightforwardly," he once proclaimed; "and if We should commit
improprieties, they are to speak out to the extreme without concealment and without fearing others."[59] Since a very large proportion of
Yüan censors were themselves Mongols,[60] their influence as remonstrators may well have been facilitated by the egalitarian comradeship
that prevailed in Mongol tribal society, and their status may have corresponded more nearly to that of semifeudal Han remonstrators than
to that of bureaucratic remonstrators in T'ang and Sung times. In
any case, the Yüan censors seem to have become diligent admonishers
of the Mongol emperors. One censor-in-chief presumed to remonstrate with Kublai Khan against a proposed attempt to invade Japan
at a time when the emperor had strong feelings on the matter and
no one else dared to argue with him.[61] And late in the Yüan period,
when the Mongol empire was beginning to fall apart, censors repeatedly warned emperors of the disaster that loomed ahead.[62]

The Ming censorial system that is considered in detail in the following chapters, blending elements from both the immediately preceding Yüan system and the more remote tradition, was not the final
phase of China's censorial history.[63] When in 1644 invading Manchus from the northeast superseded the Ming emperors with their
Ch'ing dynasty (1644–1912), they retained the Ming governmental
structure almost wholly intact, including the censorial system.[64] Their
only major innovations that are relevant here were (1) completing the
trend toward coalescence of surveillance and remonstrance functions
by moving supervising secretaries into the structure of the metropolitan Censorate, and (2) allowing Provincial Surveillance Offices to

drift almost entirely into non-censorial roles, following a Ming trend that will be discussed later. Even after republican revolutions over-threw the Ch'ing dynasty and destroyed most of the old regime along with it, the censorial tradition persisted, and it persists into our own time.[65] The Nationalist government dominated by Chiang Kai-shek since 1927 has included a so-called Control Yüan among the five coequal organs at the top of its administrative structure; and the Con-trol Yüan, directly descended from the imperial Censorate, remains active and influential in the Nationalist refuge on Taiwan.[66] More-over, when the Chinese Communist Party drove the Nationalists from the mainland and established the People's Republic of China in 1949, they incorporated into their governmental structure several types of surveillance organs, notably a hierarchy of Committees of People's Supervision and a hierarchy of People's Procuratorates. These, though patterned most directly after Soviet Union models, have at least terminological connections with the traditional system, and they still function on the mainland.[67]

Nevertheless, there is reason to consider the censorial system of Ming times as the culminating achievement of the old tradition. The Manchus disrupted the inherited system by thrusting "racial" con-siderations upon the Censorate, insisting that every Chinese censor be paired with a Manchu counterpart. And both the Nationalist Con-trol Yüan and the various censorial agencies of Communist China have been instruments of authoritarian, partisan control. They have served exclusively as surveillance organs, having no vestiges of the remonstrance functions that marked traditional censorial operations. Therefore, however deserving of study all these post-Ming systems may be for their own sake and for their relevance to the problem of control practices in modern government, they do not represent as well as the Ming system does the unique Chinese censorial tradition that developed through the imperial age.

The chapters that follow describe the organizational structure and the personnel arrangements of the Ming censorial establishment (Chapter 2); explain the operational workings of the system (Chapter 3); analyze what the censorial officials actually attempted and accom-plished in two contrasting periods, 1424–34 and 1620–27 (Chapters 4 and 5); describe the various ways in which they were distracted from and caused to suffer for the pursuit of their censorial duties (Chapter 6); and finally, offer some tentative evaluations of the system in reference to the functioning of Ming government and the vicissi-tudes of Ming political history in general (Chapter 7).

Chapter two

The Ming Censorial Establishment

The Ming dynasty (1368–1644) governed China and dominated the whole of East Asia during a long age when, on the opposite end of the Eurasian continent, dramatic events in quick succession were transforming medieval Europe. When the Ming dynasty arose in 1368, the Black Death still threatened much of the West. The Medici ruled Florence. Petrarch and Boccaccio were alive. The papacy endured its "Babylonian captivity" at Avignon. Charles IV was keeping the Holy Roman Empire together. The Black Prince and Du Guesclin were harassing each other in the early stages of the Hundred Years' War, and the Hanseatic League was at the peak of its power in the north. When the Ming dynasty gave way to Manchu conquerors in 1644, Richelieu had just died and Oliver Cromwell dominated England. The Thirty Years' War between the Germanic and Scandinavian principalities was drawing to a close. The Romanovs had come to power in Russia. The British and Dutch East India Companies were rising to supremacy in South and Southeast Asia, and Roger Williams was uniting Rhode Island. Feudalism had given way to mercantilism, land barons to nation-states, the Renaissance to the Reformation. The great age of discovery and invention had dawned, and the West had begun its rise to world leadership.

While Europeans were suffering from the instability and turbulence of all these transformations, Ming Chinese were enjoying peace, stability, and tranquil prosperity. The hated Mongols had been thrown out and no longer posed a major threat. Japan flexed its muscles in piratical raids on China's coast and in an invasion of Korea during the 1590's, but the Japanese were too often embroiled in civil wars at home to dream of annoying China, and the Chinese could not take a Japanese challenge very seriously in any case. Toward the strange, newly arrived "Franks" and "red-haired barbarians" from the little understood but obviously uncouth West, the Chinese could afford to be tolerant, sometimes paternalistically benevolent, and usually amused. Throughout the Ming period, the Chinese felt an almost unprecedented security.

With the Mongols out of the way, the Ming Chinese self-consciously set out to restore and reassert the glorious traditions of the past—notably of the T'ang (618–907) and Sung (960–1279) eras. They had no wish to participate in adventures or to make progress toward anything new. The important thing was to shake off the bad memories of the Mongol century. In doing this, the Chinese committed themselves to a conservative mode of thinking and living, which the perspective of history shows was clearly out of step with the pace of dynamic change in the rest of the world, and which doomed China to be eventually overwhelmed by the aggressiveness and technological prowess of the West. To the Ming Chinese, however, their stability was undoubtedly comfortable, and to their contemporaries in the West it was certainly enviable. Who on either side would have supposed that the wealthy, genteel, sophisticated Chinese need see anything worth emulating in the brash, brawling way of life of the Westerners, who crudely ate flesh with their fingers?

The unusual self-satisfaction and conservative outlook of the Ming Chinese should not suggest that they had lost all their flexibility and creativity. The general stability that marked Chinese life throughout the Ming era was achieved by many changes in traditions. Especially in the realm of government, the Ming Chinese were notably and realistically adaptable. Not only the Ming censorial apparatus, but the whole of the Ming governmental establishment, though nominally patterned after T'ang and Sung models, was a distinctive and ever-changing structure.[1]

GENERAL PATTERNS OF MING GOVERNMENT

The Emperor

As at all other times throughout the history of imperial China, it was understood in Ming times that ultimate power to make decisions affecting society at large—a power virtually free of legal limitations—rested with the emperor, secluded with a host of consorts and attendants in the Forbidden City, a city within a city at the national capital. The founder of the dynasty established his capital and central government at Nanking, on the Yangtze River near the coast. But in 1421

The Ming Emperors

Temple name	Personal name	Reigned	Era name
T'ai-tsu	Chu Yüan-chang	1368–98	Hung-wu
Hui-ti	Chu Yün-wen	1398–1402	Chien-wen
Ch'eng-tsu	Chu Ti	1402–24	Yung-lo
Jen-tsung	Chu Kao-chih	1424–25	Hung-hsi
Hsüan-tsung	Chu Chan-chi	1425–35	Hsüan-te
Ying-tsung	Chu Ch'i-chen	1435–49	Cheng-t'ung
Ching-ti	Chu Ch'i-yü	1449–57	Ching-t'ai
Ying-tsung (restored)		1457–64	T'ien-shun
Hsien-tsung	Chu Chien-shen	1464–87	Ch'eng-hua
Hsiao-tsung	Chu Yu-t'ang	1487–1505	Hung-chih
Wu-tsung	Chu Hou-chao	1505–21	Cheng-te
Shih-tsung	Chu Hou-tsung	1521–66	Chia-ching
Mu-tsung	Chu Tsai-kou	1566–72	Lung-ch'ing
Shen-tsung	Chu I-chün	1572–1620	Wan-li
Kuang-tsung	Chu Ch'ang-lo	1620 (one mo.)	T'ai-ch'ang
Hsi-tsung	Chu Yu-chiao	1620–27	T'ien-ch'i
Chuang-lieh-ti	Chu Yu-chien	1627–44	Ch'ung-chen

Peking, north of the Yellow River, became the capital, and from that time on Nanking had the status of an auxiliary capital. The regions around Peking and Nanking were directly administered "metropolitan areas," whereas the remainder of the country was divided into thirteen provinces.

The Ming imperial line began with a peasant orphan and Buddhist mendicant monk named Chu Yüan-chang (posthumous temple designation T'ai-tsu, "Grand Progenitor"). He led the uprising that expelled the Mongols from China and reigned from 1368 to his death in 1398. The succeeding 15 emperors (see accompanying list of Ming emperors) were his direct descendants in the male line and considered themselves conservators of his heritage. Although they varied considerably in ability, effectiveness, and aggressiveness, they were alike in that their authority to act on any matter as they saw fit could be challenged only at the risk of indictment for treason. The penalty for treason was certain death and perhaps death for all one's relatives and associates. Though the emperors living or dead were not thought of as divinities, their persons and their authority were nonetheless sacred for all practical purposes.

This unchallengeable and virtually unlimited governmental power was sanctioned in theory by the Neo-Confucian orthodoxy of the times, which considered the emperor to be the earthly legate of

Heaven. In practice, his power depended upon the customary obedience of the two groups of people who, as his delegates, enforced governmental decisions: the personnel of a vast military establishment, which included perhaps one hundred thousand officers and four million soldiers at the peak of its strength; and the personnel of a civil-administration establishment, which included at most approximately fifteen thousand "commissioned" officials and one hundred thousand "non-commissioned" lesser functionaries or sub-officials.

The Military Service

Ming military forces (see accompanying chart of Ming military hierarchy) were scattered throughout China in local garrisons called Guards, which were subdivided into Battalions and then Companies. The Guards were concentrated at the national capital and along the northern frontiers. With a few exceptions, notably the Guards at the capital, Guards were supervised by Regional Military Commissions on the provincial level, which at the maturity of the system numbered sixteen—one for each of the thirteen provinces and one in each of three vital zones along the northern frontier. At the beginning of the Ming period the Regional Military Commissions were in turn subordinate to one Chief Military Commission in the central government. But after 1380 this agency was fragmented into five coordinate Chief Military Commissions of equal rank, the ranking officers forming a kind of Joint Chiefs of Staff. Each Commission had administrative jurisdiction over a specified group of Regional Military Commissions.

Characteristically, the officers and soldiers who served in these units were hereditary military men. From the beginning of the dynasty, certain families were designated "military families" and were

The Basic Military Hierarchy of Ming Times

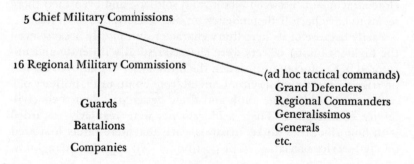

5 Chief Military Commissions

16 Regional Military Commissions   (ad hoc tactical commands)
     Grand Defenders
Guards   Regional Commanders
     Generalissimos
Battalions   Generals
     etc.
Companies

obliged to provide one son from each generation for permanent service as a soldier. In consideration of such service, the family was granted certain tax exemptions or reductions. Lower-ranking posts as military officers passed directly from father to eldest son, and higher-ranking posts were filled by special merit selections from among the holders of the hereditary offices. Before being certified for appointment to a hereditary office, the son of an officer had merely to demonstrate competence in such military techniques as riding and archery. After 1478 the pool of hereditary officers was supplemented with officers recruited in open, competitive examinations, which superficially resembled the civil-service examinations but emphasized only competence in military skills. Since most candidates seem to have been officers' sons not eligible for inheritance, the examinations did not significantly change the hereditary character of the officer corps. Hereditary soldiers, however, did not prove adequate for defense purposes in the late Ming years. The frontier forces in particular had to be augmented and were finally almost superseded by auxiliaries lured or coerced into service for pay.

In their garrisons, the military forces engaged in training exercises, provided local police and bandit-suppression service when needed, and theoretically supported themselves by part-time farming on state lands specially set aside for their use. They were periodically rotated to special training divisions at the capital and when the occasion arose were also sent to tactical commands for frontier defense duty or for large-scale campaigning. In such tactical service, soldiers were commanded by officers who were not of their own garrisons, but who were delegated on an ad hoc basis from permanent assignments in supervisory agencies of the military hierarchy. In time, some tactical commands became semipermanent posts themselves, but only in the late Ming decades, with the extensive use of mercenary auxiliaries, did there develop any semblance of "personal armies," with continuing close attachments between officers and soldiers; and even then there seems to have been little tendency toward warlord-like separatism.

Partly because of its hereditary character, but mostly because even the highest-ranking officers were characteristically illiterate and untutored in Confucian proprieties, the military service enjoyed far less prestige than the civil service. Ranked from 6b up to 1a, military officers usually held higher rank and drew better pay than their civil-service counterparts. Their achievements were regularly rewarded with honorific titles (duke, marquis, earl) that were rarely bestowed on civil-service officials (except posthumously); and their daughters, unlike those of civil-service officials, might aspire to selection for the entourage of imperial consorts. Nevertheless, the military service was clearly under the overall control of the civil service. Perhaps at no other time in Chinese history was the principle of civilian supremacy over the military so respected as in the Ming dynasty. Local garrisons were at the beck and call of civil-service magistrates and prefects, and even tactical commands were subject to the orders of civil-service supreme commanders. The military establishment was a force to be reckoned with and had a certain self-perpetuating autonomy, but in prestige and practical power it yielded to the civil service.

The Civil Service

In accordance with what had by then become a firmly established tradition, the Ming civil service consisted of highly educated men recruited in a series of open, competitive, written examinations administered periodically by the government at the local, provincial, and national levels.[2] By demonstrating their grasp of the Confucian principles on which government service was based, candidates were successively awarded the equivalents of bachelors', masters', and doctors' degrees. They thus won places on the roster of certified literati who were appointed to civil-service positions when vacancies occurred. From the 1440's to the end of the dynasty, civil servants recruited in this fashion were the only officials who could hope to have distinguished governmental careers. Prior to the 1440's, before the newly restored examinations could be routinely counted on to staff the bureaucracy, there was no discrimination against men admitted to the service in less formal ways—by "direct commission" upon the special recommendation of existing officials or by completion of study programs in state-supported schools. Throughout the dynasty, some men inherited official status, but they were never appointed to important positions or given high rank; and from 1450 to the end of the dynasty, some men also purchased literati status, but their titles were almost entirely honorific and had little relation to the functioning bureaucracy.

The careers of "commissioned" civil servants advanced through eighteen ranks, ranging from 9b up to 1a, to which their salaries were keyed. Every civil-service post was also ranked; so that, for example, when a 5b office fell vacant a 5b official was chosen to fill it. Once appointed to a post, an official served a maximum nine-year term in three-year segments, though at any time, if circumstances warranted, he could be transferred, promoted, demoted, or dismissed from the service. Progress up the career ladder was normally slow and often hazardous; it depended upon evaluations of service by one's superiors and by censorial officials. If by merit or luck one eventually attained the highest rank, he served as a very prestigious adviser and minister directly under the emperor, and his personal power could be immense.

The executive-like civil-service officials were assisted in all agencies by "non-commissioned" lesser functionaries who performed clerical and technical tasks. Unlike officials, they were ordinarily locally recruited for specific government agencies and permanently attached to them. Officials moving from one assignment to another necessarily depended heavily on them for detailed knowledge of the particular conditions and procedures of each locality and agency; thus the lesser functionaries could directly or indirectly wield significant influence. But they had little prestige and were paid little official attention.

The hierarchy of agencies in which civil officials served was complex, neatly articulated, and relatively "modern" in its provision for well-differentiated specializations. Although the humanistically educated literati were basically generalists and proudly so, the agencies they served in had specialized functions, so that every new assignment gave an official new on-the-job training. On the basis of their functional differentiations, the agencies can be thought of most conveniently as comprising several relatively autonomous hierarchies or groups: (1) a censorial-judicial hierarchy, (2) an educational-literary hierarchy, (3) a relatively unintegrated and somewhat less autonomous group of "service" agencies, and (4) a tightly integrated hierarchy of general-administration agencies—the line administration agencies, so to speak—extending from counties at the lowest level up through many intermediary agencies to six Ministries in the central government at the national capital.

Aside from the specialized censorial agencies proper, which are the subject of this book, the censorial-judicial hierarchy most notably included a Grand Court of Revision (rank 3a).* This provided a final check, short of imperial review, on the propriety of judicial findings and sentences throughout the empire.

The hierarchy of agencies concerned with education and officially sponsored literary activities included state-supported schools scattered throughout the empire.[3] These were staffed with teachers who

---

* Chinese texts commonly assign ranks to agencies as well as to official positions. The rank assigned to each agency corresponds to that of its highest-ranking official position.

characteristically had no formal civil-service status but constituted a semiprofessional service all their own. More important for purposes of the present study, this hierarchy also included several prestigious and influential agencies at the national capital. One was the Supervisorate of Imperial Instruction (3a), which was in charge of educating the heir apparent and thus exerted great long-term influence on the persistence of Confucian values and traditions within the imperial family. Another was the National University (4b), which admitted students recommended by local schools and gave them final preparatory training either for taking the civil-service examinations or for direct entrance into bureaucratic service as probationers. Also, there was a Hanlin Academy (5a) staffed with eminent civil-service litterateurs who, among other things, drafted and polished proclamations, compiled imperially sponsored histories, and read and explained the Confucian classical and historical writings to the emperor in what were intended to be daily continuing-education sessions. Top-ranking graduates of the civil-service doctoral examinations were normally appointed to Hanlin offices and had continuous Hanlin careers, eventually being rewarded with honorific titles or with nominal, concurrent appointments to high posts in the line administration agencies.

The "service" agencies, many of which were administratively subordinate to line administrative agencies, constituted something like an imperial household administration, with highly specialized service functions. They included a Court of Imperial Sacrifices (3a), a Court of Imperial Entertainments (3b), a Court of the Imperial Stud (3b) with several branches in good horse-pasturing parts of the country, a Court of State Ceremonial (4a), a Directorate of Astronomy (5a), an Imperial Academy of Medicine (5a), a Directorate of Parks (5a), a Music and Dance Office (6a), and several lesser agencies concerned with the imperial seals, the imperial treasury, and so on.[4] In this group, too, were Princely Establishment Administration Offices (5a), one to supervise the affairs of each imperial prince other than the heir apparent. These were scattered throughout the country, since every prince not expected to inherit the throne was required upon attaining maturity to live outside the capital and refrain from interfering in court affairs.

The line administration agencies were both more numerous than the censorial-judicial, educational-literary, and "service" agencies and more directly organized in a hierarchical structure (see the accompanying chart of the Ming civil-administration hierarchy). At the low-

The Basic Civil-Administration Hierarchy of Ming Times

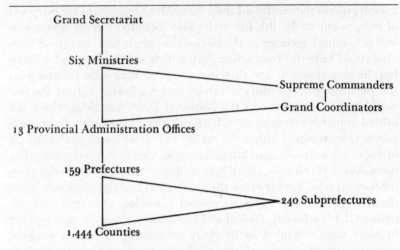

Grand Secretariat

Six Ministries

Supreme Commanders

Grand Coordinators

13 Provincial Administration Offices

159 Prefectures

240 Subprefectures

1,444 Counties

est level was the county (sometimes called district), whose magistrate (7a) was the local representative of the emperor in all realms of government. At its full development the Ming empire comprised 1,144 counties. These were subordinate to 159 prefectures (4a), in some cases through intermediate subprefectures (5b). For general administrative purposes, the prefecture was the essential territorial unit in the empire, and the prefect's post was a highly responsible one.

Prefects were accountable directly to Provincial Administration Offices (2b), one in each of the 13 provinces. The Provincial Administration Office shared supervisory control over its province, in a rather loose consultative arrangement, with a Provincial Surveillance Office and a Regional Military Commission. These three agencies were popularly known as "the three provincial offices," no one of them being equivalent to a provincial governor's office. Such disunity in provincial administration led to the emergence, during the fifteenth century, of two levels of higher supervisory officials. Thus every province—and, in addition, each of several strategic areas superimposed upon the provincial grid—came to have a grand coordinator (technically holding office in a central government agency and only temporarily delegated to provincial duty), who by the late Ming years had become a virtual provincial governor. And regional combinations of two or more provinces came to have still more prestigious coordinators known as supreme commanders (also, officially, temporary delegates from the central government) who, though civil servants, had principal responsibility for regional military concerns.

The Provincial Administration Offices thus became accountable to the capital through grand coordinators and supreme commanders, although they continued to report directly to the central government in the case of much administrative routine.

Correspondence from and to the provinces was handled in the capital by a message center called the Office of Transmission (3a). But the apex of the line administration hierarchy was a group of six coordinate Ministries (2a), differentiated by functional specializations. Each had a group of subordinate Bureaus, and some supervised service agencies of the types already mentioned (see the accompanying lists of the Ministries' subordinate agencies and of a typical Ministry staff). The Ministry of Personnel was in general charge of appointments, merit ratings, promotions, and demotions of all civil officials and lesser functionaries. The Ministry of Revenue was responsible for

The Ming Ministries and Their Subordinate Agencies

Ministry of Personnel
  Bureau of Appointments
  Bureau of Honors
  Bureau of Records
  Bureau of Evaluations
Ministry of Revenue
  Chekiang Bureau, etc. (one such bureau for each of 13 provinces, each with identical sections)
    Statistics Section
    General Accounts Section
    Special Accounts Section
    Granary Section
  Superintendency of Paper Currency
  Office of Currency Supply
  Office of Plate Engraving
  Warehouses, granaries, custom-houses
Ministry of Rites
  Bureau of Ceremonies
  Bureau of Sacrifices
  Bureau of Receptions
  Bureau of Provisions
  Messenger Office
  Court of Imperial Sacrifices
    College of Translators
    Music and Dance Office
  Court of Imperial Entertainments

Ministry of Rites (cont.)
  Court of State Ceremonial
  Office of Seal Engraving
  Office of Music
  Central Buddhist Registry
  Central Taoist Registry
Ministry of War
  Bureau of Personnel
  Bureau of Operations
  Bureau of Equipment
  Bureau of Provisions
  College of Interpreters
  Court of the Imperial Stud
  Pasturage Offices
Ministry of Justice
  Chekiang Bureau (one such bureau for each of the 13 provinces)
Ministry of Works
  Bureau of Construction
  Bureau of Forestry and Crafts
  Bureau of Irrigation and Transportation
  Bureau of State Lands
  Armory
  Mint
  Offices of Produce Levies
  Warehouses, manufactories, etc.

Staff of a Typical Ming Ministry

---

1 minister (2a)	Record Office
1 vice minister (3a)	1 record clerk (8a)
Each subordinate Bureau	1 collator (9a)
1 director (5a)	General Services Office
1 vice director (5b)	2 office managers (9b)
1 secretary (6a)	

the census of population and of cultivated lands, the assessment and collection of taxes, and the handling of government revenues. The Ministry of Rites was in charge of state ceremonies, rituals, and sacrifices and also the reception of envoys from tributary states. The Ministry of War was responsible for military administration in general: the appointments, promotions, and demotions of military personnel, the maintenance of military installations, equipment, and weapons, the operation of the postal system, etc. The Ministry of Justice supervised judicial and penal processes. The Ministry of Works was in charge of government construction projects, the conscription of artisans and laborers for periodic state service, the manufacture of government equipment, the maintenance of waterways and roads, the standardization of weights and measures, and the exploitation of natural resources. Throughout most of the Ming period, the executive ministers of these six Ministries, together with the censor-in-chief of the Censorate, held the highest-ranking functional posts in the civil service. Except in the earliest years of the dynasty, ranks 1a and 1b were reserved for honorific titles given to such ministers and other personages without reference to their duty assignments—such titles as grand preceptor, grand tutor, and grand guardian.

At the very beginning of the Ming dynasty the six Ministries remained what they had been in Mongol times and earlier—subordinate agencies of a unitary Secretariat, whose grand councilors corresponded to prime ministers or premiers. In 1380, however, the Secretariat was abolished because of a threatened rebellion under the leadership of a grand councilor, and the Ministries became autonomous. Such a fragmented central administration prevented any one minister from gaining power sufficient to threaten the throne, but it made burdensome demands on the emperor. Therefore, emperors gradually began to rely heavily on officials of the Hanlin Academy to serve as secretarial intermediaries between them and the ministries, and by the middle of the fifteenth century this informal, unofficial group of grand secretaries, known as the Grand Secretariat, had come to serve in practice as a powerful executive body much like the Secretariat in earlier dynasties. Throughout the remainder of the Ming era, strong grand secretaries repeatedly gained almost dictatorial power, and the fact that their careers were spent almost entirely in the educational-literary agencies of government created much suspicion and hostility between them and the ministers and other officials whose careers had been spent in the line administrative agencies. Giving the grand secretaries nominal, concurrent titles as ministers or vice ministers raised their rank and in some measure blunted such antagonisms; but the grand secretaries could never quite escape the stigma of being an "inner court" with interests hostile to those of the line officialdom or "outer court."

Irregularities in the Exercise of Power

In the normal course of events, the Ming civil-service officials had governmental affairs well in hand. There was no other group either in the state structure or in the society at large that could legitimately wield greater influence on the emperor or more routinely shape his decisions. Though omnipotent in theory, the emperor was not expected to initiate policy. When a problem arose that required more than routine action, the immediately responsible official submitted a full report to his superior, recommending a possible solution. The more difficult problems were passed up the administrative hierarchy to the appropriate Ministries. Some were eventually presented to the emperor via the grand secretaries, who submitted each memorial with an attached suggestion for a suitable rescript. It was expected that the emperor would either confirm the decision proposed by the grand secretaries or reach agreement on a different decision in consultation with them. Similarly, when a vacant post had to be filled, the Ministry of Personnel or the Ministry of War proposed an eligible replacement for the emperor's approval; or, if the post was a high-ranking one, submitted a list of two or three qualified men from among whom the emperor could choose. Before making any kind of decision, the emperor might ask for open discussion in general court audience, might summon one or more trusted officials for private or semiprivate consultation, or might convoke a large group of high-ranking officials for a formal "court deliberation."[5] As a matter of fact, the administrative regulations of the dynasty forbade the making of any important policy decision without recourse to such a court deliberation. Participants were sometimes provided in advance with abstracts of the problems on the agenda. Each participant seems to have had an equal voice, and each voted by submitting a formal written opinion. Unanimity was hoped for. When it was achieved, custom apparently dictated that the assembly's decision was binding on the emperor. In the case of major bureaucratic appointments, senior officials were called on to make guaranteed recommendations of eligible men, which similarly influenced or determined the emperor's choice. Thus, although the civil-service establishment was legally restricted to advisory rather than legislative powers, the normal administrative routine gave it some significant procedural checks on imperial irresponsibility or arbitrariness. The right to make final decisions was always the emperor's, but the civil servants normally prescribed the alternatives among which the emperor could choose.

Governmental conditions, however, were seldom normal in Ming times. Jen-tsung (1424–25), Hsüan-tsung (1425–35), and Hsiao-tsung (1487–1505) were model Confucian rulers—unaggressive, benevolent, trustful of the civil-service officials. But most other Ming rulers were a difficult lot for the bureaucracy to manage. They were often tyrannical, often cruelly oppressive, often angrily resentful of and inattentive to their responsibilities. They capriciously sent one honest official after another into disgrace or exile, subjected dozens and even hundreds of officials at a time to humiliating open-court floggings, and on some horrible occasions put thousands of innocents to death without any semblance of due process. So flagrantly did they ignore or disrupt prescribed governmental procedures that throughout much of the Ming period officials close to the throne must have lived in a perpetual state of apprehension verging on terror. That Ming China prospered and survived as long as it did testifies to the remarkable resiliency of the political system that the emperors abused so callously.

The founding emperor, T'ai-tsu (1368–98), set the despotic tone that most of his successors emulated. In his later years, terribly sensitive about his humble origins and suspicious of the lieutenants who had helped him win the empire, T'ai-tsu began to see insults and threats in even the most innocent acts and instituted a series of pogroms that reportedly cost 30,000 lives in one case and 15,000 in another.[6] Before his reign was half over, according to a contemporary, officials of the capital always bade their wives and children farewell on leaving for court audience each morning, and if evening came without disaster they congratulated one another on surviving another day.[7]

A complete catalogue of Ming emperors' aberrations would be long indeed. Hsien-tsung (1464–87) stuttered so miserably that he was ashamed to appear at court audiences and avoided contact with his officials whenever possible. Wu-tsung (1505–21) was a frustrated adventurer. He loved gaiety and sport, and he often wandered about the capital in disguise, seeking thrills in the company of sycophants. Military adventures pleased him especially; he staged special campaigns for no purpose other than to give himself the thrill of field leadership. In consequence of fancied victories, he then conferred upon himself ever more distinguished military titles. When court officials protested against his wasteful and undignified pastimes, he had them imprisoned, flogged, or otherwise humiliated. Shih-tsung (1521–66) supported a retinue of Taoist alchemists in a prolonged search for an elixir of immortality and for twenty years withdrew almost entirely from governmental cares, leaving all decisions to an unpopular grand secretary. Shen-tsung (1572–1620) was even more inattentive—so much so that modern students, trying to peer through the veils of traditional historiography that shroud emperors' personal lives, have speculated that he suffered glandular disorders that made him grossly obese, or that he might have been an opium addict. For 25 years—from 1590 to 1615— he conducted no general audiences at all, and he once went for ten years without even consulting in person with a grand secretary. One grand secretary, finally seeing the emperor for the first time, became so agitated that he emptied his bladder on the palace floor and fell into a coma that lasted for several days.[8] What was most disruptive of all was that Shen-tsung, petulantly determined not to be harassed by the officialdom, pigeonholed memorials in the palace and refused to make decisions even on appointments, so that large numbers of offices fell permanently vacant and much governmental business could not be carried on at all. Hsi-tsung (1620–27) refused to let governmental duties interfere with his principal hobby, carpentry.

It must be admitted that emperors lived trying and frustrating lives. They were reared in seclusion and always catered to by hosts of personal attendants, but were expected to endure elaborate court rituals beginning at dawn. They continually had to listen to the lectures of moralistic Confucian officials who were probably dour and seldom entertaining. Naturally, they often resented their constricting responsibilities and were vulnerable to any self-seekers who offered to divert them. The civil service was always on guard against the machinations of such would-be palace favorites within its own ranks or from outside, and the Ming system did successfully prevent the parents or patrons of palace women from causing interferences of sorts that sometimes disrupted other dynasties. But at the same time the system itself bred one class of people whose irregular influences could not be checked, though the danger was well understood and amply illustrated in a succession of debacles in earlier dynasties. These were palace eunuchs, who in Ming times repeatedly gained influence over emperors to such a degree that normal government procedures were wholly undermined and the civil service found itself deprived of access to real power.

Eunuchs were the only male attendants permitted to live in the Forbidden City and with the grand secretaries constituted the "inner court" par excellence.[9] It was the founding emperor's original intention that the eunuch staff should not exceed one hundred persons, but it did not remain at this low level. By the end of the fifteenth centry, eunuchs apparently numbered ten thousand; late in the sixteenth century groups of three thousand or more were regularly recruited at a time; and by the end of the dynasty it has been estimated that their number had grown to more than seventy thousand. Throughout the dynasty they were forbidden by law to interfere in government affairs on pain of death, but in practice they were regularly used for special assignments outside the palace. They came to be employed as special investigators, tax collectors, supervisors of foreign trade, directors of state-operated manufactories, and even as military commanders. Eunuchs finally became a dominant factor in Ming political history. Four famous eunuch dictators arose in succession: Wang Chen in the 1440's, Wang Chih in the 1470's, Liu Chin in the early 1500's, and finally the most notorious of all, Wei Chunghsien, in the 1620's. These great eunuchs terrorized the officialdom at large through the activities of the Eastern Depot and the Western Depot, palace agencies that were like imperial secret service headquarters, responsible for investigating treasonable offenses. They had the willing cooperation of the personal military bodyguard of the emperor, called the Embroidered-Uniform Guard, whose officers exercised almost unlimited police and judicial authority and maintained a special palace prison that became, especially in late Ming times, a feared torture chamber.[10]

Ming emperors relied on eunuchs principally for the same reason that English kings of the fourteenth century relied on celibate clerics to manage household agencies such as the exchequer and the chancery: family concerns did not dilute their loyalty to the throne since they had no heirs to provide for.[11] Moreover, since eunuchs necessarily came from the lowest classes in society and were objects of revulsion to persons of respectable background, they had little hope of attaining status or esteem except through faithful and pleasing service to their imperial master. They were not affected by public opinion, and they were never influenced by the moralistic considerations that colored the literati's every act. They had nothing whatsoever to gain by opposing the emperor's whims and everything to gain by acquiescing in them. They were therefore totally subservient, and emperors seem to have considered them to be singularly trustworthy.

Since the emperor relied on eunuchs for the satisfaction of personal, everyday wants, they had no difficulty in gaining access to him. And since they were the only males who were permitted to have informal daily contact with him, they had unequaled opportunities to become his confidants. Young or weak emperors, therefore, easily fell under the influence of strong-willed eunuchs, and dilatory emperors gladly used vigorous and clever eunuchs to do much of their work for them. When such emperors as Shih-tsung and Shen-tsung secluded themselves for long periods, eunuchs became go-betweens essential to the maintenance of even remote contact between the emperor and the officialdom. At such times, imperial decisions were transmitted to the Grand Secretariat on papers carried by eunuchs shuttling in and out of the remote recesses of the palace, and sometimes they were even transmitted orally. Improper eunuch influence on state affairs was almost unavoidable.

The officialdom seems to have been helpless in this situation. Even under conscientious and diligent emperors, grand secretaries found it advisable to have friends among the eunuchs who were always at the emperor's side. And at times grand secretaries had no choice but to connive with influential eunuchs to maintain essential governmental activities, which depended heavily on obtaining from the throne prompt decisions or confirmations of decisions. Such conditions could only promote distrust of the grand secretaries among the "outer court" civil servants.

Other irregularities in governmental activities grew out of divisiveness within the civil service itself: it was honeycombed with partisan cells based on informal personal relationships. For example, officials who had passed the same doctoral examination ("the class of 1526") considered themselves lifelong comrades who owed political loyalty to one another, and for their whole careers they were like politically subservient disciples of the senior officials who had been their examiners. Similar bonds of informal political clientage persisted between one-time superiors and inferiors in governmental agencies. Thus the adherents of one powerful minister intrigued against those of another, or officials from one region intrigued against those of another region, or officials of one agency against those of others, or literati associated with one philosophical movement against those associated with another, and so on.[12] Since partisan wrangling could only be resolved by one clique's winning imperial favor and ousting its adversaries from positions of influence, these struggles served merely to weaken the officialdom's resistance to the irregularities of the emperor or his eunuch favorites. Destructive partisanship could only have been suppressed by strong disciplinary leadership within the civil-service ranks, of the sort presumably given by the grand councilors or prime ministers in earlier dynasties. But such leadership could not come from the Ming grand secretaries, alienated from the officialdom at large by their "inner court" affiliations. Thus Chinese historians are fond of blaming the abolition of the old-style Secretariat in 1380 for the gradual decay of Ming governmental effectiveness and the collapse of the dynasty in 1644.[13]

On the local levels, still other kinds of irregularities interfered with normal governmental procedures. Relatives and friends of palace eunuchs and other imperial favorites, as well as of powerful officials and officers of the civil and military services, used their connections to advantage in dealing with local magistrates. Of course, retired or temporarily unassigned officials had to be treated delicately. Moreover, as in all governmental systems, the wealthy families of every locality were not averse to protecting their special interests as best they could—by intimidation, social courtesies, or bribery, as circumstances suggested. The lowest functionaries must have been especially vulnerable to such influences. But civil-service magistrates as well were susceptible to manipulation by the local gentry. Because he came from the educated elite that provided candidates for the civil-service examinations, a "gentleman" could claim an official's sympathy on the grounds that they shared common values and a common responsibility for maintenance of the whole Confucian heritage. It would be naïve to suppose that such relationships were not often exploited to selfish advantage and to the disadvantage of proper governmental operations, even though legally all citizens rich or poor were wholly at the mercy of the government.

To discover the particular realities of political power in any system —to pinpoint the complex motivations and pressures that influence any political action—is of course no easy matter. After all, government documents everywhere reflect an assumption that events occur in regular, legitimate ways; they ask to be taken at face value. Ming

China is no exception in this regard. Perhaps Ming government functioned as it was supposed to function to a greater degree than any other contemporary government. But the historical record makes it clear that irregularities like those mentioned often made the formal process of government little more than a facade behind which informal, illegitimate arrangements determined the course of events, and these irregularities led to the eventual destruction of the Ming dynasty.

Since it was the special charge of the censorial system to maintain the regularity and legitimacy of governmental operations by denouncing the intrusion of deviations at any level, it follows that the system was ultimately ineffective. How relatively effective it was at any particular time may be impossible to judge objectively. Nevertheless, as an organization it was certainly equipped to fight a good fight.

STRUCTURE OF THE CENSORIAL ORGANS

In 1368, and for several years thereafter, Ming forces were still actively campaigning to wrest control of all China from the Mongols; and the necessity of getting an operational government established in a hurry prevented the founding emperor, T'ai-tsu, from altering very quickly the Yüan dynasty's existing patterns of administration. It was not until the 1380's that a series of reorganizations produced a distinctive Ming governmental structure. Before attaining their characteristic Ming forms, therefore, the censorial institutions underwent several transformations.

The Censorate

The earliest Ming Censorate was almost a replica of the Yüan organ.[14] It bore the traditional designation Tribunal of Censors and was headed by two censors-in-chief, differentiated as censor-in-chief of the left (senior) and censor-in-chief of the right (junior), both of civil-service rank 1b. The staff also included two vice censors-in-chief of left and right (2a); an unprescribed number of associate censors (2b); one secretarial censor (3a); unprescribed numbers of palace censors (5a) and investigating censors (7a); and five types of non-censorial administrative personnel—a registrar (5b); a chief clerk (7a); a record clerk (8a); and a translator and an usher (both ungraded). As in earlier times, investigating censors constituted a Court of Surveillance, but there is no evidence of any formal recognition of the traditional Court of General Affairs and Court of Palace Affairs. Also, in one notable departure from the Yüan pattern, the Ming government did not establish any branch Censorates.

The first significant change in the Censorate's organization occurred in 1376, when the offices of associate censor, secretarial censor, and palace censor were discontinued. This left a staff consisting only of censors-in-chief, vice censors-in-chief, and a Court of Surveillance comprising the investigating censors. Then in 1380 the Censorate was seriously affected in the sweeping reorganization of the whole central government that followed conviction of the grand councilor Hu Wei-yung for treason. The Censorate suffered particular imperial disfavor because the censor-in-chief Ch'en Ning and the vice censor-in-chief T'u Chieh were among the officials who were put to death as partisans of Hu.[15]

It was also in 1380 that the old-style unitary Secretariat was abolished, leaving the six Ministries as a fragmented central administration, and the old-style unitary Chief Military Commission was split into five Chief Military Commissions. In the first stage of this reorganization the Censorate suffered only the loss of its positions of censors-in-chief. The posts of vice censors-in-chief remained, and the former posts of associate censors were even restored. This in effect reduced the Censorate from its previous rank of 1b to that of 2a. Within four months, however, the posts of vice censors-in-chief and also of associate censors were abruptly done away with, in what is usually described as the abolition of the Censorate. The designation Tribunal of Censors was no longer used. Only the formerly subordinate Court of Surveillance, with its investigating censors, remained.[16]

In 1382 a new form of organization began to appear. Investigating censors dropped in rank from 7a to 9a and were reorganized into twelve offices called Circuits, which were named after the twelve current provinces. This does not mean that the investigating censors were actually sent out to duty in the provinces for which their Circuits were named. Censors of the Chekiang Circuit, for example, did have certain responsibilities regarding the affairs of Chekiang province; but they characteristically remained in the capital and, if sent into the provinces at all on temporary duty, might be sent anywhere. Three, four, or five investigating censors were assigned to each Circuit. At the same time, eight chief investigating censors appeared as a new type of executive official (7a), and the designation Chief Surveillance Office was assigned to the Censorate as a whole for the first time.[17]

Steps were taken to restore some of the Censorate's diminished prestige in the following year, 1383, when it was "promoted" and again reorganized. Chief investigating censors were then abolished, and the investigating censors were placed under eight new officials: two old-style censors-in-chief of left and right, rank 3a (but with new Chinese designations*); two vice censors-in-chief of left and right (4a); and four assistant censors-in-chief, two each of left and right (5a). In 1384, Censorate ranks again were raised. Censors-in-chief attained rank 2a, vice censors-in-chief 3a, and assistant censors-in-chief 4a. Investigating censors were restored to their former rank of 7a.

The Chinese source materials seldom spell out justifications for these successive transformations of the Censorate, and it is often difficult to see any special significance in the various changes of titles and ranks. But an overall significance emerges. In the early 1380's T'ai-tsu was restructuring his government so that no broad area of governmental activity could be dominated by any one official. Abolition of the Secretariat and the Chief Military Commission meant that there was no longer the possibility that a grand councilor might monopolize civil administration or a military commissioner-in-chief might monopolize military control. The so-called "abolition" of the Censorate —meaning removal of its executive superstructure—similarly removed the possibility that a high-ranking censor-in-chief might acquire monopolistic domination over surveillance activities.

But the subsequent treatment of the Censorate differs from that of the Secretariat and the Chief Military Commission. Neither control over civil administration nor control over military affairs was ever restored to a unified executive body in the top level of the central government, but the Censorate's executive superstructure was quickly reconstituted. Perhaps this was because unified control over surveillance activities might not pose as great a threat to imperial authority as unified control over civil administration and military affairs. It could even be argued that a strongly integrated and centralized surveillance apparatus tended to serve monarchical interests in checking the civil and military hierarchies.

It would seem that the Censorate weathered T'ai-tsu's reorganization of the central government without suffering any basic change in its structural integrity. But, despite a superficial continuity between the old Tribunal of Censors and the new Chief Surveillance Office, during the 1380's the Censorate actually experienced a lasting fragmentation comparable to that in other hierarchies of the government.

---

* The traditional titles such as *yü-shih ta-fu*, "chief of the censors," were not reinstated. Henceforth the Censorate's executive officials had the Chinese titles *tu yü-shih* (censor-in-chief, literally "chief censor"), *fu tu yü-shih* (vice censor-in-chief), and *ch'ien tu yü-shih* (assistant censor-in-chief).

It is clear that henceforth the executive officials of the Censorate did not exercise centralized direction of surveillance activities. They remained superiors of the investigating censors for purposes of personnel administration within the organization; however, in maintaining surveillance over the officialdom, investigating censors were individually and directly agents of the throne. Whereas the Yüan Censorate, and presumably the pre-1380 Ming Censorate, were empowered to appoint, demote, and promote their own personnel,[18] in the system that developed after 1382 all personnel matters affecting investigating censors required action by the emperor.[19] Censors to be sent out into the provinces were selected by the emperor, and when they returned to the capital they reported directly to the throne before reporting to the Censorate.[20] Their independence of the censors-in-chief was emphasized even in titular identifications. For example, there were officials called secretaries of the Chekiang Bureau of the Ministry of Justice; but investigating censors were called investigating censors of the Chekiang Circuit, never investigating censors of the Chekiang Circuit *of the Censorate*.[21] They were not in any sense agents of the censor-in-chief.

After Ch'eng-tsu (1402–24) moved the Ming capital to Peking, Nanking became an auxiliary capital with a skeleton replica of the central government and an auxiliary Censorate.[22] And as the boundaries of Ming provinces changed before settling into their standard 13-province pattern, the number of Circuits for investigating censors changed from 12 to 14 and in 1435 to a standard 13.[23] Otherwise, the Censorate organization that emerged in the 1380's did not change substantially thereafter.[24]

From 1421 until the end of the dynasty, then, the metropolitan Censorate at Peking normally consisted of the following staff:

2 censors-in-chief of left and right (2a)[25]
2 vice censors-in-chief (3a)
4 assistant censors-in-chief (4a)[26]
110 investigating censors (7a) divided among 13 Circuits*
Registry: 1 registrar (6a), 1 chief clerk (7a)[27]
General Services Office: 2 office managers (9b)[28]
Record Office: 1 record clerk (8a), 1 collator (9a)[29]
Prison Office: 1 prison superintendent (9b)[30]

In addition to these graded civil-service officials, the Censorate staff included at least 168 ungraded lesser functionaries serving in various

---

* Yunnan Circuit, 11 men; Chekiang Circuit, 10; Kiangsi Circuit, 10; Shantung Circuit, 10; Honan Circuit, 10; Hukwang Circuit, 8; Shensi Circuit, 8; Shansi Circuit 8; Kwangtung Circuit, 7; Fukien Circuit, 7; Szechwan Circuit, 7; Kwangsi Circuit, 7; Kweichow Circuit, 7.

clerical capacities and perhaps as many as 250 advanced students of the National University who were serving novitiates in surveillance processes.[31] Often men who had recently passed the doctoral examinations were also attached to the Censorate for a period of tutelage and observation before being assigned to their first substantive positions.[32]

The staff of the auxiliary Censorate at Nanking was smaller, but adhered to the same pattern. It consisted of the following:

1 censor-in-chief of the right (2a)
1 vice censor-in-chief of the right (3a)
1 assistant censor-in-chief of the right (4a)[33]
30 investigating censors,[34] divided among 13 Circuits*

The Nanking Censorate also included a Registry, a General Services Office, a Record Office, and a Prison Office, comparable to those in the Peking Censorate, and at least 103 ungraded lesser functionaries serving in clerical capacities.[35]

During the last two centuries of the Ming period the number of officials who bore the titles censor-in-chief, vice censor-in-chief, and assistant censor-in-chief became increasingly abundant; and in the last Ming decades the holders of such titles who actually performed duties in the Censorate were so rare that contemporary chroniclers found it advisable to identify them by appending to their titles the phrase "in charge of Censorate affairs."[36] The proliferation of these censorial titles resulted from the practice of giving them to grand coordinators and supreme commanders, the highest-level supervisory administrators in the provinces.

The offices of grand coordinators and supreme commanders originated in the fifteenth century, when vice ministers and other high-ranking officials of the central government were temporarily detached on special trouble-shooting commissions in the provinces. Gradually the positions became more regular, so that from about the beginning of the sixteenth century grand coordinators and supreme commanders were permanent fixtures of the provincial administrative hierarchy. But the men who held these positions were still officially considered on commission in the provinces and remained nominal members of central government organs, as has been noted. Beginning in 1453, they were regularly given concurrent nominal

* Yunnan Circuit, 2 men; Chekiang Circuit, 2; Kiangsi Circuit, 2; Shantung Circuit, 2; Honan Circuit, 2; Hukwang Circuit, 3; Shensi Circuit, 2; Shansi Circuit, 2; Kwangtung Circuit, 3; Fukien Circuit, 3; Szechwan Circuit, 2; Kwangsi Circuit, 3; Kweichow Circuit, 2.

status in the Censorate, and by the last years of the Ming period it
had become a standard practice for all grand coordinators and supreme commanders to have censorial titles as their principal nominal titles.

Consequently, it is sometimes said that these provincial officials
were Ming equivalents of the branch Censorates of Yüan times.[37] But
this was not actually the case. The grand coordinators and the supreme commanders did not have specialized censorial responsibilities. Neither did they have dealings with the metropolitan Censorate
and the local surveillance organs comparable to the dealings of the
Yüan branch Censorates. They were territorial administrators on a
large scale, and they were given censorial titles only "to facilitate
their affairs."[38] This meant, for one thing, that they could feel free
to submit memorials directly to the throne, bypassing normal document-control processes; but this consideration seems to have been
secondary. Grand coordinators were granted censorial titles in the
first place, in 1453, because they were being harassed too much by
regional inspectors—investigating censors on special provincial commissions (whose functions will be discussed in Chapter 3). It was felt
that giving grand coordinators titular high rank within the censorial
establishment itself might help to protect them from such harassment.[39]

Since the grand coordinators and the supreme commanders were
not primarily functioning censorial officials,[40] their activities will not
be discussed further in this study.

The Offices of Scrutiny

The tradition of speaking officials was revived to some extent in
Ming times after its deterioration under the Mongols. Even a Sung-
style Bureau of Remonstrance was briefly reconstituted. It did not
appear at the beginning of the dynasty, but in 1380, when it may have
been thought preferable to the Censorate, which had just been "abolished." Its staff was small, consisting only of two admonishers and
four monitors, of ranks 7a and 7b respectively. These titles, both of
which were inherited from the Sung system, were supplemented in
1382 by the even more ancient one of grand remonstrator. But almost
immediately thereafter, all these offices of remonstrators were discontinued—just at the time when the Censorate was restored to its former imposing status.[41] The traditional offices of omissioners and reminders were briefly reconstituted under Hui-ti (1398–1402), but the
Bureau of Remonstrance did not reappear.[42]

Supervising secretaries, however, were important censorial officials throughout the Ming period. For a brief time in T'ai-tsu's reign they had subordinate positions in the Office of Transmission, but at all other times they enjoyed organizational autonomy.[43]

The office of supervising secretary appeared in the first national government that T'ai-tsu created in 1367 but may not have been filled until 1373, when twelve officials were appointed.[44] In the latter year the supervising secretaries were for the first time distributed among six Offices of Scrutiny, each given a functional jurisdiction comparable to that of a Ministry. From 1389 until 1393 the supervising secretaries bore the unprecedented title "source officials," because they were considered to be "the root and source of governmental affairs."[45] But in 1393 the former designation was restored, and it remained in use throughout the rest of the dynasty. The Offices of Scrutiny were also reorganized to include chief supervising secretaries and left and right supervising secretaries as executive officials. In 1421, as in the case of the Censorate, two groups of Offices of Scrutiny emerged, one at Peking and one at Nanking.

In mature form, each Office of Scrutiny at Peking had one chief supervising secretary (7a), and one left and one right supervising secretary (7b). In all, there were 40 supervising secretaries (7b), whose number was reduced to 32 in the 1580's, as indicated below.

	At maturity	Later Ming decades
Office of Scrutiny for Personnel	4 men	4 men
Office of Scrutiny for Revenue	8 men	6 men
Office of Scrutiny for Rites	6 men	5 men
Office of Scrutiny for War	10 men	7 men
Office of Scrutiny for Justice	8 men	6 men
Office of Scrutiny for Works	4 men	4 men

The Nanking Offices of Scrutiny had only one supervising secretary each except for the Office of Scrutiny for Revenue, which had two. None had chief supervising secretaries or left and right supervising secretaries.[46]

There is no evidence that the staffs of Offices of Scrutiny included any ungraded lesser functionaries.

Provincial Surveillance Offices

Provincial Surveillance Offices[47] had the official designation of their early Yüan counterparts, literally Office for Punishments and Surveillance, which linked them terminologically to both judicial intendants of Sung times and surveillance commissioners of T'ang times. During the brief reign of Hui-ti (1398–1402) they had the variant designation Office for the Rectification of Administration and for Surveillance. Most commonly, they were known simply as Office for Surveillance, although the somewhat literary designation Office of the Fundamental Law was also occasionally used. They existed in all thirteen provinces alongside the Provincial Administration Offices and the Regional Military Commissions and shared with them the collective popular designation "the three provincial agencies." A fourteenth Provincial Surveillance Office, for the province of Chiao-chih (Annam), existed between 1407 and 1430.

These local surveillance organs appeared in T'ai-tsu's first national government in 1367. When the Censorate was "abolished" in 1380, they also were done away with; but they were restored in 1381 and experienced no further organizational vicissitudes.[48]

Each of the Provincial Surveillance Offices was organized on the following pattern:

> One surveillance commissioner (3a)
> Variable numbers of surveillance vice commissioners (4a)
> Variable numbers of assistant surveillance commissioners (5a)
> Registry: 1 registrar (7a), 1 chief clerk (8a)
> Record Office: 1 record clerk (9a), 1 collator (9b)
> Prison Office: 1 prison superintendent (9b)

Vice commissioners and assistant commissioners were normally in charge of branch offices detached from the principal office at the provincial capital, to provide closer surveillance over the prefectures, subprefectures, and counties. Their numbers varied greatly from province to province.

Like the Censorate, each Provincial Surveillance Office had a large clerical staff of ungraded lesser functionaries.[49]

RELATIONS AMONG THE CENSORIAL ORGANS

The extreme centralization of the censorial agencies that characterized the Yüan system did not persist into Ming times. The Censorate, the Offices of Scrutiny, and the Provincial Surveillance Offices were substantially independent of each other.

Within the Censorate itself, although investigating censors were subject to some administrative supervision by censors-in-chief, "they were nevertheless not their subordinate officials," one late Ming writer insisted.[50] The individual independence of action that censors enjoyed was apparently intended to facilitate their surveillance of one another.[51] But it was understood that censors-in-chief, who did give censors merit ratings upon completion of their tours of duty, should not normally submit impeachments of investigating censors during their service. Investigating censors, on the other hand, freely impeached the senior officials of the Censorate. "If a current censor-in-chief ought to be impeached," a contemporary wrote, "they forthwith impeach him and on withdrawing from court hand him a duplicate copy of the impeachment. The censor-in-chief does not dare reject it. Thus he is unable to gag or restrain them." In all such impeachments they "could act independently, without the censor-in-chief having any foreknowledge." Among supervising secretaries the same spirit of independence prevailed. Not only were the various Offices of Scrutiny totally independent of each other; even within any given Office of Scrutiny, the chief supervising secretary had no more control over his associates than did the censors-in-chief over the investigating censors.[52]

There were close working arrangements between the Offices of Scrutiny and the Censorate. Censors and supervising secretaries often served jointly on special investigatory missions, and in official documents they were commonly referred to by abbreviated collective designations that suggest they were thought of as a single homogeneous group.[53] The principal differences between them were their specializations. The supervising secretaries chiefly devoted themselves to their traditional controls over documents sent to and from the throne. Also, although they had long been regular officials of the "outer court," they were still considered to be intimate attendants of the imperial household, so that no emperor made public appearances without having supervising secretaries in close attendance, theoretically to counsel and remonstrate with him if need be. Censors, on the other hand, although they had nominal status as speaking officials, were chiefly concerned with much broader surveillance duties directed specifically at the officialdom.

Nonetheless, the distinction between censors and supervising secretaries had diminished greatly after T'ang and Sung times. Ming censors exercised remonstrance functions just as freely as supervising secretaries did, and supervising secretaries' document-control activities attracted them more and more to disciplinary surveillance over the officialdom and to submitting impeachments. But they remained organizationally separate. The trend toward amalgamation of the different censorial functions did not reach its natural culmination until the succeeding Ch'ing period, when supervising secretaries were at last incorporated into the Censorate, perhaps in an attempt to blunt rivalries that may have existed in Ming times.[54]

The Censorate's relationship with the Provincial Surveillance Offices was closer than its relationship with the Offices of Scrutiny, and its relationship with the Provincial Surveillance Offices changed more notably during the Ming period.

The Surveillance Offices were established at the beginning of the Ming era to serve as Censorate-like surveillance organs in the local government hierarchy. They were collectively called "the Outer Censorate," and their personnel, along with censors, were known as "guardians of the customs and fundamental laws," whose prescribed duty was "to rectify administration and enforce the laws."[55] The Surveillance Offices "repressed the myriad bureaucrats and awed the myriad functionaries," and their senior officials "were counterparts of the censor-in-chief and had equal authority."[56] Ming writers were fond of pointing out the distinction between the censorial functions of the Surveillance Offices and the administrative functions of the Provincial Administration Offices. "Surveillance is in their title because surveillance is their function," one proclaimed.[57] An elaborate code of regulations was drawn up to govern the conduct of surveillance commissioners and representatives of the Censorate in maintaining joint surveillance over local officials.[58]

The Surveillance Offices, however, were not directly subordinate to the Censorate, as their Yüan counterparts had been. In Yüan times the censorial hierarchy had been so integrated that the Censorate was empowered to promote and demote surveillance commissioners.[59] This close administrative relationship may have persisted into the earliest Ming years, but it is quite clear that at least after the reorganization of the Censorate in the 1380's, the Censorate did not have such tight control over the Surveillance Offices. For this reason, the Surveillance Offices are considered to have been independent of rather than subordinate to the Censorate.

Nevertheless, they were far less independent than the Offices of Scrutiny, for there were numerous procedural links between the Surveillance Offices and the Censorate. The Censorate was the channel through which the Surveillance Offices received instructions from the throne, just as Provincial Administration Offices received instructions through the six Ministries, and Regional Military Commissions received instructions through the Chief Military Commissions.[60] Moreover, routine correspondence from Surveillance Offices to other agencies was routed through the Censorate, and Surveillance Offices had to submit to the Censorate reports on their judicial and record-checking activities.[61]

Such was the early Ming system; but it changed. By the end of the sixteenth century, writers were complaining that Surveillance Offices were no longer exercising their surveillance functions.[62] These organs had from the outset performed judicial as well as censorial duties, and the judicial function had now become the predominant one. European visitors to late Ming China consistently described the Surveillance Offices as judicial agencies.[63] One contemporary Chinese complained: "Criminal cases from all over the empire are submitted for review to the Censorate, yet people have never regarded the Censorate as a judicial agency. Why should the Surveillance Offices alone become so?"[64] The Surveillance Offices' actual surveillance continued to decline during the seventeenth century until, in the words of a contemporary, by the end of the Ming period "the surveillance commissioners became merely administrative officials."[65] Chronicles of the 1620's, for example, no longer reveal significant procedural links between the Surveillance Offices and the Censorate; the surveillance commissioners were becoming more and more like their counterparts in the Provincial Administration Offices, from whom they differed only in having a judicial specialization.

During the succeeding Ch'ing dynasty, which perpetuated the general governmental structure of the Ming era, the divorce of the Surveillance Offices from the censorial hierarchy seems to have become complete. Surveillance commissioners of the Ch'ing period, consequently, are generally called provincial judges by Western writers.[66]

CENSORIAL PERSONNEL

Since censorial positions carried high prestige and subjected appointees to the special temptations and pressures encountered by all men responsible for criticizing others, finding suitable personnel for the various censorial offices posed problems for the Ming rulers. Ying-tsung (1435–49, 1457–64) once observed that in comparison with other officials, "the guardians of the customs and fundamental laws are of especial importance."[67] No one seems to have considered the possibility of creating a special censorial personnel corps with its own recruitment procedures and a permanent monopoly of censorial offices; and strong arguments could have been made against any such separation of censorship from the civil service. But it was recognized that recruitment into the civil service did not necessarily qualify one for specialized censorial positions. Ch'eng-tsu (1402–24) once emphasized this point:

As censors We must employ incorrupt, cautious, resolute, and upright men. If incorrupt, they will not be self-seeking. If cautious, they will not be irresponsible. If resolute and upright, they will dare to speak out. Censorate officials who are not like this should be demoted without delay.[68]

Many similar proclamations reveal the Ming emperors' persistent concern with finding just, honest, intelligent, virtuous, and responsible men for the Censorate, the Offices of Scrutiny, and the Surveillance Offices alike.[69] This concern led to the promulgation of a series of special eligibility regulations for censorial appointments, which were the only appointments distinguished in this way.[70]

Eligibility Qualifications

Positions in the Surveillance Offices and the offices of censors-in-chief, vice censors-in-chief, and assistant censors-in-chief were all of relatively high rank. Ordinarily, no one could be appointed to any of these offices without having many years of successful experience in lower-ranking civil-service positions. Men could be selected, therefore, with the reasonable certainty that they would conduct themselves properly once appointed. It was harder to screen men for appointments as investigating censors and supervising secretaries. Since these offices were ranked very low on the scale, appointees were necessarily in the early years of their civil service careers, and there could be far less certainty about the selections. The special regulations for censorial personnel, consequently, were aimed at minimizing this particular risk. They did so by successively narrowing eligibility according to two criteria: (1) the manner in which a man had originally entered the civil service, and (2) the extent of his prior experience in government. Throughout the Ming period, there was apparently an additional rule that relatives of all high-ranking officials were automatically ineligible for appointments as censors or supervising secretaries.[71]

The founding emperor, T'ai-tsu, seems to have established only one restriction on censorial appointments, and that a very vague one—that only men who were virtuous, upright, and incorrupt should be selected. In 1409 Ch'eng-tsu added the specification that men who had come into the civil service from original status as ungraded lesser functionaries were not to be considered.[72] Thereafter for several decades men who had entered the service as doctoral-examination passers, provincial-examination passers (licentiates), or National University graduates were all eligible; but during the latter half of the Ming period licentiates and National University graduates were periodically ruled ineligible. As a general rule, the official *Ming History* states, such men might be appointed to the Censorate but not to the Offices of Scrutiny, and even among appointees to the Censorate they were at most one in four.[73] Finally, in the last Ming decades, persons who had won the doctorate in examinations so dominated the entire civil service that a non-doctor had very little hope of obtaining any position, let along a censorial one.[74]

Parallel to the increasing emphasis on obtaining doctoral graduates for the censorial posts was an effort to limit eligibility to men who had some previous experience in government service. In 1425 Jen-tsung suggested that censors should be selected only from among men who were experienced and who showed understanding of governmental practices.[75] In 1435 it was specifically ordered that thereafter newly employed men should not be appointed as censors, and from the 1440's on eligibility was increasingly restricted to men who had from three to six years of experience in specified offices.[76] Experience as prefectural judge or county magistrate became increasingly esteemed as preparation for duty in the Censorate.[77] Beginning in 1502, these rules were made applicable to the appointments of supervising secretaries as well as censors.[78] That such regulations were actually enforced is well borne out by analyses of reported appointments.[79]

The growing emphasis on obtaining experienced men for the censorial posts did not alter the basic character of the censorial service. Censors and supervising secretaries remained, characteristically, young and relatively inexperienced, in accord with the long tradition already mentioned. The eligibility requirements merely prevented censorial offices from being filled by men who were too young and too inexperienced to be effective. The men who did fill them were normally in their second civil-service appointments, and though still relatively young, they were at that stage in their careers when their bureaucratic futures lay in the balance and aggressiveness was needed.

It is possible that the imposition of experience qualifications on censorial appointments reflects a decline, after the early decades of the dynasty, in the average ages of doctoral graduates. Unfortunately, we do not yet have statistical studies of Ming bureaucratic careers, which might confirm such a possibility. Except for a reference by a memorialist in 1530 to an old rule that men under the age of thirty might not be appointed supervising secretaries, I have found no evidence of age qualifications for censorial appointees.[80] But I am inclined to believe that in general men were winning their doctoral degrees at earlier ages in the 1600's than in the 1400's. Experience requirements may therefore have had the effect of merely setting the age level of appointees back to the earlier norm.[81]

In addition to restrictions about manner of original recruitment and prior experience in government, there was a third series of regulations which, from 1441 on, established a general rule that appointees as investigating censors must serve a probationary period before being given substantive appointments. The first step of this sort was taken in 1428, when Hsüan-tsung ordered that the Censorate let recommended men gain experience in the various Circuits for three months, after which time they were to be graded in three classes. Those rated in the upper or middle classes could then be appointed censors, whereas those in the lower class would be sent back to the Ministry of Personnel for reassignment.[82] In 1439 and 1441 similar orders were issued, and the probationary period was extended to six months.[83] Thereafter investigating censors' appointments followed the pattern Hsüan-tsung had suggested. The Ministry of Personnel nominated men for probationary service of six months or for acting appointments of one year. At the end of the designated period, the censors-in-chief rated the probationers on their conduct. Those who were considered satisfactory were then given substantive appointments.[84] This procedure persisted even after the requirement of prior service experience had been instituted—in fact to the end of the dynasty—though in late Ming practice the probationary period was often very short.[85] At no time, however, were rules about probationary appointments applied to supervising secretaries. Moreover, they did not apply to Hanlin bachelors—post-doctoral students and observers in the Hanlin Academy—when they were appointed investigating censors.[86]

When Censorate vacancies required filling, it was sometimes even ordered that censors-in-chief and investigating censors submit guaranteed recommendations of men they knew were qualified.[87] And in late Ming times officials of the Censorate, in conjunction with representatives of the Ministry of Personnel, occasionally gave special qualifying examinations to nominees for positions in the Censorate and the Offices of Scrutiny before approving them. The examinations sometimes dealt with current government problems and sometimes concentrated on the form in which memorials had to be submitted.[88]

It is noteworthy that the welter of special rules applying to censorial appointments apparently did not include any restrictions on the geographical origins of candidates. The Ming government was very sensitive about disproportionate regional representation in the civil service as a whole, and it especially tried to prevent examination candidates of the rich and cultured southeastern provinces from monopolizing the doctoral pass-lists, as they might have done in any wholly "open" competition. Pass quotas were eventually assigned on a large regional basis, allowing southerners to have a majority (55 per cent) of doctoral degrees but ensuring that northerners (35 per cent) and even westerners (10 per cent) could get fair representation in proportion to the regional populations.[89] Perhaps it was assumed that such control over admission to the service made unnecessary any further geographical quotas in actual appointments, even to the sensitive censorial offices. And in practice it worked out that geographical representation in appointments seems to have been roughly proportional to the regional examination quotas (see Appendix Tables, Table 1). In any event, no rules were ever promulgated to make native place a factor in eligibility for censorial office.

In general, according to a summation of the situation in the *Ming History,* whenever civil-service reassignments were being considered there was an effort to assign the best young men to the Offices of Scrutiny, the next best to the Censorate, and the third best to the Ministries.[90]

Tenure and Continuity of Service

As was the case with officials in general, censorial officials normally held their posts for nine years and then were promoted or demoted as circumstances warranted. There was no requirement, however, that they be retained in service for full nine-year terms; they had no guaranteed tenure. Every three years they were given merit ratings by their administrative superiors in conjunction with the Ministry of Personnel, and it was common for a good official to be promoted or a bad one demoted after three or six years in a post.[91] In actual practice, censorial tenure seems to have been relatively long. Nine-year tenure was not uncommon.[92]

Senior officials of the Offices of Scrutiny were consistently chosen from among the lesser supervising secretaries. Appointees often served in unbroken succession as supervising secretaries, right supervising secretaries, left supervising secretaries, and finally chief supervising secretaries. The fact that all these offices were of low rank permitted this sort of steady stepping-stone progress. But in the Censorate things were different. There was a significant gap in rank between investigating censors (7a) and the lowest of the senior officials, the assistant censors-in-chief (4a). It was quite rare, therefore, for investigating censors to be promoted directly into the senior positions. My tabulations of data in the basic chronicles reveal only two such cases between 1424 and 1434 and none at all between 1620 and 1627. Nevertheless, the senior Censorate officials were normally men who had backgrounds in the censorial services.[93] Thus there was some measure of continuity and cumulative expertise in the system.[94]

In the early Ming years, such continuity of censorial service was often achieved by promoting investigating censors or supervising secretaries into Provincial Surveillance Offices and then, after suitable intervals, promoting them further into the executive offices of the Censorate. But in the latter half of the dynasty, as the Provincial Surveillance Offices grew away from their original censorial roles, other devices had to be found. This sometimes meant that an investigating censor or a supervising secretary was promoted nominally, as a supernumerary, into a non-censorial office at the capital (usually in an imperial household "service" agency such as the Court of the Imperial Stud) and authorized to carry on with his former censorial duties, pending a time when it might be appropriate to promote him again into an executive office in the Censorate.[95]

This change in career prospects was undoubtedly a change for the better from the point of view of the censors and supervising secretaries themselves, since in late Ming times any kind of position at the capital seems to have been preferred to a provincial position. By the 1620's there had developed a practice called "annual provincial transfers," whereby four supervising secretaries and eight investigating censors each year were promoted into provincial offices, entirely outside the normal processes of perodic merit ratings, promotions, and demotions. How and why the practice originated is not clear, but senior officials of the Censorate and the Offices of Scrutiny seem to have used it to rid their staffs of men who, though not deserving disciplinary action, were unwanted for some reason. The victims of these "annual provincial transfers" clearly considered themselves punished. One investigating censor who suffered such a promotion to the post of assistant surveillance commissioner (5a) petitioned vigorously and was later graciously permitted to resume his former lowly office of censor (7a) in the capital.[96]

Censorial Careers

The fact that senior censorial officials had usually held previous censorial positions, and that there was consequently some accumulation of experience within the censorial system, does not mean that any one official could expect to be a career censor. The censorial agencies were staffed with men who belonged to the civil service as a whole, and their careers were characteristically diversified.

The career of one early Ming censor-in-chief, Ku Tso, came about as close to being a specialized censorial career as was possible in Ming times. A native of Honan province in the Yellow River plain, Ku won his doctoral degree in 1400 and was promptly appointed magistrate of a county in far northwestern Kansu province. In 1402 he was called to Nanking (then the capital) to be an investigating censor. In this role he had periods of detached service in Kwangsi province in the far southwest, in Szechwan province in west central China, in Peking, and along the northern frontiers. Before 1425 he had also served successively as surveillance vice commissioner of Kiangsi province in the southeast, prefectural governor of Nanking and then Peking, and surveillance commissioner of Kweichow province in the southwest. In 1425 he was recalled to the capital (Peking) to be commissioner of the Office of Transmission, and in 1428 Hsüan-tsung appointed him censor-in-chief of the right. Except for taking more than a year of sick leave in 1433–34, he served in that office until he retired from active duty in 1436. He died in retirement eight years later. Ku probably spent well over half of his long career in the Censorate and in Surveillance Offices.[97]

Long service in the Offices of Scrutiny was relatively common, as has been noted above. An illustrative career is that of Li Chün of Shensi province. A doctoral graduate of 1469, Li was directly appointed to the Office of Scrutiny for Personnel and thereafter through successive promotions became its chief supervising secretary, having continuous service in the same agency for some fifteen years. But then, in 1485, he was transferred out of the capital, and he spent the remainder of his career in Provincial Administration Offices of Hukwang and Shansi provinces.[98]

The most famous of all Ming censors, Yang Lien, entered censorial service twelve years after winning his doctoral degree, and then had an intensive and varied, but still not unbroken, censorial career. Yang was a Hukwang man who passed his doctoral examination in 1607 and had a full nine-year tour as a county magistrate in the Southern Metropolitan Area beginning in 1608. It was not until 1619 that he was called to Peking to be a supervising secretary in the Office of Scrutiny for Revenue. A highly controversial figure in a series of partisan struggles, he quickly rose to the position of left supervising

secretary and then was chief supervising secretary of the Office of
Scrutiny for War (1620), chief supervising secretary of the Office of
Scrutiny for Rites (1622), supernumerary vice minister of the Court
of Imperial Sacrifices (1622), assistant censor-in-chief (1623), and vice
censor-in-chief (1624). Then, for denouncing the notorious eunuch
dictator Wei Chung-hsien, he was dismissed from the service and
finally in 1625 was put to death in the prison of the imperial bodyguard.[99]

A more representative career, including varied kinds of censorial
service but mostly spent in other governmental realms, was that of
Sun Wei, a Shensi man awarded his doctoral degree in 1577. In that
year he was appointed a lowly messenger (8a) in the Messenger Office
at Peking, and in 1582 he was promoted to the Office of Scrutiny for
War as a supervising secretary (7b). After only a year and a half in
this post, he went home on extended sick leave. Recalled in 1586,
he filled a vacancy as supervising secretary in the Office of Scrutiny
for Revenue; but four months later he took unauthorized leave of
absence to mourn his mother's death and was demoted. In 1590, after
his mourning was completed, he began his career anew, as an assistant
county magistrate (9a) in Hukwang province, virtually at the bottom
of the civil-service hierarchy. Five months later he was promoted to
the post of prefectural judge (7a) in Kwangtung province, and in
1591 he was recalled to Peking to be secretary (6a) of the Bureau of
Provisions in the Ministry of War. In 1592 he was transferred to the
Seal Office as assistant director (6a), and then in 1593 promotion made
him vice director (5b) of the same agency. He subsequently became
a vice minister (5a) of the Court of Imperial Entertainments in 1594,
a vice minister (4a) of the Court of the Imperial Stud in 1595, a vice
minister (4a) of the Court of Imperial Sacrifices in 1598, and chief
minister (3b) of the Court of Imperial Entertainments a month later.
In 1601 he was promoted to the office of prefectural governor (3a) at
Peking, and before the end of that year he was transferred to the
Court of Imperial Sacrifices as chief minister (3a).

After these ten years in the capital, Sun was promoted in 1602 to
the post of grand coordinator of the strategic Pao-ting frontier area
near Peking with the nominal office of vice censor-in-chief of the
right (3a). While he still served in this capacity his salary was increased to the level of rank 2a in 1605, and in 1607 his nominal title
was changed to vice minister of war (3a) and concurrently assistant
censor-in-chief of the right (4a). The following year promotion made
him supreme commander for provisions along the northern frontier,

with nominal office as censor-in-chief of the right (2a) and concurrently vice minister (3a) of revenue. In 1611 his nominal title became minister of war (2a), and in 1612, still with that title, he was assigned the duties of the censor-in-chief of the left in active charge of the Censorate. After one year of that duty he went home on sick leave, no doubt anticipating a deserved retirement after 36 years in the bureaucracy.

In 1621, however, Sun was recalled to duty as Nanking minister of personnel (2a) and then was promptly transferred to the office of minister of war (2a) and grand adjutant at Nanking, thus becoming a member of a viceregal triumvirate in command of the auxiliary capital. Summoned again to Peking in 1623 as minister of justice (2a), he was transferred almost immediately to the position of minister of personnel (2a) assigned to the duties of censor-in-chief of the left, in active charge of the Censorate. He pleaded for months to be retired, without getting the emperor's permission, and finally died in office late in 1624, some 52 years after entering the service, and probably approaching his eightieth birthday.[100]

Sun Wei's career, though by no means of typical longevity, is representative in its variety. Relatively few men lived so long or attained such high distinction, but the vast majority of civil servants experienced the same sort of zigzag progress up, down, and across the bureaucratic hierarchy, with interruptions for parental mourning and for sick leaves. A large proportion of them undoubtedly held censorial offices at least for brief periods in their lives. But no one could expect to serve indefinitely in the censorial agencies, or indeed in any particular kind of agency.

The combination of diversified career backgrounds and unpredictable future expectations that characterized the censorial staffs had both advantages and disadvantages for the system. On one hand, the censorial officials of any period collectively had direct, personal knowledge of the work of almost all the branches and levels of government that they were charged with investigating. They were not inexperienced idealists; it should not have been easy for a wayward official to hoodwink them. On the other hand, a censor or supervising secretary necessarily had to be mindful that a year hence or a decade hence he might find himself the direct subordinate of any line administrative official whom he might harass. The youthful zeal that investigating censors in particular were expected to display could only be somewhat tempered by such considerations.

Chapter three

Censorial Surveillance Techniques

The Ming censorial establishment was always comparatively small. Not counting lesser functionaries, or novices on detached duty from the National University and the Hanlin Academy, or personnel of such internal-administration agencies as the Registry, the Record Office, and the General Services Office, the normal roster of active censors—the investigating censors and the various levels of censors-in-chief—included 118 men in the metropolitan Censorate and 33 in the Nanking Censorate. The six Offices of Scrutiny were normally staffed with 50 to 58 men in Peking and 7 in Nanking. The various kinds of surveillance commissioners assigned to the empire's 13 Provincial Surveillance Offices fluctuated greatly in number and proliferated in the last Ming decades, but into the sixteenth century they normally numbered about 177.[1] Thus there were fewer than 400 men working as censorial officials in a civil service that regularly included from 10,000 to 15,000 "commissioned" officials.

Nevertheless, the censorial staff bore awesome responsibilities. The Censorate's officials were relied upon as "the ears and eyes of the emperor." They and surveillance commissioners were "guardians of the customs and fundamental laws"; and censors and supervising secretaries comprised the "avenues of criticism" upon which the well-being of the state was thought to depend. Such terms, though derived from centuries-old traditions, were not meaningless clichés. As they imply, the censorial agencies were charged with keeping under surveillance all agencies and operations of the whole governmental hierarchy, military as well as civil, and with requesting or instituting whatever preventive, corrective, and punitive measures were called for to maintain the proper and effective conduct of government in all spheres. No other group of institutions in the Ming government had such far-reaching, many-faceted responsibilities.

THE PROBLEM OF ACCESS TO INFORMATION

In order to fulfill their responsibilities, the censorial agencies natural-ly had to have access to information about governmental activities. Unfortunately for them, public news media, inadequate even in mod-ern China, were almost nonexistent in Ming times. As in other pre-modern societies, the public generally had to reply on the reports of travelers—such as merchants, officials, entertainers, and mendicant monks—for even regional news; and the Chinese empire was so vast that the populace had little awareness of national news. The literacy rate was low, and there was no public postal service and no public press. As a well-known proverb put it, "Heaven is high, and the em-peror is far away."

On the other hand, among the educated classes, and especially among officials, there was a lively private exchange of information. As a glimpse into any of the collected writings of eminent men will reveal, the literati were avid correspondents. Responsible travelers no doubt carried a heavy freight of letters to be delivered or relayed en route. Moreover, the literati frequently traveled, for official and unofficial reasons. Consequently, the level of information about pub-lic affairs was perhaps higher among the Chinese literati than among even the elite classes of any other contemporary society. It would be impossible to measure the extent to which censorial officials relied in these ways upon associates and correspondents to obtain "inside information" about events; but it should be kept in mind that such unofficial sources were manifold.

At least by late Ming times the need for information throughout the officialdom was served more effectively by a periodical, semi-offi-cial court circular, distributed to all capital agencies and throughout the provinces. It reproduced in detail important memorials submitted to the throne and edicts and rescripts issued from the throne. This embryonic newspaper, which perhaps had antecedents as early as T'ang times, eventually developed into the *Peking Gazette,* familiar to all foreigners in China in the nineteenth century.[2] We do not yet know its history, and we can only guess at its early form and method of distribution. Something like it may have existed from early Ming times. At least from the 1590's on it was a common source of informa-tion throughout the government.[3] By the 1620's, censorial officials were regularly citing in their memorials things they had read in the court circular, which had become their only major independent source of information.

Even in these late Ming years, however, the censorial agencies had to rely primarily upon their own information-gathering devices and processes. The techniques that they developed were sophisticated and apparently sufficient for surveillance purposes. There were three basic techniques: direct observation, routine receipt of reports and complaints, and checks on the flow of government documents.

DIRECT OBSERVATION

It was obviously impossible for the censorial staff to subject all governmental activities to continuous, direct, personal surveillance. But the system was so arranged that censorial officials were always present at state functions of a public sort that were considered important; and they always participated directly, at the provincial level as well as at the national capital, in formal deliberations about major government problems and policies. And all other government activities were subjected to at least periodic censorial visitations.

Censorial Participation in Major Governmental Functions

The main focus of state affairs was the imperial court. There in normal times, capital officials had daily audiences with the emperor. The founding emperor, T'ai-tsu, met officials in audience three times a day—at dawn, noon, and night. Later emperors omitted the evening audiences, and some did not hold noon audiences. As mentioned in Chapter 2, a few emperors did not personally participate in daily audiences at all for long periods. But officials were always required to attend if they were on duty in the capital, and it was at such audiences that state policies were announced and discussed. In addition to such "regular" audiences, there were more ritualistic court assemblies: to observe the coming of the new year and the changing of the seasons, to celebrate birthdays of the emperor and his close relatives, to formalize the appointments of empresses and heirs apparent, to lament eclipses, and so forth.

Like all other officials, censors and supervising secretaries were required to attend all imperial audiences, whether regular or irregular. Not only were they able to observe all that went on, but some of them also had special assignments to enforce the ritual regulations, which were carefully spelled out for each type of audience.[4] It was common that audiences were not adjourned until these special "ritual police" (2 supervising secretaries and from 4 to 24 investigating censors at each audience) had been called on to point out ritual irregularities, if any. Irregularities by low-ranking officials were denounced immediately in the emperor's presence, whereas those committed by officials of the third or higher ranks were memorialized about.[5]

Ritual irregularities in audience that were denounced included "disrupting the order of precedence, speaking out in a hubbub, violating the prescribed ceremony, and not being appropriately costumed."[6] For example, in 1428 one investigating censor in open court denounced two young Ministry officials for violating procedural rules in reporting on a courier mission, and in 1621 a supervising secretary submitted a memorial impeaching a vice minister of the Court of the Imperial Stud who had been "listless and clumsy" while attending audience.[7] In 1427, the investigating censor Hsiung Chien denounced 21 high-ranking military officers, 12 of whom held noble titles, for failing to attend audience at all. At the same time, he impeached the senior officials of the Court of State Ceremonial, who served as masters of ceremony at all audiences and other important state functions, for having conducted audience sloppily.[8]

Censorial officials were not exempt from the prohibition against outsiders' visiting the inner recesses of the palace, but no emperor could properly make any public appearance at all without having both supervising secretaries and investigating censors in close attendance. Thus they were present at all the imposing ceremonial appearances that encumbered the imperial calendar, including the great sacrifices at the suburban altars to Heaven and to Earth, the imperial plowing rite that inaugurated the planting season, the visits to the tombs of the imperial ancestors in the hills outside Peking, and the great military reviews in the capital.[9] Such surveillance was facilitated by the fact that supervising secretaries were still considered "inner court" personal attendants, specifically obliged to remonstrate with the emperor whenever appropriate. Investigating censors were present, theoretically, to prevent or denounce offenses against the emperor. In practice, both types of censorial officials submitted both impeachments and remonstrances on the basis of their observations.

When officials met outside of the imperial presence to deliberate about major policy problems or to nominate civil officials for the highest-ranking posts, censorial observation was assured. There was a standing regulation that both investigating censors and supervising secretaries had to participate in all official gatherings of the top capital officials.[10] More select official gatherings for deliberation and consultation ordinarily included the senior censor-in-chief. He and the ministers of the six Ministries, constituting an informal group called the "seven chief ministers" were usually expected to advise emperors about matters not entrusted to more general assemblies. He was also the Censorate representative in the "three judicial offices" (the Censorate, the Ministry of Justice, and the Grand Court of Revision), which had to consult before any death sentence could be ratified. It was obviously intended that no formal official consultations about any aspect of state administration could occur in the capital without censorial officials being directly involved in some fashion.

In the provinces, direct censorial participation in and observation of major public functions was most routinely provided by the Provincial Surveillance Offices. At least during the first century of the dynasty, the senior surveillance commissioners were provincial counterparts of the censors-in-chief at the capital, joining in deliberations about all important matters with senior officials from the other two provincial offices (the Provincial Administration Offices and the Regional Military Commissions).[11] After the middle of the fifteenth century, the three provincial offices declined somewhat in importance, and the new grand coordinators, who themselves had nominal status as censors-in-chief, presided over major deliberations. Then direct surveillance at the provincial level increasingly became the responsibility of regional inspectors, who were investigating censors sent out from the capital to extended duty in all provinces. Thus major functions and deliberations at the provincial capitals, as at the national capital, were closely observed by one censorial official or another.

This routine, almost automatic involvement of censorial agencies in major decision-making processes kept the censorial officials informed about governmental policies and operations in general and provided data that could be used in impeaching and remonstrating. But the charge laid upon the censorial system required much more particular investigatory surveillance over governmental operations. This was provided by more specific investigatory assignments for individual censorial officials.

Special Investigatory Assignments in Surveillance Offices

As the structure of the censorial hierarchy suggests, the basic responsibility for close surveillance at all levels, except at the two capitals, belonged to the Provincial Surveillance Offices. Consequently, whereas the senior surveillance commissioner stayed at the provincial capital to oversee general business and to consult with the Provincial Administration Offices and Regional Military Commissions, the vice commissioners and assistant commissioners were characteristically assigned to more specific tasks. Since the circumstances and needs of the provinces varied, the number of these officials varied from province to province. Some had responsibility for particular categories of affairs on a province-wide basis. Others were responsible for geographic jurisdictions, either as general field representatives of the home office or as inspectors of particular categories of affairs on a local level. All were expected to tour their overlapping jurisdictions regularly to keep close watch over developments at the grass roots.[12] Their counterparts in the Provincial Administration Offices were similarly distributed about the provinces in branch offices, to provide closer supervision of the general administration of prefects and magistrates than could be provided from the provincial capital.[13] The specific jurisdictions of all these detached officials—some defined territorially, others defined functionally—were called Circuits, and the officials were commonly referred to as circuit intendants. The Chinese term for circuit intendant, *tao-t'ai,* eventually entered the vocabulary of all foreigners in nineteenth-century China.

In general, every Surveillance Office had three Circuits with province-wide responsibilities. The first, an Education Intendant Circuit, had an intendant responsible for inspecting schools, examining students, and awarding the lowest-level civil-service degrees (the bachelors' degrees) that qualified candidates for triennial examinations in the provincial capital. The second was a Troop Purification Circuit, whose intendant kept watch over the continuing process of obtaining troop replacements from responsible "military families" of the province. The third was a Postal Service Circuit, whose intendant watched over the operation of all remount and runner stations, which constituted a government communications network noted for its rapid service but not available to the general public.

In addition to these Circuits with province-wide functional jurisdictions, each Surveillance Office generally had several territorially defined General Surveillance Circuits, Record Checking Circuits, and Military Defense Circuits. A General Surveillance Circuit was an all-purpose field branch of the Surveillance Office covering a territory usually encompassing several prefectures; there were as few as three in one province and as many as nine in another. Record Checking Circuits, from two to seven per province, engaged in intensive document-control processes of a sort to be discussed later in this chapter. Military Defense Circuits, whose intendants maintained censorial surveillance over all routine military activities in their jurisdictions, originally numbered from one to twelve per province but eventually became so numerous that in late Ming times, in the words of the official *Ming History,* they "overflowed the empire."[14] Still other kinds of branch offices or Circuits existed in particular provinces to deal with matters of local importance: there were Irrigation Control Circuits, Coastal Patrol Circuits, Salt Control Circuits, River Patrol Circuits, and so on. Some of these were more or less permanent, but others were transitory. For example, when a military campaign was undertaken in a province, a special Army Inspecting Circuit was set up, the intendant being required to check the accuracy of all military reports relating to the campaign.

Since the province-size "metropolitan areas" surrounding Peking and Nanking were not in provinces and were not organized under their own provincial-level administrations, circuit intendants of various sorts were assigned from the Provincial Administration Offices and Provincial Surveillance Offices of the neighboring provinces to oversee their prefectures. In the Northern Metropolitan Area surrounding Peking, four surveillance Circuits were provided from Shantung province to the east and six from Shansi province to the west. In the Southern Metropolitan Area surrounding Nanking, three Circuits were provided from Shantung province to the north and five from Hukwang, Kiangsi, and Chekiang provinces to the west and south. Thus no part of the empire was omitted from the close scrutiny of the Surveillance Offices, and because in all areas Circuits defined functionally overlapped those defined territorially, the surveillance net was finely woven indeed. Every locality could expect visits at regular intervals from several types of Surveillance Office representatives.

In addition to carrying out routine activities in their various Circuit assignments, officials of the Provincial Surveillance Offices were commonly bombarded with orders from the emperor for special, ad hoc investigations—for example, to report on the extent of a drought in Shansi province and the advisability of granting tax remissions because of it, to inventory government silk stored in Szechwan province that had reportedly been damaged by worms, or to verify whether or not a government-owned residence in Shensi province that had been petitioned for by an imperial prince was in fact unused.[15] Especially in the first century of the dynasty, emperors commonly reacted to all reports or complaints about local matters by referring them for investigation to the appropriate Surveillance Offices, which often acted in conjunction with their respective Administration Offices. As early as 1430 a surveillance vice commander of Kiangsi province complained that special, ad hoc assignments were distracting the intendants from their proper functions.[16]

The Provincial Surveillance Offices had some judicial functions at all times, and these also occupied the time of the vice commissioners and assistant commissioners who continuously toured the provinces.

Moreover, although these officials were in theory solely surveillance officials, other non-censorial administrative responsibilities inevitably fell upon them or were seized by them; and as the decades passed, the whole provincial surveillance apparatus was diverted more and more from its original censorial character. Given the present state of our knowledge, it is not possible to determine to what degree at any given time the apparatus provided a genuine censorial service. Clearly it did in early Ming times.

Special Investigatory Assignments of Censors and Supervising Secretaries

A system of duty assignments kept officials of the Censorate and of the Offices of Scrutiny also moving on special inspection tours, in the provinces as well as in the capital. To some extent this counteracted the local slack that appeared in the surveillance net later in the dynasty because of the changing role of the Provincial Surveillance Offices. Supervising secretaries of the Offices of Scrutiny were less active in this regard than were the Censorate's investigating censors. There were fewer supervising secretaries and they probably had a heavier burden of routine paperwork; furthermore, the fact that they had not completed their transition from inner-court speaking officials to full-fledged surveillance officials also kept them from too-frequent investigatory assignments away from court. But for investigating censors, such assignments were by far the most important aspect of their service.

The practice of granting special investigatory commissions to individual investigating censors, which had a long pre-Ming history, was revived very early in the dynasty and was quickly standardized.[17] Eventually there were many different types of commissions. Some were regularly filled for specific terms such as one year, and a censor assigned to such a commission could not terminate it without being relieved by a replacement. Other commissions were filled only at intervals of three months or one year or three years or even five years; as soon as the task was accomplished, the assigned censor was available for other duty and no replacement was assigned until the next scheduled time for the commission came around. Still others were irregularly filled on an ad hoc basis, and usually for indefinite, short terms.

Commissions were graded in three categories: major, ordinary, and minor, according to the esteem in which they were held.[18] Assignments to commissions were rotated among the investigating censors on the basis of seniority, and censors were generally not permitted to take a major commission without having completed an ordinary commission.[19] As a rule, an investigating censor had to complete three commissions before he could be considered for promotion. In 1623 the requirement was reduced to two commissions. Supervising secretaries were apparently required to complete one commission before being considered for promotion.[20]

For each vacant major or ordinary commission, the Censorate was required to nominate two investigating censors, and the emperor personally chose one of them for assignment. The senior Censorate officials were permitted to make assignments to minor commissions independently.[21] When a censor returned to the capital after completing a commission in the provinces, he was required to submit a report directly to the emperor before turning in any report to the Censorate.[22] Censors on commission were therefore considered independent agents of the emperor rather than field representatives of the Censorate. Sometimes censors-in-chief complained that censors returning from commissions did not bother to report to the Censorate at all.[23]

It must be noted that commissions were not themselves official posts, nor were they used to indicate one's rank in the civil service. An investigating censor officially of the Shensi Circuit, for example, might be assigned to any type of commission and sent to any geographical area. He might even be commissioned as regional inspector of Fukien province. His functional designation would then be investigating censor (serving as) regional inspector of Fukien, or in abbreviated form, Fukien regional-inspecting censor. But such titles were not rank-titles; they merely designated one's temporary functional assignment. The omission of any reference to the censor's official Circuit also emphasized the fact that censors on commission were agents of the emperor and were neither representatives of the Censorate nor representatives of its Circuits.

Investigating censors of the Nanking Censorate were assigned to certain commissions peculiar to their own agency but if needed could also be assigned to commissions by the metropolitan Censorate at Peking.[24]

Irregular commissions to which investigating censors and supervising secretaries were assigned could be enumerated endlessly. Many were related to the censorial system's special judicial role, which will be considered separately in Chapter 6. Many others were occasioned by large-scale natural disasters—floods, droughts, earthquakes, and so on—which called for investigations and reports. The always considerate emperor Hsüan-tsung, after leading a successful military campaign to put down the rebellion of a prince in 1426, sent censors, supervising secretaries, and some other officials out along the route of the army to check on damage to private property, with instructions to request tax remissions for all farmers whose fields had been trampled by the troops.[25] In general, whenever an emperor wanted special information or verification of reports submitted by the line military and administrative officials, whether or not another censorial official was already on the scene to be queried, he often ordered an investigating censor, or a supervising secretary, or both to undertake a special investigatory mission and report. And sometimes such ad hoc commissions grew into extended tours of duty.

Many of the more regular commissions were created to assure close censorial surveillance over governmental realms that were considered especially vital to the well-being of the state or especially susceptible to abuse. Several kinds of commissions concentrated censorial attention on the military establishment, and several others concentrated attention on the handling of state revenues and property.

Surveillance over the military establishment. One important group of censorial commissions focused on the recruitment, training, and tactical employment of the empire's military forces, activities that were naturally among the great continuing concerns of the Ming government.

Recruitment processes were the special concern of censorial officials assigned to "troop-purification" commissions.[26] Positions in the Guard and Battalion garrisons were constantly becoming vacant because of deaths or desertions, and it was required that new men be provided from the military families who were originally responsible for the positions vacated. The conscripting of replacements was largely the business of village headmen,* and they apparently had ample

---

* Ironically, censors themselves were sometimes responsible for abuses. The case of the troop-purification investigating censor Li Li is one example. He was dispatched to the Southern Metropolitan Area in 1428 and, thinking that the emperor's only wish was to obtain troops, high-handedly threw himself into the actual recruitment process. When he discovered that a particular military family owing a replacement to a particular Guard had in fact become exhausted, he arbitrarily conscripted men who happened to have the same surname, men who were distantly related, or even men who were connected only through having taken over the exhausted family's lands. Village headmen who protested were punished cruelly. When Li's abuses were finally denounced at court, 159 men whom he had improperly impressed were released, and 1,239 others, having already joined the Guards to which he had assigned them and having accepted pay, were ordered to continue serving only for their own lifetimes—that is, without having to transmit their military obligations to their heirs as was the general rule. (HTSL 89.2b, 89.3a–b.)

opportunities for corruption in the sale of exemptions, the concealment of returned deserters, and so on.[27]

Once on duty in a Guard garrison, soldiers had to put up with many
more abuses. Some of the common ones are pointed out in an imperial
exhortation of 1434 to all Provincial Surveillance Offices and all regional inspectors:

Military administration is one of the most urgent national concerns. From
the time of the ancestors, laws have been perfected for the encouragement
and lenient treatment of soldiers and for the setting in order of military
defenses. We have repeatedly warned the inner and outer military officers
to observe the law and to take appreciative care of the troops, but in recent
times the officers of the Provincial Military Commissions, the Guards, and
the Battalions have devoted themselves to nothing but graft. When there
are campaigns, they send off the poor and sell exemptions to the rich; and
when requisitions are levied they pass along tenfold demands. Some convert
soldiers into their private attendants. Some make them pay in ["kick back"]
their monthly salaries. Some permit them to engage in trade. Some usurp
their monthly rations. Some hold back the issuance of winter uniforms. Their
exactions and harassments are of myriad sorts, so that soldiers become so
desperate for clothing and food that they even abandon their wives and
children to slip away and escape.[28]

On one occasion in the 1420's it was reported that of 15,716 men conscripted in Shansi province and sent to join the Guards around T'ai-
yüan city, 1,713 had deserted within a short time.[29]

From an early time in the reign of T'ai-tsu, the government, recognizing the prevalence of such abuses, sent out a steady stream of troop-
purification supervising secretaries and other officials. Troop Purification Circuits were established by almost every Provincial Surveillance Office and almost every Provincial Administration Office as
well, but additional special checks were still necessary. In 1426, 15
high-ranking officials, including one vice censor-in-chief, were distributed among the provinces to rectify military conditions.[30] In 1428
there was a mass assignment of 14 investigating censors and 14 supervising secretaries to inspect military-service conditions in two-man
teams.[31] Such ad hoc commissions were given until 1440, when 17
standard troop-purification commissions were established for investigating censors, stretching a surveillance net over all provinces and
both metropolitan areas. A one-year term was prescribed. In 1458 the
term of duty was extended to three years and in 1560 to five years. By
the latter period the number of these commissions had been reduced
to 14. In Nanking, one censor, one supervising secretary, and one
Nanking Ministry of War official made up an additional three-man

team for troop-purification duty; they were appointed for three-year terms.[32]

Although the eventual breakdown of the original heredity-based military system was clearly foreseen, the government could not prevent it and finally turned for survival to a system of mercenaries, but in vain.[33] By the 1620's, censorial officials of the capital were no longer being assigned to the traditional troop-purification commissions. Instead, they were busily occupied in the active recruitment of mercenaries to shore up the tottering frontier defenses, as will be noted in Chapter 6.

Maintaining surveillance over training exercises in the scattered garrisons of the empire was principally the responsibility of Troop Purification Circuits of the Provincial Surveillance Offices, but special censorial commissions were established to keep watch on the great training divisions at Peking and Nanking. These training divisions were operated by the Chief Military Commissions, and troops from garrisons all over the empire were regularly rotated into them for temporary, intensive tactical instruction. Even early in the dynasty, the training divisions were found to be highly susceptible to graft and other abuses. Officers commonly inflated the number of troops on duty so as to profit personally from the surplus rations, and they often employed the troops for their own private purposes. Training was generally neglected, so that the divisions were seldom the large bodies of combat-ready forces they were supposed to be. By the late 1500's, they had degenerated into pools of mistreated unfortunates whose most common official employment was in labor gangs.[34]

As early as the 1420's, investigating censors and supervising secretaries were occasionally given ad hoc commissions to inspect conditions in the training divisions.[35] It was apparently not until 1464 that these commissions were put on a regular, continuing basis, with one investigating censor and one supervising secretary assigned in Peking and one each also assigned in Nanking. In general, the term of duty seems to have been one year, though for a period after 1528 it was three years.[36] In the 1620's, censorial officials assigned to inspect the training divisions were busily trying to make them into effective instruments for defense purposes. In a year's tour of duty in 1622–23, a single supervising secretary named P'eng Ju-nan submitted nine major memorials outlining proposed reforms in the operations of the Peking training divisions. Among other things, P'eng insistently urged military use of so-called "flying stones," perhaps a reference to some form of cannon.[37] The Nanking supervising secretary Yen

Wen-hui, while on duty inspecting the Nanking training divisions in 1620, had the unhappy experience of being physically assaulted in his office by discontented troops, who burned two imperial proclamations and even his sleeping quarters.[38]

The major routine tactical assignment for military forces throughout the Ming period was to defend the Great Wall. The Wall shielded China from the nomadic Mongols to the north and in the late decades of the dynasty was the last zone of frontier defense against the Manchus to the northeast. For the most part the frontier defense posts were manned on a temporary, rotating basis by troops from permanent garrisons in the northern tier of provinces. Beginning in 1432, two investigating censors were regularly commissioned to one-year terms as inspectors of the frontier passes. They divided the Great Wall into eastern and western sections and each reported on the staffing of the passes and beacon stations, the condition of weapons, and the general state of defense readiness in his section.[39] This commission was of great importance in the late Ming years, and in the 1620's censors assigned to it sent a steady stream of reports, complaints, and proposals to the court.[40] In areas other than the northern frontier zone, surveillance over permanent tactical defense arrangements was routinely maintained by Military Defense Circuits of the Provincial Surveillance Offices and by regional inspectors.

When actual military campaigning was in progress, there were always special ad hoc censorial commissions—to submit reports of successes or failures independent of those submitted by the line commanders, to denounce the unworthy, and to recommend honors for all who conducted themselves with distinction. When campaigns were only local in extent, officials of the Provincial Surveillance Offices were assigned, as has been noted above; but army-inspecting censors from the metropolitan Censorate were assigned to major campaigns.[41] In its last decades, the Ming government was in an almost continuous state of war against the Manchus and against domestic rebels as well, and army-inspecting commissions became regular and increasingly numerous.[42] The army-inspecting censors of Liaotung (modern Manchuria), which the Manchus had made a permanent war theater, normally served there as concurrent regional inspectors, and were very influential.

One of the most famous and active of the army-inspecting censors was Fang Chen-ju (1585–1645), a native of modern Anhwei province. He passed the doctoral examination of 1613 and was appointed an investigating censor of the Kwangtung Circuit in 1620. By this time the Manchus had taken much of Liaotung, and the Ming court, already racked by the bureaucratic strife that culminated in the rise of the notorious eunuch dictator Wei Chung-hsien, was gradually awakening to the seriousness of the threat from the northeast. Characteristically, the court was beginning to wrangle about what ought to be done to salvage the fast-deteriorating situation. Fang plunged eagerly into these controversies; it is said that in one day alone he submitted 13 different memorials about Liaotung problems. In the spring of 1621 he asked to be assigned to the frontier and was promptly sent out on an ad hoc commission to distribute imperial gifts among the troops to build up morale. Returning to Peking full of news and zeal in late summer, he was quickly sent back to the front as army-inspecting censor for Liaotung. He had little to observe except continued Chinese reverses, which led to the loss of the Liaotung headquarters at Kuang-ning and to a pell-mell retreat inside the Great Wall not far north of Peking in early 1622; but during his tenure he bombarded the court indefatigably with reports, proposals, criticisms, and impeachments. He personally tried to rally defenses for Kuang-ning after it had been abandoned by its commander, but in vain. In the third month of 1622 he was given sick leave and his commission was terminated. Subsequently attacked by henchmen of Wei Chung-hsien, he was arrested and imprisoned and finally, in 1626, sentenced to strangulation. Before the sentence could be carried out the reigning emperor died, Wei Chung-hsien was toppled, and Fang was exonerated. He later became grand coordinator of Kwangsi province but died soon after the fall of Peking to the Manchus, reportedly of grief.[43]

The intensity of Fang's activity in Liaotung is suggested by the following sequence of entries about him in the *Shih-lu* chronicles for 1621–22:[44]

4 (4th lunar month, 1621) Requests assignment to the frontier.
5 Sent on morale-building mission to Liaotung.
7 Reports on his Liaotung mission, asks for issuance of more weapons to the troops.
7 Proposes emergency frontier-defense measures.
7 Reports on expenditures of funds in Liaotung.
8 Appointed army-inspecting censor for Liaotung.
8 Reports on recent Liaotung losses, asks that more military equipment be provided.
10 Proposes emergency defense measures.
10 Reports on poor army morale, urges stern admonitions.
11 Submits report and recommendations about current frontier problems.
12 Impeaches two military officers, recommends promotion of another.

1 (1st lunar month, 1622) Proposes new defense measures.
1 Reports loss of the Ming position at P'ing-yang.
1 Asks help for Liaotung refugees.
2 Proposes new defense measures.
2 Criticizes various Liaotung commanders for recent losses.
2 Proposes new defense measures.
2 Reports on a personal inspection tour at the front.
3 Granted sick leave; commission terminates.

Among the things for which Fang was eventually criticized was his failure to give his life in the defense of Manchuria.[45] His predecessor as army-inspecting censor in Liaotung, Chang Ch'üan, had done just that. When the city of Liao-yang fell in the third month of 1621, Chang was personally active in its defense to the last, but he was captured by the Manchus, and soon afterward committed suicide out of shame.[46]

Along with the problems of recruitment, training, and tactical employment of forces, the problem of supplying the forces was crucial. Originally, the Ming emperors tried to make the military establishment self-sufficient by providing every garrison with state lands, which soldiers were required to farm for their own upkeep. In the early Ming reigns it was customary for 60 to 80 per cent of a garrison's troops at any one time to be engaged in farming, while the remainder performed military duties; and the agricultural production was reportedly adequate.[47] By the middle of the fifteenth century, however, this condition no longer prevailed, and particularly along the northern frontier, the garrisons had to be allocated special funds from the national treasury. By the middle of the sixteenth century, tax revenues in grain from the whole northern tier of provinces were regularly assigned to support the frontier forces, whereas revenues from South China were delivered to the capital. Even so, increasingly large allocations in silver from the national treasury had to be made to the frontier defense forces by the early seventeenth century. In the troubled late Ming decades, grain revenues coming to the capital along the Grand Canal were often diverted to support the defense of Liaotung against the Manchus.[48] New taxes were imposed, and beginning in 1618 the rates of traditional land and other taxes were increased to meet the new defense needs. Whereas in the late sixteenth century the annual defense allowance from the national treasury at Peking had been around 3 million tael units of silver, between 1618 and 1627 a massive total of 60 million taels had to be allocated to Liaotung alone, and thereafter defense expenditures skyrocketed.[49]

From the first reign of the dynasty, Provincial Surveillance Offices and the regional inspectors dispatched by the Censorate had the responsibility of checking on military agricultural operations, and special Circuits for this purpose were maintained by the Surveillance Offices of Kiangsi, Honan, and Szechwan provinces.[50] Beginning in 1468, investigating censors of the Nanking Censorate were regularly commissioned to such special duty in the Southern Metropolitan Area for three-year terms, and after 1529, investigating censors of the metropolitan Censorate similarly toured the Northern Metropolitan Area.[51] In 1551 (1569 in Nanking) this commission was combined with another, first established in the middle of the fifteenth century, which imposed upon censors the duty of supervising the breeding, maintenance, and branding of government horses scattered in the pastures of the Court of the Imperial Stud.[52] Censors undertaking these combined commissions remained active even in the 1620's, although the military establishment no longer relied significantly on its own agricultural production.[53] A more important role in maintaining censorial surveillance over military supply activities was now played by investigating censors and supervising secretaries commissioned to oversee the provisioning of the defense forces in Liaotung. These commissions became regularized in 1620.[54] One ration-expediting censor of this type, Chiang Jih-ts'ai, even had the temerity to suggest in 1622 that the emperor cut down on his palace expenditures to provide defense necessities without making further demands on the people.[55]

On lesser commissions relating to the military system, investigating censors and supervising secretaries watched over the distribution of salaries and supplies to the capital Guards in both Peking and Nanking and over the special military units that guarded the four gates of the imperial palace in Peking.[56]

Surveillance over state revenues and property. The large Ming governmental establishment naturally required enormous revenues for its support. What was annually delivered to Peking alone, in normal times, included about 4 million piculs of rice and other grains (a picul being approximately 133 pounds) and about 4 million taels (ounces) of bulk silver, not to mention many other types of "tribute" articles. Even larger amounts were retained by the provincial and prefectural authorities or shipped to the frontiers. Maintaining surveillance over the collection, transportation, storage, and disbursement of all these government valuables was certainly as important a responsibility as overseeing the military system; and a group of special censorial commissions focused on vital aspects of the state fiscal apparatus.

State revenues derived from many kinds of assessments. There were corvée levies based on persons, which after the middle Ming period were largely commuted to payments in silver. There were various taxes based on proprietorship, of which the most important by far were land taxes; they were originally collected in produce but increasingly throughout the dynasty were also commuted to payments in silver. There were also various assessments on production or consumption—taxes on merchants, a salt gabelle, internal customs duties, and so on. Revenues were accumulated in granaries and storehouses in all localities, and the large quantities remitted to Peking were shipped from the Yangtze valley along the complex of rivers and canals that we call the Grand Canal, across the Yellow River and on northward to T'ung-chou just east of the capital. Several thousand canal boats and approximately 120,000 men were constantly engaged in this transport operation; the laborers were soldiers rotated from their regular garrisons to special transport divisions.[57] Grain transported north in this fashion was stored in great granary depots at T'ung-chou and Peking—almost never falling below a two-year reserve supply—and silver and other valuables were accumulated in storehouses in the imperial palace.

Several censorial commissions were related specifically to the transport and handling of this "tribute" grain and silver. The Nanking Censorate seems to have had special responsibility for keeping watch over the lower Yangtze valley region, where the tribute revenues were collected, assembled, and loaded for transport to the north. One of its senior officials was always on commission as controller of the river, to oversee the administration of the army's transport divisions, to direct anti-piracy patrolling, to watch over the work of the shipyards that built and repaired the government's canal transport fleet, and so on.[58] Two Nanking investigating censors regularly held river-patrol commissions to keep still closer surveillance over shipping and storage along the lower Yangtze. One was based at An-ch'ing west of Nanking and the other at Chen-chiang east of Nanking, precisely where the Yangtze opened into the Grand Canal itself.[59] Other Nanking censors were specifically commissioned to audit and oversee the great lower Yangtze granary depots from which the canal boats were loaded.[60] For some time after 1567 the Nanking censors were assisted by specially commissioned "loading expediters" from the Peking Censorate, who were charged to check on the delivery of revenues from the rich southeastern areas to the Yangtze granaries as well as their load-ing into canal boats for the journey north.[61]

The general operation of the canal transport system between the Yangtze valley and Peking was the responsibility of a civil-service supreme commander who was concurrently grand coordinator of a large area north of Nanking and who held the nominal title of censor-in-chief. At least in normal times, his post was undoubtedly the most important civil-service office outside the capital.[62] Surveillance over his transport system was provided by investigating censors and super-vising secretaries commissioned from Peking. Through much of the fifteenth century two censors patrolled the canal, one in the southern sector and one in the northern sector.[63] In 1472 their functions be-came the responsibility of salt-control censors in the area, but by the 1620's there were again general transport-control commissions for both censors and supervising secretaries.[64]

The final delivery and storage of tribute goods at T'ung-chou and Peking came under the special scrutiny of one granary-inspecting censor in each city and of storehouse-inspecting censors and super-vising secretaries who concentrated on the imperial treasury in the palace.[65] From 1529 on, the T'ung-chou granary inspector was even expected to oversee the operation of the whole northern sector of the canal system, but his commission was abolished in 1626 on the grounds that granary-inspecting censors gave too much trouble to the transport personnel and also had been made obsolete by the more broadly responsible transport-control censors.[66] The former impor-tance of the granary-inspecting commission is illustrated by troubles once caused when the lax emperor Shen-tsung (1572-1620) failed to commission a granary-inspecting censor at the proper time, which meant that the canal boats could not be unloaded.[67]

The production and distribution of salt, properly carried on only under strict state licensing, provided substantial additional revenues for the government but was highly susceptible to corruption; con-sequently, it was another important focus of censorial surveillance. Beginning as early as 1416, one investigating censor was regularly commissioned to keep watch over each of the four major salt-produc-ing regions of China—the coastal areas of Chekiang, the Southern Metropolitan Area, the Northern Metropolitan Area, and the dry-salt-bed areas of Shansi province. The four salt-control censors, serv-ing one-year terms, were expected to make particularly sure that salt was issued only to licensed salt merchants and that the salt revenues were promptly remitted to the capital.[68]

Investigating censors were also regularly commissioned to inspect and audit the accounts of the Offices of Produce Levies in the areas near Peking and Nanking.[69] Such agencies, scattered throughout the empire, levied on forest products taxes in kind that were used for ship-building by the Ministry of Works. Other censors regularly super-vised the government stations in northwestern Shensi province that traded tea to the Mongols in exchange for horses.[70] Whenever great government construction projects were undertaken in the capital, censors and supervising secretaries were commissioned to keep watch over them, and by the 1620's regular commissions of this sort had become established for supervising secretaries.[71] The Court of Im-perial Entertainments, which was akin to an official catering service for the palace and the whole central government, was subject to the constant surveillance of one investigating censor and one supervising secretary, who served one-year terms.[72] The Nanking Censorate also assigned its personnel to a variety of lesser regular commissions—to check on irrigation systems, to audit the national land-tax registers that were stored in Nanking, to oversee the payments of salaries to Nanking personnel, and so on—in some cases in collaboration with Nanking supervising secretaries.[73]

Other government fiscal activities, though not singled out for the special attention of censorial commissions, were by no means neglected. Provincial Surveillance Offices and regional inspectors, in their normal routines, kept watchful eyes on them.

Surveillance over schools and examinations. The Confucian tra-dition made sponsorship and guidance of education one of the major obligations of the Chinese state, and competitive examinations of educational achievement were vital to civil-service recruitment and played some role in the recruitment of military officers. Therefore, guarding against irregularities in the nation's schools and in the ex-aminations was one of the most important responsibilities of the cen-sorial system. To a large extent, routine surveillance was assured by the Education Intendant Circuits of the Provincial Surveillance Of-fices and by the general field surveillance provided by the regional inspectors, but there were also special censorial commissions devoted to this realm.

Among the few commissions ranked as major commissions were those of education intendants assigned by the Censorate to the two metropolitan areas. First established in 1436, these commissions were given for three-year terms.[74] Such censors were required to approve the admission of students to state schools at all levels, to test and classify them periodically, and to select those qualified to take the triennial civil-service examinations. It was always understood that the censors assigned to such duty had to be distinguished by their learning and their exemplary conduct.[75] Late in the dynasty a second education intendant for the Southern Metropolitan Area was added, and in 1622 it was even proposed that special Censorate education intendants be commissioned to every province as well as to the metropolitan areas in order to stimulate scholarship.[76]

When provincial civil-service examinations were conducted every third year in all provincial capitals, distinguished officials were always sent out from Peking to serve as examiners. Supervising secretaries were often among them.[77] The Censorate's regional inspectors normally served as proctors at the provincial examinations, but four censors were specially assigned to proctor the examinations in the Northern Metropolitan Area, and four Nanking censors proctored those in the Southern Metropolitan Area.[78] When, soon after the provincial examinations, the Ministry of Rites conducted the metropolitan examination in the capital at which doctoral degrees were awarded, both censors and supervising secretaries served as proctors.[79] Similarly, two censors were regularly assigned to proctor military-service recruitment examinations.[80]

Surveillance over the capital cities. The dual capitals of the Ming empire, Peking and Nanking, were in a category different from other cities, and each had special administrative arrangements. Each was divided into five Wards, and in each Ward there was a Warden's Office, administratively responsible to the Ministry of War, which provided police patrols and fire watchers. There was also in each Ward a ward-inspecting investigating censor, commissioned for a one-year term, who maintained rosters of residents and kept a close, police-type watch over all activities. He was especially charged with suppressing thievery, guarding against subversive activities or threats to the palace, and keeping the local population contented.[81]

The ward-inspecting censors were involved in many dramatic escapades in Ming times and obviously were influential personages. The censor Fang Chen-ju, after completing a term of this service, once wrote in a memorial:

The imperial court is ringed round with the Five Chief Military Commissions and the Six Ministries. The people know nothing of these; they only know there is a ward-inspecting censor, and that's all. The capital is adorned by marquises, princes, grand guardians, and grand tutors. The people do not stand in awe of these, but only stand in awe of the ward-inspecting censor, and that's all. Such petty things as children's quarrels and such commonplace things as ricebowl arguments are not terminated except by recourse to the censor; fleeting flareups on the street and lifelong animosities alike are resolved only by recourse to the censor. . . . Thus the ward inspector's function is essential, and his authority is great; and therefore, without taking time to pursue all ramifications but merely getting at fundamentals, I say that ward rules must be made worthy of respect, ward prohibitions must be made severe, and ward personnel must be chosen with caution.[82]

The all-round surveillance of regional inspectors. As important as all these specialized censorial commissions were, the unchallengeably supreme commissions were those given to regional inspectors. Regional inspectors were investigating censors distributed throughout the empire as all-purpose surveillance agents, "the ears and eyes of the emperor" par excellence. They were traditional China's equivalents of the missi dominici of Charlemagne, the fiscals of Frederick the Great and Peter the Great, and in a certain sense the party commissars of modern totalitarian regimes. No doubt every well-developed bureaucratic system has had comparable surveillance agents, but it is unlikely that the degree of organization of any other system has surpassed China's.

Certainly, the regional inspectors greatly impressed early modern European visitors to China. Matteo Ricci wrote of them:

The office of [the regional inspector] would correspond to that of a commissioner or a royal investigator. Representing the King, as he does, he is responsible for the conduct of the entire province. He visits all cities and military centers, inspects the offices of all magistrates, and has power to punish and to demote those of minor rank. His reports go directly to the King, and having the power to impose capital punishment, he is naturally respected and feared by everyone.[83]

C. Alvarez Semedo also wrote in awe of the regional inspector's office:

We have no Office in Europe, that is answerable [comparable] to it: he is, as it were, Visitour of the Province. It lasteth only a yeare, it is of great rigour and much feared. He hath authority to take Cognizans of all causes both Criminall and civill; of the militia; of the King's Patrimonie; in a word, of all. He visiteth, enquireth, and informeth himself of all, even to the Vice-roy himself [the grand coordinator or provincial governor]: the inferiour Mandarines and Judges he may punish, or turne them out of their places. Concerning the greater Mandarines, if there be cause, he is to give in Memorialls, and they are from thence forward suspended from the function of their Offices, till the Kings answer come from Court. . . . It belongeth also to him to visit the Wals, Castles, and publick places etc. He setteth forth with a great traine and pomp, having banners carried before him and other Ensignes of Rigour and Majestie.[84]

Galeote Pereira, who came to the general conclusion that Ming China "may be worthily accounted one of the best governed lands in all the world," wrote that the regional inspectors "where they come, are so honoured and feared, as though they were some great princes."[85]

The Chinese have traditionally considered the Censorate's regional inspectors substitutes for the "imperial progresses" or imperial tours of the country that ancient rulers personally undertook on occasion and that were revived by some of the Manchu emperors in the seventeenth and eighteenth centuries.[86] The regional inspectors were not an innovation of the Ming rulers, but had a tradition going back at least to the T'ang dynasty. The designation reappeared in 1377, and in fact censors may have carried out regional-inspecting functions on an ad hoc basis almost from the very beginning of the dynasty.[87] At first they may have been regularly established only in the metropolitan area around Nanking, leaving Provincial Surveillance Offices to monopolize censorial surveillance in the provinces.[88] But by the 1390's, regional inspectors were regularly assigned everywhere.[89]

Throughout the Ming period there were generally 21 regional inspectors' jurisdictions. One inspector was assigned to each of the 13 Ming provinces, one to Liaotung in the northeast, one to Kansu in the northwest (not a separate province in Ming times), and one to the Hsüan-ta region along the northern frontier in the vicinity of modern Kalgan, principally encompassing the prefectures of Hsüan-fu and Ta-t'ung. The Northern Metropolitan Area was divided between two regional inspectors, one based at Peking and the other at Chen-ting to the southwest. Three censors toured the Southern Metropolitan Area; one was based at Nanking, one worked to the north in the region of the Huai-an and Feng-yang prefectures, and one concentrated on the rich Yangtze delta region of the Su-chou and Sung-chiang prefectures near modern Shanghai.[90]

Regional inspectors were assigned for one-year terms, during which they were expected to make personal visits to every locality under their jurisdiction.[91] They interviewed prisoners and checked their trial records, inspected all agencies of local government, observed the conditions of the people, freely interrogated officials and commoners alike, accepted complaints and petitions from the people, audited all government records, and advised, admonished, or commended local authorities as they saw fit. They had the power to send directly to the emperor memorials impeaching anyone, and they freely submitted to the throne proposals for new government policies. On their own initiative they could instruct local officials to undertake, cease, or modify minor activities; and they were empowered to inflict bodily punishment on low-ranking officials and lesser functionaries without awaiting trial or ratification. They were consulted by the regular provincial authorities on all major policy matters, and they engaged in joint deliberations with the grand coordinators in their areas. In general, they "honored what was good and repressed abuses and corruption so as to rectify public morale and activate governmental principles."[92] The prestige of regional inspectors was so great that it was repeatedly necessary to warn them that they should not unceremoniously order about the senior officials of the Provincial Administration Offices and the Provincial Surveillance Offices, should not be abusive or rude toward the high-ranking regional military authorities, should not humiliate or insult local authorities who observed the law, and should not permit prefects (who outranked the inspectors by several grades) to kneel down before them.[93] It was to prevent the low-ranking investigating censors who served as regional inspectors from intimidating even the grand coordinators that the latter dignitaries after 1453 were always given nominal titles of vice censors-in-chief or assistant censors-in-chief.[94]

The investigatory responsibilities of regional inspectors were prescribed in detail in extensive regulations first issued in 1393 and revised or added to at intervals thereafter. These rules even spelled out the ceremonial rites that were to be observed when censors met various types of local officials, and they clarified the division of responsibilities between regional inspectors and grand coordinators.[95] The regulations applied generally to the local surveillance provided by both regional inspectors and officials of the Provincial Surveillance Offices, and it appears that the two types of officials acted jointly in many ways. In practice, regional inspectors probably left many county-level investigatory affairs to the discretion of Surveillance Office circuit intendants while they themselves concentrated on provincial affairs, though they were by no means expected to do so. When the late Ming censor Chang Su-yang tried to defend himself against charges of having made poor recommendations while serving as regional inspector of Chekiang province by saying that he had to rely on information given him by circuit intendants, the censor-in-chief Chao Nan-hsing retorted that regional inspectors would be unnecessary if circuit intendants were to do all the surveillance work.[96]

The regulations make it clear that the highest-priority responsibilities of a regional inspector on arriving in any particular locality were (1) to review local criminal cases, (2) to audit local administrative records, (3) to inspect local ritual sites such as sacrificial altars, (4) to look into the care of orphans, widows, and the aged, (5) to inventory local granaries and storehouses, and (6) to examine students in the local schools. But these tasks were not his only responsibilities. He must also take note of the levying of corvée services, the condition of irrigation and flood-control installations, the progress of wasteland reclamation, the condition of the postal service's remount and runner stations, the condition of bridges and roads, the administration of all taxes and the census, the requisitioning of military supplies, the administration of state manufactories, the standardization of units of measurement, the handling of litigations in the magistrate's court, the requisitioning of local government-office personnel, the existence of notably filial sons and notably chaste wives, the functioning of village self-government institutions, the validity of all official seals and warrants, and the reputation left by the previous year's inspector. He had to make suitable interrogations to see that every official properly understood both the general laws and the particular regulations pertaining to his office. He was also required to prepare a detailed map of his jurisdiction and a personnel file for every official in it.[97]

The full scope and impact of the regional inspectors' activities is perhaps best reflected in the pattern prescribed for the reports they were required to submit upon completion of their terms of duty. As fixed in revised form in 1534, the pattern called for itemized reports of all the censor's activities in the following categories:[98]

1. How many civil and military officials had been recommended.
2. How many civil and military officials had been commended.
3. How many civil and military officials had been impeached.
4. How many civil and military officials had been admonished.
5. How many notably filial, righteous, and chaste persons had been discovered.
6. How many civil and military officials had been tried and removed from office.
7. How many granaries and storehouses had been inventoried.
8. How many students in the schools had been found to be of great promise.
9. How many advantageous and disadvantageous things, in both civil and military spheres, had been promoted and removed, respectively.
10. How many orphans and aged persons had been given care.
11. How many prisoners had been given judicial review.
12. How many offenders had been tried and sentenced, by categories of punishments.
13. How many stolen goods had been recovered and fines levied, by categories of dispositions.
14. How many captures of local thieves and bandits had been directed.
15. How many repair projects on city walls, moats, dikes, embankments, and ponds had been directed.
16. In how many instances intimidation and exploitation by powerful and influential local personages had been stopped.

17. In how many instances the employment of illegal punishments had been terminated.
18. In how many instances military officers had been stopped from abusing their troops.
19. In how many instances misappropriations and thefts from granaries had been stopped.
20. How many malicious litigations had been stopped.
21. How many abusive and illegal tax impositions had been terminated.
22. In how many instances excessive disciplinary action against soldiers or civilians had been stopped.
23. How many delays and hindrances in court litigations had been corrected.
24. In how many instances abuses in the levying of corvée services had been terminated.
25. In how many instances hoodlumism and gangsterism had been terminated.
26. In how many instances gambling for money and other wrongdoings had been terminated.
27. In how many instances extravagant living among the people had been terminated.
28. How many special instructions had been fulfilled.

These reports were expected to be more than mere statistical tabulations. The censor was required to provide full details about every item tabulated, even if a detailed impeachment based upon it had already been submitted. In the case of orphans and aged persons, for example, the report had to name persons admitted to asylums in each prefecture, each subprefecture, and each county, and the specific circumstances suggesting such action in each case had to be explained. And in recommending officials, censors were urged not to rely on the vacuous phraseology of efficiency reports but to specify actual facts that justified the recommendations.

Not only did regional inspectors have all these general responsibilities; they were often asked to perform concurrently the functions that were normally assigned to special troop-purification censors, record-checking censors, salt-control censors, army-inspecting censors, or still others. Moreover, they constantly received "special instructions" of the sort referred to in the report form above—that is, special orders from the throne to make investigations, verify reports, and so forth. The censor Hsü Ch'üan, objecting to this practice in a memorial of 1429, reviewed the heavy responsibilities that a regional inspector bore as a matter of routine and then added:

In recent years, whenever the Five Chief Military Commissions or the Six Ministries have had some item of business that has not been fully carried out, whether great or small or trifling or essential, they have offhandedly memorialized requesting that the appropriate regional inspector be charged to expedite the matter. Yet each of the Five Commissions and the Six Ministries has many of its own officials and functionaries who could be sent out, whereas the regional inspector is just one solitary being. If he complies with all that he is charged with and undertakes to direct all the work of the local authorities everywhere, how can he do justice to his censorial duties?[99]

Hsü begged that the practice be modified substantially, and the emperor agreed that in the future special charges should not be lightly imposed upon regional inspectors; but the *Shih-lu* chronicles give abundant testimony that the practice continued throughout the remainder of the dynasty. "Special instructions" rained down upon the regional inspectors at all times, and when they returned to the Censorate upon completion of their provincial tours they were rated inadequate if they had not fulfilled at least seventy per cent of all special tasks assigned them.[100]

Despite Semedo's observation that the regional inspector "setteth forth with a great traine," regulations severely limited the corps of assistants who might travel with him. Each regional inspector was allowed only one clerk. In addition, he might be accompanied by a few National University students serving their novitiates, probably not more than two. Other attendants were prohibited, except that a bodyguard of soldiers was assigned to escort the regional inspector when he was actually traveling from place to place. Censors assigned to record-checking commissions were allowed two clerical functionaries to assist with the paperwork, and presumably regional inspectors who concurrently undertook these duties could correspondingly expand their staffs.[101] Nevertheless, one late Ming provincial budget book still extant lists salaries for 44 attendants assigned to the regional inspector, including 12 sedan-chair bearers and parasol holders and 24 lictors.[102] This suggests that the limitations referred to in the regulations applied only when the censor was actively on tour and did not apply during those periods when he was in residence in the provincial capital.

At least while on tour, the regional inspector was expected to conduct himself as a model of frugality and probity. He was authorized to travel on postal-service horses and courier boats but was prohibited from riding in sedan chairs and public passenger boats. The clothes and other personal belongings that accompanied him were not to exceed 100 catties in weight (about 133 pounds) or what could be carried on a single shoulder-pole. He could not take relatives with him, could not receive private letters, and could not attend private dinner parties.[103] He could not permit local officials to leave their city walls to welcome him or bid him farewell, could accept no gifts, and could not invite undue influence by marrying or taking as a concubine any woman of his territorial jurisdiction.[104] In short, censorial officials were expected to conduct themselves impeccably while on tour. "If they commit improprieties even of the most minute sort," the regulations stated, "then others can hardly be criticized."[105]

The activity of regional inspectors in fields touching every realm of government and virtually every aspect of Chinese life is amply illustrated by even random samplings from the *Shih-lu* chronicles, in which their memorials, and imperial pronouncements about them, bulk larger than any other category of references to the censorial system. The range of activities reflected in these entries can perhaps be suggested by a few specific cases:

1432: The regional military commissioner Hua Ying of Kwangtung province was reported to have accepted a substantial gift of money from one of his subordinate battalion commanders, and the regional inspector Ch'en Jui was ordered to look into the matter. Ch'en reported that the accusation was true and urged that Hua be punished.[106]

1623: The Fukien inspector Ch'iao Ch'eng-chao reported successful military actions against the "red-haired barbarians" (the Dutch), who were then active in Taiwan and the Pescadores.[107]

1625: A licentiate of Shensi province, after getting into trouble and being sentenced to frontier duty as a common soldier, turned up in the capital and got himself appointed to a county magistracy in Shantung province. The Shensi inspector Liu Ch'i-chung sent a memorial bringing the man's background to the attention of the emperor, who then ordered the Shantung grand coordinator and regional inspector to arrest him and send him to the capital for trial.[108]

1428: A lesser functionary on duty in the Ministry of Justice submitted a memorial reporting that when he was a student in a state school he had been examined by a touring regional inspector at a time when he happened to be ill. He was consequently unimpressive, and the inspector ordered that he be removed from school and assigned to functionary duty. He requested a re-examination, and it was now granted.[109]

1428: The Shantung inspector Pao Te-huai impeached the regional military commissioner of Liaotung and various subalterns for failing to prevent Mongol raids on frontier settlements.[110]

1620: The Kiangsi inspector Chang Ch'üan requested that the

emperor officially honor the Wu family of Nan-ch'eng County as exemplary citizens, because eight generations of the family were living together.[111]

1425: The Shansi inspector Keng Wen reported on the decay of military agricultural projects in his province.[112]

1626: The Yunnan inspector Chu T'ai-chen asked that new state schools be opened in six areas where the population was rapidly growing.[113]

1622: The Szechwan inspector Chang Lun submitted blueprint-like plans for two new types of catapults to be used for defense on city walls and sent to the capital for employment a Szechwan craftsman skilled in their construction.[114]

1431: The Shantung inspector Li Lu impeached an assistant administration commissioner for having accepted betrothal presents from county officials of his jurisdiction and a surveillance vice commissioner for having intimidated merchants into selling him silks at an unfairly low price.[115]

1621: A Northern Metropolitan Area inspector, Tso Kuang-tou, proposed that the paddy-rice techniques of southern China be introduced into the Yellow River plain.[116]

1620: The Kwangtung inspector Wang Ming-hsüan reported extensive earthquake damage in the province and asked for tax remissions to relieve the population.[117]

One full *Shih-lu* entry of 1433:

The Fukien regional inspector Chang P'eng memorialized: "In Ning-te County of Fu-chou Prefecture there is a local spirit to whom sacrifices are offered. Upon investigation I have discovered that the spirit's name is Huang Yüeh and that [the family] had lived for generations in the county's Fei-luan village. He mastered study of the classics, the hexagrams of the *Book of Changes,* the T'ai-hsüan commentary, and calendrical calculations. At the time of Huang Ch'ao's rebellion [against the T'ang dynasty late in the ninth century], when the people were in great distress, he gave out generous gifts. He had the manner of a natural leader. The Prince of Min [a regional-autonomy leader in Fukien] heard about him and tried to entice him into his own service, but he said, 'I am a servant of the T'ang and cannot serve a pretender,' and forthwith sank into an abyss. Thus he became a spirit and dwells in a temple where the people offer sacrifices to him. The Sung rulers canonized him Loyal Unto Death Prince. Moreover, at the Pao-feng silver mine sacrifices are offered to yet another spirit. I beg that [both these spirits] be canonized and that official food offerings be made to them in spring and autumn."

When the memorial was received, the emperor ordered that the Ministry of Rites and the Hanlin Academy should deliberate about the matter. The minister of rites Hu Jung, together with the junior tutor and minister of war and concurrently grand secretary of the Hua-kai Pavilion, Yang Shih-ch'i, and the junior tutor and minister of works and grand secretary of the Chin-shen Pavilion, Yang Jung, reported as follows: "The meritorious conduct of these spirits is not recorded in the histories, nor were they enrolled in the sacrificial canon in the Hung-wu period [the reign of the founding emperor, T'ai-tsu]."

The emperor then decreed: "Rather than report about distress among the people, this censor only obsequiously wishes to serve ghosts and spirits, seeking his own good fortune. Should a guardian of morale and discipline do such as this? Disapproved!"[118]

In a comparable vein, the censor Wang Tsun-te in 1621 called to the emperor's attention the strange fact—no doubt of significance as an omen—that the farmland of a citizen in Kwangtung province had suddenly split open and bloody water had gushed forth.[119]

Thus touring, inspecting, impeaching, commending, reporting, the regional inspector symbolized in his own commission the whole scope of surveillance by direct observation, the keystone of the censorial structure. It is no wonder that the fifteenth-century scholar Yeh Sheng would write in awe, undoubtedly speaking for the host of his informed countrymen, "Is this not indeed a vital office?"[120]

The direct observation of government operations that was provided by all these censorial assignments and commissions entailed some inevitable overlappings and duplications. It was hoped that the Surveillance Office personnel and the supervising secretaries and investigating censors who were on tour would not hinder one another. They were repeatedly urged to cooperate, and they were particularly warned to discuss in private any differences that might develop among themselves.[121] When there were regional inspectors and other censors simultaneously on commission in the same territory, they were warned not to infringe upon each other's responsibilities.

However the surveillance work may have been divided in practice, it would have been an insignificant government activity indeed that did not at regular intervals come under the personal scrutiny of some censorial official.

RECEIPT OF ROUTINE REPORTS AND COMPLAINTS

But personal observation by censorial officials was not the only means of obtaining information. One element in the general sophistication and bureaucratization of government in traditional China was its heavy reliance on written reports of all sorts. Probably no other contemporary government was equally concerned with documenting all its activities; written instructions flowed down through the administrative hierarchy in a flood, and written reports flowed back up through the hierarchy in even greater volume. And in the process most reports from the field passed at some point through censorial hands.

It is here that there was real significance in giving province names to the investigating censors' Circuits. For example, the Chekiang Circuit was so designated because—quite irrespective of the activities of the Chekiang regional inspector (who might actually belong to the Shansi Circuit)—it was responsible for maintaining surveillance over the routine paperwork relating to all judicial, military, and general-administration operations in Chekiang province. In addition, it was arbitrarily charged with keeping watch over one of the five Chief Military Commissions in the capital, over specified prefectures and military garrisons of the metropolitan areas, and over specified units of the Capital Guards, since all agencies in the capital and the metropolitan areas were distributed among the Circuits for routine surveillance. The Censorate itself was the responsibility of the Honan Circuit.[122] Certain kinds of reports therefore came to the Circuits from agencies in the corresponding provinces. Moreover, apart from these routine procedures of the Censorate, the six Offices of Scrutiny (themselves under the surveillance of the Kwangsi Circuit) maintained their own type of surveillance over the six Ministries,[123] receiving routine reports of activities, receipts, disbursements, manufactures, and so on from all agencies throughout the empire that were responsible to the Ministries.*

General personnel evaluation was one realm of censorial responsibility in which there was heavy reliance on routine reports. Since one principal purpose of all censorial surveillance was to make sure that government officials were properly qualified for their posts and conducted themselves effectively, the personnel-evaluation processes were among the most carefully planned censorial activities.

The state tried to get proper men into the civil and military services through the competitive examinations and other recruitment techniques already mentioned. Once they were in the services and appointed to offices, officials were subjected to regular periodic eval-

* In some degree, the receipt of reports by the censorial agencies related to their surveillance over judicial administration, which will be discussed in Chapter 6; and in perhaps even greater degree it contributed to the censorial agencies' document-control processes, which will be discussed later in this chapter.

uations by their administrative superiors.[124] Every county and sub-prefectural magistrate sent an evaluation of every subordinate official to his prefect once a month; and at the end of every year the prefect submitted a consolidated evaluation of all personnel of the prefecture to the Provincial Administration Office. Military commanders evaluated their subordinates in similar fashion, though on a different timetable. These routine evaluations were especially supposed to note eight particular shortcomings: avarice, cruelty, frivolity or instability, inadequacy, overage, illness, weariness, and inattention. On the basis of these reports and any other available information, every third year the Provincial Administration Offices, Provincial Surveillance Offices, and Regional Military Commissions made evaluation reports to the grand coordinator and regional inspector of each province, and they in turn collaborated in compiling a great personnel register evaluating every official in their jurisdiction. Their register was then submitted to the capital for joint consideration by the Ministry of Personnel and representatives of the Censorate.

All this was in preparation for what was called the "outer evaluation," a great gathering of provincial and local officials in the capital every third year, when they were received in special imperial audiences and the unfit were demoted, dismissed, or otherwise punished. In preparing their final recommendations, the officials of the Ministry of Personnel and the senior Censorate officials relied on both the provincial evaluation registers and special statements prepared by all officials coming to audience and submitted in advance to the Office of Scrutiny for Personnel.[125] The accumulated personnel notations from the annual reports of successive regional inspectors must also have contributed to the pool of information available for the evaluations.

Matteo Ricci, who had opportunities to observe several outer evaluations while he was residing in Peking from 1600 to 1610, described them as follows:

Every third year the ranking officials of all provinces, districts, and cities . . . must convene in Pekin [sic] to express their solemn fealty to the King. At that time a rigorous investigation is made concerning the magistrates of every province in the entire kingdom, including those present and those not called. The purpose of this inspection is to determine who shall be retained in public office, how many are to be removed, and the number to be promoted or demoted and punished, if need be. There is no respect for persons in this searching inquisition. I myself have observed that not even the King would dare to change a decision settled upon by the judges of this public investigation. Those who are punished are by no means few or of lower grade. After this general inquiry took place in 1607, we read that sentence was passed upon four thousand of the magistrates, and I say read because a list of the names of those concerned is published in a single volume and circulated throughout the land.[126]

Officials on duty in the capital underwent a comparable "capital evaluation" every sixth year. Capital officials of the fourth and higher ranks, however, were not reported on by anyone else for this purpose; they submitted their own evaluations of their service.

In every case, after the routinely processed evaluations had been offered to the throne, individual censors and supervising secretaries were called on to play the traditional role of "omissioners"—that is, to impeach those officials whose offenses had been overlooked or concealed in the evaluations, or to exonerate those officials who had been evaluated unfavorably on the basis of false accusations or biased judgments.[127]

Entirely apart from these "outer evaluations" and "capital evaluations," an even more routine efficiency-report process was conducted simultaneously. As each official completed his third year in office he was given an efficiency rating by his immediate superior. He was similarly rated again upon completing 6 years and finally 9 years of service, if he remained that long in one post. In such merit ratings officials were classified as superior, adequate, or inadequate. As a rule— whether at the end of 3, 6, or 9 years—those in the first category were promoted, those in the second were continued in rank, and those in the third were demoted. The final recommendations were made jointly by the Ministry of Personnel and the Censorate, to which the efficiency ratings were routinely submitted. When an official completed a full nine-year term and was sent to the Ministry of Personnel for reassignment, he was required to present to the Office of Scrutiny for Personnel a volume reproducing all the instructions he had received from his superiors during his tenure and all the reports he had made. In these individual cases, as in the mass evaluations, the supervising secretaries could impeach or recommend anyone whose faults or merits were not taken properly into account in the routine rating processes.

Thus, for judging the worthiness of officials and officers, the censorial agencies not only had the benefit of direct observation by individual censorial officials but also accumulated an awesome bulk of reports from administrative superiors at all levels, from individual officials themselves, and from generation after generation of regional inspectors and Surveillance Office circuit intendants.

The censorial officials also accepted complaints both from members of the bureaucracy and from the public. Censors on commission and Surveillance Office circuit intendants were urged not to rely wholly on complaints but to make inquiries of all kinds about official conduct and general conditions wherever they went, on their own initiative, with diligence and in secrecy if need be.[128] However, much of the time of any conscientious censor on tour must have been taken up with matters brought to him by complainers and informers. The general rule was that people who had complaints against any government personnel could freely submit them either to the appropriate administrative superiors or to the Surveillance Office circuit intendants or regional inspectors.[129]

Two specific categories of complaints were discussed at length in the regulations that governed censorial surveillance. One was the complaint that a popular local official was being transferred away. It happened quite commonly that the citizens of a locality besieged the regional inspector with appeals for the retention of an official beyond his normal term, and it seems to have been realized by all that such "retention requests" could on occasion be less spontaneous and sincere than appeared on the surface—that they could, in fact, reflect self-seeking machinations by the official concerned.[130] Regional inspectors were therefore told to investigate meticulously all circumstances relevant to such requests and to submit detailed memorials.[131]

Complaints of injustice in judicial processes comprised the other category extensively dealt with in the censorial regulations. In general, complaints about maladministration of justice were supposed to be made "through channels"—that is, to prefects if county magistrates were to blame, to Provincial Administration Offices if prefects were to blame, to Provincial Surveillance Offices if the Administration Offices were to blame, and only then to regional inspectors. It was in this sequence that judicial cases were routinely reviewed in appellate processes, and regional inspectors were not expected to intervene unless provincial-level appellate possibilities had been exhausted. Therefore, whenever judicial complaints were brought to them, they were expected to turn the cases over to the appropriate appellate jurisdictions. Or, if a decision had not yet been reached in the court of original jurisdiction, an inspector could set a deadline for a ruling by the appropriate magistrate.[132]

Technically, anyone who failed to go through the proper appellate channels and appealed directly to a censorial official about a judicial matter was guilty of a misdemeanor and could be punished. The regional inspector Chang P'eng in 1433 protested in a memorial that the Fukien Surveillance Office seemed to have no wish to rectify injustices, because every time a complainer appeared it harshly invoked the law about going "out of channels" and sentenced him to military service at the frontier. At Chang's request, an order was promulgated that henceforth complaints made out of proper channels would be considered punishable only if on investigation they were found to be unjustified and malicious.[133]

"Proper channels" for complaints about injustice extended even beyond the provincial level. If a complainer failed to get redress from a regional inspector, he could appeal further through the communications channels of the Office of Transmission, which was supposed to turn such matters over to the Censorate itself for reinvestigation. If even that failed, one could then submit a complaint directly to the throne.[134]

There were two ways in which a common citizen could get the attention of the emperor. First, it was provided by law that any citizen could submit a sealed memorial directly to the emperor by handing it in at any government office. There was one vague but important condition: that the petitioner must have something to say that was worth the emperor's attention.[135] Though one could expect to be punished for abusing this privilege, the Ming rulers prided themselves on maintaining this means by which the court could retain contact with the general public. Historical data suggest that the privilege was indeed used and abused. In 1429, for example, the Provincial Surveillance Office of Szechwan complained that the people of Szechwan were exceedingly fond of litigations and often on the slightest pretext submitted sealed memorials to the throne. The result was that the matters were consistently referred back to the Surveillance Office for investigation and clarification. It reported that in a period of less than four years, more than 200 such cases had arisen in Szechwan alone, and it asked for more stringent prohibitions against abuse of the privilege.[136]

The other possibility open to a victim of real or fancied injustice was, as a last resort after normal appellate processes had been exhausted, to strike a Complaint Drum that was set up outside the imperial palace. The Complaint Drum had a traditional place in Chinese judicial practices and in former dynasties had been tended by a special governmental agency all its own.[137] The first Ming emperor re-established the drum but ordered that it be attended daily by an investigating censor, and before the end of his reign he transferred it to the control of the Offices of Scrutiny, whose supervising secretaries were required to attend it in rotation. When a citizen struck the drum, the attending supervising secretary had to submit the complaint directly to the palace.[138] As with complaints submitted through the Office of Transmission, the usual procedure was for the Censorate to be ordered to reinvestigate the matter and submit an extremely detailed report to the throne.[139] It was forbidden that anyone interfere with the submission of such complaints. When one supervising secretary reported that most cases brought to the emperor's attention in this fashion had already been dealt with thoroughly by the regular judicial authorities, so that the Complaint Drum served no purpose but to harass the emperor uselessly, he was rebuked and warned that if the attendants at the drum became guilty of any concealment or obstruction they would be punished severely.[140]

It was specifically provided that whenever a criminal was scheduled to be put to death, if any relation or friend struck the Complaint Drum and claimed injustice, the attending supervising secretary was to order a stay of execution, pending imperial reconsideration. Some dramatic cases reported in the *Shih-lu* chronicles attest that the Complaint Drum was occasionally used to save innocent persons from the death penalty. In 1426, for example, nine soldiers were saved from execution for armed robbery. The tale that ultimately unfolded was a complex one. One of the men's wives had committed adultery. When the husband learned of this from friends, he beat her cruelly. In furious retaliation, she then told the local magistrate that her husband, in collusion with all those who had informed on her, were guilty of a recent, still unsolved robbery. But all these circumstances did not come out until a relative of the husband struck the Complaint Drum in the capital. The thorough investigation that ensued revealed that all of the supposed robbers had well-supported alibis for the time at which the robbery occurred.[141]

DOCUMENT CONTROL

The most extreme form of surveillance routinization in Ming times appears in the provisions made to keep watch over the flow of documents through the various hierarchies. This involved two different practices: (1) a complicated surveillance maintained by supervising secretaries over outgoing edicts and orders and incoming memorials and reports, and (2) the record-checking activities of investigating censors and Surveillance Office personnel.

The responsibilities of the Offices of Scrutiny and their supervising secretaries included a multitude of minor inspection visits to government activities in the capital, the more substantive commissions already mentioned, and even such tasks as carrying certificates of nobility to the heirs of imperial clansmen and taking diplomatic messages to foreign rulers. But by far their principal responsibility was to see to it that memorials submitted to the court met with some response and that orders issued from the court were acted upon.[142]

Memorials and reports from lesser agencies to the six Ministries or to the throne were normally handled by the Office of Transmission, which sent certain "secret and urgent" documents directly to the palace but distributed the vast majority to the Offices of Scrutiny, in accordance with their functional specializations in personnel matters, revenue matters, etc.* The Offices of Scrutiny in turn distributed routine reports to the appropriate Ministries. Memorials addressed to the throne, however, were noted in registers by the Offices of Scrutiny and passed along to the Grand Secretariat. The grand secretaries studied the memorials and drafted rescripts; their drafts were written on separate slips of paper that were pasted onto the memorials, which were then presented to the emperor. He made notations in vermilion ink indicating either his approval of the suggested decisions or his alternative decisions, and the documents were then returned to the Offices of Scrutiny. More often than not, an imperial rescript called for deliberation and advice from a Ministry. The supervising secretaries gave a copy of the memorial and its appendages to the Ministry concerned. When the Ministry responded, the rescript-drafting process was repeated, and some sort of action was finally ordered. Again, the supervising secretaries saw to it that the appropriate Ministry was informed.

The volume of paperwork handled in this fashion by the Offices of Scrutiny must have been enormous. It was reported early in the dynasty that during one period of only eight days the supervising secretaries handled 1,660 memorials dealing with 3,391 separate matters.[143] As the years passed and the bureaucracy grew in size, the burden of paperwork in the Offices of Scrutiny could only have grown heavier.

At several points, the supervising secretaries exercised significant checks on documents. When a memorial first appeared, they had the right to "veto" it either because of its form or because of its substance. Officials were sometimes denounced merely for miswriting a character

---

* The Office of Transmission itself had some authority to "veto" memorials in the fashion of the Offices of Scrutiny (See TMHT 212.) The Chinese term that I render "veto" is *feng-po*, literally "blocking and annulling."

in a memorial.[144] Even the tyrannical emperor Ch'eng-tsu (1402-24) once lost patience because supervising secretaries paid so much attention to trifles. He complained to a group of them:

You have all recently made an endless fuss about petty errors in memorials, and have rejected the memorials for this reason. This is really too much! Paperwork annoyances accumulate in bureaucratic work, and one's energy is sometimes exhausted by them, so that it is difficult to avoid errors. Hereafter, whenever memorials include erroneous characters in numbers, dates, and so forth, just block them out and rectify them in marginal notations. There is no need to inform me![145]

The more benevolent Hsüan-tsung (1425–35) also had occasion to complain to supervising secretaries that they should not impeach an official because "just once in a fluster he omitted a dot."[146] "Vetoes" based on the substance of memorials usually took the form of protests against whatever a memorialist was proposing. Thus the supervising secretary Wang Chi-tseng once vetoed the recall to duty of two high-ranking officials by the Ministry of Personnel on the grounds that both had been proved unfit in previous evaluations, and in 1623 the supervising secretary Lo Shang-chung vetoed the nomination of Han Ts'e for supreme commander because in Lo's view, although Han had great talents, his temperament was too volatile.[147] None of these Office of Scrutiny vetoes seem to have actually prevented the memorials from reaching the emperor; they were merely protests or impeachments attached to memorials that the supervising secretaries considered offensive.

When memorials were returned from the palace, supervising secretaries were similarly empowered to veto the imperial decisions. This meant that the supervising secretaries could return rescripts to the palace for reconsideration before distributing them to the appropriate Ministries—again, either because of their form or because of their substance. Thus in 1523 Huang Ch'en vetoed an imperial rescript because it was erroneous in terminology and had no Grand Secretariat draft attached.[148]

There was one circumstance that actually required supervising secretaries to hold up the issuance of imperial orders. Whenever eunuchs delivered orders to the Offices of Scrutiny, supervising secretaries were ordered to memorialize for confirmation before taking further action, to prevent any usurpation of the imperial authority by eunuchs.[149] This regulation, enacted in 1426, was honored in principle even during those periods when such eunuchs as Wei Chung-hsien completely dominated the palace.

The most important routine work of the Offices of Scrutiny was checking on the Ministries to see that imperial orders were implemented. When imperial rescripts were made available to the Ministries, the supervising secretaries entered the orders in a register. Similarly, when orders were issued orally by emperors in audience, supervising secretaries were expected to enter them in the registers.[150] As a general rule, responses from the Ministries were to be made within five days; when made, the supervising secretaries were to cancel out the orders in their registers.[151] Sometimes even shorter time limits were specially imposed.[152] Any failure to comply with the assigned time limit was to be called to the attention of the emperor by the supervising secretaries in an impeachment of the official responsible.

The last Ming emperor, Chuang-lieh-ti (1627–44), complained that this procedure had deteriorated: that the Offices of Scrutiny took too long in getting copies of orders to the Ministries and that Ministries delayed too long in making responses. He warned that he would expect strict compliance with a regular time limit of ten days.[153] That the process had indeed become ineffective is indicated by a recorded case of 1622. The supreme commander of the southwestern provinces, who was engaged in putting down a widespread rebellion, urgently requested the dispatch of additional troops to his command. His memorial was sent to the Office of Scrutiny for War to be copied and delivered to the Ministry of War, with orders to deliberate and propose action. Three months passed without a response. When the emperor then inquired what had become of the matter, the Ministry of War complained it had never received the order from the Office of Scrutiny. The Office of Scrutiny retorted that officials of the Ministry paid no attention to their business. But the apparent fact was that the supervising secretaries had allowed three months to pass without impeaching anyone in the Ministry for failure to respond. The emperor ordered that the time limits should be observed and enforced more effectively in future.[154]

In addition to these responsibilities, which focused on the flow of documents between the throne and the Ministries, the Offices of Scrutiny kept watch over the instructions sent from Ministries to subordinate agencies throughout the empire and the reports sent back to the Ministries. The kinds of surveillance they provided varied according to the specialized functions of the different Ministries, but in general the Offices of Scrutiny endorsed, registered, and filled in time-limit notations on all instructions sent out by the Ministries, and then canceled out their register entries as reports returned from the field.[155] For example, no warrant for arrest issued by the Ministry of Justice was valid without an endorsement and a time-limit notation by the Office of Scrutiny for Justice, and no certificate in which the Ministry of Personnel ordered an official to duty was valid without comparable endorsement and notation by the Office of Scrutiny for Personnel. Assignments of tax quotas sent out to all local tax collectors by the Ministry of Revenue were approved and registered by the Office of Scrutiny for Revenue, which subsequently compared its registers with reports of receipts submitted by all granary and storehouse depots to which taxes were delivered. Moreover, if any instructions prepared by a Ministry seemed to be illegal or irregular, the supervising secretaries could veto them by sending them back to the Ministry to be redrafted.

In general, correspondence between capital and provincial agencies was conducted on registered documents, somewhat comparable to the chirographs used in medieval times in the Western world, which allowed prompt and easy authentication. Each local office was provided with a register or stub book prepared by the imperial treasury. Each page of the register bore half the impression of a treasury inscription and seal. The other half of the inscription and seal was on a sheet of paper that had previously been partially inserted into the register so that the inscription and seal could be applied at the point of overlap. The loose sheets were retained in the imperial treasury for issue to the agencies of the central government whenever they had correspondence to send out. Upon receipt by a local office, correspondence was authenticated by the perfection of the impression at the point of overlap between the sheet of paper from the capital and the correspondingly numbered stub sheet in the local register. Conversely, local offices were issued supplies of sheets of paper for which there were corresponding stub registers in the capital, and on these sheets they submitted their reports to the capital offices.[156] It was by controlling the distribution of these registered documents or "tallies" to the Ministries that the Offices of Scrutiny were able to enforce their power of surveillance over the outgoing correspondence of the Ministries.

At the other end of the administrative axis, the investigating censors and Surveillance Office circuit intendants assigned to record-checking duties kept watch over the flow of documents in and out of the agencies that acted upon instructions from the Ministries. Their specific charge was to go through the correspondence files of all government agencies to determine whether business had been transacted as ordered, without delay and without malpractice, and also whether proper records of such business were maintained.[157]

To accomplish this intensive scrutiny of government files at the lowest levels of the hierarchy, each Provincial Surveillance Office maintained several Record-Checking Circuits or branch offices: 2 in Chekiang, 5 in Kiangsi, 4 in Fukien, 5 in Kwangtung, 4 in Kwangsi, 4 in Szechwan, 7 in Hukwang, 4 in Shantung, 4 in Honan, 6 in Shensi, 5 in Shansi, 4 in Yunnan, and 4 in Kweichow. And the Surveillance Offices regularly sent reports to the appropriate Circuits in the Censorate about their record-checking work. Moreover, all regional inspectors commissioned by the Censorate had the concurrent duty of checking records, except during limited periods when other censors were specially commissioned to record-checking duty.[158] For the most part, record-checking censors in the provinces left the bulk of this particular type of surveillance work to the Surveillance Office intendants and concentrated their own efforts on the provincial-level agencies.[159] In the metropolitan areas, the record-checking censors themselves checked government files down to the county level.

The capital agencies gave the Censorate its heaviest record-checking responsibilities. Censors even checked records in the Ministries, thus duplicating some of the surveillance provided by the supervising secretaries. As has been noted above, each Circuit in the Censorate had record-checking jurisdiction over specified agencies in the capital as well as over the province for which it was named, and censors were regularly commissioned to record-checking duty in the capital in the same way that they were commissioned to various assignments in the provinces or metropolitan areas. All of the censors who were thus commissioned were considered to constitute a Metropolitan Circuit, but this was a duty assignment only and did not have the organizational status of the regular Circuits named after the provinces.[160] The Metropolitan Circuit commission was considered the most honored of all the censorial commissions, the great prestige and power of the regional inspectors notwithstanding.[161]

In some cases, capital agencies made itemized reports of all their transactions and submitted them periodically to the appropriate Censorate Circuit for checking. But usually the censors visited the offices they were to check records in, in the capital as in the provinces. For assistance in checking records, 178 National University students were normally made available to the Censorate as novices.[162] One censor was reported to have had ten such student novices with him on a specific record-checking assignment.[163] On tour in the provinces, a record-checking censor was additionally allowed two lesser functionaries serving as clerks.[164]

For each transaction an office made, there was supposed to be a specific file. The process of checking records involved determining whether or not the transactions had been completed according to instructions. Each file was to be investigated and then classified in one of five categories:

(1) Transaction terminated without violation or error.

(2) No violation or error, but transaction cannot yet be terminated.

(3) Transaction could have been terminated but has not yet been terminated.

(4) Transaction terminated with violation or error, but without willful evasion of law.

(5) Willful evasion of law, such as deliberate failure to undertake some transaction that should have been undertaken.

The record-checking censor accordingly marked each file: "complied with," or "in progress," or "delay," or "error," or "evasion."[165] Officials of the inspected offices were required to make sworn statements that no records had been withheld from inspection; and those responsible for delays, errors, or evasions were punishable according to the seriousness of their offenses.[166]

The record-checking regulations included, for the guidance of inspectors, hypothetical cases in all of the six major realms of government business. One of these cases, concerned with revenues, can be summarized as follows: Suppose a certain prefecture received instructions from the Ministry of Revenue to undertake extensive land-reclamation projects, offering citizens three-year exemptions from land taxes on all fields newly brought under cultivation. The prefecture should have sent suitable orders to its subordinate counties and should have set up a file pertaining to this item of business, to which it should have added the counties' reports indicating which specific citizens had reclaimed what specific lands. Then, when the three-year exemption period had ended, this file should have been compared with the registers of tax assessments and the reports of taxes paid. When the file is eventually checked by an inspector, if the transaction was properly carried out by all the local authorities and taxes were properly assessed and paid, then the file should be marked "complied with," so that subsequent record-checking officials can consider it a closed case. If at the time of checking the three-year exemption period had not passed but the file is otherwise in order, it should be marked "in progress." If the file reveals that the counties failed to undertake reclamation projects promptly as ordered, or if the prefecture itself failed to expedite the matter, then the file should be marked "delay." If the reports from counties show careless clerical mistakes, for example indicating a tax assessment of 1,000 piculs rather than 10 piculs (the Chinese characters for 10 and 1,000 differ by only a single stroke), then the file should be marked "errors." Finally, if the file reveals that taxes were not assessed and collected when the exemption period ended or that tax assessments were finally made on the basis of either more or less land than had originally been reported as being reclaimed or that there were other sorts of irregularities in carrying out the transaction, then the file should be marked "evasion."[167] The record-checking official had to see to it that the irregularities and errors revealed in the file were corrected and that the persons responsible were punished.

The volume of work required for this type of surveillance is suggested by one report that censors on record-checking duty in the capital investigated files on 64,812 transactions dated between the beginning of 1426 and the end of 1429 and found a total of 19,742 punishable violations for which 5,116 different persons were responsible to some degree.[168]

When record-checking activities of such intensity are added to the checks that supervising secretaries exercised over memorials and rescripts, and when all these types of document-control surveillance are added in turn to the censorial receipt of routine reports and complaints and the direct censorial observation described above, the result becomes a truly formidable surveillance net stretched over the entire governmental apparatus. However deficient the public news media were, there seems to have been no reason for the Ming censorial system to lack information on which to base its efforts to "rectify administration."

Chapter four

Censorial Impeachments and Counsel in a Tranquil Era, 1424–34

The censorial officials "rectified administration" principally in two ways: (1) by evaluating, recommending, and denouncing all types of government personnel, which without too much distortion might simply be categorized as impeaching; and (2) by recommending changes in government policies and operations, which might simply be categorized as counseling. In both cases, the general instrument of censorial action was the petition or memorial submitted to the throne. This could be presented orally in open audience, but it was most commonly offered in writing, if necessary under seal to be broken only in the imperial presence.[1] There was a common saying about two fifteenth-century censors noted for their forthrightness, "Everyone dreads Tso Ting's hand and Lien Kang's mouth," indicating that Tso excelled in written denunciations and Lien in oral ones.[2]

Although impeachment was traditionally the specialty of surveillance officials, and counsel was traditionally the specialty of speaking officials, in Ming times all censorial personnel were active in both realms.

Impeachments of powerful personages and daring remonstrances with the emperors were their most dramatic activities, and many famous cases testify to the aggressive zeal of censorial impeachers and remonstrators in Ming times.[3] All the great eunuch dictators who successively disrupted the government—Wang Chen in the 1440's, Wang Chih in the 1470's, Liu Chin in the early 1500's, and Wei Chung-hsien in the 1620's—were repeatedly denounced, as were the civil-service ministers who occasionally came to wield extraordinary power for good or ill—Hu Wei-yung in the 1370's, Yü Ch'ien in the

1450's, Yen Sung in the 1540's and 1550's, and Chang Chü-cheng in the 1570's. From T'ai-tsu's time on, Ming emperors were also denounced for tyranny, debauchery, wastefulness, or laxity, by courageous remonstrators. Many an emperor must have felt as Hsien-tsung (1464–87) felt about the tireless supervising secretary Mao Hung. Weary with his remonstrances, the emperor finally exclaimed to another official after audience, "Yesterday Mao Hung; today Mao Hung! Whenever I happen to disagree with him, he argues on and on and never gives up!"[4]

As instructive as it might be to catalogue all the dramatic denunciations by the most famous Ming impeachers and remonstrators, a more balanced understanding of the censorial routine and its impact on government must be sought elsewhere. My purpose in this chapter and the one following is to seek this understanding by analyzing the whole spectrum of censorial impeachments and counselings, dramatic or otherwise, in two selected periods of the Ming dynasty, one noted for its tranquillity and the other for its political turbulence.

THE PERIOD 1424–34 IN GENERAL

The quieter period, spanning the reigns of the fourth and fifth Ming emperors, Jen-tsung and Hsüan-tsung, extended from the eighth month of 1424 through the end of 1434.* By this time the formative years were over, years when T'ai-tsu and Ch'eng-tsu founded and secured the dynasty and dominated the government with their dynamic, strong-willed, suspicious, and often harsh personalities. Still in the future was the era of notable decline, which began when Ying-tsung permitted himself to be led almost to destruction by the eunuch Wang Chen in 1449. On the whole, the reigns of Jen-tsung and

---

* Dates given here and elsewhere in the text do not exactly correspond to their apparent Western equivalents. To be more accurate one could speak, for example, of the eighth lunar month of the Chinese year usually identified with the Western year 1424. This Chinese year actually extended from the Western dates February 1, 1424, through January 20, 1425, and was designated as the twenty-second year of the reign period Yung-lo. To avoid confusing the general reader with exclusively Chinese dates and at the same time to preserve for the specialist dates that are meaningful in their Chinese contexts, I adhere to the following system: Years are indicated by the Western years to which they roughly correspond and with which they are commonly identified. Months are indicated by their Chinese sequence, as "first month," "sixth month," and so on, rather than by the Western names January, February, etc. When there is reference to an "intercalated fourth month," it indicates an extra month inserted in the calendar following the fourth month and preceding the fifth month. Days are indicated either by their numerical sequence in the month or by their sequence in the sexagenary cycle of so-called "stems and branches," beginning with the combination *chia-tzu.*

Hsüan-tsung constituted an interval of peace and stability. Both emperors have been considered able rulers, and they were assisted by an unusual number of highly regarded ministers. The decade was one that later Chinese were to look back on as "the good old days."

This does not mean that China had no troubles under Jen-tsung and Hsüan-tsung. In the political realm there was one major setback, the loss of Annam. This southern state, part of modern Vietnam, had been in and out (most often out) of the Chinese domain since the Han dynasty. Ch'eng-tsu's forces conquered it anew in 1407. Thereafter it remained an uneasy province of the Ming empire, racked by almost continual uprisings; and by the beginning of Jen-tsung's reign an Annamese chieftain named Li Li had become the scourge of the Chinese occupation forces. During 1424, 1425, and 1426, he won battle after battle against the Chinese. Reinforcements were sent to no avail. Finally in the ninth month of 1427 the Chinese suffered an overwhelming defeat, and in the following month the Ming generalissimo concluded a peace treaty with Li Li and abandoned Annam to him. It was never again incorporated in the Ming empire; and although the Chinese for some time talked about recovering Annam to save face, the loss does not seem to have caused great sorrow. Its abandonment, though humiliating, was a practical solution to a difficult and costly problem.[5]

The major event of China's domestic history in the decade was an abortive uprising by Chu Kao-hsü, Prince of Han, in the eighth month of 1426. The prince was an envious brother of Jen-tsung who decided, when his young nephew Hsüan-tsung succeeded in 1425, to seize the throne—just as his father, Ch'eng-tsu, had seized it from a nephew in 1402. But the prince's plot was quickly discovered, and Hsüan-tsung reluctantly took decisive steps to defend himself. When a vast imperial army appeared at the prince's Shantung base, he promptly capitulated. Brought to the capital, he was placed under rather lenient house arrest and eventually died of natural causes.[6]

Military troubles also arose intermittently in the southwest and on the northern frontier. On one hand, hostile aboriginal natives of Kwangsi, Kweichow, and Szechwan provinces erupted in noteworthy rebellions at least thirteen times during the decade. On the other hand, Mongol tribesmen made at least seven noteworthy raids on Chinese outposts along the northern frontier from Kansu to Liaotung.[7] Neither group, however, posed a serious threat to the stability of the empire.

Aside from the Annamese situation, two problems claimed most of the government's attention between 1424 and 1434. One was agricultural distress aggravated by inflation. China may have been passing through one of its cyclical periods of climatic misfortunes, since droughts and floods, with resultant famines, were recurrent local disasters. The government had an almost continuous program of relieving the agricultural population by remitting taxes in famine areas, canceling tax debts, attempting to resettle farmers who had been forced to abandon their lands, and fostering various kinds of governmental economies. Prices of goods in general were said to be "several tens" of times higher than they had been under T'ai-tsu.[8] Nevertheless, there is no evidence of any widespread suffering. Rather, the decade was marked by general contentment.[9] The government's great concern for farm problems may merely reflect a lack of any more urgent problems to deal with.

Conditions in the army, the other major worry of the time, were probably more genuinely worthy of concern. The early Ming system of hereditary, self-supporting military forces was fast deteriorating. There was great corruption in the army, and this resulted in wholesale troop desertions and in abuses by military officers of discipline and recruitment procedures.[10] It is noteworthy that in Annam, their only real test of the period, Chinese forces failed utterly. Recognition of the basic military weaknesses prompted, among other reform efforts, the creation of "troop-purifying" commissions for investigating censors and supervising secretaries in 1427. But deterioration continued unchecked until in 1449, only 15 years after Hsüan-tsung's death, Ying-tsung foolishly campaigned against the Mongols and was captured. The Mongols were surprised and even less prepared than the Chinese, or they probably would have reconquered at least North China.[11]

Perhaps the most ominous portent of the decade 1424–34 was the growing influence of palace eunuchs. Active eunuch participation in government affairs had begun during the reign of Ch'eng-tsu, but under Jen-tsung and Hsüan-tsung it became more and more common. The famous eunuch admiral Cheng Ho, whose fleets had repeatedly traversed the Indian Ocean under Ch'eng-tsu's orders, was made almost a viceroy in Nanking in 1425 with the title grand commandant.[12] Eunuch military commanders became familiar figures in the provinces; at least three eunuch generals were involved in the Annamese disaster.[13] Eunuchs were also frequently used for a variety of special assignments—to requisition government supplies, to supervise state lumbering projects, to travel as envoys to foreign states, and so on.[14] Hsüan-tsung admitted his generous treatment of eunuchs and regretted that even high-ranking provincial authorities and censorial officials were somewhat afraid of them.[15] In 1429 he even opened a Literary Bureau or school in which young eunuchs might be taught to read and write.[16] Later Chinese historians have consistently pinpointed this act as the seed from which later eunuch dictatorships grew; but in Hsüan-tsung's own time eunuch influence seems to have remained only a potential threat to government stability and was not significantly disruptive.

China's general tranquillity in this decade in large part reflects the interests and personalities of the two emperors, who enjoy reputations among traditional Chinese historians as conscientious, Confucian-minded rulers respectful of their ministers and benevolent toward the people.

Jen-tsung, whose personal name was Chu Kao-chih, came to the throne as a mature, experienced man in his forty-sixth year, on the fifteenth day of the eighth month of 1424; and he died suddenly on the twelfth day of the fifth month of 1425.[17] During his father's campaign for the throne in 1402 he had served ably as a military commander, and during Ch'eng-tsu's reign he had been left in charge of the government as regent on the many occasions when the emperor was away from the capital campaigning against the Mongols. He thus came to the throne with long experience in government and with the respect of the officialdom and the esteem of the people.

Jen-tsung's primary concern as emperor was to alleviate distress among the people. Once, when a local famine was reported and the Ministry of Revenue proposed that grain from state granaries be issued to the needy as loans, Jen-tsung retorted, "Forthwith issue it in relief! What would loans accomplish?"[18] On another occasion when popular distress was reported to him he promptly told his chief adviser, the grand secretary Yang Shih-ch'i, to order tax remissions and the cessation of government requisitions in the area. Yang pointed out that it was proper for the Ministry of Revenue and the Ministry of Works to be consulted before issuing any such orders. Jen-tsung replied angrily, "Be patient! Relieving people's poverty ought to be handled like rescuing from fire or saving from drowning. One cannot hesitate. But the authorities, worried about possible insufficiencies for the state's needs, are always stolid and indecisive. You just be still, sir!" He sent a eunuch after paper and ink, had Yang write out a proclamation on the spot, affixed the imperial seal, and sent it off with a runner. Only then did he turn back to Yang and say, no doubt with a smile, "Now, sir, you may inform the Ministry of Revenue and the Ministry of Works that We have ordered remissions and cessations."[19]

Jen-tsung's impulsiveness, however well intentioned, sometimes gave him cause for regret. He repeatedly urged his officials to speak up about current problems and if necessary to remonstrate with him vigorously about his own mistakes.[20] However, he sometimes became terribly angry when they did so. Less than a month after making one urgent plea for fearless remonstrance, he flew into a rage at an official of the Grand Court of Revision named I Ch'ien for speaking out "provocatively" and barred him from subsequent audiences. Soon thereafter he noticed that the officials in audience were not participating in discussion and complained that he could not rule effectively if his ministers would not tell him things. On Yang Shih-ch'i's advice, he then restored I Ch'ien's rights to come to audience and proclaimed that the officials should not take I's regrettable case to be a prohibition of remonstrance.[21] Yet only two months later Jen-tsung was overcome by anger once more. His victim on this occasion was Li Shih-mien, a low-ranking member of the Hanlin Academy. Li submitted a memorial in which, among other things, he observed that during the mourning period the emperor should not be intimate with his concubines. He was immediately summoned, beaten, and demoted; and soon he was cast into the palace prison of the imperial bodyguard, where he remained for more than a year before Hsüan-tsung restored him to office.[22]

Jen-tsung's irascibility put a great strain on the atmosphere of freedom that, on the whole, he tried to foster. His redeeming grace was that he recognized and repeatedly apologized for his aberrations; and they seem to have been completely overshadowed by his many benevolent acts and his sincere eagerness to serve the public interest. The official *Ming History* praises his goodness and compares him to the Han dynasty's emperors Wen and Ching, traditional paragons of simplicity, kindness, and earnestness.[23]

Hsüan-tsung, Jen-tsung's eldest son, personally named Chu Chan-chi, took the throne in 1425 at the age of twenty-seven and died on the third day of the first month of 1435.[24] As a youth he had been the favorite of his grandfather, Ch'eng-tsu, and his tutors had uniformly reported that he showed great promise. In the last months of Jen-tsung's reign he had served as imperial deputy at Nanking.

As emperor, Hsüan-tsung closely followed the policies laid down by his father. He was continuously concerned about the people's well-being and about the quality of government personnel in the prov-inces.[25] He, like his father, emphasized the importance of the cen-sorial "avenues of criticism," especially as a means for him to learn of conditions among the people.[26] For example, in 1426 he rebuked the censor-in-chief Wang Chang, who had been sent out to "tour and soothe" the area between Peking and Nanking, for reporting only insignificant matters. Then Hsüan-tsung turned to the officials in attendance and complained:

The two capitals, southern and northern, are several thousand *li* apart. We are constantly fearful that postal couriers going and coming might cause oppression and harassment, or that there might be calamitous damages from flood or drought or diseases, so that people suffer and starve. All these things We want to hear about. Yet ministers go and return and censors make tours and none reports about them. We sent Wang Chang to tour and inspect, hoping to learn the truth. Now he speaks only of petty trifles of no essential significance. If great ministers can do no better than this, what can We any longer hope for?[27]

Hsüan-tsung frequently jaunted into the countryside to observe conditions for himself, and on at least two occasions he made inspec-tion tours of the northern frontier.[28] In the late summer of 1428, while on a tour in the Northern Metropolitan Area, he learned of a nearby raid by Mongol tribesmen. Leading 3,000 specially chosen troops through a frontier pass, he overtook the raiders and inflicted a crushing defeat on them. It is said that on this occasion he personally killed three men in the fighting.[29] While traveling on another occa-sion, Hsüan-tsung got interested in a plowman working in the fields and paused to try his own hand at the plow. Then he said to his attendants, "We have given the plow only three pushes, and already We are unequal to the labor. What if one does this constantly! Men always say there is no toil like farming, and they are right!" Subse-quently he handed out money to all the farmers he met on the road.[30] It was probably incidents of this sort that gave rise to a later tradi-tion that Hsüan-tsung habitually mixed among the people in dis-guise.[31]

Hsüan-tsung was especially noted for lenience and mercy. During his reign almost all crimes except venality by high officials could be re-deemed by commutation payments of grain according to prescribed scales.[32] He repeatedly ordered judicial reviews for criminals current-ly imprisoned and generously gave reductions in punishments and granted pardons.[33] When he heard of Li Shih-mien's case, at first he became angry and ordered him beheaded for insulting the former emperor, but after learning the substance of the offending memorial he restored Li to office and praised his loyalty.[34]

Though lenient, Hsüan-tsung was by no means gullible. He was generally skeptical of surface appearances and at times shrewdly read between the lines of proposals and accusations.[35] Moreover, though generally inclined toward mildness and tolerance, he could be stern indeed when necessary. It is for this reason that officials do not seem to have worried much about eunuch influence during his reign, for Hsüan-tsung never let the situation get out of control. In 1427, the eunuch Chang Shan was put to death for corruption and abuses while on commission in the provinces, and in 1431, when it was discovered that the eunuch Yüan Ch'i had organized a large-scale network of graft, he was put to death by slow torture and ten of his eunuch associates were beheaded.[36]

Both of these emperors profited from having as advisers some of the most distinguished and able officials of the entire dynasty. Most important of these were the "three Yangs," with whom, according to the *Ming History,* any discussion of worthy Ming statesmen must begin. They served in high office in the best Confucian tradition. Though unrelated, they were like-minded and harmonious; and they are regularly described in the terms most esteemed by Chinese historians—diligent, humble, resolute, honest, respectful, unostentatious, and utterly without lust for power.[37]

Yang Shih-ch'i, a native of Kiangsi, was recommended and first employed under the second Ming emperor, Hui-ti, and became an influential adviser of Ch'eng-tsu, during whose reign he developed great admiration for Jen-tsung, then heir apparent. He served continuously in the Hanlin Academy and the Supervisorate of Instruction; then under Jen-tsung he was named vice minister of rites and concurrently grand secretary of the Hua-kai Pavilion. He successively held the honorific titles of junior guardian, junior tutor, and junior preceptor; and in 1425, retaining the position of grand secretary, he became minister of war. He died in the third month of 1444 at the age of seventy-nine. He was a constant and intimate counselor of both Jen-tsung and Hsüan-tsung, who respected him highly. In fact, it was largely because of his influence that Jen-tsung repented his treatment of I Ch'ien and that Hsüan-tsung realistically agreed to abandon Annam. He participated in or supervised compilation of the *Shih-lu* chronicles for the reigns of T'ai-tsu, Ch'eng-tsu, Jen-tsung, and Hsüan-tsung; and he was recognized as an able scholar and author in his own right.

Yang Jung, a native of Fukien, attained his doctoral degree in 1400 and thereafter served in the Hanlin Academy and the Supervisorate of Instruction with successive promotions. Under Ch'eng-tsu he became the youngest member of the embryonic Grand Secretariat. In 1420 he was made grand secretary of the Wen-yüan Hall while retaining his former post of chancellor of the Hanlin Academy. Under Jen-tsung he acquired the additional duties first of chief minister of the Court of Imperial Sacrifices and then of minister of works. He was successively granted the honorific titles of junior tutor of the heir apparent, junior tutor, and junior preceptor. He died in 1440 in his sixty-ninth year. Although he was personally rather intolerant of other men's mistakes, he nevertheless exerted on the emperors an influence for tolerance and lenience. He gave advice noteworthy for its shrewd common sense. He and Yang Shih-ch'i were jointly responsible for calm recognition of the loss of Annam, and Hsüan-tsung's personal campaign against the rebellious Prince of Han was Yang Jung's stratagem.

Yang P'u, a native of Hukwang, also attained the doctoral degree in 1400 and entered the Hanlin Academy. He became a favorite counselor of the future ruler Jen-tsung. In 1414 Ch'eng-tsu cast him into the palace prison of the imperial bodyguard as a scapegoat for a mistake by the heir apparent. During ten years in prison he studied assiduously, and it is said that he read through the classics, the histories, and the philosophers several times. As soon as Jen-tsung came to the throne, Yang was released and made Hanlin chancellor. The emperor treated him with special favor because of his long suffering. He was soon named concurrent chief minister of the Court of Imperial Sacrifices, and under Hsüan-tsung he entered the developing Grand Secretariat—almost twenty years later than Yang Shih-ch'i and Yang Jung. In 1434 he was promoted to the concurrent office of minister of rites; and in 1438 he became junior guardian, minister of rites, and concurrently grand secretary of the Wu-ying Pavilion. He died in 1446 in his seventy-fourth year. Perhaps his most notable characteristic was humility; it is said that when he entered the audience chambers he walked next to the wall unobtrusively. His greatest contributions in government seem to have been as a peacemaker adept at moderating differences among other ministers.

The three Yangs were the elder statesmen of their era; their prestige was unchallenged. Current opinion was that Yang Shih-ch'i was distinguished by his erudition, Yang Jung by his quick discernment, and Yang P'u by his fine deportment. It was Hsüan-tsung's trust in these three men that brought into full-scale existence the Grand Secretariat system of drafting imperial rescripts that characterized Ming administration thereafter.

CENSORIAL OPERATIONS IN GENERAL

Under the emperors Jen-tsung and Hsüan-tsung, counseled by such ministers as the three Yangs, the censorial establishment had an opportunity to function in a relatively normal governmental environment. The emperors behaved as the Chinese traditionally hoped emperors would behave. Motivated far more by benevolence than by malice, they held the reins of government securely, not delegating them or letting them slip away into improper hands, but listening to their ministers with respect. Therefore, the government operated without any major irregularities like those that disrupted it in other periods. The officialdom was not distracted by great partisan controversies, and the court was not shaken by acrimonious debates about major policies. The state was not seriously threatened from any source, and there were neither great heroes to fawn upon nor great malefactors to fear. If such conditions constitute the state of normalcy that people everywhere have always seemed to yearn for, then the decade 1424–34 was probably the only substantial era of normalcy in the whole Ming dynasty.

Moreover, by the 1420's the procedures and organization of the censorial agencies were already fully matured in the patterns described in Chapters 2 and 3. To be sure, not all of the various censorial commissions described in Chapter 3 had yet become regularly established. But regional inspectors were everywhere, and in addition, the system provided for routine censorial assignments to check records, proctor civil-service recruitment examinations, inspect the palace gate guards, supervise salt distribution, inspect the Court of Imperial Entertainments, and inspect the capital granaries. Two important commissions were added in Hsüan-tsung's time: purifying the troops and inspecting the frontier passes. And many surveillance commissions that subsequently became regular were filled on an ad hoc basis between 1424 and 1434: inspecting military agricultural projects, inspecting construction projects, inspecting the army's training divisions at the capital, supervising the collection of taxes in the Southern Metropolitan Area and the transport of tax grains via the Grand Canal to Peking, and others. In short, the surveillance net was almost as extensive as it was in any later period; and since the Provincial Surveillance Offices were notably more active in censorial work than they were two centuries later, the censorial system was in one of its best-organized periods of the Ming dynasty.

This decade was not the best of times in all regards, however. From the beginning of the period until late in 1428 the Censorate itself was dominated by a holdover censor-in-chief from the reign of Ch'eng-tsu named Liu Kuan, who seems to have been one of the most corrupt and venal high officials in Ming history. As will be seen in detail in Chapter 6, Liu's corruption was exposed in 1428 with severe consequences for both the Peking and Nanking Censorates. An honest and rigid disciplinarian, Ku Tso (whose total career as a bureaucrat has been outlined in Chapter 2), was brought in as a reformist censor-in-chief, and within a few months 30 investigating censors of the Peking Censorate and 13 more of the Nanking Censorate were removed from office. Therefore, it must be understood that for a full third of the period (as long as Liu Kuan was in office) the censorial establishment did not enjoy normal internal conditions and could not have functioned with optimum effectiveness.

What did the censorial officials actually accomplish in the decade 1424–34? The best available answers to this question come from the *Shih-lu* chronicles for the two reigns. Compiled soon after each emperor died, by officials of the Hanlin Academy who had personal knowledge of the events of the time and had access to relevant government records, the *Shih-lu* are day-by-day records of imperial activities and of events that came to the emperor's attention. For the most part, they chronicle memorials submitted to the throne and rescripts issued from the throne, but they do so selectively. Not all memorials are noted, and not all the memorials that are noted are represented even by substantial abstracts. Matters of a routine nature are not noted at all (for example, the reports submitted by regional inspectors upon completion of their tours, the evaluations of officials at the conclusion of three or six or nine years of service in their posts, and so on). The assignments of censorial officials to commissions were apparently considered too routine for inclusion, even in cases that required imperial ratification. In particular, routine provincial affairs discussed in reports to the Ministries or other capital agencies, rather than in memorials to the throne, were almost never noted in the *Shih-lu,* though they might have been of great historical significance. Thus the records of events offered in the *Shih-lu* are imperfect and incomplete. But they constitute a fuller and more detailed record of events, and of censorial activities in particular, than any other available source or the combination of all other available sources.

As incomplete as they may have been, the *Shih-lu* for the reigns of Jen-tsung and Hsüan-tsung reveal that in the decade 1424-34 censorial officials were responsible for the demotion of more than 240 officials in personnel-evaluation procedures and for the appointment, recall, or promotion of at least 32 persons; they submitted 247 impeachment memorials denouncing at least 659 officials and at least 17 other persons; and they submitted 251 memorials offering counsel and remonstrance.

PERSONNEL EVALUATIONS

The system of personnel evaluations described in Chapter 3 was fully developed by the 1420's, and both Jen-tsung and Hsüan-tsung repeatedly emphasized its importance. Great outer evaluations were conducted in 1427, 1430, and 1433; and on at least twelve occasions regional inspectors were reminded and exhorted to make irregular evaluations of provincial officials.[38] Late in 1424, fourteen censors were even sent out for the specific purpose of evaluating local officials.[39]

The results of these evaluations are no doubt the most inadequately and incompletely recorded censorial concerns in the *Shih-lu*. For each of the outer evaluations of 1427 and 1430 there is merely a record that the Ministry of Personnel and the Censorate submitted joint memorials about unspecified offenders and the emperor ordered that offenders should be demoted or otherwise dealt with as proposed; not even the numbers of officials affected are given.[40] For 1433 it is reported that the six Ministries, the Censorate, and the six Offices of Scrutiny all submitted impeachments of provincial and local officials coming to triennial court audiences and that the emperor, urging them to reform, pardoned all offenders.[41]

The evaluations that are noted in some detail in the *Shih-lu* were therefore all of the irregular sort. The more than 240 persons who were demoted in consequence of such censorial action included 184 capital officials, 12 provincial-level officials, 24+ prefectural and county officials, and 20 military officers. The capital officials were a very mixed lot made up principally of secondary-level appointees; but they included 15 investigating censors and 6 directors of Bureaus in the Ministries. The demoted provincial-level officials included 1 surveillance commissioner, 2 surveillance vice commissioners, 3 assistant surveillance commissioners, 4 administration vice commissioners, and 2 assistant administration commissioners. The military officers who were demoted were all members of Wardens' Offices in the capital. The number of prefectural and county officials who were demoted is indefinite because *Shih-lu* entries often merely indicate, for example, that "X and other county officials" were demoted. Counting each such instance as 1+ in the tabulation is inevitably misleading. In all cases, only very general reasons are given for the censorial actions: most often inadequacy, but occasionally inattention, ignorance, indolence, venality, and even oppressiveness.

The more than 32 persons appointed, recalled, or promoted because of censorial recommendations were an even more mixed lot. Those called to duty in the government for the first time included an unspecified number of private scholars recommended by a regional inspector, more than ten private scholars recommended by the censor-in-chief Liu Kuan, and an unspecified number of "worthy and talented men" recommended by a supervising secretary. One county magistrate was recalled from mourning on recommendation of a Provincial Surveillance Office. Eighteen low-ranking officials became investigating censors as a result of guaranteed recommendations by existing members of the Censorate; and one erudite of the National University was made vice director of a Bureau in the Ministry of War on the basis of a censor's recommendation.

Aside from these cases in which censorial officials were clearly and singly responsible for action taken, they shared with non-censorial officials in recommendations that affected a much larger number of people. Nine officials were promoted to the office of prefect in 1430, after they were specially recommended by the senior officials of the six Ministries and the Censorate.[42] In 1433 a total of 29 military officers were promoted after being recommended by various regional inspectors, Provincial Surveillance Offices, and provincial military superiors.[43] And in 1428 a total of 704 retired military officers were recalled to active duty after being rated as still employable by a board on which the Censorate, the Chief Military Commissions, and the Ministries were represented.[44] It is impossible to determine how many promotions that actually resulted from censorial influence were recorded without explanations or were not recorded at all.

Not all censorial recommendations were approved. A Provincial Surveillance Office submitted one recommendation of eight local officials that was turned over to the Ministry of Personnel to be investigated before any action was taken.[45] The investigating censor

Hsieh Yao once submitted a recommendation of several persons he thought worthy of official appointments but erred in writing one of the surnames. Hsüan-tsung exclaimed, "If he does not know their names, how can he know their worthiness? And if he is as careless as this, how can he measure up to the responsibilities of a censor?" Hsieh himself was demoted.[46] On another occasion the censor Yin Ch'ung-kao recommended a private scholar, Liu Chia-hui, for employment as an educational official. Liu was summoned to the capital but on arrival protested that he was eighty years old and unfit to serve. Hsüan-tsung laughingly said, "Well, Fu Sheng [a Han dynasty scholar] edited the classics at ninety; is being an educational official at eighty impossible?" But then he added: "Confucius said, 'The aged should be made content.' Though the nation encourages learning and needs teachers, cannot this one man be done without? Let him go home and take his ease!"[47]

In 1429 Ch'en Chih, as surveillance commissioner of Shensi province, recommended that a prefectural registrar, Liu Chien, be considered for higher office because of his great abilities. The Ministry of Personnel reported that efficiency ratings revealed Liu to be an inferior calligrapher and urged that Ch'en be punished for making an inappropriate recommendation. When ordered to explain himself, Ch'en memorialized, "When I recommended Liu Chien I had only observed him performing public tasks and making plans and dispositions; there was much to be observed. The fact is I had not been aware of his calligraphic deficiencies." Hsüan-tsung then told the Ministry of Personnel, "What Ch'en Chih says makes sense. Human talents are not uniform. Some are good at this but wanting at that; they cannot be judged by a single standard." Liu was apparently not promoted, but Ch'en was not punished.[48]

IMPEACHMENTS

Of the 247 impeachment memorials that censorial officials submitted to Jen-tsung and Hsüan-tsung, as noted individually in the *Shih-lu* chronicles, 188 were initiated by censors, 11 by supervising secretaries, 11 by censors and supervising secretaries jointly, and 37 by Surveillance Office officials. They met with imperial responses as follows:

No punitive action taken	36 (14%)
Investigation or trial ordered	40 (16%)
Punitive action directly ordered	171 (70%)

Whether impeachments originated with censors, with supervising secretaries, or with surveillance commissioners, there was no significant variation in the pattern of imperial responses. For example, emperors impulsively ordered punitive action to be taken in response to 70 per cent of impeachments submitted by censors, 55 per cent of impeachments by supervising secretaries, and 76 per cent of impeachments by surveillance commissioners.

The statistics clearly suggest that Jen-tsung and Hsüan-tsung were more inclined to take action on impeachments promptly, whether by pardoning or by punishing, than to turn them over to judicial agencies for clarification and consideration. But this conclusion requires several qualifications. Although the *Shih-lu* entries often give in relatively clear detail the grounds on which impeachments were based, and although they usually specify the names and offices of both the accusers and the accused, they frequently provide only sketchy information about the action or lack of action that resulted. This is undoubtedly because the compilers of the *Shih-lu* concerned themselves with affairs almost exclusively from the emperor's point of view, so that little attention was given to whatever followed issuance of an imperial decision. When the emperor ordered that an accused man be forgiven, that certainly terminated the matter. But in any other case, the ultimate effect of an imperial decision is by no means clear. It was frequently ordered that an accusation be investigated—sometimes by censors or supervising secretaries, sometimes by other officials, and sometimes by unspecified persons. In some cases emperors ordered that the accused be tried by the Ministry of Justice, by the Censorate, by individual censorial or other officials, or merely by "the legal offices" without more specific identification. In either case, whether investigations or trials were ordered, the *Shih-lu* rarely make any subsequent reference to the matter. Whatever may have happened eventually, it can no doubt be assumed that the victims would have preferred to be pardoned outright; and we can safely assume that all unpardoned cases involved some measure of punishment or admonition. In response to most impeachments, however, emperors forthwith ordered that the accused be fined, imprisoned, demoted, disgraced, dismissed, or simply "punished" without specific identification of the action to be taken. Thus it is clear that some accused persons were subjected to disciplinary or punitive action without benefit of what in the West is normally considered due process of law. Yet it is also apparent that oftentimes orders that accused persons be punished actually called for some sort of trial. Although the common decision, "punish him according to the law," no doubt signified more of a prejudgment than did a decision to have an impeachment investigated or even to have an accused person tried, the regular judicial authorities had roles to play before any punishment was actually carried out, despite the *Shih-lu*'s silence about follow-up action. Consequently, there is probably less distinction between such categories as "tried" and "punished" than the terms ordinarily imply. At the same time, it cannot be denied that Jen-tsung and Hsüan-tsung had little hesitance in judging a case on the merits of an impeachment memorial alone.

Persons denounced in the 247 recorded censorial impeachments can be categorized as follows:

Civil officials	261+
Military officers	398+
Others	17+
Total	676+

These figures do not give full value to two extraordinary mass impeachments submitted by investigating censors—one involving 12,729 unspecified officials and lesser functionaries denounced for record-keeping violations, and one involving 530 unspecified officials and functionaries denounced for fraud in the payment of laborers and artisans employed in the capital.[49] Including such large numbers in the tabulation would distort it to such a degree that it would be almost useless for any comparative purpose.

The alleged offenses that gave rise to all the censorial impeachments were highly varied. Among the most commonly cited offenses were inattention to duty, venality, greed and coercion, failure to take proper action, and misappropriation of state funds and property. Others included ignorance of the laws and regulations, lying, dissoluteness, concealing crimes, usurping authority, ritual errors, errors in maintaining records, disrespect, injustice, and contentiousness. Tabulating only the times an offense was mentioned, not the number of persons involved, the offenses can be grouped into major categories as follows:

Personal character or attitudes	96
Malfeasance	64
Incompetence	77
Crimes	104
Partisanship	7

Impeachments of Civil Officials

The censorial impeachments of civil-service officials, and the consequences of these impeachments, are analyzed in Table 2 according to the official ranks of the accused, and in Table 3 according to wheth-er the accused served in the capital or in the provinces. (All statistical tables are grouped together in the Appendix.) The analyses show that the censorial officials did not stand in awe of high rank or prestige. When it is considered that high-ranking officials were far outnum-bered by middle- and low-ranking officials and that capital officials were outnumbered by provincial officials, it begins to seem that the likelihood of an official's being impeached did not decrease but actu-ally increased in direct proportion to his prominence. High-ranking officials were more often impeached than their juniors, and capital officials more often than provincial officials.

This general impression must be qualified by two considerations. For one thing, the likelihood that an impeachment would be noted in the *Shih-lu* must have increased as the prominence of the accused increased. Moreover, as will be shown in Chapter 6, censorial officials were empowered to take direct punitive action against low-ranking officials for relatively unimportant offenses and thus did not have to rely on impeachments in their cases as often as in the cases of their seniors. General conclusions drawn from the tabulations must there-fore be tentative. Even so, it is quite clear that prominent officials were by no means immune from censorial harassment.

Neither were prominent officials immune from punishment in con-sequence of censorial impeachments. High-ranking officials seem to have been more often forgiven for their offenses than were their jun-iors, but not extraordinarily so; and on the whole, capital officials seem to have been less often forgiven than were provincial officials.

The largest single category of civil-service officials who were im-peached was that of censorial officials themselves, principally because of the Censorate purges that were provoked by Liu Kuan's venality. Censors-in-chief were impeached twice, vice censors-in-chief three times, an assistant censor-in-chief once, and investigating censors 67 times. Supervising secretaries were impeached by other censorial offi-cials five times and officials of Surveillance Offices 36 times. These cases will be considered in Chapter 6.

Impeachments of others holding important offices notably includ-ed the following:

In the capital	*In the provinces*
Ministers, 3	Administration commissioners, 15
Vice ministers, 12	Administration vice commissioners, 5
Directors of Ministry Bureaus, 9	Assistant admin. commissioners, 11
	Prefects, 6

However, no civil-service officials of this era were subjected to any sustained censorial attacks. Impeachments were generally isolated and, on the whole, businesslike and unimpassioned.

The minister of justice Chin Ch'un was denounced in 1428 by a group of censors and supervising secretaries because, at a time when a great judicial review of prisoners in the capital had been ordered, he paid no attention but enjoyed himself in feasting and drinking. He was sent to the palace prison of the imperial bodyguard and subsequently was forced to retire from service.[50]

A somewhat more representative case is that of the Nanking minister of justice Chao Hung and his vice minister Yü Shih-chi, both impeached in 1430 by the censor Chang K'ai. Various lesser officials in the Nanking ministry had been found guilty of abuses and injustices. Chang urged that the minister and vice minister, as persons generally responsible for the ministry's activities, also be punished. They were consequently relieved of their duties, summoned to Peking, and then forced to retire from the service.[51]

Another vice minister in Peking, P'ei Lien, was denounced in 1425 by the censor Yen Chi-hsien because of his general evasion of duty. Yen claimed that when ordered to make an inspection visit to one of the imperial tombs P'ei had feigned illness to avoid going out in the summer heat. When it rained he again reported he was ill. He neither attended audience nor went to his office. Instead, every day he had clerks bring official documents to his home for signature, while he himself did little but "rest his feet." Thereafter P'ei was alternately ill and well as suited his convenience. Yen denounced his lack of either respect or fear and requested that he be punished. Hsüan-tsung ordered P'ei sent to the palace prison, and two months later he was demoted to the office of subprefectural magistrate.[52]

Some common types of misconduct that censorial officials denounced are represented in the following *Shih-lu* entry from 1431, translated in its entirety:

Fourth month, the day *ping-shen*: The regional inspector of Shantung, Li Lu, memorialized: "The assistant administration commissioner Shen Ting, supervising public affairs in Ch'ung-chou Subprefecture, on arrival at the subprefecture acquired a concubine, whereupon officials of Chin-hsiang County gathered together silver and presented it to him as a wedding gift. Also, the surveillance vice commissioner Kan T'ing-i bought 16 rolls of pongee with 300 strings of currency in the Wu-ch'eng County, underpaying to the disadvantage of the people. I request that both be punished."

The emperor proclaimed to officials of the Censorate: "If one serves as a provincial authority and behaves like this, how can he be an example to the prefectures and counties? Order Li Lu to seize and punish them."[53]

When there was a fire in the quarters of the Court of Imperial Entertainments in 1433, censors and supervising secretaries joined in impeaching its assistant minister Ni Ts'ung for carelessness. He was tried and sentenced to temporary banishment; moreover, he was required to make good the things that had been destroyed by the fire. But the emperor annulled this sentence and let Ni return to duty on suspended salary.[54]

Such was the general tenor of censorial impeachments of civil-service officials under Jen-tsung and Hsüan-tsung. They seldom became dramatic issues.

Impeachments of Military Officers

Censorial impeachments of military officers and the consequences of those impeachments, analyzed in Table 4, generally followed the same pattern as the cases of civil officials. High rank did not deter either censorial harassment or imperial punishment. However, Hsüan-tsung was noticeably reluctant to punish military officers severely, especially if they held noble titles; items tabulated as "otherwise punished" include a large number of mere rebukes. Hsüan-tsung refused to hold military officers to the same standards of conduct as civil officials because they were often illiterate and characteristically unversed in the niceties of Confucian propriety that civil officials so esteemed.

Military officers who were impeached in the period 1424–34 included 3 dukes, 18 marquises, and 19 earls; 18 commissioners-in-chief, 5 vice commissioners-in-chief, and 7 assistant commissioners-in-chief of the Chief Military Commissions; and 46 senior officers of Regional Military Commissions in the provinces. The bulk of the "not clear" category consists of two groups, one of 166 unspecified officers and another of 35 unspecified officers, all of whom were ordered punished in varying degrees.

By far the military man most harassed by censorial officials of this era was an officer named Ch'en Huai.[55] Ch'en, a native of modern Anhwei province, inherited the post of battalion vice commander and under Ch'eng-tsu quickly rose in the military hierarchy, partly because of service in Annam. When Jen-tsung took the throne, Ch'en was made a vice commissioner-in-chief posted to Shensi province. The censor-in-chief Liu Kuan impeached him in 1426 for utilizing troops for private excursions beyond the northern frontier and for beating a guard commander who halted them. Hsüan-tsung ordered Ch'en to explain himself, but the *Shih-lu* give no clue about any subsequent action.[56]

By 1430 Ch'en had become a commissioner-in-chief serving as regional commander in Szechwan province, and censorial officials began a sustained campaign against him. In the fifth month of that year censors "of every Circuit," according to the *Shih-lu,* impeached him for interfering with civilian affairs in Szechwan and humiliating officials of the Provincial Administration Office and Provincial Surveillance Office who happened to offend him. Because Ch'en had "come up from the ranks," Hsüan-tsung replied, he should not be sentenced; but it was ordered that the impeachment be sent to him for perusal, and the emperor further sent him a warning to restrict himself to military matters. It was patiently explained that the provincial officials held important posts and must be treated with propriety, and Ch'en was informed that if other officials were doing wrong he should impeach them, not insult them.[57]

In the second month of 1431 the vice censor-in-chief Hu I, then checking on a state lumbering project in Szechwan, complained of military laxness in the province. Although Ch'en Huai was not specifically mentioned in the memorial, he was again rebuked.[58] The investigating censor Wang Li soon carried on the fight by impeaching Ch'en for bribery, sheltering criminals, illegal seizures of land, extortion, and gross abuses of authority. Hsüan-tsung sent the impeachment to Ch'en, asking if the abuses referred to had stopped. Ch'en confessed his errors, and in the fourth month the emperor pardoned him inasmuch as he was a military man lacking in proper education.[59] But in the next month the regional inspector of Szechwan, Wang Ao, added a request that Ch'en be ordered to go personally to the Sung-p'an frontier area of Szechwan to direct campaigns against border raiders. It was so ordered.[60] Later in the same month Wang Ao complained again, this time about Ch'en's having brought more than 260 military men along with him into Szechwan from his prior post in Shensi, as his personal followers. Wang reported that they served no purpose and wasted government supplies. Hsüan-tsung ordered Ch'en to send them back to their original garrisons.[61]

The weight of successive accusations finally overwhelmed Ch'en. The climax, together with a résumé of all his offenses, is recorded in the *Shih-lu* of 1433 as follows:

Eighth month, the day *jen-ch'en:* The commissioner-in-chief Ch'en Huai was found guilty and for the first time was sent to prison. In the beginning, Ch'en Huai was ordered as regional commander to guard Szechwan. He was exceedingly extravagant and overstepped his authority. He established an elegant headquarters, opened an audience chamber, and ordered officials of the three provincial offices and their subordinates each morning to place themselves to east and west in separate ranks, standing in attendance. If they had any business, they had to kneel to explain it. Ch'en Huai sat in the center and disposed of matters in imperial style. Moreover, because of private vexations, he beat and killed a government soldier. He accepted bribes and released the guilty. He confiscated the fields and houses of soldiers and civilians. Day by day he drank wine to greater excess. As for the defense of the various Sung-p'an localities, his strategies were ineffective, so that raiders violated the borders and captured walled cities and stockades by assault. When the regional inspector and the Provincial Surveillance Office made all this known, Ch'en Huai was summoned to return. When he arrived at the capital, censors and supervising secretaries successively impeached him in memorials demanding that he be punished for his crimes. The emperor ordered that the great civil and military ministers should jointly try him. Now the Ch'eng-kuo duke, Chu Yung, and others memorialized that Ch'en Huai's crimes were all substantiated and that, by law, he should be beheaded. He was accordingly sent to the Censorate's prison.[62]

In the second month of 1434 the case was reconsidered when Ch'en complained of injustice. He was then excused from the death penalty but was dismissed from the service.[63] The censorial officials' victory had no lasting effect, however; for in 1437, after Hsüan-tsung's death, Ch'en was restored to his former rank, and subsequently he was even enfeoffed as an earl. He died in Ying-tsung's disastrous campaign of 1449 against the Mongols.

The hereditary Chen-yüan marquis, Ku Hsing-tsu, was another frequent target of censorial impeachments.[64] Soon after Hsüan-tsung's accession, he was named regional commander in Kwangsi province, and almost immediately the Censorate denounced him for molesting the widow of a junior officer and for other offenses. He was ordered to explain himself.[65] In the seventh month of 1427, an order for his arrest was given when, having been impeached on 15 counts by the regional inspector Wang Ching-ming, he was unable to explain himself satisfactorily and did not reform. The charges included failure to give effective relief to the harassed Chinese forces in Annam, falsely claiming the capture and killing of a bandit chief, extortion of gold, silver, and horses from aboriginal tribesmen, confiscation of people's homes, intimidation of women, and others.[66] When he arrived at the capital late in the year, many censors and supervising secretaries again impeached him, attributing to him partial responsibility for the loss of Annam. He was tried by an assemblage of officials from the Censorate, the Ministry of Justice, and the Grand Court of Revision as well as various dukes, marquises, earls, and commissioners-in-chief of the Chief Military Commissions; and he confessed.[67] In the spring of 1428, after the defeated generals from Annam had arrived and been sentenced, he was confined to the palace prison.[68] Late in 1429, however, the emperor pardoned him in consideration of his illustrious forebears.[69]

Sun Chieh, the Ying-ch'eng earl, was another noble sent to prison in consequence of censorial impeachments. His imprisonment occurred in 1430, when he was found guilty of taking bribes from officials who feared his oppressive punishments.[70] After one month, however, he fell ill and was released so that he might recuperate.[71] Then in the fifth month of the year he was restored to his noble rank after performing punitive labor to atone for his crimes and to escape the prescribed punishment of temporary banishment.[72] Again in 1433 he was impeached for taking bribes, but he was pardoned.[73]

Impeachments of Other Persons

The bulk of the people other than civil officials and military officers who were impeached by censorial officials in 1424-34 were the two groups of 12,729 and 530 "officials and lesser functionaries" who were denounced in the mass impeachments mentioned above. Not counting these, there were 15 censorial victims of miscellaneous categories:

Imperial clansmen, 2	Students, 3
Imperial in-laws, 2	Former official, 1
Eunuchs, 2	Soldier, 1
Aboriginal chieftain, 1	Buddhist official, 1
Lesser functionary, 1	Relative of an official, 1

All were ordered punished with the following exceptions: one imperial clansman was pardoned and the other was tried; one eunuch, the soldier, and the Buddhist official were ordered tried; and the aboriginal chieftain was pardoned.

One of the imperial clansmen referred to was the rebellious Prince of Han, Chu Kao-hsü. When the prince had been subdued and brought to the capital as a prisoner in 1426, the Censorate as well as other agencies of the central government submitted routine impeachments of him.[74] The prince was subsequently tried. The other imperial clansman, not specified by name in the *Shih-lu,* was denounced by the investigating censor Chang Chü for illicit trading in silver. No action was taken against the clansman, but Chang was demoted for his presumption.[75]

The two imperial in-laws who were impeached were both consorts of imperial princesses. One, Mu Hsin by name, was impeached by the censor-in-chief Liu Kuan in 1424 for misappropriating government property, mistreating soldiers, and encroaching upon common people's lands; he was severely admonished.[76] The other, Chiao Ching, was impeached by the investigating censor Wu Tsung-yüan for misappropriating government horses. He was sent to the palace prison, though later pardoned.[77]

The two impeachments of eunuchs that censorial officials submitted were equally undramatic. One eunuch, Liu T'ung, had connived with a military commissioner-in-chief to make private use of 74 horses and 5 camels that belonged to the state; an investigating censor impeached them. Hsüan-tsung replied, "Such mean fellows are not worth profound rebukes. Just have the judicial authorities seal up the censor's memorial and show it to them, so that they may mend their ways."[78] The other impeachment was submitted by the Provincial Surveillance Office of Honan province, which complained of unspecified illegalities committed by the eunuch Ch'en Shih, who was attached to the household of the locally resident Prince of I. Hsüan-tsung ordered the matter turned over to the administrative officials of the prince's establishment for disposition but added a stern warning that the censorial agencies would be called on to take drastic action if the prince's establishment could not police itself.[79]

The impeached Buddhist official was Ta Wang, a titular clerk in the Central Buddhist Registry, an agency through which the Buddhist clergy was expected to discipline itself. He was impeached in 1432 by the censor Li Te-ch'üan for proselytizing, giving sanctuary to scoundrels and registering them as monks, and in general permitting monks to be "avaricious, gluttonous, obscene, and vile." Though tried and sentenced to beheading, Ta Wang was released by the emperor with stern warnings about the continuance of such abuses.[80]

One interesting case in this category involved the wife of the investigating censor Fu Ching. The Censorate reported in 1431 that she had fought with one of her husband's concubines and had so hurt her with a blow "at a vital point" that the concubine had strangled herself and died. Hsüan-tsung exclaimed, "How can murder be tolerated! Punish her according to the law." Then he added, speaking to the officials in attendance, "Wifely jealousy is an evil thing. How much more extreme is the evil of murdering because of such jealousy!"[81] There are no other references in the *Shih-lu* of this era to the censor's wife or, for that matter, to the censor Fu Ching himself.

COUNSEL AND REMONSTRANCES

The 251 counseling memorials that censorial officials submitted in 1424–34 were not always separate documents from their 247 impeachment memorials. The different kinds of memorials did not have differentiated forms, and many memorials served dual purposes: to request correction of certain harmful practices and simultaneously to denounce particular persons who were thought responsible for the practices discussed. Or, conversely, a censorial official might denounce someone for particular offenses and then proceed in the same document to suggest corrective action that might prevent the recurrence of such offenses in general. Consequently, there is some overlapping in the two categories of memorials.

The censorial memorials that are tabulated as counselings or remonstrances were of varied sorts. Some, at least as noted in the *Shih-lu,* were little more than reports for the emperor's information—for example, about damage done by natural disasters, or about the activities of bandits. They did not explicitly call for action on the emperor's part, though the emperors usually responded to requests that were implied in such reports. Others might call for action, but action so vague and general that the emperor could be expected to react only by agreeing in principle (for example, that all high-ranking officials should exert themselves to purify their minds and do their jobs more effectively). Still other memorials might call for adoption of new general policies in certain government realms; and those of yet another type might request very specific, limited actions. Any one memorial might include proposals or requests representing several of these types, ranging from the most general to the most specific, and might include a number of proposals falling into totally different categories of subject matter.

It is especially difficult to differentiate what might properly be called remonstrances from other sorts of counseling memorials. Any memorial that suggested a change in governmental policies or operations could have been understood by the emperor to be at least an indirect criticism of himself; almost any proposal could have been intended or received as a protest. I have therefore not attempted to separate the *Shih-lu* data into these two categories for tabulation purposes. In the interests of simplicity, I label all counselings and remonstrances simply as proposals.

Reactions to censorial proposals, as noted in the *Shih-lu,* fall into four categories: (1) approval, ranging from a laconic indication of assent to the issuance of detailed instructions about implementing proposals; (2) deliberation, representing orders that "the relevant Ministry," or "the Ministries and the Censorate," or "the proper authorities," or specifically identified agencies or officials take note of proposals, or consider and report on them; (3) disapproval, ranging from the most mild to the most violent; and (4) no action, so far as the records indicate.

Table 5 shows how the 251 censorial proposals of this era were initiated and how they were received. Such analysis suggests that censors had by Ming times become speaking officials to a startling degree, or conversely that supervising secretaries, the supposed speaking officials par excellence, had become absorbed in other than "speaking" duties to a startling degree. Regardless of the fact that the Censorate employed a larger number of officials than did the Offices of Scrutiny, it is clear that supervising secretaries were laggards in submitting proposals, compared to their colleagues in the Censorate or, for that matter, in the Provincial Surveillance Offices.

Table 5 also confirms, as analysis of censorial impeachments suggested, that Jen-tsung and Hsüan-tsung were quite vigorous personal decision-makers. Some 77 per cent of all censorial proposals were forthwith approved or disapproved by the emperors. In only 16 per cent of the cases did the emperors entrust proposals to their ministers for deliberation. Although most of the proposals tabulated as "approved" could only have been implemented by line agencies, so that the responsible bureaucratic authorities presumably had some opportunity to modify them in details, and although some censorial proposals were themselves the results of previously ordered deliberations, nevertheless it must still be concluded that the emperors displayed remarkable decisiveness. Moreover, Table 6, dealing with the subject matter of proposals, reveals that the pattern of imperial decisiveness —and of general imperial approval of what was proposed—did not vary to any significant degree from one subject-matter category to another.

To summarize, Jen-tsung and Hsüan-tsung consistently approved a majority of proposals submitted, whatever the subject matter; they infrequently requested ministerial advice before taking action on a proposal; and they rarely disapproved of what was proposed.

Counsel Concerning Imperial Conduct

Forthright remonstrances of the type acclaimed by admirers of the censorial system were not frequently offered to Jen-tsung and Hsüan-tsung. One of them, despite being well known because it brought disaster upon the memorialist, is not even mentioned in the *Shih-lu* at all and thus does not appear in my tabulations. This was submitted by the investigating censor Ch'en Tso in 1431, when the empire was untroubled and Hsüan-tsung was devoting much time to hunting and other sports. Ch'en urged him not to neglect his literary studies and especially directed his attention to the ancient classic *The Great Learning*, which, as expanded by Sung dynasty scholars, had become a revered handbook of governmental ideals. The emperor was outraged that anyone should intimate he was unacquainted with so important a book and ordered Ch'en cast into prison. Eventually several of Ch'en's close relatives were also imprisoned because of Ch'en's offense, and it was not until after Hsüan-tsung's death in 1435 that the Ch'ens regained their freedom. Meanwhile, Ch'en Tso's father had died of illness in prison.[82]

Of the five memorials reported in the *Shih-lu* that are tabulated in the category of counsel concerning imperial conduct (Table 6), two were protests against decisions made by Hsüan-tsung about wayward officials. One was submitted by the supervising secretary Nien Fu, who in 1433 protested obstinately and at length when the emperor pardoned Tuan Min, a vice minister of justice in Nanking who had been found to be disproportionately lenient in dealing with offenders. Hsüan-tsung responded to Nien's protest with characteristic aplomb and good humor: "What you say is indeed true. However, We have already pardoned him and have no wish to reconsider the matter now."[83] The other remonstrance of this type was offered by the censor-in-chief Hsiung Kai in 1434, protesting the emperor's similar tolerance in the case of an assistant minister in the Court of State Ceremonial, Liu Ch'ing. Liu had accepted bribes from a friend and made representations on his behalf to the Ministry of Works, for which offense he had been sentenced to strangulation by the judicial authorities. Hsüan-tsung set aside that sentence and ordered Liu dismissed from the civil service instead. Hsiung Kai protested that this treatment was entirely too lenient, especially in the case of a personal imperial attendant who had committed such an offense. The emperor in this instance changed his mind and ordered that Liu be sent to prison, presumably pending review of the case.[84]

Two other censorial protests focused on the emperors' reliance on eunuchs. Late in 1424 the supervising secretary Kuo Yung-ch'ing, in a memorial dealing with five different problems, included a recommendation that palace eunuchs should not be sent out into the provinces on special assignments, but that matters should be left in the hands of the provincial authorities. No details of the memorial are provided in the *Shih-lu,* but it is noted that Jen-tsung assented.[85] The next year the investigating censor Yin Ch'ung-kao, then serving as regional inspector of Chekiang province, complained that eunuchs, sent there by the emperor to requisition commodities required by the court, annoyed the people, amassed far more than was required, and disrupted trading conditions. Yin proposed that the eunuchs be withdrawn and that local authorities be relied on for requisitioning whatever was required. Hsüan-tsung, exclaimed, "How could We have foreseen that they would make trouble like this!" and put an immediate stop to the eunuchs' activities.[86]

The fifth censorial memorial in this category did not have the tone of remonstrance at all. It was respectful counsel offered to Jen-tsung in 1424 by the investigating censor Hu Ch'i-hsien, who suggested that the auxiliary capital, Nanking, was of such strategic importance to the state that allowing any official to dominate it could be dangerous. Hu proposed that the heir apparent be posted there with viceregal powers.[87] No response is indicated in the *Shih-lu,* but the heir apparent was in fact subsequently sent to Nanking, only to be recalled in a few months to succeed to the throne as Hsüan-tsung.

Several other censorial memorials noted in the *Shih-lu* of this era, though not tabulated in this category, might have been remonstrances. We are told that the investigating censor Chiang Ssu-ch'eng was transferred to the post of county magistrate in Yunnan province in 1427 because in memorializing about affairs he did not please the emperor; but what Chiang's memorial consisted of is not indicated.[88] Another censor, Chang Ts'ung, was demoted in 1432 partly because of venality, but also partly because he "memorialized about matters that were not true."[89] Again, what was actually memorialized about is not indicated.

In 1432 the supervising secretary Nien Fu in collaboration with the censor Ch'eng Fu submitted what might be considered a remonstrance-warning; it also is not tabulated as a remonstrance. The Ning-yang marquis, Ch'en Mou, serving as regional commander of the Ning-hsia region on the northern frontier, had been impeached for extortion, theft, accepting bribes, and other offenses. Hsüan-tsung ordered that the impeachment be sent to Ch'en for his perusal but also ordered him to report to the capital. The two censorial officials, apparently foreseeing a pardon, memorialized that Ch'en's crimes were so serious they could not properly be pardoned. Hsüan-tsung responded that the marquis's crimes were serious, to be sure; but he nevertheless pardoned him, requiring only that he return the goods stolen and that the bribes he accepted be confiscated.[90]

Counsel Concerning General Administration

The censorial proposals tabulated in the category of general administration emphasize primarily the problems of economic distress that have been discussed above. The censorial officials consistently urged that tax and corvée burdens be alleviated for people who for whatever reason had fallen on bad times. Requests for relief in areas that had suffered natural disasters comprised only one group of these memorials. In 1425 a censor requested that special requisitions of provincial commodities for court use—which apparently always involved losses for the sellers—be suspended except in periods when harvests were abundant and general conditions prosperous.[91] A regional inspector in 1427 requested that civilians who had been conscripted to repair the walls of a local garrison be released from the labor until the busy harvest period was over.[92] In 1433 a Provincial Surveillance Office complained that Buddhist and Taoist monasteries accumulated great estates and protected their tenants from various state levies, thus creating an intolerable burden for the general population. It proposed that such estates be carefully investigated with a view toward redistributing their lands among the landless or registering their tenants for regular corvée service.[93] In 1431 one censor urged that officials be deputed to work out a redistribution of agricultural lands in the Ta-t'ung area of Shansi province, where good farming soil was scarce and had been monopolized by military garrisons.[94] In addition, the regional inspector of Shansi province asked at the same time that Shansi lands that had formerly been devoted to government-controlled production of such luxury goods as saffron and indigo be diverted to the production of necessities for the local population.[95]

Twice during the period censorial officials advocated the operation of emergency-reserve granaries, which in some form were traditional fixtures in Chinese government. For example, in 1430:

Fifth month, the day *ping-ch'en*: The Censorate's assistant censor-in-chief of the left, Li Chün, said: "During the Hung-wu era [T'ai-tsu's reign] reserve granary depots were established in the Metropolitan Area, Honan, Shansi, and other regions. Accordingly as the times were prosperous or bad, stores were alternately accumulated and issued, all to the general advantage. Then, whether floods or droughts occurred, the people did not starve. But in recent times the authorities of the various localities have not been able to carry on this virtuous plan, and the granary stores have all been dissipated. Thus, if a poor harvest occurs, the people have nothing to rely upon. I beg that the local authorities be ordered according to the law to refurbish the granaries, that government funds be provided, and that grains be laid in at current prices to provide for emergency needs. It would be advantageous." It was approved.[96]

Adjustments and remissions of taxes in special circumstances, aside from those created by natural disasters, were common subjects of censorial proposals. Shansi province seems to have been a notably depressed area and a frequent focus of censorial concern. For example, in 1426:

Second month, the day *hsin-wei*: The Shansi regional inspector, Chang Cheng, said: "Among the people of every locality there were formerly those who deserted, abandoning their fields and defaulting on their taxes. Now an imperial proclamation of amnesty and pardon has been received, ordering that they return to their occupations and that all accumulated tax debts be remitted. Joy soars, and people are returning home from far and near. However, upon coming to Shansi . . . I have found most people still gloomy and downcast. This is undoubtedly because at the time when they originally deserted, the local authorities, afraid of being blamed, never reported the matter to the Ministry of Revenue, which therefore has not authorized remissions; the taxes that were previously defaulted are still assessed. The fact is that the people's old properties have been abandoned for a long time, and now, although they are returning, they are still without resources. If they are still dunned for the taxes and persecuted, then I fear they will have no choice but to desert again. I cannot neglect to report this."

The emperor said to the minister of revenue, Hsia Yüan-chi, and others: "When deserted people first return home, they should certainly be treated with lenience and pity. Why were the tax debts not canceled after the great amnesty? How can debts spanning several years be assessed for payment insistently when it is admitted that they were formerly not reported for remission? How can the people bear it? Let the authorities be ordered that all should immediately be granted remissions."[97]

The same censor four months later requested that some remaining tax arrears be accepted in cloth rather than in grain, for the convenience of the people. The Ministry of Revenue protested that if this were done it might cause a shortage of grain for military use, but the emperor responded, "Tax debts exist only because of the people's poverty. Let us be guided by the people's advantage."[98]

The only censorial memorials in the general-administration category that were disapproved were proposals that emperors felt would be of disadvantage to the people. In 1428, the censor-in-chief Liu Kuan, who seems to have had a strong Legalistic preference for rule by strict laws and punishments, proposed that regulations concerning paper money (which the government had long tried to put into general circulation but which the people distrusted) should be enforced by an elaborate scale of heavy fines levied in paper money and by sentencing offenders to one month in the cangue (an instrument of torture like the stocks, in which certain types of criminals were displayed in public). Hsüan-tsung disapproved, saying: "To assess fines in paper money serves no purpose other than to force the circulation of paper money, and to put offenders in the cangue for one month is very severe. Just circulate a notice to be displayed, so that people will be warned."[99]

Thirteen of the 28 memorials in the "personnel matters" subcategory were reports from regional inspectors or Provincial Surveillance Offices about popular appeals that local officials be retained beyond their normal duty terms. Others in this subcategory were a diverse lot. For example, in 1432 the censor-in-chief Ku Tso requested that a stern warning be issued against bias in evaluating personnel.[100] In 1430, the censor Chin Lien proposed that T'ai-tsu's old practice of giving rewards to excellent local officials be resumed.[101] In the same year the regional inspector of Hukwang, Ch'en Po, recommended that new standards for rating local educational officials be established. The standard in use had been fixed at a time when an unlimited number of licentiate degrees were granted each year at the provincial examinations, but meanwhile rigid quotas of degrees per province had been established. This worked a hardship on the educational officials, who were mainly rated according to how many of their pupils succeeded in the provincial examinations during their nine-year terms. The problem was deliberated by the minister of rites and others, and a new formula was promulgated. It provided that to be rated superior, a prefectural instructor had to produce only five licentiates instead of nine; to be rated average, three instead of four, and so on.[102] In 1429 Hsüan-tsung approved a proposal submitted by Wu Na, the regional inspector of Kweichow, that postal-service officials in the distant provinces of Kweichow and Yunnan be required to go to the capital for evaluation only every ninth year rather than every third year, since the journey to and fro occupied so much time that the postal services easily deteriorated in their absence.[103]

Memorials tabulated in the "waterways and transport" subcategory most often proposed that the Grand Canal and other waterways systems be improved in various ways: by the repair of dikes, by the dredging of silted channels, by the installation of locks and

glacises and capstans, by the assignment and reassignment of transport labor units, and so on.[104] One censor in 1430 requested that
tax grain collected in the K'ai-feng region of Honan be transported
only to granaries at Lin-ch'ing on the Grand Canal to the east rather
than northward to Peking because of the excessive cost of transport
across Honan, where boats were scarce.[105] In one of the several memorials concerning land transport, the regional inspector of Shansi
province, Ho Ching, in 1427 proposed that three new transport stations be established along the heavily traveled route from Peking
across Shansi into Shensi province. The Ministry of War agreed that
such action would be desirable, and Hsüan-tsung ordered that it be
done.[106]

The censorial officials of this era were not greatly troubled about
educational and examination problems, but some of their proposals
about schools are worth noting. In 1424 the Shantung Provincial
Surveillance Office reported a shortage of educational officials in that
province and urged that every civil official of rank 7 and above be
required to recommend one qualified person; this would provide a
pool from which vacancies could be filled.[107] Six years later, the supervising secretary Li Pen of the Office of Scrutiny for War suggested,
to the contrary, that the number of educational officials ought to be
reduced. If by chance he aimed to please the emperor by advocating
government frugality, he misjudged Hsüan-tsung's temper. The emperor disapproved and commented: "In regard to educational officials, We are not worried about having a surplus; We are only worried lest the proper men not be obtained."[108] About doing away with
one superfluity, however, Hsüan-tsung had no qualms. When the
Kwangsi regional inspector Shen Ch'un reported that repeated aboriginal uprisings had virtually depopulated two counties and there
were no students, he readily agreed that the local schools might as well
be abolished.[109]

Other memorials about education included one from a regional
inspector in Shensi urging that Confucian schools in the military garrisons of that province be revitalized and brought up to the standards
prevalent in the prefectural and county schools, and one from a regional inspector in Szechwan urging that long-neglected community
schools, a traditional aspect of state-promoted self-government at the
village level, be reorganized and re-emphasized.[110] And in 1429 the
investigating censor Chang Ch'un complained that some students had
spent ten or even twenty years in the National University at Nanking
without ever graduating and being given duty assignments. He re-

quested that they promptly be given at least probationary appointments.[111]

In the same complex memorial Chang Ch'un made a rather vague proposal of a sort that accounts for several items in the "Miscellaneous" subcategory—that is, proposals relating to the censorial system itself. He wrote:

Guardians of the Customs and Fundamental Laws [i.e., censors and surveillance commissioners] have ear-and-eye responsibilities vital to the disciplinary principles: to impeach the host of officials and to rectify the multitude of governmental policies. Their zealous spirit should be nourished so that it will fortify them in their functioning. But in recent times the Guardians of the Customs and Fundamental Laws have for the most part clung to fears and scruples; they have seldom offered policy criticisms. I request that an edict be issued encouraging them and commanding each to state his views. Then the disciplinary principles might be revived and the avenues of criticism might not be blocked.

To this typically flowery and vague proposal, Hsüan-tsung responded by lecturing the censor-in-chief Ku Tso:

According to the dynasty's established law, officials of all agencies and even the hosts of laborers and artisans are permitted to speak out about affairs. How much more should those with the responsibilities of Guardians of the Customs and Fundamental Laws! The avenues of criticism are what We rely on and trust; how can there be anything to fear or have scruples about? You instruct them in their duties, and if anyone has cause to speak out but does not, have him punished for neglecting his duty!

One of the other diverse memorials tabulated in the "miscellaneous" subcategory came from a regional inspector returning to the court upon completion of his duty term. He reported that en route he had encountered the Prince of Ning-hua, who begged him to request help from the emperor for his mother, who was quite old and seriously ill, and for whom no suitable physician was available. Hsüan-tsung immediately ordered that a physician of the Imperial Academy of Medicine be dispatched by fast-post facilities.[112] On another occasion, the supervising secretary Huang Chi complained about many abuses committed by Central Asian merchants who came into China falsely claiming to be tribute bearers. (Tribute bearers were the only foreigners authorized to carry on trade in Ming China.) Jen-tsung approved Huang's suggested preventive measures and then severely rebuked the minister of rites Lü Chen, whose ministry was in general charge of foreign relations, because Lü was a native of the far northwestern Shensi province and should have had a better understanding of the wiles of Central Asian traders.[113]

Another *Shih-lu* entry that defies regular classification, though it is representative of well-established Chinese practices of Ming and other times, is the following, from 1425:

Ninth month, the day *wu-shen*: A testimonial of merit was issued for the virtuous woman Madame Meng. Madame Meng was a daughter of a citizen of Chu-chi County (in Chekiang province); her given name was Yün. In the beginning she was betrothed to a government student of the county, Chiang Wen-sheng. But before she became his, Chiang was chosen and sent to enter the National University. He subsequently became a censor but then fell ill and died. Thus Meng Yün's life was over at twenty! Weeping bitterly, she joined the Chiang household and undertook mourning for three years. She served her intended parents-in-law with complete filial devotion, and she voluntarily maintained her grief and chastity. When she had attained sixty years of age the regional inspector Yin Ch'ung-kao found out these facts. He memorialized requesting issuance of a testimonial of merit.

The emperor said to officials of the Ministry of Rites: "Women who preserve their chastity are rare enough in the world. This woman was no more than betrothed and yet was able to observe the ritual obligations of a wife; and she held to her commitment without going to another. She can truly be called a virtuous woman! Since this is what people find difficult, those who are capable of it should be given testimonials of merit to promote morality."[114]

Counsel Concerning Military Matters

Censorial proposals about military matters dealt almost exclusively with relatively routine military-administration affairs. There was no visible concern about major defense policies, even as regards the embarrassing military situation in Annam. When memorialists touched on the Annamese problem, they most often considered only its logistical aspects, as in the following, from 1427:

First month, the day *hsin-hai*: Ch'en Jui, the regional inspector of Chiao-chih [i. e., Annam], memorialized: "The headquarters of the Ch'iu-wen Guard is located in the Liang-shan prefectural city. This area is an important passage route in Chiao-chih, but the grain from the granary barely provides for the officers and soldiers of the local Guard. I request that the abundant granary grain in those parts of Kwangtung and Kwangsi that are near Liang-shan be transported to Liang-shan to provide for the grand army, so that its activities will not be impeded." This was approved. It was ordered that the Ministry of Revenue delegate officials to supervise the transport.[115]

The attention of censorial officials, and undoubtedly of the court in general, was much more clearly focused on the more traditional source of trouble, the northern frontier. On at least two occasions censors requested repair of defense walls at specific localities along the northern border.[116] In 1429 the supervising secretary Tai Sheng of the Office of Scrutiny for War complained that defense forces sta-

tioned along the important sector of the frontier from Shan-hai-kuan
on the coast to Chi-chou devoted themselves only to military training;
he urged that they be held responsible for dividing their time between
military duties and farming, so as to become self-supporting.[117] Making the frontier forces independent in a different sense was the aim
of another censorial proposal of the following year, 1430:

Eleventh month, the day *wu-wu*: The investigating censor Liu Ching memorialized: "Government troops are deployed to guard the frontier passes at
Shan-hai, Lung-ch'ing, and Yüan-shan; but local civilian authorities have
increasingly been forced to post civilian workmen to tend the fire-beacons
in those regions—seven or eight men, or five or six men each. This is an imposition on the civilian population, and I beg that it be stopped. It would
be advantageous."
   The emperor proclaimed to the minister of war Chang Pen and others:
"In general, troops are to protect civilians, and civilians are to support the
troops; both have their proper responsibilities. Why should civilian energies
be improperly diverted, with hindrances to agricultural pursuits? Let the
posting of civilian workmen in this way be stopped. None but soldiers should
be detailed to tend the beacons."[118]

In 1429 the regional inspector of Shantung, Pao Te-huai, recommended the strengthening of defenses in Liaotung:

The Liaotung area faces the outer frontier and is stealthily watched for raiding opportunities. Between Kao-ling and Ling-ho there are seven post stations to facilitate traveling to and fro, and each one is harassed by raiders.
I request that a Guard be created at Yang-ch'ih east of the Ts'ao-chuang post
station; that a Battalion be assigned to each of the seven post stations; and
further that half the troops be available to protect travelers and the other
half to produce crops in camp for subsistence. Then the unexpected might be
guarded against.[119]

A convocation of capital officials recommended that comment on this
proposal be sought from the regional commander of Liaotung, and
finally in the next year action was taken that substantially complied
with Pao's request.[120]
   Another regional inspector of Shantung, Chang Ts'ung, in 1433
made the following proposal to strengthen defenses by curbing desertions from the military garrisons in Liaotung:

Most of the soldiers serving in Liaotung have been sent there in disgrace because of their crimes to guard the frontiers. Some disappear and hide. This is
because they are villainous fellows, who falsify their native places when first
enrolled and sent off to service. As soon as they are delivered to their Guards,
they desert. When recoveries are attempted, the home authorities report no
knowledge of any such persons. The troop ranks are therefore vacated. I request that the regional commander of Liaotung and the Regional Military

Commission be commanded by the emperor to investigate and record the names and native places of all soldiers who have deserted from the various garrisons and report them to the Chief Military Commissions and the Ministry of War for verification or correction, so that the records might facilitate making recoveries. Hereafter, whenever men are sent off to serve as soldiers, the Ministry and the Chief Military Commissions should determine the facts of their background, and should compile registers, by categories, of all those sent to serve under the [Liaotung] Regional Military Commission. They should also issue warrants and delegate men to take charge of the delivery; and these men should, relying on the registers, verify the facts that persons have been received and that they have been conducted to specified Guards to serve as soldiers. Then these escorts should prepare a register of the Guards and Battalions to which the men were assigned, and return it to the Ministry of War. And the Ministry of War should then notify the government offices at the men's native places of the reasons for which they were sentenced to serve as soldiers and of the Guards or Battalions in which they provide frontier-guard service—all this so that villainy and corruption will be prohibited and stopped, and soldiers will find concealment impossible.[121]

Hsüan-tsung approved this proposal.

The majority of censorial memorials about banditry related to uprisings among the aboriginal tribesmen of Kwangsi, Yunnan, Szechwan, and Hukwang provinces. Many such memorials were little more than reports comparable to the aforementioned reports about natural disasters. But in at least one instance there was a proposal about procedures for dealing with banditry in general. This was submitted in 1428 by the censor-in-chief Liu Kuan and reveals again his penchant for Legalistic governing. Liu memorialized:

For the capture of fierce bandits there already are rules about promotions and rewards, but the law about capturing bandits should emphasize severity [in the event of failure]. If it is severe, then men will not dare to become bandits and the pursuers on their part will exert themselves zealously. Henceforth, whenever fierce bandits plunder and pillage an area, officials and lesser functionaries of the garrisons and civil offices and also the village and neighborhood chiefs should all be sent out to serve as soldiers so that captures might be effected. If they make captures within two months they will escape punishment, but if they have failed to do so when the time limit has expired, then, in accordance with the rules, they should be turned over for punishment. Moreover, when fierce bandits have been captured they should be asked during trial to identify the Guards or Battalions or Subprefectures or Counties in which they were formerly registered. If they had been soldiers, then those in charge of the appropriate garrisons should be punished. If they had been civilians, then the appropriate civil officials, lesser functionaries, village elders, and neighborhood chiefs should be punished. If this is done then men will know what to dread.[122]

Hsüan-tsung, who was decidedly not inclined to be Legalistic, commented that such action would be severe indeed, and ordered that it be carefully considered by an assembly of capital officials. The tenor of the proposal is notably at variance with the spirit in which Hsüan-tsung often received reports of banditry or uprisings. He preferred to order that officials be delegated to visit the offenders and read to them "soothing edicts" in the hope that they might be peacefully persuaded to desist and resume law-abiding life.[123]

Among other censorial proposals about military affairs were requests that city walls be repaired throughout the empire, that forts be installed along the Kwangtung coasts, that additional Police Offices be established in certain strategic areas, that soldiers be relieved of burdensome horse-tending duties, that troop training be improved, that physicians be made more available to military units, and that judicial procedures in military units be improved.[124]

The general weakness of the hereditary system of obtaining military officers apparently prompted the censor Pao Te-huai to recommend creation of military recruitment examinations comparable to the civil service examinations. He wrote:

Each human being is born with some specialized talent, and if he excels in something he is worthy of employment. Now in the families of military personnel—aside from the eldest sons, who inherit by the system called "protection"—how can it be that the other sons are not talented in the military arts? Their talents in this line must surpass those of the masses; but, however they might wish to win fame, they have no channel through which to enter the service. I recommend that military examinations be instituted and that, except for men entitled to inherit posts and men who have committed offenses, those who are skilled in archery and horsemanship and versed in strategy should be permitted to go to the Regional Military Commissions for competitions in which the most capable could be selected. The Ministry of War should then re-examine them. If they are actually worthy of employment, they should first be given acting appointments in frontier-guarding posts. As soon as they demonstrate and establish their merit they should uniformly be given substantive appointments. If this is done, then men of talent might all find employment.[125]

Hsüan-tsung reserved this proposal for deliberation by assembled ministers. They reported that the establishment of military examinations was contrary to the traditional system; and no further action was taken at this time.[126] As has been noted in Chapter 2, it was not until 1478 that what Pao Te-huai had in mind actually came into being.

Counsel Concerning Judicial Matters

The largest single group of censorial memorials tabulated in this category dealt with a system of commuting punishments into payments of rice, a system that was used sporadically in this era. Sometimes censorial officials requested that it be employed to augment food supplies in the frontier garrisons.[127] But Hsüan-tsung considered the commutation system a means to alleviate the plight of unfortunates who might suffer undeservedly, always excepting what were called "true criminals rating the death penalty."[128] Thus in 1429 he ordered the Ministry of Justice, the Censorate, and the Grand Court of Revision to regularize the commutation system, with these prefatory remarks:

Punishments are instruments for aiding government. Great crimes are the worst of great evils and are dealt with severely according to the laws, not being excused or pitied. But as for those who, being misled and implicated, have difficulty in escaping from the law and yet whose cases have extenuating circumstances, morning and night We ponder means to be lenient and take pity on them.[129]

Before long the censor-in-chief Ku Tso and colleagues in other agencies submitted a proposal spelling out a system of regular commutations that took account of differences in status among the offenders and the varying difficulties of transporting commutation rice to designated depots in different areas. This proposal ran as follows:

As regards paying in rice to redeem crimes, water transport in the Nanking area is excellent and advantageous, whereas land transport in the Peking area is rather difficult. We have deliberated and propose that:

When arrested and brought to the Peking legal offices or to Ho-chien Prefecture or any other of the eight prefectures of the Northern Metropolitan Area, as well as to Honan and Shantung, officials, lesser functionaries, soldiers, and civilians who rate the death penalty only as secondary criminals, and all lesser offenders [i. e., all offenders of any status except "true" criminals rating the death penalty, whose guilt was considered so great that their punishments could not be subject to commutation] should pay in rice to the Peking granaries in accordance with the following scale:

For the death penalty as a secondary criminal: 50 piculs
For permanent banishment: 10 piculs less than for the death penalty [i. e., 40]
For temporary banishment, five degrees:
    three years: 35 piculs
    the lower four degrees [two and a half years, two years, one and a half years, one year]: progressively reduced 5 piculs each [i. e., 30, 25, 20, 15]
For beating with the heavy bamboo, five degrees:
    100 blows: 10 piculs
    the lower four degrees [90 80, 70, 60 blows]: progressively reduced 1 picul each [i. e., 9, 8, 7, 6]
For beating with the light bamboo, five degrees:
    50 blows: 5 piculs
    40 blows: 1 picul less than 50 [i. e., 4 piculs]
    30 blows: 5 pecks less than for 40 [i. e., 3½ piculs]

20 blows: 1 picul less than for 30 [i. e., 2½ piculs]

10 blows: 5 pecks less than for 20 [i. e., 2 piculs]

When sentenced to the death penalty only as secondary criminals, or to lesser punishment, by the Nanking legal offices or by Hukwang or Kiangsi, as well as by the T'ai-p'ing Prefecture or other prefectures, subprefectures, or counties of the Southern Metropolitan Area south of the Yangtze River, officials should be sent to Peking; lesser functionaries, soldiers, and civilians should pay in rice to the Nanking granaries. When sentenced to the death penalty only as secondary criminals, or to lesser punishments, by Chekiang or by the four prefectures Su-chou, Sung-chiang, Ch'ang-chou, and Chen-chiang of the Southern Metropolitan Area, as well as by the Feng-yang Prefecture or other prefectures, subprefectures, or counties of the Southern Metropolitan Area north of the Yangtze River, officials should be sent to Peking; lesser functionaries, soldiers, and civilians should pay in rice to the Huai-an granaries. Those of Hsü-chou should pay in rice to the Lin-ch'ing granaries. All these should comply with the Nanking rules:

For the death penalty:

officials and lesser functionaries: 100 piculs

soldiers and civilians: 20 per cent less than that [i. e., 80 piculs]

For permanent banishment: 40 per cent less than for the death penalty [i. e., 60 piculs]

For temporary banishment, five degrees:

three years: 50 piculs

two and a half years: 40 piculs

the lower three degrees [see above]: progressively reduced 5 piculs each [i. e., 35, 30, 25]

For beating with the heavy bamboo, five degrees:

100 blows: 20 piculs

90 blows: 15 piculs

80 blows: 12 piculs

70 and 60 blows: progressively reduced 2 piculs each [i. e., 10 and 8]

For beating with the light bamboo, five degrees:

50 blows: 6 piculs

the lower four degrees [i. e., 40, 30, 20, 10 blows]: progressively reduced 1 picul each [i. e., 5, 4, 3, 2 piculs].

When the paying in has been completed, military personnel sentenced to the death penalty as secondary criminals should be posted to the Guards [in their former status, or as common soldiers?]; civil-service personnel, both officials and lesser functionaries, should all be dismissed from the service. Of those sentenced to permanent or temporary banishment: military officers should be restored to their duties; civil-service officials should be demoted one degree; lesser functionaries should be reassigned. Of those sentenced to beating with the heavy or light bamboo: civil-service and military officials and functionaries should alike be restored to their posts. But those who repeatedly offend should be dealt with as prescribed in the law. And those who steal provisions for which they themselves are responsible or who appropriate goods unlawfully; those soldiers, prisoners, artisans, cooks, etc., who desert; and all those who are unable to pay in rice should be dealt with as prescribed in the former rules.[130]

This sophisticated formula for commutations was approved. There was also a commutation system that permitted officials and lesser functionaries to redeem certain kinds of offenses by performing punitive labor (literally called "transporting tiles") on palace-construction projects in the capital. When they completed their labor, they could resume their posts.[131]

No censorial official of this period demanded abolition of these commutation practices, but some censors were quick to point out their unjust aspects. Commutation seems to have been required, not merely permitted; and for this reason commutation wrought hardships on some persons who were better able to endure the prescribed punishment than to make the commutation payments or perform the duties demanded. At the same time, the system unduly favored persons of means, to whom commutation payments might mean little. Hsüan-tsung himself was aware, as he stated in 1426, that "offenders are unequal in richness and poorness."[132] In 1429 the censor Wang Ao proposed that officials and lesser functionaries who committed offenses involving venality be demoted or dismissed rather than be restored to their posts after completing the prescribed labor service.[133] The censor Cheng Tao-ning in 1428 complained that poor people who were required to pay in rice to commute punishments suffered unreasonably in practice: being unable to pay, they were held in confinement indefinitely. He reported that he knew of 96 men who had died in such confinement during the previous eight months. The emperor approved his proposal that artisans be permitted to make up commutation payments by work and soldiers by special duties and that others be permitted to return to their homes, where they might have some hope of accumulating the prescribed payments.[134] The next year the censor Chang Ch'un urged that persons of no means be punished according to the original laws rather than be held pending commutation payments, as was still done in Nanking. This, too, was approved.[135]

In many other ways censorial officials showed concern about mistreatment of people in judicial processes. On several occasions the Censorate requested that physicians be assigned to treat prisoners who were ill.[136] The Shansi surveillance commissioner Chang Cheng once complained that malicious persons often lodged unfounded complaints for the purpose of getting enemies imprisoned pending trial and then absented themselves from the area. The consequence was that innocent persons sometimes languished in prison indefinitely while fruitless searches for their accusers were undertaken. He won the emperor's approval for a policy that any accused person should be released immediately if his accuser disappeared.[137] The censor-in-chief Hsiang Pao also once won approval for a policy to prevent malicious badgering of innocent officials. It provided that if any local official were implicated in an accusation, he would not be arrested until trials of his alleged associates conclusively verified his complicity.[138] Hsüan-tsung also approved the supervising secretary Li Yüan-chin's recommendation that stern prohibitions be issued against mistreatment of prisoners being transported cross-country by the government's postal-service personnel.[139]

SOME TENTATIVE EVALUATIONS

The proper function of the censorial system in the traditional Chinese state was to help restrain undesirable elements in the government and to help foster desirable elements, to the end that peace, justice, and the Confucian ideal of good government might prevail. The judgment of Chinese historians has been that relatively good government did prevail in the decade 1424–34, and the present study provides no basis for contradicting it. Thus it is pertinent to consider to what degree the censorial system itself deserves credit for the prevailing good government.

Quantitative data presented in this chapter suggest at least that the censorial officials were active in carrying on their prescribed duties and that the emperors generally approved both their impeachments and their counsel. The censorial officials brought about the removal or punishment of a large number of government personnel whose conduct they considered detrimental; and in a large number of cases they brought about the institution or modification of government policies or procedures in ways that they considered advantageous. If imperial approval can be equated with meritoriousness, then in a large majority of instances the censorial officials' work in impeachment and counseling can be considered to have contributed to the general welfare.

To evaluate censorial achievements in qualitative terms is necessarily far more difficult. But the emperors of this era do seem to have generally acted in a very conscientious spirit, so that their approval or disapproval can probably be taken with confidence as a valid measure of the merit of any censorial memorial. Moreover, without any apparent and significant variation during the period, the substance of the memorials is prima facie evidence of meritoriousness. Censorial officials made proposals designed to strengthen the state's military defenses and to eradicate banditry, and they seized upon laxness in defending the frontiers and in dealing with banditry as grounds for impeaching officials and military officers. They proposed action to alleviate disaster conditions by the remission of taxes and by the issuance of government stores as relief, and they proposed means of preventing such distress from recurring frequently. They denounced unjust punishments, and they recommended changes in commutation practices to abolish those aspects that favored the rich at the expense of the poor. Extortion, oppression, and the improper exploitation of citizens and soldiers were frequently cited in their denunciations as grounds for disciplinary action. Given the facts we have, their sustained attack against the corrupt military commissioner-in-chief Ch'en Huai was justified and commendable, and their perseverance in the face of Hsüan-tsung's reluctance to punish Ch'en can count only to their credit.

At times, of course, censorial memorials were disapproved. But in many such instances the censorial officials were chided by the emperors only for being too zealous or too severe. When one considers the nature of the censorial responsibilities, such good-humored rebukes cannot be counted to the officials' discredit. Conversely, the fact that the censorial officials' only real quarrel with the emperors of this period was their disapproval of what they considered Hsüan-tsung's unreasonable leniency may be to the emperor's credit but reflects no discredit on the censorial officials.

Consideration of what censorial officials neglected to do, however, throws a somewhat different light on their service during this decade. Inasmuch as conditions were generally good, it is perhaps understandable that censorial officials did not bring about, or try to bring about, any major departures in general governmental policies or operations—Pao Te-huai's attempt to introduce competitive examinations for the recruitment of military officers being perhaps the only exception. But that they failed to protest more vigorously, or to protest at all, about those disadvantageous conditions and tendencies which did exist seems difficult to excuse.

The beginning of this chapter mentions the severe punishment that Jen-tsung inflicted on Li Shih-mien for memorializing forthrightly about the emperor's personal conduct; and it notes Jen-tsung's temperamental reaction, subsequently repented, to I Ch'ien's "provocative" remarks. These actions appear in the historical records as clear instances of imperial impropriety. Although it is possible that the statements that actually provoked Jen-tsung to anger were not known publicly, the circumstances suggest that censorial officials must have been aware of the general nature of the cases. Yet not a single censorial official is reported to have reproved Jen-tsung for either of these aberrations. It seems particularly discreditable that Li Shih-mien remained in prison for more than a year after Hsüan-tsung's accession without a single censorial official's calling his case to the attention of the new and obviously kind-hearted emperor, and that no censorial official ever seems to have protested Hsüan-tsung's later imprisonment of the censor Ch'en Tso and his relatives when the emperor felt he had been insulted by Ch'en's educational advice.

It has also been pointed out above that this era witnessed a notable advance toward the expansion of eunuch power that ultimately became an important factor in the decay and fall of the Ming dynasty. Eunuchs were given positions of prestige and authority as military commanders in some provinces, one was named grand commandant at Nanking, and in 1429 Hsüan-tsung instituted a practice of teaching young eunuchs to read and write. All these things were in direct violation of the founding emperor's insistence that palace eunuchs be prevented from interfering with government affairs and that to this end they be kept illiterate. Reliance on eunuchs by Jen-tsung and Hsüan-tsung does not seem to have posed a grave threat to the national welfare at the time, to be sure; but historical examples of eunuch abuses would have justified some alarm about the prevailing trend. Moreover, when eunuch disruptiveness was brought to his attention, Hsüan-tsung reacted vigorously, as has been noted: he recalled eunuchs from commodity-requisitioning missions in Chekiang in 1425, and he put to death Yüan Ch'i and ten of his eunuch associates in 1431. One would suppose that the emperor's attitude on such occasions might have emboldened remonstrators to speak out aggressively about the growth of eunuch influence, without fear of endangering themselves. And at the very beginning of Hsüan-tsung's reign one administration vice commissioner of Hukwang province, Huang Tse, did so quite decisively, saying:

The emotions of castrated men are dark and secret, and their thinking is dangerous and cunning. Their greatest villainy simulates loyalty, their greatest falseness simulates truth, and their greatest artfulness simulates stupidity. To be entirely intimate with them is like drinking wine without realizing its power to intoxicate, or like biting into sweet dried meats without realizing their power to poison. To favor them is easy; to keep them at a distance is most difficult. For this reason, in antiquity eunuchs were not permitted to command troops or to interfere in the government. This is how disaster was guarded against before it had sprouted. But if the bubbling brook is not stopped up, it will become a great river. They ought altogether to be kept at a distance, not being permitted to get control of affairs. What happened in the Han and T'ang dynasties is certainly well known.[140]

Censorial officials utterly failed to take up Huang Tse's refrain. For that matter, they were not even responsible for the exposure of Yüan Ch'i and his henchmen. As Hsüan-tsung himself had occasion to remark, they seemed somewhat afraid of eunuchs.[141]

The humiliating if realistic abandonment of Annam is another matter that might have been, but apparently was not, a subject of censorial criticism. It may be that, since the abandonment came as a welcome relief to almost everyone, there was no good reason to oppose it. But if such was the case, it may justifiably be wondered why censorial officials failed to protest previously, when efforts were being made to hold Annam at great expense and at the cost of many lives. In short, censorial officials took no stand at all on the Annamese question.

Aside from their failure to remonstrate significantly with the emperors, did the censorial officials neglect to denounce officials who deserved to be denounced? This question cannot be answered in general terms on the basis of the present analysis, but one highly significant omission does call for comment. That is the apparent failure of censors to impeach Liu Kuan while he was in active charge of the Censorate. Liu's many offenses, which will be discussed in Chapter 6, were such that censors cannot but have known of them; indeed, many were offenses against the general body of censors themselves, and they seem to have been matters of public knowledge. Yet it was not until Liu had been absent from Peking on provincial duty for three months that censors at last stepped forward with the evidence that in part led to his dismissal. At this time, it is true, Hsüan-tsung referred to "secret memorials" that had previously exposed much of Liu's venality, some of which may have come from censorial officials. Nevertheless, that Liu's corruption was allowed to continue for so long without any open protest, especially since it interfered in some degree with the performance of their own proper functions, is an unquestionable adverse reflection on either the courage or the integrity of the censors who served under him.

In this connection, it is perhaps noteworthy that neither the pace of censors' activity in submitting impeachments and proposals nor the patterns of imperial responses changed significantly after the Censorate purges that followed Liu Kuan's exposure and dismissal. The reigns of Jen-tsung and Hsüan-tsung covered a combined total of 129 months. Liu Kuan was senior official of the Censorate during the first 49 of those months, Ku Tso during the remaining 80 months. During Liu Kuan's regime, Censorate personnel submitted 83 impeachment memorials at a rate of 1.7 per month and 70 counseling memorials at a rate of 1.4 per month; under Ku Tso the pace was slowed slightly, to 116 impeachments at 1.4 per month and 108 proposals at 1.3 per month. Imperial responses to these memorials varied only slightly, as is indicated in Table 7. It is clear that in the emperor's judgment at least memorials from the Censorate were not significantly more or less appropriate and reliable after the Censorate purges than they had been before.

In sum, it appears that censorial officials under Jen-tsung and Hsüan-tsung, considering only their activities in denouncing way-ward officials and giving counsel, were on the whole conscientiously active and responsibly true to their calling. But they were less aggres-sive than circumstances seemed to require them to be, even though prevailing conditions at court gave them little cause for timidity.

Chapter five

Censorial Impeachments and Counsel in a Chaotic Era, 1620–27

In striking contrast to the relatively tranquil era of Jen-tsung and Hsüan-tsung, the reign of Hsi-tsung from 1620 to 1627 was a turbulent period of grave military emergencies, imperial irresponsibility in its most extreme form, ruthless eunuch disruptiveness, and impassioned bureaucratic struggles. If the decade 1424–34 had been the most normal of Ming times, 1620–27 was the most abnormal; and the Confucian state system sank to what was probably its historic low point in morale and effectiveness. The purpose of this chapter is to analyze the censorial response, in impeachments and counselings, to such conditions.

THE PERIOD 1620–27 IN GENERAL

Hsi-tsung, who reigned from the ninth month of 1620 until his death of natural causes in the eighth month of 1627, was the next to last Ming emperor. His brother and successor, known as Chuang-lieh-ti, inherited from him a state whose socioeconomic base was so deteriorated, whose officialdom was so corrupt and demoralized, and whose foreign and domestic enemies were so powerful, that he was destined merely to preside over its gradual disintegration. However, Hsi-tsung himself cannot be blamed for all of the late Ming troubles. When he came to the throne in 1620 the seeds of decay had already produced very sturdy sprouts.

During the century and a half that followed Hsüan-tsung, though China had been repeatedly irritated and occasionally humiliated by Mongol raiders, Japanese pirates, and small-scale domestic rebellions, there had been no substantial threat to the established order. Although none of his successors had Hsüan-tsung's combination of vigor and conscientiousness, and although eunuch influence or other irregularities had often disrupted administration, the established patterns of government operation had not been significantly upset. The military system deteriorated and inequities in land distribution and taxation accumulated, but the government had instituted no drastic changes. The prevalent mood was conservative. State and society did change, but slowly.

Then in the 1570's there was a reinvigoration. A nine-year-old boy, posthumously known as Shen-tsung, inherited the throne in 1572 and for ten years was dominated by a strong-willed grand secretary, Chang Chü-cheng.[1] Under Chang's leadership, two great generals, Li Ch'eng-liang and Ch'i Chi-kuang, reorganized the frontier defenses and the military establishment until China was as strong and secure as it had ever been in Ming times, and it was no longer dependent on an inadequate hereditary soldiery. Lands were surveyed and taxes restructured until the national economy was perhaps sounder than it had ever been during the dynasty, and the government enjoyed a regular surplus of revenues. A money economy flourished, silver having replaced grain as the basic unit of exchange and taxation. Largely by sheer force of character, but partly by a stubborn disregard for traditional procedures when they interfered with efficiency, Chang Chü-cheng cowed both the emperor and the officialdom into a state of well-disciplined alertness that had been lacking in the government for more than a century. All in all, under young Shen-tsung, guided firmly by Chang, China had an exemplary government of a sort not enjoyed since Hsüan-tsung's time.

But Chang Chü-cheng died in 1582, and things changed. Shen-tsung, released from Chang's stern guidance and sometimes harsh tutorship, rapidly degenerated into a self-indulgent and irresponsible despot. The officialdom, reacting in its own fashion to a decade of stern discipline, rapidly degenerated into numerous cannibalistic factions, as group struggled against group to prevent the emergence of a new leader like Chang. The emperor so lost patience with his officials, and especially with the speaking officials of the censorial establishment, that he ignored the bureaucracy as much as possible and relied more and more on trusted eunuchs to get essential business done. Left to themselves, the officials became steadily less responsible and more cannibalistic. By the time of Shen-tsung's death in 1620, conditions had deteriorated to such an extent that a new revival might have been impossible, as the official *Ming History* comments, "even for the most resolute, enlightened, and heroically vigilant ruler."[2] But a worn-out profligate, Kuang-tsung, came to the throne.

Though he initiated some promising changes, he promptly fell ill and then died before a month had passed, leaving his fifteen-year-old son, Hsi-tsung, confronted with several imminent disasters.

The problems that Hsi-tsung faced upon his accession, and which dominated his seven-year reign, were basically of three types: 1) military challenges to the national security, coupled with economic distress; (2) bureaucratic factionalism that made effective government action impossible; and (3) eunuch intrusions into government that quickly led to the ruthless dictatorship of Wei Chung-hsien.

Wars, Rebellions, and Economic Distress

The stability achieved in Chang Chü-cheng's time had long since disappeared. In the 1590's, military challenges had arisen on many sides, and the government had been forced to engage in extensive campaigning against Mongol rebels in the northwest, against aboriginal tribesmen in the southwest, and in support of China's vassal Korea when it was invaded by the ambitious Japanese warlord Toyotomi Hideyoshi.[3] And then had come the rise of Manchu power in China's northeastern territories.

The Manchus (related to the Jurchen tribes that had ruled much of northern China in the pre-Mongol Chin dynasty, from 1115 to 1234) had been peaceful tributary settlers on the far frontier of Liaotung, north of Korea, since the early 1400's. Their prominence in Chinese affairs began with the chieftain Nurhaci, who inherited the leadership of a minor tribe in 1583. Under the patronage of Li Ch'engliang, the dominant Ming authority in Liaotung, Nurhaci gradually extended his authority over other tribesmen, and in 1608 he won from the Ming court recognition of his own domain, an area adjoining Liaotung. Though at first humbly subservient, he eventually became hostile toward China, and in 1616 he proclaimed himself khan of a revived Chin dynasty, thus renouncing his former tributary status and in effect challenging the legitimacy of the Ming emperor. In 1618 he openly denounced the Chinese court and conducted a raiding expedition into Liaotung, defeating the Chinese forces there in several encounters; and when a Chinese punitive expedition appeared the following year Nurhaci decimated and dispersed it. From then on, the Ming state was on the defensive against the Manchus.[4]

Nurhaci and his successors were vigorous, imaginative generals, and they were also expert organizers. Patterning their government after that of the Ming and honoring the Chinese social and ideological traditions, the Manchus quickly learned that they could compete for the allegiance of the Chinese people by providing more honest and effective government than did the demoralized Ming officialdom. Through the 1620's and 1630's, as conditions worsened in the interior, Chinese of some regional importance in the northeast steadily defected to the Manchu cause, and in the end, in 1644, the Manchus were able to march into China proper as the proclaimed saviors of the Confucian state system from its domestic despoilers.[5]

When Hsi-tsung came to the Ming throne in 1620, however, the situation in the northeast was by no means lost. Shen-tsung had from the beginning paid little attention to the danger that Nurhaci posed, and the grand army that was sent to punish him in 1619 was badly managed. Even so, only the northeasternmost portion of the Liaotung territory had yet been affected by the Manchu threat. Moreover, effective Chinese action seemed about to be taken. When the grand army was defeated, Hsiung T'ing-pi, a former censor who had given futile warnings about defense needs while serving as regional inspector in Liaotung a decade earlier, was recalled from early retirement and made supreme commander of Liaotung with full powers to restore peace.[6] A tall, powerfully built man skilled at archery as well as literary pursuits, Hsiung exuded competence and confidence; and for a year he worked to strengthen the defenses and shore up sagging discipline and morale in the ranks.

Unfortunately for Hsiung, he was an arrogant man who tended to be contemptuous of the court ministers. He made few friends, and in his career he had made many partisan enemies. Soon after Shen-tsung's death they began to complain at court about his failure to take dramatic action, and he retorted in bad temper. He was soon dismissed.

Hsiung T'ing-pi's successor, Yüan Ying-t'ai, was overwhelmed by the Manchus as soon as spring came in 1621, and the two key settlements in central Liaotung, Shen-yang (modern Mukden) and the territorial headquarters town Liao-yang, were both captured.[7] The Manchus thus won control of all the territory east of the Liao River, and the whole Ming defense establishment in the northeast seemed to be collapsing. Yüan committed suicide, and the court at Peking, in considerable alarm, soon recalled Hsiung T'ing-pi. He was reappointed supreme commander of all northeastern military affairs and stationed at the strategic coastal pass north of Peking, Shan-hai-kuan. A younger official who had shown some distinction in Liaotung affairs, Wang Hua-chen, was made grand coordinator in the forward area, with headquarters at the principal Ming fortress west of the Liao River, Kuang-ning.[8]

From the beginning of their association, Hsiung T'ing-pi and

Wang Hua-chen were at odds with each other. Hsiung was defense-minded. He wanted to concentrate all available army strength at Kuang-ning, to hold that fortress against any assault and thus prevent further Manchu moves westward and southward toward Peking. He wanted simultaneously to build up naval fleets at Tientsin and in the Teng-lai area on the northern Shantung coast, hoping that from these bases they might in time be able to transport substantial forces across open sea to attack the Manchu flank and rear. He also hoped that the Koreans might be induced to join in an eventual pincers movement. He advocated patience and careful preparation in the meantime. Wang Hua-chen, on the other hand, was vaingloriously offense-minded. He promised that the Mongols, whom Hsiung distrusted, were ready to send 400,000 horsemen to join him in an assault on the Manchus, if properly bribed; he insisted that the residents of the lost areas, whom Hsiung had come to distrust because of their defections, were ready to rise up in a massive assault on the Manchus from within; and he dispatched an adventurous officer named Mao Wen-lung to organize refugees in north Korea for raids on the Manchu rear as soon as possible.[9] When Mao successfully carried out a daring attack, Hsiung protested that his only accomplishment was to arouse the Manchus into retaliatory massacres of innocent villagers, and that he had so offended the Koreans that they were unlikely to be of any future help; but the court at Peking was eager to think the tide was turning, and Wang Hua-chen's views got influential support. In particular, the minister of war, Chang Hao-ming, favored Wang over Hsiung. Wang was consequently emboldened to try several sorties across the Liao River without the sanction of his nominal superior, Hsiung; all his attacks were repulsed by the Manchus.

Finally, in the first month of 1622, Wang notified Hsiung that he was launching a major attack, and Hsiung frantically moved his small force northward to give what support he could. The Manchus poured across the Liao River, and Wang's army disintegrated for lack of leadership. Wang himself, abandoning Kuang-ning, fled southward pell-mell. When he encountered Hsiung, in a show of bravado he proposed making a gallant last stand at Ning-yüan, the only remaining fortress north of Shan-hai-kuan. Hsiung, however, set fire to all supplies and equipment that could not be carried and then shepherded what remained of the Liaotung armies into the security of Shan-hai-kuan, to protect Peking in any eventuality. The pursuing Manchus ran out of supplies not far south of Kuang-ning and withdrew, but the court was thrown into a state of panic. Hsiung and Wang were both arrested, tried, and convicted of deserting their posts, and both were eventually executed after long delays.

Fortunately for the Chinese, the Manchus were not yet ready in 1622 to capitalize on Ming weakness and panic. Nurhaci, though he established his capital at Liao-yang in 1624 and then at Shen-yang in 1625, apparently never dreamed of actually overthrowing the Ming dynasty, and there was much for him to do in consolidating his newly won territories in Liaotung. Consequently, for the remainder of Hsi-tsung's reign the Ming-Manchu front remained fairly stable. From late 1622 until late 1625 there was vigorous and competent leadership on the Chinese side from Sun Ch'eng-tsung, who served simultaneously as grand secretary, minister of war, and supreme commander at Shan-hai-kuan.[10] Sun even re-established Ming control north of the pass in the fortresses of Ning-yüan and Chin-chou, with the help of his principal subordinate and eventual successor as supreme commander, Yüan Ch'ung-huan.[11] In 1626 and 1627 Yüan held both positions against heavy Manchu attack, and he then stubbornly refused to negotiate a peace treaty with Abahai, who dominated the Manchus after Nurhaci's death in 1626. Although both Sun and Yüan in turn lost favor at court and were dismissed, the end of Hsi-tsung's reign found China indebted to them for a temporary respite from the succession of military disasters that had seemed in the early 1620's to portend the dynasty's quick collapse. But Liaotung was irrevocably lost.

While confronted with the Manchus in the north, China under Hsi-tsung was concurrently shaken by domestic rebellions in other outlying regions. The most serious of these was a grand uprising of restive aboriginal peoples in the southwest, begun by the chieftain She Ch'ung-ming in Szechwan in late 1621 and joined by the chieftain An Pang-yen in Kweichow in 1622. The major southwestern cities Chengtu, Chungking, and Kweiyang were at various times captured or besieged by the rebels, and Yunnan province was affected as well. Throughout the remainder of Hsi-tsung's reign, government forces met many reverses in their attempts to pacify the aborigines; and the rebellion was not suppressed until the reign of Chuang-lieh-ti.[12]

In mid-1622, just when the Liaotung crisis and the southwestern rebellion were at their peaks, another rebellion broke out in Shantung province, under the banner of the old fanatical religious movement called the White Lotus Society. The rebel forces quickly mushroomed to a strength of more than 100,000 men, and at one time they severed the Grand Canal transport route, on which the whole northern defense system relied heavily for logistical support. But prompt and effective action by the local authorities suppressed the rebellion before the end of 1622.[13]

No sooner had the Shantung rebellion been put down, however, than trouble arose on the far southeastern coast, in the persons of the Dutch (whom the Chinese called "the red-haired barbarians" to distinguish them from the Portuguese). The Portuguese had been profitably established at Macao (near Canton) since the 1550's, and the Dutch, who were developing a mercantile empire in Indonesia, wanted to get into the China trade also. In 1622 a Dutch fleet attacked the Portuguese at Macao but was driven off, whereupon the Dutch proceeded eastward and established themselves on the sparsely populated Pescadores Islands, between the Fukien coast and the large island of Taiwan. When the Chinese authorities in Fukien refused to negotiate a trade agreement with them, the Dutch retaliated by seizing Chinese ships and looting along the coast. Though the Ming court never took the Dutch menace very seriously, it had to divert forces into Fukien to deal with them, and it was not until 1625 that the Dutch were forced to abandon the Pescadores. They then retreated to Taiwan, where they remained until 1663.[14]

All these military difficulties were accompanied by natural disasters, which were all the more demoralizing because the Chinese took them to be omens of Heaven's displeasure. There were earthquakes at Peking in 1623, 1624, and 1626, and at Nanking in 1624 and 1626. Fires destroyed pavilions and halls in the imperial palace complex in 1620, 1621, and 1626, and in the Nanking palace in 1623. Throughout Hsi-tsung's reign there were recurrent reports of floods, droughts, hail storms, and locust infestations throughout the country.[15]

The fiscal demands made on the state by these varied troubles were extraordinary, and the sense of prosperity and abundance that had prevailed in Chang Chü-cheng's time did not persist. Shen-tsung's military campaigns in the 1590's reportedly required special expenditures of 10 million taels of silver from the state treasury, and from 1618 through 1627 defense against the Manchus in the northeast is reported to have cost 60 million taels.[16] The Ministry of War stated that in the brief period from the fourth month of 1618 into the tenth month of 1620 alone, just short of 20 million taels had been issued for Liaotung expenditures.[17] Imperial extravagance added to the burden. When Shen-tsung married, the ceremonies cost the state an estimated 90,000 taels. Celebration of the birth of a daughter in 1577 required 100,000 taels. The investiture ceremonies for Shen-tsung's various princes cost more than 12 million taels, and the marriages of imperial princesses in Shen-tsung's time cost another 120,000 taels. When Shen-tsung rebuilt some burned palace buildings, expenditures on wood alone are reported to have amounted to more than 9 million taels, and palace-construction projects in Hsi-tsung's time seem to have cost approximately 6 million more taels, perhaps in a single year.[18] The necessity of building monumental tombs for both Shen-tsung and Kuang-tsung in quick succession in the early 1620's must also have been an enormous drain on the court's resources.

When measured against a normal empire-wide annual revenue of some 14 million taels of silver, expenditures at these levels meant real fiscal trouble.[19] The extent of the trouble is suggested by a calculation that allocations for the various defense areas along the northern frontier west of Liaotung, which normally exceeded 3 million taels, steadily fell short as costs in Liaotung mounted, so that by 1626 and 1627 they were deficient annually in excess of 2 million taels.[20] Besides causing this heavy drain of silver from the state treasury to pay the troops, the struggle against the Manchus, by Hsi-tsung's time, was also causing a portion of the grain revenues that were transported northward on the Grand Canal to be diverted from Peking to the war zone to feed the troops; and merely the overland shipping of these grain supplies to Shan-hai-kuan and beyond required an enormous expenditure of silver.[21]

The government responded to these needs by increasing taxes. Wars and palace-reconstruction work in the 1590's caused Shen-tsung to send out special eunuch expediters to supervise tax collections and to levy a variety of new emergency taxes—on mines, on shops, on boats, and so on. Then, beginning in 1618, special increments to meet Liaotung needs were added to the basic land-tax rate. By 1620 such cumulative added assessments totaled more than 5 million taels. In 1621, because it was felt that landowners could bear no heavier burdens, the need for more revenues led to comparable increments to other tax rates—domestic customs tolls, salt taxes, and others. Throughout Hsi-tsung's reign, though conditions prevented the collection of all these extraordinary assessments in full, the government seems to have regularly collected between 4 and 6 million taels per year over and above the normal base revenues of 14 million taels.[22]

The imposition of such added tax burdens on a national economy that had never been noted for its flexibility could only have been disastrous to the morale of the people. The concentration of land in fewer and fewer hands, which had been a tendency throughout the whole Ming dynasty, undoubtedly accelerated, and problems of tenancy and bonded servitude grew worse. Retired officials and the relatives and hangers-on of high-placed ministers increasingly took advantage of their prestige and of the special privileges and exemptions that were the traditional prerogatives of the literati. They found it easy in times of lax government to oppress the common people by extortion, violence, and the disruption of judicial processes; and conscientious local officials found efforts to restrain them useless or dangerous because of the indolence or the susceptibility to bribery of their own superiors.[23] The armies came to be made up largely of distressed peasants, who yielded to recruitment as their only hope of making a living but who readily deserted in large numbers when called upon to fight. Such deserters, together with other peasants who disdained army service, readily turned to banditry, which in turn could easily grow into widespread rebellion.

Even so, Ming China might have met and overcome its challenges even as late as Hsi-tsung's time with proper leadership from the official class, if not from the emperor. Without this, conditions continually deteriorated. No sooner had Chuang-lieh-ti taken the throne following Hsi-tsung's death in 1627 than a new rash of domestic rebellions broke out. Gradually consolidated under two cunning leaders, Li Tzu-ch'eng and Chang Hsien-chung, rebels ravaged such large tracts of central and western China in the 1630's that the government's ability to resist anywhere steadily eroded away; and in the end it was not the Manchus but the rebel Li Tzu-ch'eng who captured Peking and terminated Ming rule in 1644, only to have the watchful Manchus step in to steal the shattered empire from him.[24]

The Rise of Bureaucratic Factionalism

The lack of effective government leadership during the latter part of Shen-tsung's reign and throughout Hsi-tsung's reign, in part attributable to the weaknesses and eccentricities of the emperors themselves, was accentuated by bitter factional partisanship within the officialdom. This principally revolved around a group that came to be known as the Tung-lin Party, which historians have consistently acclaimed for its ultimately disastrous opposition to the eunuch Wei Chung-hsien.[25]

Open partisanship, to the extent that it could be interpreted as conspiracy and sedition, was of course intolerable in the Chinese state, and any group of officials who acted as we expect a modern political party to act could anticipate vicious denunciations and severe punishments. Yet the nature of China's traditional social order, with its emphasis on familism and other sorts of small-group interrelationships, made it inevitable that certain tendencies toward rudimentary party-like relationships were present at all times in the bureaucracy. As was mentioned earlier, officials who had passed the same doctoral examination considered themselves lifelong comrades who owed political as well as personal loyalty to one another and to their old examiners. Similar bonds of political patronage and clientage persisted between former superiors and inferiors in particular government agencies. Thus the adherents of one powerful minister were expected to support him against the machinations of any other; officials from one region were expected to support each other against the machinations of those from other areas; the officials of one agency felt a common cause against those of other agencies; literati associated with one philosophical movement suspected those associated with another; and so on. All this was considered normal and proper; and in fact, violating obligations that derived from such relationships was frowned on as being vaguely akin to unfilial conduct. Moreover, to differentiate these manifestations of "proper human feelings" from conspiracy and sedition must have been difficult at any time. But it was relatively easy, especially in times of imperial laxness, for quite legitimate informal associations of bureaucrats to begin large-scale partisan controversies of the most vengeful sort. This is what happened under Shen-tsung and Hsi-tsung.

The partisan conflict originally took the form of a struggle between the "inner court," especially as represented by the Grand Secretariat, and the "outer court," especially as represented by the censorial officials, whose prescribed duties of impeachment and remonstrance naturally inclined them toward polemics and legitimated their engaging in disputes. The struggle was rooted in antagonisms that developed in the time of Shen-tsung's powerful grand secretary, Chang Chü-cheng.

To achieve a well-disciplined and effective officialdom, Chang Chü-cheng stepped on many outer-court toes. In particular, he suppressed what he considered irresponsible censorial criticism. Outer-court antagonism toward him, or what might be called anti-administration sentiments (i. e., anti-Grand Secretariat sentiments), boiled over in 1577, on the occasion of the death of Chang's father. The Confucian tradition required that when one of his parents died, an official had to leave office and observe mourning in retirement for 27 months; and this was the general practice. Chang accordingly requested permission to depart. But Shen-tsung, who was only fourteen years old at the time, ordered that the regular mourning period and procedure be waived and that Chang remain on duty. Many contemporaries and subsequent historians believed that Chang himself was responsible for this order. At least, he did not protest as dramatically as might have been expected, but agreed to a compromise that permitted him to observe mourning and perform his Grand Secretariat duties simultaneously, merely being excused from personal participation in court audiences.

Four officials of the outer court protested this "violation of human feelings," accusing Chang of being so jealous of his powerful position that he forgot his parents. All four were beaten in court, imprisoned, and in the end banished into frontier military service. A new doctoral graduate serving his apprenticeship in the Ministry of Justice, Tsou Yüan-piao (eventually a leader of the Tung-lin Party), was similarly beaten and banished when he memorialized in their defense. In the remaining years of Chang's regime his supporters dominated the outer court, and his influence was so great that opposition was not shown openly. But as soon as Chang died in 1582, long restrained censorial officials began to attack his closest adherents, and Shen-tsung listened to the critics with sympathy. Before a year had passed, Chang himself was posthumously disgraced, and officials who had been banished during the mourning controversy were recalled.

During the next 25 years, Chang Chü-cheng's successors as senior grand secretaries were constantly embroiled in court disputes. There was a series of frenzied controversies over merit evaluations for civil-service personnel, over the activities of eunuch tax collectors, and over a host of seemingly trivial incidents related to what the antagonists called "the root of the state."[26] This term referred to the status of the eldest imperial son, whose investiture as heir apparent was peevishly and repeatedly delayed by Shen-tsung, though increasingly insisted upon by the outer court. It was widely known that Shen-tsung was enamored of one of his concubines whose own son, later known as the Prince of Fu, might indeed have been designated heir apparent despite his juniority. Although Shen-tsung ultimately gave in, he was so irritated by the impertinences of his critics that he became steadily more inattentive and less manageable. Year after year dozens of outer court spokesmen were degraded or banished; the grand secretaries found themselves hopelessly caught in the cross fire between the palace and the outer court; and Shen-tsung finally ceased seeing even his closest ministerial advisers. For the last half of his long reign the flow of documents to and from the throne was handled solely by eunuchs, and the emperor pigeonholed any memorials that he chose not to deal with.

Meanwhile, the court controversies had gradually changed in character. By the beginning of the seventeenth century they were no longer primarily expressions of friction between the Grand Secretariat and outer-court officials intent on preventing the grand secretaries from attaining the predominance that Chang Chü-cheng had enjoyed. Moral issues had colored the controversies from the start; and at this time the institutional alignments tended to be submerged in a new struggle, essentially within the outer court itself, that had a distinctively moral tone. What brought this moral tone into prominence was the development of the Tung-lin Academy.

The establishment of private academies, at which private scholars and scholar-officials gathered for philosophical discourse and where some private tutoring of examination candidates was undertaken, had become one of the most notable aspects of Chinese intellectual life by the late sixteenth century, largely because of the influence of the famous philosopher-statesman Wang Yang-ming (1472–1529). The Tung-lin or "Eastern Grove" Academy was established in 1604 at Wusih (Wu-hsi) in the culturally rich Yangtze delta region of modern Anhwei province.[27] It was started by a group of scholar-officials living in the area, almost all of whom had been ousted from the government during the controversies of the prior decade. The founder and leading philosopher of the academy, Ku Hsien-ch'eng, deplored what he considered the political immorality of the court.[28] He attributed it to a general relaxation of Confucian standards by Wang Yang-ming's followers, and called for a kind of moral crusade that might restore control of government to "good elements" or "upright men" or "honest critics" and unseat what he and his followers considered the vindictive, opportunistic sycophants then in power. Ku lectured throughout the southeast and wrote political tracts that got wide circulation, while his friends still in service kept the court boiling with controversies. By 1610 the old anti-administration group in the government had aligned itself with the Tung-lin group and was being openly referred to by its enemies as the Tung-lin Party.

The capital evaluations conducted in 1611 marked a turning point in the factional developments. Tung-lin men held strategic positions as grand secretary and as minister of personnel when the evaluations occurred, and they proposed that the leaders of opposing factions be removed from office. But when they pressed this recommendation and got imperial approval, such a barrage of attacks was launched against the Tung-lin men that most withdrew into voluntary retirement. By 1614 the Tung-lin group was in almost total eclipse. Thereafter the only grand secretary on duty was a weak, vacillating man named Fang Ts'ung-che, of whom the official *Ming History* says, "Shen-tsung actually paved the way for the Ming collapse, but Fang Ts'ung-che was principally responsible."[29] Fang seems to have been little more than the servile tool of allied factions of anti-Tung-lin men from Shantung, Hukwang, and Chekiang provinces. The supervising secretary Chi Shih-chiao, a Shantung man, had become the acknowledged leader of these factions.

A dramatic controversy in 1615 put the few remaining Tung-lin partisans into the emperor's bad graces. A commoner had rushed into the palace residence of the heir apparent and clubbed some eunuch attendants, but had been seized before he could do any further harm. The judicial authorities concluded that the attacker was an irresponsible madman, but Tung-lin partisans insisted that "the case of the attack with the club," as it came to be known, was actually a plot to do away with the heir apparent so that the Prince of Fu could supplant him after all.[30] For thus impugning anew the emperor's intentions toward the heir apparent, the Tung-lin men were ousted in the capital evaluations of 1617. Meantime, the death of Ku Hsien-ch'eng in 1612 had robbed the Tung-lin group of its vigorous intellectual leadership. Kao P'an-lung, who succeeded as master of the academy, though himself an ousted official, did not have Ku's intense interest in current politics.[31]

Thus the last years of Shen-tsung's reign were marked by the almost unchallenged supremacy of the three anti-Tung-lin factions, which did not interfere with the emperor's inclination to let things drift. Memorials were not answered, and official vacancies were not filled. At one time only 4 supervising secretaries were on duty in the six Offices of Scrutiny, and the absence of any supervising secretaries at all in the Offices of Scrutiny for Personnel and for War held up thousands of recommended appointments in both the civil and military services. Only five investigating censors were on duty in the Censorate, and some regional inspectors served terms as long as five years because they were not replaced. Although the censorial offices suffered particularly because of Shen-tsung's determination to quell their harassment, vacancies crippled all other government hierarchies.[32] Once in 1618 Fang Ts'ung-che, irritated by some criticism, sulked at home for more than forty days, during which time there was no one at all on duty in the Grand Secretariat itself. Shen-tsung's refusal to approve appointments was not new; vacancies had been accumulating since the turn of the century, when the emperor's irritation with court critics turned him against speaking officials in general. But in his last years nothing prodded him into action except the Manchu attack on Liaotung in 1618, in response to which he authorized official appointments for a while.

Once the appointments log-jam was broken, the dominant factions could not wholly prevent the slow infiltration of a new generation of idealistic "good elements" with Tung-lin sympathies, and in 1619 two new "minority leaders" became influential at court. One of these was Yang Lien, whose career has been outlined in Chapter 2.[33] A native of Hukwang, Yang won his doctoral degree in 1607 and was appointed county magistrate in the vicinity of Wusih, site of the Tung-lin Academy. He regularly attended meetings there and became a devoted disciple of Ku Hsien-ch'eng and Kao P'an-lung. He was called to the capital in 1619 and appointed a supervising secretary in the Office of Scrutiny for Revenue, and he quickly became friends with the investigating censor Tso Kuang-tou.[34]

Tso, a native of modern Anhwei province in the southeast, had won his doctoral degree in the same examination as Yang Lien, but only after prior failures in 1601 and 1604. From 1607 to 1613 he served as a drafter in the Central Drafting Office, and during this period he was apparently favorably impressed by the Tung-lin group, though he was not then active in controversies. In 1613 he was nominated for the post of investigating censor, but he had to wait at home until 1619 before this nomination got imperial approval. He then joined the Chekiang Circuit. One of his first censorial acts was to memorialize requesting that the emperor make a personal appearance at court audience.

Yang Lien and Tso Kuang-tou, both committed to reforming the court, found a willing helper waiting for them in the capital. This was Wang Wen-yen, who eventually became the object of much anti-Tung-lin agitation.[35] An orphan from Anhwei province, Wang served for a time as a clerical functionary in a local office and then through a mutual friend became a close associate of Yü Yü-li.[36] Yü, an anti-administration polemicist of the 1590's, had been removed from office in 1603 because of a strange minor controversy known as "the case of the subversive book," but he continued from afar his dabbling in court politics. Yü was an ardent supporter of a popular supreme commander of the Grand Canal transport system, Li San-ts'ai, who had made himself controversial through his attacks on an unpopular grand secretary at the turn of the century.[37] Li was so regularly championed by Tung-lin partisans that by 1610 one's attitude toward him seemed prima facie evidence of one's political affiliation in general. Yü Yü-li and Li San-ts'ai were the supreme political manipulators of the Tung-lin movement. As Yü's disciple, Wang Wen-yen met all of the important Tung-lin men and himself became an ardent and adept politician. In 1613 Yü Yü-li had sent Wang to Peking as a political spy and agent for the ousted "good elements," and he had purchased status as a National University student. He cultivated the acquaintance of Wang An, the chief eunuch in the household of the heir apparent, who was favorably inclined toward the Tung-lin partisans because of their long championing of the heir apparent. When Yang Lien and Tso Kuang-tou appeared in the capital in 1619 determined to rescue the "good elements" from oblivion, Wang Wen-yen became their zealous aide. Through strategies worked out by Yang and Tso, and with Wang An's support in the palace, Wang Wen-yen engaged immediately in a series of intrigues that provoked internal antagonisms within the opposition ranks, got the Hukwang faction at odds with the Chekiang and Shantung factions, and thus paved the way for unobstructed recalls of the Tung-lin partisans when Shen-tsung died in 1620.

Kuang-tsung's death after only a month on the throne not only disheartened the Tung-lin group; it precipitated two more ugly controversies, the echoes of which reverberated throughout Hsi-tsung's reign. One is known as "the case of the red pills," the other as "the case of the removal from the palace."[38]

"The case of the red pills" had to do with the manner of Kuang-tsung's death. Within a week of his accession, the new emperor fell ill. Rumor in the capital had it that Madame Cheng, the envious favorite of Shen-tsung who had long hoped to put her own son, the Prince of Fu, on the throne, had sent a congratulatory present of eight beautiful palace maidens to Kuang-tsung, a known lecher, and he had promptly fallen ill of exhaustion. In any event, the emperor was slow to recover, and Madame Cheng hovered constantly at his side, conniving with his favorite consort, Madame Li, to prevent the officials from having access to him. They had a eunuch physician, Ts'ui Wen-sheng, give the emperor a laxative, which seemed to worsen his condition. There were frantic court assemblies. Led principally by Yang Lien and Tso Kuang-tou rather than by the ineffective grand secretary Fang Ts'ung-che, the officials insisted that Madame Cheng remove herself and that Ts'ui Wen-sheng be punished. Finally, after two weeks, a delegation of officials was able to visit the emperor's bedside. For another two weeks the emperor's condition fluctuated. Then, on the last day of the eighth month, at the emperor's insistent order, a minor official of the Court of State Ceremonial, Li K'o-shao, was allowed to give him some red pills of his own making that Li made great claims for; and early the next morning Kuang-tsung died. For years following, there were factional disputes about who was responsible for the emperor's death.

"The case of the removal from the palace" followed immediately. On learning of Kuang-tsung's death, a host of officials marched into the palace to do obeisance to the fifteen-year-old successor, Hsi-tsung. But Madame Li had taken him into her custody in the imperial residence hall, and her eunuch attendants barred the way. Yang Lien, always impetuous, roared and cursed at the eunuch guards, and the friendly eunuch Wang An finally by a ruse whisked the boy emperor out of Madame Li's presence and into the custody of the officials. Though the officials promptly began to quarrel among themselves about when the emperor should be formally enthroned, and feelings rose to such a pitch that Tso Kuang-tou even spat in Yang Lien's face, they reunited quickly when Madame Li refused to move out of the imperial residence hall and announced that she would screen all government documents for Hsi-tsung. Yang Lien, Tso Kuang-tou, and others protested so vigorously against the possibility of a female usurpation of the throne that her friends and relatives finally persuaded her to yield and move out so that Hsi-tsung could move in unchaperoned. The crisis then ended, but for years court factions argued about the propriety of what had been done.

The recall to duty of banished Tung-lin partisans, begun under Kuang-tsung, continued under Hsi-tsung. It included many men who had been in enforced retirement for more than 20 years—Tsou Yüan-piao (a critic of Chang Chü-cheng in 1577), Chao Nan-hsing (an anti-administration victim of 1593), Kao P'an-lung, and others.[39] Even Li San-ts'ai, by now almost a symbolic standard of Tung-lin partisanship, was at last recalled after prolonged arguments at court, though he died before actually resuming office. The new ascendancy of the "good elements" was signaled late in 1621 by the reappearance as senior grand secretary of Yeh Hsiang-kao, who had been the principal Grand Secretariat defender of Tung-lin interests from 1607 to 1614.[40] Fang Ts'ung-che had been removed from the Grand Secretariat at the end of 1620 under insistent Tung-lin attack for his roles in the "three great cases" of 1615 and 1620; and in the cap-

ital evaluations of 1623, under the vengeful leadership of Chao
Nan-hsing, the Tung-lin men succeeded in removing from the capital many of their remaining enemies of former days, beginning with
the Shantung faction leader, Chi Shih-chiao. By the latter part of
1624 the key posts at court were all held by Tung-lin partisans. Yeh
Hsiang-kao was a highly prestigious senior grand secretary, Chao
Nan-hsing was minister of personnel, and Kao P'an-lung was censor-
in-chief.

The Tung-lin partisans, however, did not at any time have complete control of the government, and they suffered several reverses.
One resulted from a controversy over the establishment in Peking
of an academy in which philosophical conferences might be held.
This was a project initiated by two of the most venerable "good element" heroes, Tsou Yüan-piao and Feng Ts'ung-wu, respectively
censor-in-chief and vice censor-in-chief at the time.[41] During a 30-
year retirement in Kiangsi province, Tsou had devoted himself to
philosophical studies, founded an academy of his own, won empire-
wide renown as a moralist, and lectured occasionally at the Tung-
lin Academy during its heyday. Feng Ts'ung-wu, a Shensi native,
had been an active anti-administration investigating censor in the
1590's and had been removed from office in 1595. In retirement he
had become a disciple of Ku Hsien-ch'eng. Neither Tsou nor Feng
was a notably vengeful partisan; Tsou Yüan-piao, as a matter of
fact, disapproved of the inflexible partisan attitudes of Chao Nan-
hsing and some others, feeling that old grudges would best be forgotten. But the presence of Tsou and Feng in senior positions in
the Censorate was a bad omen for the Tung-lin opponents as the
1623 evaluations approached. When in 1622 Tsou and Feng opened
a Tung-lin type academy in Peking and summoned their friends to
meetings, which Kao P'an-lung and many other Tung-lin men attended, it could only be construed by the opposition as a flagrantly
partisan demonstration right at the foot of the throne. Tsou and
Feng were vigorously attacked in memorials and were forced to
retire.

This episode was perhaps more of an embarrassment than a griev-
ous setback for the Tung-lin "good elements." But the rise to power
of the eunuch Wei Chung-hsien was a different matter indeed.

The Rise and Dominance of Wei Chung-hsien

Wei Chung-hsien was a native of Su-ning in the Northern Metropolitan Area, probably born in 1568.[42] He seems to have had a dis-

solute, restless early life; and after he had attained maturity he had himself castrated and was accepted among the thousands of eunuchs engaged in palace service in Shen-tsung's time. He quickly proved to be an adept tactician in palace politics, winning the favor and patronage of a succession of influential chief eunuchs. He finally became a protégé of Wang An, who dominated the household of the heir apparent who was to become Kuang-tsung. With Wang An's help Wei became manager of foodstuffs in the establishment of the consort Madame Wang, the mother of Kuang-tsung's eldest son— the future Hsi-tsung. During Kuang-tsung's short reign Wei closely attended the ambitious consort Madame Li, repeatedly offended the officials who opposed her ambitions, and was repeatedly humili- ated by Yang Lien. When Madame Li was finally forced to abandon the imperial residence, Yang Lien denounced Wei and a eunuch colleague for rifling the imperial treasure-chests as they left the hall.[43]

Because of his involvement with Madame Li, and even more be- cause he was apparently illiterate, Wei Chung-hsien should not have expected to gain much influence in the palace under Hsi-tsung. But he did his politicking well. Through depravities, the only recourse of eunuchs in such relationships, he won the passionate favor of the boy Hsi-tsung's nursemaid, one Mistress K'o. It has been suggested that Wei and Mistress K'o introduced the young emperor-to-be to a life of profligacy. However that may be, through Hsi-tsung's fondness for Mistress K'o, Wei Chung-hsien became the emperor's trusted ad- viser in 1621 and 1622. He had his old patron Wang An degraded and then murdered in 1621. Honors of various sorts were increasingly heaped upon Wei and Mistress K'o, despite growing protests from the officialdom; and in 1622 Wei even got the emperor's approval to be- gin training a eunuch army within the palace. At the end of 1623 he was made chief of the Eastern Depot, the notorious secret-service headquarters in the palace which, in collaboration with the imper- ial bodyguard, had at intervals since the fifteenth century instituted short-lived reigns of terror.[44]

It was the character of Hsi-tsung himself that made possible Wei Chung-hsien's rise to power. Prior to taking the throne, because of his youth and his apparent remoteness from succession, Hsi-tsung had never been exposed to the distinguished litterateur-officials whose tutorship was normally imposed on heirs apparent. His training had been entirely in the hands of such attendants as Mistress K'o. He had therefore not been subjected to Confucian indoctrination. As a matter

of fact, it is probable that he was illiterate and remained so throughout his reign. But he had an absorbing interest in carpentry, and Wei
Chung-hsien found it easy to encourage him to while away his time
in the workshop, with interruptions for other less innocent pleasures.
After his first few months on the throne, Hsi-tsung rapidly wearied
of the demands that government made on him and let Wei be his
intermediary with the Grand Secretariat, with less and less supervision. Not all of these developments were immediately known by the
outer court, for at all times outsiders had difficulty in finding out exactly what was happening in the palace. But the Tung-lin partisans
did not like what little they learned about palace goings-on.

Among Ming officials, as has been noted previously, collaborating
with eunuchs had long since become a recognized and often inescapable practice. The Tung-lin partisans had no misgivings about coop-
erating with Wang An, and they may have tried to cultivate another
eunuch as a rival to Wei Chung-hsien after Wang An's murder.[45] But
Wei's obvious purpose was to pursue his own aggrandizement rather
than to encourage an unstable emperor to do his duty, so that collaborating with him was out of the question for the Tung-lin men. As
his influence grew their objections became sharper, and Wei then
sought to find allies in the outer court who might join him in silenc-
ing his critics. Since the Tung-lin group at this time was busily root-
ing out "rascals," willing helpers were not hard for Wei to find among
the opposition officials, and unwitting tools were also at hand in the
persons of officials who found partisanship distasteful and sought neu-
trality.

Thus the years 1622 and 1623 were uneasy years. Despite their
grasp on key positions, the Tung-lin partisans were steadily being
undermined by a multitude of complicated intrigues that linked Wei
Chung-hsien to dissatisfied elements in the outer court. The crisis
came in the sixth month of 1624, when Yang Lien (by then having
risen to the rank of vice censor-in-chief) submitted a long denunciation of Wei in which he itemized "twenty-four great crimes." Yang
chose a moment when according to rumor the emperor had become
peevishly annoyed with Wei over some trifle, but even so Yang's
friends did not unanimously encourage him. It seems that both Tso
Kuang-tou, now assistant censor-in-chief, and Miao Ch'ang-ch'i, an
official of the Supervisorate of Imperial Instruction who had been associated with the Tung-lin cause since 1615, helped draft Yang's memorial.[46] But others tried to dissuade Yang. The investigating censor
Huang Tsun-su, who had himself barely escaped being beaten in

open court just a few months before, told Yang, "Anyone who tries to clear away the ruler's side must have inside help. Do you have it? If you once strike and do not succeed, the villain will just intervene more."[47] The respected grand secretary Yeh Hsiang-kao also urged caution for fear of disastrous reprisals.[48] But Yang went ahead, and when he was severely rebuked for his audacity, the "good elements" presented an almost united front in defending him and reiterating his accusations. One defender, Wan Ching, a Bureau director in the Ministry of Works, was beaten in court in an effort by Wei to cow his attackers, and died four days later.[49] The conflict between the Tung-lin men and Wei Chung-hsien finally became open battle. With Hsi-tsung on the throne, it was a hopelessly one-sided battle.

At about this time an investigating censor named Lin Ju-chu, a fellow-provincial and protégé of Yeh Hsiang-kao, was so annoyed by two eunuchs that he had them seized and beaten. Knowing that there would be retaliation, he went into hiding. Wei Chung-hsien sent a small army of eunuchs to surround Yeh Hsiang-kao's residence, where he suspected Lin was concealed.[50] In humiliation, Yeh submitted his resignation and left Peking to go home. There rapidly followed a great purge of Tung-lin men, many of whom had previously been shielded from harm only by the grand secretary's influence. Chao Nan-hsing, Kao P'an-lung, Yang Lien, and Tso Kuang-tou all departed in disgrace. Those whom they had suppressed or removed were promoted or recalled. Long lists of Tung-lin sympathizers were drawn up, beginning with Ku Hsien-ch'eng and Li San-ts'ai and including men who had been on the same side as the Tung-lin group in any of the controversies since the one over "the root of the state" in the 1590's. The lists were presented to Wei Chung-hsien to guide him in the purge. In all, more than 700 names were listed.[51]

One of the men who now became a principal outer-court tool of Wei Chung-hsien was a Shensi man and old Tung-lin enemy, Wang Shao-hui.[52] As a supervising secretary in the early 1600's, Wang had been one of the chief attackers of Li San-ts'ai and had been removed from the capital in the evaluations of 1611. Returning to service under Hsi-tsung in 1620 through Fang Ts'ung-che's influence, he was repeatedly attacked by the Tung-lin group and was finally forced to go home on sick leave. After the purge of Tung-lin men began in 1624 he was recalled to replace Tso Kuang-tou as assistant censor-in-chief and compiled one of the most important Tung-lin blacklists.

Not all the men who now became active partisans of Wei Chung-hsien, however, were long-standing enemies of the Tung-lin group.

Wei Kuang-wei, for example, was the son of an old-time anti-administration champion who was a close friend of Li San-ts'ai.[53] Wei Kuang-wei was nevertheless one of the earliest civil officials to seek Wei Chung-hsien's favor; as early as 1623, he entered the Grand Secretariat as a poorly masked spokesman for the eunuch. The Tung-lin minister of personnel, Chao Nan-hsing, despised and repeatedly snubbed him; and when Wei Kuang-wei supported Wei Chung-hsien's determination to punish Yang Lien in 1624, he was viciously impeached by Tung-lin men. Afterwards Wei, like Wang Shao-hui, devoted himself to preparing Tung-lin blacklists and assisting in the purge.

Another leading antagonist of this period was Ts'ui Ch'eng-hsiu.[54] Appointed an investigating censor in 1620, Ts'ui sensed that the Tung-lin group was coming into power and tried in various ways to get in its good graces, principally by recommending the recall to service of Li San-ts'ai. But the "good elements" judged him a corrupt opportunist and rebuffed him. When he returned to Peking in 1624 upon completion of a censorial commission, he was denounced for venality by Kao P'an-lung, and Chao Nan-hsing urged that he be disgraced and sent to serve as a common soldier at the frontier. Terrified, Ts'ui fled to Wei Chung-hsien for help and pledged himself to be Wei's adopted son. Wei had him restored to duty, and Ts'ui—eventually rising to the rank of censor-in-chief—came to be the eunuch's most feared outer-court agent.

As the purge went on, Wei Chung-hsien and his adherents ceased to be satisfied with mere dismissals. Their enemies were pursued with more and more accusations. Honors were posthumously stripped from those who had died. Those who had been dismissed were now "erased from the rolls" and thus deprived of their status as literati. Chao Nan-hsing and some others were sent to serve as common soldiers at the frontier. But even this was not enough. Wang Wen-yen (the former spy for the Tung-lin party and confidant of the murdered eunuch Wang An) was arrested, imprisoned, beaten in court, and dismissed; then he was again imprisoned, tortured, and finally put to death in prison—all in an effort to extort testimony about corruption on the part of Yang Lien and Tso Kuang-tou.

Though Wang Wen-yen had not given the desired evidence, early in 1625 Wei Chung-hsien ordered the arrests of Yang Lien, Tso Kuang-tou, and four other Tung-lin men on charges that they had accepted bribes from the disgraced Liaotung supreme commander Hsiung T'ing-pi, then awaiting execution in prison. All were brought to Peking, thrown into prison, and tortured. None survived. In 1626 more arrests were ordered. The master of the Tung-lin Academy, Kao P'an-lung, learning that his time had come, drowned himself in a pond at his home to avoid the disgrace of arrest; but seven other Tung-lin men were tortured to death that year in the palace prison.[55] Afterwards the families and friends of the victims were hounded for punitive damages assessed in the thousands of taels.

By such ruthlessness and terrorism Wei Chung-hsien reduced the entire civil service to submission. Some of the earlier neutrals, aghast at the brutalities committed in 1625–26, drifted out of the government after helping to deliver control to Wei. Even such leaders as Wei Kuang-wei and Wang Shao-hui had misgivings; Wei Kuang-wei retired under suspicion late in 1626. But Wei Chung-hsien found less scrupulous associates. By the end of Hsi-tsung's reign all memorials offered to the palace necessarily included specious praise of the powerful eunuch, whose capacity for absorbing flattery was apparently limitless. Provincial authorities competed with one another in erecting temples in his honor and in offering sacrificial prayers for his long life. Titles and honors were heaped upon him and his forebears; his relatives were granted official posts, then honorific titles, then higher and higher grades of noble rank. The unprecedented title "supreme duke" was invented for Wei himself. It was even proposed that Wei Chung-hsien be ranked on a par with Confucius in ritual observances, and a unicorn (an omen always associated with the emergence of a great sage) was speciously reported to have appeared in Shantung, Confucius' own homeland. Imperial rescripts drafted by the Grand Secretariat usually began: "We and the palace minister . . . ." Finally one of Wei's nephews even substituted for the emperor in performing sacrifices in the imperial temple—the most flagrant possible disrespect for the throne. Men wondered who was emperor. And, as the *Ming History* comments, "Those who were murdered are beyond calculation; on the streets men used only their eyes" (dared not speak).[56]

The all-but-eclipsed emperor suddenly died in the autumn of 1627. What prevented seizure of the throne by Wei Chung-hsien and saved China from the humiliation that would have resulted can only be guessed at. Hsi-tsung's brother Chuang-lieh-ti was enthroned, and conditions gradually became somewhat better. Chuang-lieh-ti, himself only seventeen years old on accession, apparently did not feel secure enough or bitter enough to order any immediate and drastic action against Wei. Only after several months of tense waiting, during which time former supporters warily submitted criticisms of Wei to test the new emperor's attitude, did Chuang-lieh-ti at last banish the eunuch to live in exile outside the capital. There were no protests. Instead, those who had previously glorified Wei now rushed to join in denunciations of him in the hope of exonerating themselves. Soon Wei's arrest was ordered, and he committed suicide. Mistress K'o was beaten to death. Their most notorious henchmen were punished, and those of their victims who were still alive were recommended and recalled.

Thereafter the court was disrupted by long bickering over the guilt or innocence of persons who had held office during Wei Chunghsien's regime, and the emperor became so sick of partisanship that he eventually found the name Tung-lin almost as distasteful as that of Wei Chung-hsien. To the very end of his reign, while domestic rebellions raged and the Manchus threatened, the court was kept in a constant turmoil by petty animosities between groups that sought to pin partisan labels on one another in efforts to arouse the emperor's indignation. Partisan bickering had become a habit, and the government stagnated.

CENSORIAL OPERATIONS IN GENERAL

When one compares the censorial system of Hsi-tsung's time with that of Hsüan-tsung's time two centuries earlier, a notable similarity is evident. The Provincial Surveillance Offices had become more administrative than censorial in practice, and in the 1620's investigating censors and supervising secretaries were regularly assigned to the full range of duty commissions that was described in Chapter 2, the development of which had been in only a rudimentary stage in the 1420's and 1430's. But in general organizational terms the censorial system had not undergone any significant changes between Hsüan-tsung's and Hsi-tsung's times.

However, anyone who browses in the *Shih-lu* chronicles of the two periods will immediately note some striking differences. And undoubtedly the most conspicuous difference is that the censorial officials of Hsi-tsung's time occupied the front and center of the political stage, as they had never done in Hsüan-tsung's time. What has already been said about governmental developments after the 1570's will have suggested as much. The censorial officials were no longer bit players, unessential to the main action. They were now the protagonists, dominating the action rather than merely casting lights and shadows by their commentary on the action.

This impression cannot be wholly confirmed by objective proofs, but quantitative evidence strongly supports it. Whereas one must hunt for page after page in the chronicles of Jen-tsung's and Hsüan-tsung's time before finding references to the censorial offices, such references clutter almost every page of the chronicles of Hsi-tsung's time, collectively overshadowing the references to any other category of officials—or even, one almost feels, the references to all other categories of officials combined. Specifically, although there are fewer than 1,400 entries pertaining to the censorial offices in the 1424–34 chronicles, those recorded for the shorter period 1620–27 total over 3,200. Whereas the chronicles note 247 impeachment memorials for 1424–34, they note 526 for the shorter period 1620–27; and whereas they record 251 counseling memorials for 1424–34, they record 1,296 for 1620–27. Transforming these figures into average monthly rates of submission, we find in the case of impeachments a startling difference between the rate of 1.91 a month for 1424–34 and 6.3 for 1620–27. Furthermore, in counselings we find an even greater difference between 1.95 for 1424–34 and 15.3 for 1620–27. Such extreme differences cannot be accounted for by any general differences in the chronicles for the two eras. In overall bulk, there is no significant variation between the chronicles, and the importance of memorials in the emperor's eyes was the principal criterion for their inclusion in the chronicles of both eras. The inescapable conclusion is that, in contrast to the situation of 1424–34, censorial officials of 1620–27 were tumultuously active, and what they did was of prime importance in state affairs.[57]

Another facet of this difference between the two periods is suggested by the tabulations just given. That is, during the later period, censorial officials were especially more active in their roles as "speaking officials." In the earlier period they submitted almost the same number of impeachment memorials as counseling memorials, but in the 1620's—while submitting more memorials of both sorts than before—they submitted more than twice as many counseling memorials as impeachment memorials, at an average rate of 15.3 per month as against 6.3 per month. Supplementing this is the fact that censorial proposals were no longer predominantly of a rather routine, particularized sort. In the period 1424–34, of 178 counseling memorials submitted by censors, the vast majority were submitted by regional inspectors (112) and by the censors-in-chief or just "the Censorate" (40); only 26, or 14.6 per cent, were offered by investigating censors on general duty in the capital. But in the period 1620–27, of a total of 674 proposals offered by censors, the vast majority (391, or 58.0 per cent) were submitted by investigating censors on general duty in the capital.

Chronology of Major Events of Hsi-tsung's Reign

Year, Month

1620	8	Kuang-tsung succeeds Shen-tsung; recall of Tung-lin partisans begins
	9	Hsi-tsung succeeds Kuang-tsung; "The case of the red pills"; "the case of the removal from the palace"
	10	Hsiung T'ing-pi removed as Liaotung supreme commander
1621	3	Shen-yang and Liao-yang fall to the Manchus
	6	Hsiung T'ing-pi recalled to be Liaotung supreme commander
	9	Aboriginal rebellion in Szechwan begins
	10	Yeh Hsiang-kao enters Secretariat, signifying Tung-lin ascendancy
1622	1	Aboriginal rebellion in Kweichow begins; Kuang-ning falls to Manchus, all Liaotung abandoned
	2	Outer evaluations: Tung-lin men in charge
	3	Training of eunuch army begins in palace
	4	Hsiung T'ing-pi tried and sentenced to death
	5	White Lotus rebellion in Shantung begins
	8	Sun Ch'eng-tsung takes command at Shan-hai-kuan
	10	White Lotus rebellion quelled
1623	1	Capital evaluations; Dutch begin harassment of Fukien coast
	12	Wei Chung-hsien takes charge of Eastern Depot
1624	6	Yang Lien leads censorial attack on Wei Chung-hsien
	7	Yeh Hsiang-kao leaves Grand Secretariat
	10	Wei Chung-hsien begins purge of civil service
1625	1	Outer evaluations: eunuch partisans in charge
	3	Trial of Wang Wen-yen
	8	Academies throughout empire ordered destroyed
	10	Sun Ch'eng-tsung relieved of command at Shan-hai-kuan
	12	Tung-lin blacklists published
1626	1	Yüan Ch'ung-huan defeats Manchus at Ning-yüan
	3	Eunuch supervisors sent to all defense commands
	6	First proposal to erect a Wei Chung-hsien temple
1627	5	Yüan Ch'ung-huan again defeats Manchus at Ning-yüan and Chin-chou; Wei Chung-hsien equated with Confucius in sacrifices
	7	Yüan Ch'ung-huan relieved of Liaotung command
	8	Hsi-tsung dies; Chuang-lieh-ti takes throne
	11	Wei Chung-hsien sent into retirement, commits suicide

Twenty-nine were submitted by censors-in-chief, 181 by regional inspectors, and 73 by investigating censors on other sorts of commissions. The implications of these data are quite clear. They suggest that in the 1620's censors were speaking out as individuals rather than as institutional representatives of the Censorate, and about general matters rather than about particular matters relating to their routine assignments. It is also noteworthy in this regard that supervising secretaries of the Offices of Scrutiny—the "speaking officials" par excellence of Ming times—though responsible even in part for only 25 of the total 251 censorial proposals of 1424–34, were wholly or partly responsible for 618 of the 1,296 censorial proposals submitted between 1620 and 1627. When all these considerations are added together, it becomes strikingly apparent that the censorial officials now saw themselves, and behaved, predominantly as shapers of policy rather than just as post facto critics of governmental operations. As a matter of fact, it would be hard to believe that censorial officials had a similar position in any other period—not merely of the Ming dynasty, but of all Chinese history. To the extraordinarily provocative political conditions of the 1620's, the censorial officials contributed as well as responded, and with extraordinary vigor.

The censorial activities of Hsi-tsung's reign can be analyzed only with constant reference to the major political events of the period (which are condensed in the accompanying chronology), and especially to the rise of Wei Chung-hsien and his purge of the Tung-lin Party. In the early part of the era the censorial organs reflected the interests of the Tung-lin men predominantly, and later they reflected the interests of Wei Chung-hsien exclusively. The point at which the general political tide turned would be difficult to pinpoint. For tabulation purposes, I arbitrarily consider the ninth month of 1624 to terminate the Tung-lin ascendancy and the tenth month to inaugurate Wei Chung-hsien's ascendancy; for it was early in the tenth month that the censor-in-chief Kao P'an-lung, the vice censor-in-chief Yang Lien, and the assistant censor-in-chief Tso Kuang-tou were all forced out of office. For the censorial agencies, this was the major turning point in the reign. Though censorial activities were just as vigorous after the purge as before it, there was a totally different quality to those activities, as shall be noted throughout the remainder of this chapter.

In overall totals, based upon the *Shih-lu* chronicles of the era, between 1620 and 1627 censorial officials brought about the demotion of more than 410 officials in personnel-evaluation procedures. They caused the appointment, recall, or promotion of at least 148 persons; submitted 526 impeachment memorials denouncing at least 975 persons; and submitted 1,296 memorials offering counsel and remonstrance.[58]

PERSONNEL EVALUATIONS

Mass outer evaluations affecting both provincial and local officials, recurring in a three-year cycle, were conducted early in 1622 and again in 1625; and capital evaluations, recurring in a six-year cycle, were conducted in 1623. As has been suggested above, the evaluations of 1622 and 1623 were utilized by the Tung-lin Party to oust many of its enemies, whereas the 1625 evaluations were utilized principally by the adherents of Wei Chung-hsien to oust Tung-lin men. The entries in the *Shih-lu* of this era that report on the evaluations at best do little more than cite the numbers of officials who were affected, and sometimes they do not even specify numbers. In sum, they indicate that more than 410 officials of the following categories suffered demotions, dismissals, or retirements in consequence of the regularly scheduled evaluations:

> 326 capital officials
> 60 provincial-level officials
> 2+ prefectural and county officials
> 22 military officers

The notation 2+ ("at least two") derives from two different entries, each of which reports the evaluation of an unspecified number of local officials.[59] In each case hundreds of officials could have been affected. Thirty provincial and local officials, who were the objects of adverse reports submitted by Nanking censorial officials in the 1622 evaluations, are not counted in these tabulations, because it is not clear what final action was taken in their cases.[60]

One of the revealing, though brief, entries utilized in these tabulations reports that 235 capital officials were penalized in the 1623 evaluations for reasons as follows:[61]

> Aged or ill, 49   Frivolous and superficial, 45
> Venal, 18   Incompetent, 29
> Cruel, 3   Weak and inactive, 2
> Careless conduct, 89

Censorial officials, of course, were not wholly responsible for the regular evaluations, but they shared in them. In this era, since adverse censorial reports on personnel all appear as impeachments rather than as evaluations, I have encountered no reports in the 1620–27 records that any officials were affected by irregular evaluations. But the records are full of personnel recommendations submitted by censors and supervising secretaries. This is not surprising, since in the earliest 1620's the formerly ousted Tung-lin men were being recalled to duty and after 1624 the ousted Tung-lin enemies were being recalled.

In all, the *Shih-lu* chronicles for 1620–27 reveal that at least 148 persons were either recalled or promoted because of censorial recommendations. They included 45 civil officials and 14 military officers who were promoted, and at least 89 former civil officials who were recalled. The latter figure includes 39 men recalled prior to Wei Chung-hsien's ascendancy and 50 recalled thereafter. The fact that one report notes the recall of "more than ten" former officials makes the total imprecise.

These tabulations only partly indicate the extent of censorial recommendations during this era, since they do not include a majority of the entries reporting censorial recommendations; for in most of these cases there is no indication of what final action was taken. In all, the chronicles present 116 censorial memorials in which personnel were recommended: 76 submitted by censors, 39 by supervising secretaries, and one by censors and supervising secretaries jointly. In only 50 cases are there clear indications that the recommendations were acted upon, and these account for the above tabulation of men recalled. Of the other 66 memorials, 33 were suspended until they could be deliberated upon by appropriate authorities; at least 19 were clearly disapproved, and the recommenders rebuked; and the remaining 14 seem to have met with wholly inconclusive responses.

In Wei Chung-hsien's era, the censorial right and obligation to make personnel recommendations was challenged, apparently for the first time. Investigating censors in particular had always been expected to call attention to worthy citizens and officials whom they encountered, as was noted in Chapter 3 in reference to regional inspectors.[62] In Hsüan-tsung's time censors were repeatedly ordered to submit such recommendations.[63] And on at least one occasion under Hsi-tsung, a minister of war requested that censors and supervising secretaries be ordered to submit guaranteed recommendations of men personally known to them as military officers who might be made use of in Liaotung.[64] On the other hand, censors were responsible for their recommendations and could be punished for poor ones. A rule established in 1532 provided specifically that a regional inspector's recommendations should subsequently be checked against evaluations; if among the men who were penalized in the evaluations there were four or more who had been recommended by any one censor, the censor was himself to be removed from office.[65] Chao Nan-hsing, while serving as vice censor-in-chief in 1623, got salary suspensions for five censors who had made "excessive" recommendations while serving as regional inspectors.[66] And censors were sometimes complained about or chided for making recommendations "just to parade their own goodness," or merely to join a partisan chorus; a common response in such instances was a brusque "Don't make a clamor!"[67] Censors could have no legitimate complaint about being held accountable for what they did in these ways. But in Wei Chung-hsien's time edicts began to suggest that censorial officials should not submit personnel recommendations at all. In 1625 the regional inspector Wei Kuang-hsü was told that his duty was to "evaluate personnel," not make biased recommendations.[68] Soon thereafter the censor Li Ts'an-jan was informed that "the duty of speaking officials is to impeach" and was warned to stop trying to court favor by making recommendations.[69] The censors Ch'en I-jui in 1625 and Wang Yeh-hao in 1626 were both explicitly told, "Supervising secretaries and censors are not permitted to recommend people."[70]

There seems to have been no support in regulations or traditions for this palace opinion, and censorial officials were not deterred by it in practice. They continued submitting personnel recommendations until the very end of the reign. Moreover, their recommendations were commended and approved whenever they suited Wei Chung-hsien's pleasure.

IMPEACHMENTS

The 526 impeachment memorials that censorial officials submitted to Hsi-tsung and that are noted in the *Shih-lu* chronicles for his reign were initiated as follows:

By censors	317
By supervising secretaries	198
By supervising secretaries and censors jointly	9
By Surveillance Office officials	2
Total	526

The almost complete absence of impeachments by Provincial Surveillance Office officials in the 1620's is one evidence of the decreasing involvement of these agencies in characteristically censorial work, but it should not be overemphasized. The censorial officials of the capital were so busy impeaching persons of great prominence that impeachments of less prominent officials submitted by the provincial authorities must have received rather low priority in the selection of material for inclusion in the *Shih-lu*. The tabulation above, therefore, probably cannot be taken as an accurate reflection, even in relative terms, of the numbers of impeachments submitted by Surveillance Offices, though it certainly does reflect, and probably with accuracy, the relative unimportance of such impeachments as measured against those offered by censors and supervising secretaries.

The impeachment memorials that are referred to above met with imperial responses as follows:

No punitive action taken	208	(39.5%)
Investigation or trial ordered	168	(32.0%)
Punitive action directly ordered	150	(28.5%)

When these figures are compared with similar figures for the period 1424–34 from Chapter 4, in terms of percentages, some noteworthy differences emerge:

	1424–34	*1620–27*
No punitive action taken	14%	39.5%
Investigation or trial ordered	16%	32.0%
Punitive action directly ordered	70%	28.5%

In Chapter 4, Jen-tsung and Hsüan-tsung were described as being relatively impulsive, in that they directly ordered punitive action in response to 70 per cent of all censorial impeachments. If the same standard is applied to Hsi-tsung's time, the conclusion must be that much greater restraint was exercised, since punitive action was directly ordered in response to only 28.5 per cent of such memorials. Put in other terms, the contrast is even more striking: whereas Jen-tsung and Hsüan-tsung took direct action in response to an overwhelming majority of impeachments, in almost precisely the same overwhelming proportion of cases Hsi-tsung did *not* take direct action.

It would unquestionably be erroneous to suggest or imply that the relatively great restraint displayed in this regard by Hsi-tsung (or his palace agent) betokens a greater humaneness on his part than on the part of Jen-tsung or Hsüan-tsung. What we know of the general history of the two eras conclusively contradicts this interpretation. The comparison should suggest, instead, that there was greater doubt about the honesty and validity of censorial impeachments in 1620–27 than in 1424–34. This accounts, in particular, for the much higher proportion of impeachments that were rejected or ignored in Hsi-tsung's time: 39.5 per cent, as against only 14 per cent for the earlier period.

The bureaucratic partisanship of Shen-tsung's reign had left two

legacies that help to explain this situation. On one hand, it had come
to be expected that censorial impeachments would have solely partisan motivations much of the time; on the other hand, it had come
to be expected that memorials of any sort would get no response from
the throne in a large proportion of cases. These expectations rein-
forced one another. Getting no response to their denunciations, censorial officials were provoked to make repeated attacks; and the more
often they attacked, the more easily could purely partisan spite be
seen in their denunciations. Considering the relatively open, declared
partisan warfare of Hsi-tsung's time, it could not be expected that
censorial impeachments would have resulted in direct imperial punitive action as often as in the 1420's and 1430's, just as it could be
expected, conversely, that censorial officials would have impeached
more clamorously.

Between 1424 and 1434, as was noted in Chapter 4, there was no
significant variation in the imperial responses to impeachments submitted by different kinds of censorial officials. But in this regard, too,
the period 1620–27 differs notably. Direct punitive action was ordered in response to impeachments by censors far more often than
in response to those by supervising secretaries:

	Supervising Secretaries	Censors
No punitive action taken	95 (48%)	108 (34%)
Investigation or trial ordered	66 (33%)	98 (31%)
Punitive action directly ordered	37 (19%)	111 (35%)

It follows from what has been said that supervising secretaries were
expected to denounce on the basis of partisan motives more often
than were censors, since such a large proportion of their impeachments were rejected or ignored. And there may be good grounds for
this interpretation. The capital was the focal point of partisan warfare, and supervising secretaries were predominantly capital-based to
a greater degree than were censors, many of whom at any given time
were active in the provinces on various commissions. It could be expected that memorials from censors would therefore reflect the partisan tensions of the capital to a lesser degree, in which case they might
be more likely to meet with direct imperial responses. To determine
whether such expectations were valid would unfortunately require
a series of value judgments about the substance of impeachments,
which would inevitably be highly subjective and arbitrary in a vast
majority of cases. I can therefore suggest this interpretation of the
situation only as a hypothesis. In any event, I know of no other way

to explain the notable variation that occurred in the responses to impeachments submitted by the two categories of censorial officials.

Persons who were denounced in censorial impeachments of 1620–27 can be broadly categorized as follows:

Civil officials	735+
Military officers	172+
Others	67+

These tabulations are not distorted by any large groups of hundreds or thousands of persons who were denounced in single mass impeachments, as was the case in 1424–34.

The alleged offenses that were cited in the censorial impeachments of the 1620's are of the same general sorts that were cited in the years 1424–34: inattention to duty, venality, and so on. But two types of offenses that were not important in the earlier period were cited insistently in the later period, as could be expected in the historical circumstances. Military failures are cited in 53 censorial impeachments: 46 times in the era of successive disasters in Liaotung before Wei Chung-hsien's ascendancy, and only 7 times thereafter during the period of relative stability on the Liaotung front. The other notable category, of course, is partisanship, which was cited in 113 censorial impeachments: 39 times in the Tung-lin era and 74 times in the Wei Chung-hsien era. Being a member of the Tung-lin Party was specifically cited in 13 impeachments of the post-1624 period.

As in Chapter 4, tabulating only the times an offense was cited rather than the number of persons who were accused of it, the offenses on which censorial impeachments of 1620–27 were based can be grouped into major categories as follows:

Personal character or attitudes	64
Malfeasance	111
Incompetence	69
Crimes	40
Partisanship	113

Impeachments of Civil Officials

Censorial impeachments of civil-service officials for 1620–27, and their consequences, are analyzed in Table 8 on the basis of the official ranks of the accused and in Table 9 on the basis of whether the accused served in the capital or in the provinces. Comparable analyses of the 1424–34 data in Chapter 4 suggested that high-ranking officials were more likely to be denounced than were their juniors and that capital officials were more likely to be denounced than were provincial officials; and the 1620–27 data reveal patterns that are identical, but much more pronounced. Capital officials were denounced almost three times more often than provincial officials in the years 1620–27, as against a two-to-one ratio for 1424–34; and officials in the very highest ranks, 2a and 2b, the victims of fewer than 10 per cent of all censorial denunciations for 1424–34, suffered more than 30 per cent of all such denunciations during Hsi-tsung's reign. In contrast to the censorial officials of 1620–27, those of 1424–34 would appear to have been almost timid.

The 1620–27 data must be presented with the same cautions that applied to those of the earlier period. That is, it must be kept in mind that the likelihood of an impeachment's being noted in the *Shih-lu* must have varied in direct correlation with the prominence or lack of prominence of the accused. Especially since there were so many impeachments of prominent persons under Hsi-tsung, there would seem to be a strong probability that impeachments of lesser persons were omitted from the *Shih-lu* to a wholly disproportionate degree. Even when such factors are taken into account, however, there is a very clear significance in the data. In the era 1620–27, in a way wholly foreign to the years 1424–34, censorial officials were concentrating their impeachment attacks on the capital officials, and on the very highest-ranking among them.

The largest single category of civil-service officials who were impeached, in fact, was the elite group in ranks 2a and 2b. This group principally included: (1) the grand secretaries and the ministers of the six Ministries, who dominated the operation of the central government; (2) the supreme commanders or viceroys who directed the defense of Liaotung, supervised the operation of the Grand Canal, and were in charge of multi-province regions elsewhere; and (3) the grand coordinators who served as governors of the provinces. In addition, some of these actually held the honorific titles that alone carried ranks 1a and 1b in the civil service. By Hsi-tsung's time this group, which had not yet been fully formed in the 1420's and 1430's, had developed into such a dominant force in government that the nobles and other military personages who had been of some independent importance in Hsüan-tsung's time were now eclipsed and relegated to quite minor roles in state affairs. But the censorial officials were quite undeterred by the immense prestige of the elite. Censorial impeachments of such officials reached the following totals:

> Grand secretaries, 56
> Ministers, 89
> Supreme commanders, 43
> Grand coordinators, 73

In general, the lower an official's rank, the more he was ignored, and lesser-ranking officials on provincial duty received the least attention of all. Even vice ministers were impeached only 49 times, and the directors of Bureaus in the various Ministries were impeached only 20 times. Thus the vice ministers and Bureau directors, though at any given moment they outnumbered the ministers at least 8 to 1, received 20 fewer denunciations than their superiors, the ministers. The *Shih-lu* records show only 8 denunciations of commissioners, vice commissioners, or assistant commissioners of all thirteen Provincial Administration Offices combined and only 12 impeachments of prefects.

As in the decade 1424–34, censorial officials were themselves common targets of their colleagues' impeachments, though censorial impeachments of censorial officials do not account for nearly as large a total as do the impeachments of the elite officials mentioned above. As will be noted in Chapter 6, investigating censors were impeached 51 times, supervising secretaries 30 times, various levels of censors-in-chief 6 times, and Surveillance Office officials 21 times.

The pattern of imperial responses to censorial impeachments of civil officials is somewhat different than that of 1424–34. Table 8 reveals that 64 per cent of all denunciations of rank 2a and 2b officials were rejected or ignored, as contrasted with only 24 per cent of the denunciations of all other officials; and Table 9 shows that 45 per cent of all denunciations of capital officials were rejected or ignored, as contrasted with 34 per cent of the denunciations of all provincial officials. To a far greater extent than in the decade 1424–34, in other words, prominent officials of Hsi-tsung's time could apparently expect the emperor to ignore censorial attacks made on them more often than those made on others, in compensation for the fact that they were attacked more frequently. But they were still by no means immune from punishment in consequence of censorial denunciations.

The attack on Fang Ts'ung-che. Hsi-tsung's reign began with a flurry of partisan recriminations about "the case of the red pills" and "the case of the removal from the palace," which focused on the role of the vacillating grand secretary Fang Ts'ung-che. Justly or unjustly, Fang was blamed for allowing the eunuch Ts'ui Wen-sheng, and then the Court of State Ceremonial official Li K'o-shao, to prescribe medicines for Kuang-tsung and for being polite toward the consort Madame Li when she refused to vacate the imperial residence hall. The direct censorial attack was led by the left supervising secretary Wei Ying-chia of the Office of Scrutiny for Justice, who was especially antagonized by Fang's suggestion that Li K'o-shao merely be fined, when the court was clamoring that he be severely punished. "Everyone says he is unworthy," Wei said of Fang in a final rhetorical flourish. "He has turned his back on the state and on the imperial grace. But the spirits of the imperial ancestors are powerful. How can he not dread retribution?"[71]

When Wei Ying-chia's attack received no response, his colleague Hui Shih-yang, right supervising secretary of the Office of Scrutiny for Works, carried on with a more pointed denunciation, harking back even to Fang's role in "the case of the attack with the club" in 1615 and claiming that in more recent times Fang had accepted bribes from eunuchs in return for supporting Madame Li. Hui insisted that Fang deserved the death penalty. The emperor responded: "When a speaking official discusses affairs, he should with a calm mind make careful investigations. Is it proper to make arbitrary judgments on the basis of mere rumors? To accuse a great minister lightly is to damage the essential principles of the state."[72] Though Fang Ts'ung-che now began to ask for dismissal or retirement, the censorial denunciations were not getting any tangible results. Wei Ying-chia thereupon resumed and broadened the attack, holding Fang responsible for the military deterioration in Liaotung as well as for the controversial palace developments at the end of Kuang-tsung's short reign. In response, Hsi-tsung commented that a grand secretary ought not be held responsible for everything, since although the grand secretaries did indeed suggest imperial rescripts, what issued from the throne was not always what the Grand Secretariat had proposed.[73]

Fang Ts'ung-che now began to submit his resignation in earnest, and repeatedly. Before it was finally accepted and he was permitted to leave office in the last month of 1620, however, the investigating censor Chia Chi-ch'un and the supervising secretary Ch'eng Chu had joined in the denunciations.[74] And even after he had retired, Fang was pursued with criticisms as the various "cases" of 1620 continued to be debated. As late as mid-1624 the censor Chang Chi-meng of the Nanking Censorate blamed Fang for the Liaotung disasters.[75]

The attack on Huang K'o-tsan. Another object of concentrated censorial attack early in Hsi-tsung's reign was the minister of justice, Huang K'o-tsan. A defender of Fang Ts'ung-che, Huang began to be attacked at about the time of Fang's departure. The censor Chiao Yüan-p'u and the supervising secretary Sun Chieh both impeached him at the end of 1620 because of his attitudes during the recent controversies, but to no avail.[76] The supervising secretary Mao Shih-lung attacked him in mid-1621, equally without effect, for his handling of important criminals in judicial reviews; and the censor Wang Yün-ch'eng promptly joined in the attack, claiming that Huang had mistreated the censor Chia Chi-ch'un, who had recently been dismissed from the civil service because of his remonstrances about "the case of the removal from the palace."[77] Huang retorted that Wang Yün-ch'eng was angry merely because Huang had opposed his wish to have the old Tung-lin hero Li San-ts'ai recalled.[78] Mao Shih-lung and Wang Yün-ch'eng pressed their charges, again without effect, and then in the tenth month of 1621 Chiao Yüan-p'u re-entered the controversy with an accusation that Huang was trying to use the hotly debated issue of Li San-ts'ai's recall as a shield to protect himself against attack. Huang in a response blamed all his troubles on the fact that early in the century he had offended Li San-ts'ai, whose adherents were now determined to get their revenge.[79] Though Huang, in accordance with propriety, had repeatedly requested dismissal while under attack, Hsi-tsung repeatedly soothed him and consistently ignored the accusations. Early in 1622, Huang was transferred, becoming minister of war.

In mid-1622 Huang K'o-tsan invited new criticisms, and brought about his own undoing, by preparing for consideration by a great assembly of officials a narrative account of the deathbed medical treatment of Kuang-tsung, which completely exonerated Fang Ts'ung-che. The supervising secretaries Hsüeh Wen-chou and Shen Wei-ping immediately attacked him for flagrant partisanship.[80] Though Hsi-tsung made it clear he was weary of all the arguments about the events of 1620, he at last permitted Huang to retire.

The welter of accusations and counter-accusations and the far-reaching ramifications of Huang K'o-tsan's case illustrate the hotly partisan climate of 1621 and 1622. But at this early time partisan lines were not yet clearly drawn. To be sure, most of the censorial officials involved in the attack on Huang were clearly identified "good elements"; but Sun Chieh, despite his attack on Huang K'o-tsan, quickly aroused Tung-lin antagonisms by becoming an outer-court spokesman of Wei Chung-hsien, and early in 1622 he was sent out to a provincial post. After the eunuch's rise to power he came back to court as a close henchman of Ts'ui Ch'eng-hsiu.[81] And Chia Chi-ch'un, who figured in both the Fang Ts'ung-che and the Huang K'o-tsan cases, played a highly independent role, being opposed by Yang Lien and Tso Kuang-tou but befriended by Yeh Hsiang-kao and several other Tung-lin stalwarts. Wei Chung-hsien later used him to establish an anti-Tung-lin version of "the case of the removal from the palace," and during the reign of Chuang-lieh-ti, Chia was officially labeled one of the "eunuch partisans."[82]

The attack on Tsou Yüan-piao. The controversy that arose in 1622 about the establishment of a Tung-lin-like academy in Peking helped to clarify the partisan lines. In addition, it revealed some antagonisms between the Censorate and the Offices of Scrutiny. The two founders of the academy in Peking—the censor-in-chief Tsou Yüan-piao and the vice censor-in-chief Feng Ts'ung-wu—were both long-established "good element" leaders. Their impeachers were three supervising secretaries: Chu T'ung-meng of the Office of Scrutiny for War and Kuo Yün-hou and Kuo Hsing-chih of the Office of Scrutiny for Works.[83] Kuo Hsing-chih even seized upon Tsou's well-known aversion to partisan vengefulness to attack him. Because Tsou had characteristically said "right and wrong are not always perfectly clear," Kuo Hsing-chih denounced him for displaying Buddhist inclinations, and requested an imperial order that if Tsou were going to teach anything he should teach Confucianism.[84] The closing of the academy by imperial order and the humiliating retirements of Tsou and Feng hardened the partisan feelings of the Tung-lin men; and all three of the Office of Scrutiny impeachers were transferred to provincial posts in 1623 or 1624.[85] All three subsequently rose to high capital posts under Wei Chung-hsien.

The attack on Hsiung T'ing-pi. The greatest single concentration of censorial impeachments during Hsi-tsung's reign were aimed at the Liaotung supreme commander Hsiung T'ing-pi, and Hsiung's case became one of the principal tests by which men subsequently came to be labeled Tung-lin sympathizers or Tung-lin enemies. However, the case is full of ironies. Early in his career—from about 1608 to 1613, while he was serving as an investigating censor—Hsiung had been associated with fellow provincials in the Hukwang faction, which opposed the Tung-lin group. He especially supported a National University chancellor named T'ang Pin-yin, who was then considered the leader of all the factions opposing the Tung-lin men, and who was also supported by Wang Shao-hui, later to be one of Wei Chung-hsien's chief adherents. Most of all, Hsiung was then intimate with the supervising secretary Yao Tsung-wen, the recognized leader of the Chekiang faction and a vigorous impeacher of the Tung-lin hero Li San-ts'ai. But in 1619 and 1620, while Hsiung was serving his first term as Liaotung supreme commander, Yao was sent on an extended inspection tour of the frontier, and the two men began to fall out; indeed, it was Yao who was principally responsible for terminating Hsiung's service in Liaotung late in 1620.[86]

Other censorial officials actually brought about Hsiung's removal, but the criticisms they submitted reflected Yao Tsung-wen's views. The attack was inaugurated in the ninth month of 1620, the very first month of Hsi-tsung's reign, by the censor Ku Tsao. Ku complained that after a year in the field Hsiung still had no concrete plans, that he concealed troubles from the court's knowledge, and that under Hsiung's command it looked as if the war with the Manchus would require endless expenditures at a rate of 8 million taels per year, which would bankrupt the empire.[87] When the emperor responded by merely urging that Hsiung T'ing-pi exert himself to do better, the censor Feng San-yüan then enlarged upon Ku Tsao's complaints, pointing out eight specific problems for which Hsiung apparently had no plans and three instances in which Hsiung had apparently failed to report the whole truth. "If Hsiung is not dismissed," he concluded, "Liao certainly will not be preserved."[88] Hsiung submitted an angry rebuttal, but before the ninth month ended, a court assembly recommended his removal, and he was ordered to remain on duty pending the appointment of a replacement.[89]

In the tenth month of 1620, having been replaced as supreme commander by Yüan Ying-t'ai, Hsiung set out to rescue his reputation. In a memorial he readily agreed that he had won no dramatic successes, but he pointed out that he had inherited from his predecessor a defeated and disorganized army that had proved itself no match for the Manchus in a series of minor engagements. He had consequently concentrated on defensive work only, simultaneously setting out to strengthen and train the army and put in order its supplies and equipment. He claimed that in consequence of his prudence the northeastern defenses were now strong and the army was revitalized. The censors Feng San-yüan and Chang Hsiu-te and the supervising secretary Wei Ying-chia (the impeacher of Fang Ts'ung-che) criticized him anew. Hsiung suggested that they be authorized to visit the front to observe conditions for themselves. The emperor thought this was a good idea but was finally persuaded to send one different man instead, the supervising secretary Chu T'ung-meng of the Office of Scrutiny for War, who was later to become a chief impeacher of Tsou Yüan-piao.[90]

Chu T'ung-meng submitted his report on Liaotung conditions early in 1621. He conceded that Hsiung should indeed be credited with the stabilization of Liaotung and with some personal heroics, but he concluded that Hsiung had demeaned himself and ruined his effectiveness by arguing angrily with court critics and in addition had proved himself to be untrustworthy by asking for retirement (the standard and expected reaction from an official who had been denounced) just at a time when his services were needed most. Chu felt that Hsiung's guilt outweighed his merits, but Hsi-tsung did not seem to agree.[91]

When the Liaotung defenses collapsed anew and both Shen-yang and Liao-yang were lost in the third month of 1621, the supervising secretary Kuo Kung promptly attacked Hsiung T'ing-pi, but the censor Chiang Ping-ch'ien responded with a defense of Hsiung and a counterattack on Kuo Kung; and in the fourth month an assembly of officials proposed that Hsiung be recalled to service.[92] One of those who strongly supported his recall was the censor Chou Tsung-chien, an independent man who was repeatedly at odds with the Tung-lin group but who eventually became one of its greatest heroes and martyrs.[93] In the sixth month, Hsi-tsung finally did recall Hsiung and reappoint him Liaotung supreme commander. His most vigorous impeachers—Kuo Kung, Feng San-yüan, and Chang Hsiu-te—were all demoted and transferred to provincial posts.[94] Hsiung's turncoat friend Yao Tsung-wen had long before been removed from office on a charge of irresponsibility and was now "removed from the register" and thus deprived of his civil-service status for having previously undermined Hsiung.[95] Both Yao Tsung-wen and Feng San-yüan subsequently became supporters of Wei Chung-hsien.

Hsiung T'ing-pi's second term as supreme commander was marred by bad feelings and disagreements between him and his subordinate, the grand coordinator Wang Hua-chen. Hsiung was repeatedly annoyed by the criticisms of censorial officials who supported Wang's views, including Sun Chieh, one of Huang K'o-tsan's impeachers.[96] These criticisms led to a great policy debate at Peking in the first month of 1622, in which Hsiung's superior, the minister of war Chang Hao-ming, proposed that Hsiung be removed and command be given to Wang. Hsi-tsung, though his confidence in Hsiung was badly shaken, did not permit such action, and censors and supervising secretaries began to attack Chang Hao-ming for worsening an already bad situation.[97]

Before another month had passed, Wang Hua-chen provoked the Manchus into action, and both he and Hsiung had to retreat within the Great Wall. With the court in a total panic, the chief supervising secretary of the Office of Scrutiny for War, Ts'ai Ssu-ch'ung, impeached both Hsiung and Wang, as well as some subordinate officials.[98] Fang Chen-ju, the censor serving as Liaotung regional inspector, also memorialized assigning blame to both Hsiung and Wang.[99]

Hsiung had a few active defenders. The supervising secretary Chou Ch'ao-jui angrily defended him against attack by an official of the Ministry of Justice; the censor Chiang Ping-ch'ien, who had defended Hsiung a year earlier, insisted that the minister of war Chang Hao-ming was more guilty than either Hsiung or Wang; and the Nanking censor Ho Chien-k'o attributed all blame to Chang and Wang but none to Hsiung.[100] Nevertheless, when the judicial authorities in Peking conducted a great trial in the fourth month, the result was that both Hsiung and Wang were sentenced to death.[101]

For reasons that are not wholly clear, the Tung-lin political agent Wang Wen-yen now began to organize last-resort support for Hsiung T'ing-pi.[102] Soon a host of censors and supervising secretaries (including Chiang Ping-ch'ien and Chou Ch'ao-jui) submitted separate memorials trying to divert blame to the minister of war Chang Hao-ming, charging that he had been so partisan to Wang and so resentful of Hsiung that he had openly urged Wang not to heed Hsiung's orders. Chang defended himself in a rebuttal but repeatedly asked sick leave, which was finally granted him in the seventh month.[103] Censors continued to criticize him.[104] In 1626 Wei Chung-hsien had Chang Hao-ming recalled and named supreme commander to quell the long-drawn-out aboriginal rebellion in the southwest. Before he took up such duties, however, Chuang-lieh-ti came to the throne, supervising secretaries attacked Chang as a "eunuch partisan," and he was permitted to retire.[105]

Chang Hao-ming's removal from Peking in 1622 did not alleviate the situation of Hsiung T'ing-pi, who remained in prison awaiting execution. In the tenth month, the censor Yang Wei-yüan (who was later to become one of the most uninhibited flatterers of Wei Chung-hsien) denounced a Ministry of War official, Ku Ta-chang, for having accepted bribes from Hsiung at the time of the trial, at which Ku had advocated lesser punishment for Hsiung than for Wang Hua-chen.[106] On the very same day, Yang Wei-yüan also protested that Hsiung was allowed too much freedom and comfort in prison—that he was actually receiving visitors.[107] In 1623 Hsiung's old enemy Kuo Kung, having been recalled to duty as a supervising secretary after a year's service in the provinces, demonstrated that he was unchastened: he attacked Hsiung T'ing-pi again and then engaged in a protracted feud with the censor Chou Tsung-chien, Hsiung's longtime defender, during which Chou openly accused Kuo of being a tool of Wei Chung-hsien.[108]

Beginning late in 1624, as Wei Chung-hsien's purge of the outer court got under way, Hsiung T'ing-pi's enemies began to insist that his long-delayed death sentence be carried out.[109] Finally in the eighth month of 1625 he was decapitated, in response to insistent demands from the supervising secretaries Kuo Hsing-chih (previous impeacher of Tsou Yüan-piao) and Chou Hung-mo and the censors Men K'o-hsin and Shih San-wei.[110] Hsiung's own family, and the families of his wife's relatives, were all ruined by government efforts to collect from them 1 million taels in punitive damages.[111] Meantime, his defenders were being dealt with harshly. Wang Wen-yen, Chou Ch'ao-jui, and Ku Ta-chang all died in prison in 1625, and Chou Tsung-chien followed in 1626.

The Tung-lin Party had never unanimously supported or defended Hsiung T'ing-pi. The revered grand secretary Yeh Hsiang-kao, for example, sympathized with Wang Hua-chen, who had won his doctoral degree in the examination of 1613, for which Yeh served as chief examiner.[112] Nor apparently did such leading Tung-lin partisans as Yang Lien and Tso Kuang-tou ever openly defend Hsiung. But those who attacked Hsiung became sycophants of Wei Chung-hsien so consistently, and those who defended Hsiung were later punished by the eunuch faction so severely, that subsequent critics considered Hsiung T'ing-pi to have been a Tung-lin hero comparable to Li San-ts'ai, despite his early involvement in anti-Tung-lin activities as a censor.

The aboriginal rebellion in the southwest provoked almost as many censorial denunciations as did the Liaotung disaster. The three most prominent civil officials who tried to suppress the rebellion—the successive southwestern supreme commanders Chang Wo-hsü and Yang Shu-chung and the Kweichow grand coordinator Wang San-shan—were all repeatedly denounced by censors and supervising secretaries for their failures to take more effective action.[113] But their cases did not become controversial issues as did Hsiung T'ing-pi's.

Censorial impeachments after Wei Chung-hsien's rise to power. The great purge of Tung-lin leaders was accomplished by Wei Chung-hsien without much need for relying on censorial denunciations to provide legitimate pretexts, but censorial officials were helpful. The initial instrument was a supervising secretary of the Office of Scrutiny for Justice, Fu K'uei, whose case illustrates the complex interrelations and motivations underlying the public activities of this troubled period.

Fu K'uei was a clansman of Fu Chi-chiao, a eunuch who was attached to the palace secret-service agency called the Eastern Depot; and through Fu Chi-chiao he got acquainted with Fu Ying-sheng, a favorite nephew of Wei Chung-hsien who happened to have the same surname. These three became close friends and even called each other "brother." Fu K'uei was also a friend of Juan Ta-ch'eng, another supervising secretary. When the post of chief supervising secretary of the Office of Scrutiny for Personnel fell vacant early in 1624, Juan Ta-ch'eng coveted it but stood only second in eligibility on the basis of seniority. He therefore called upon his friend Fu K'uei to intervene with his palace friends, and word soon spread that Juan would indeed get the post. But Tso Kuang-tou, then serving as assistant censor-in-chief, knew Juan as a fellow townsman and distrusted him. Probably through Tso's influence (at least, Juan understood so) the minister of personnel Chao Nan-hsing announced that Juan was scheduled to be transferred to a provincial post and that the position of chief supervising secretary would be given to the man who stood third in eligibility by seniority. This was Wei Ta-chung, who, since his appointment in 1621 as a supervising secretary in the Office of Scrutiny for Works, had become one of the most aggressively partisan Tung-lin supporters.[114]

Thus thwarted, Juan Ta-ch'eng went immediately to Wei Chung-hsien and plotted with him to get rid of the Tung-lin partisans. Juan reportedly presented Wei with portraits of the leading Tung-lin men and coached him on the importance and weaknesses of each.[115] Then the two men prevailed on Fu K'uei to submit an impeachment, and Fu denounced both Tso Kuang-tou and Wei Ta-chung for conspiring illegally with Wang Wen-yen and with the late eunuch Wang An.[116] Wei and Tso submitted rebuttals, Tso denouncing Fu K'uei for conspiring with Fu Chi-chiao.[117] The censor Yüan Hua-chung, who had aligned himself with the "good elements" earlier by denouncing the grand secretary Fang Ts'ung-che and by warning against eunuch influence, memorialized in support of Wei Ta-chung and Tso, complaining that Fu K'uei was determined "selfishly to expel all worthy men so that the entire state might be emptied."[118]

No action was taken against Wei Ta-chung or Tso Kuang-tou in response to Fu K'uei's denunciation, but Wang Wen-yen was arrested and sent to the palace prison of the imperial bodyguard for full interrogation. This was in accord with Wei Chung-hsien's strategy, which was to rely on Wang Wen-yen for evidence that would undermine many of the Tung-lin partisans, including the grand secretary

Yeh Hsiang-kao, one of Wang's patrons. But Wang gave no such evidence, and Yeh Hsiang-kao's influence was still great enough to prevent disaster. Wang was beaten in court and dismissed from the civil service, but no one else suffered for the time being.

The Wang Wen-yen incident was followed closely by Yang Lien's open denunciation of Wei Chung-hsien, the court beating and subsequent death of Wan Ching, and the humiliation and retirement of Yeh Hsiang-kao. Then in the ninth month of 1624, the censor Ts'ui Ch'eng-hsiu returned to Peking after a tour of duty as regional inspector and salt-control censor in the Huai River region. He was denounced for corruption by the censor-in-chief Kao P'an-lung and threatened with disgrace by the minister of personnel Chao Nan-hsing; and to protect himself he joined Fu K'uei and Juan Ta-ch'eng as one of Wei Chung-hsien's protégés.[119] In the tenth month, some of the Tung-lin men disagreed about the nomination of a new grand coordinator for Shansi province, and pressed by Juan and Ts'ui to take advantage of this flimsy pretext, Wei Chung-hsien had Wei Ta-chung demoted and transferred to a provincial post and Kao P'an-lung removed from office.[120] A few days later, Yang Lien and Tso Kuang-tou were dismissed from the civil service and various other Tung-lin men were removed from office.[121] A denunciation by the censor Chang Na paved the way for Chao Nan-hsing's removal in the twelfth month.[122]

Having thus removed from the court all the Tung-lin leaders, Wei Chung-hsien decided to pursue them even more ruthlessly. It was the censor Liang Meng-huan who opened the way. At the end of 1624, the issue of Wang Wen-yen still rankled, and Liang brought it up once more.[123] This led to Wang's rearrest and death by torture, and through his trial to the deaths by torture of Yang Lien, Tso Kuang-tou, Wei Ta-chung, and many other Tung-lin heroes in 1625–26.[124] Liang Meng-huan remained on duty in the Censorate until Hsi-tsung's death in 1627, regularly submitting memorials praising Wei Chung-hsien and his chief partisans, and in the words of the *Ming History* generally "serving Wei as a father."[125]

Once Wei Chung-hsien was in full command of the government, the censorial officials continued to ferret out and denounce Tung-lin men who still remained unpunished.[126] "If Wei Chung-hsien happened to forget someone," the *Ming History* comments, "his partisans were always able to dredge up some affair from the past to make Wei angry about him."[127] The retired grand secretary Yeh Hsiang-kao was the only major Tung-lin sympathizer who, though repeatedly attacked by censorial officials, was allowed to live unmolested until his death in 1627.[128]

Among Wei Chung-hsien's chief adherents there eventually developed jealousies and disagreements, and censorial officials were again relied on to lend an air of legitimacy to the intrafactional feuds. The chief troublemaker in this regard was Ts'ui Ch'eng-hsiu, who rose under Wei Chung-hsien's patronage to become censor-in-chief. In 1626 Ts'ui aspired to be made a grand secretary, but his ambitions were thwarted by the senior grand secretary Feng Ch'üan and the minister of personnel Wang Shao-hui. Feng was a second-generation enemy of the Tung-lin group who eventually became doubly notorious by serving as a grand secretary under the Manchus. Wang was a longtime Tung-lin enemy who had been removed in the capital evaluations of 1623 but was recalled by the eunuch faction, only to have many misgivings, especially about Wei Chung-hsien's cruel punishments. Ts'ui Ch'eng-hsiu's chief adherents among the investigating censors—Ch'en Ch'ao-fu, Liu Wei, Lu Ch'eng-ch'in, and Li Ts'an-jan—successively impeached Feng Ch'üan for venality and abuse of authority.[129] And others—Yüan Ching, Chang Wen-hsi, and Kao Ssu-t'u—successively impeached Wang Shao-hui.[130] Ts'ui thus got both Feng and Wang removed from their posts. Though he himself did not get into the Grand Secretariat after all, Ts'ui remained securely in Wei Chunghsien's favor and became probably the most arrogant and feared of the "five tigers," as Wei's chief henchmen were popularly known. When Chuang-lieh-ti took the throne, however, some of Ts'ui's own former lieutenants denounced him. He was given permission to retire and then strangled himself when orders for his arrest were subsequently issued.[131]

Impeachments of Military Officers

Censorial officials were much more active in impeaching civil officials in the years 1620–27 than in the decade 1424–34; but as Table 10 indicates, they were much less active in impeaching military officers, despite the great importance of military affairs in Hsi-tsung's time. The explanation of this is implied in what has already been said. To be sure, the censorial officials might have devoted more attention to military matters had they been less absorbed with civilservice factionalism and palace problems; but they were by no means inattentive to military affairs, as the censorial attack on Hsiung T'ing-pi attests. What they neglected, relatively, was not the military establishment as such, but the military officer class; and they neglected military officers because, as a class, military officers were no longer of any particular importance in state affairs. Since military control had passed into the hands of civil-service supreme commanders and grand coordinators such as Hsiung T'ing-pi and Wang Hua-chen, the status of the military officer class had become clearly subordinate. Though they still enjoyed high ranks and prestigious titles, and even perpetuated their monopoly on noble titles, military officers in the 1620's functioned merely as technicians and had little more significance in the military realm than clerical functionaries had in the general-administration realm.

This decline in stature of the military officer class was probably one of the important factors in the general military decline of late Ming times. To censorial officials, who were increasingly inclined to concentrate their attacks on the men at the top of any particular power structure, it meant that military officers were no longer worth the kind of attention they got between 1424 and 1434. It also meant that Hsi-tsung could treat military officers with a good deal more contumely than Jen-tsung and Hsüan-tsung exhibited. Under Hsi-tsung it was relatively rare for a military officer to be forgiven when he was denounced. In a vast majority of instances, and in contrast to the patterns of responses to impeachments of civil officials, denunciations of military officers during the years 1620–27 met with immediate responses in the form of demotions or other punitive action.

The very nature of the *Shih-lu* entries in this category—concise, uncluttered with details—reveals their relative unimportance in contemporary minds. The following entry from 1622 is typical:

Fifth month, the day *hsin-ch'ou*: The investigating censor Hou Hsün memorialized impeaching the regional commander Hsü Shih-ch'en, who was ordered forthwith to return to his Guard garrison.[132]

Even the nobility got short shrift in the chronicles. This is from 1621:

Third month, the day *chi-yu*: The Ministry of War responded to memorials from Nanking supervising secretaries and censors rectifying omissions in military evaluations: the P'ing-chiang earl, Ch'en Ch'i-ssu, vice commandant at Nanking in charge of the Chief Military Commission for the Rear; the regional vice commander at Ta-t'ung, Yang Chen; and the assistant commissioner of the Hukwang Branch Regional Military Commission, Yang Yü-k'ai, were all removed from their posts.[133]

There were no "great cases" among the impeachments of military officers in the 1620's. The most common offense cited was venality, and the most common punishment that was meted out in response was that the accused officer was relieved of his tactical command and sent back to garrison duty in his home Guard. Officers on duty in the Liaotung theater and in the southwestern rebellion area were among those denounced—for venality, or cowardice, or ineffectiveness.[134] Two earls were punished for privately engaging in the salt trade.[135] A field commander in the Yen-sui northern frontier region was denounced for failing to report a Mongol raid.[136] An officer in Fukien was denounced for criminal negligence in dealing with the Dutch threat from the Pescadores.[137] But so little was the importance attached to impeachments in this category that for the most part no explanations appear in the *Shih-lu* at all.

Impeachments of Other Persons

Censorial denunciations of persons other than civil officials and military officers in the period 1620–27 are analyzed in Table 11. Impeachments in this category are of interest principally because they include the most famous censorial acts of the period, the denunciations of Wei Chung-hsien.

The only imperial clansman denounced in this era was Chu Shen-chieh, a distant relative of the emperor, who was impeached in 1626 by the censor T'ien Ching-hsin because he had visited the capital, in violation of the general rule that clansmen must remain in their assigned localities except when the court specifically authorized them to travel. It was ordered that he be sent to the Princely Establishment having jurisdiction over him, to be tried according to the law.[138]

One of the imperial in-laws impeached by censorial officials was Cheng Yang-hsing, brother of the Madame Cheng who had been Shen-tsung's favorite consort. Ever since 1620, when Madame Cheng seemed to try to speed Kuang-tsung's death, there had been continuing suspicions that she and her supporters had designs on the throne. Her brother was denounced in 1622 by the censor Wen Kao-mo and the supervising secretary Lo Shang-chung for abusive conduct, for creating anxieties by lurking around the capital, and even for negotiating with the Manchus; and when their attacks brought him to trial early in 1623 he was sentenced to live in permanent exile away from Peking.[139]

The other imperial in-law included in these tabulations is Chang Kuo-chi, father of Hsi-tsung's empress, Madame Chang. Wei Chung-hsien, after coming to power, feared lest Madame Chang's influence over Hsi-tsung undermine his own. He thus had the sycophantic censor Liang Meng-huan denounce her father in the hope that action against him would intimidate her. Liang accused Chang of oppressing people by abusing his influence, and even of murder. By an imperial edict that was obviously Wei's handiwork, Chang was ordered to leave the capital, return to his native place in Honan province, and concentrate on reforming his character.[140]

This category also includes a denunciation of Madame Li, Kuang-tsung's favorite consort and protégé of Madame Cheng, made at the time of "the case of the removal from the palace," by Yang Lien, then a supervising secretary.[141] The category also includes a single direct denunciation of the notorious imperial nursemaid, Mistress K'o, submitted late in 1621 by the investigating censor Ma Ming-ch'i. Intervention by the Grand Secretariat was all that saved Ma from severe punishment; he escaped with a one-year salary suspension.[142]

In other impeachments in this category, stonemasons employed by the Ministry of Works were denounced for falsifying accounts; a son of a grand secretary was attacked for operating a savings and loan society to which people contributed money; three students of Kwei-chow province were denounced for joining the rebellion there; and a merchant was reported for concealing 42,600 catties of saltpeter that was essential for military defense.[143]

Impeachments of eunuchs included several denunciations of the eunuch physician Ts'ui Wen-sheng, who was thought to have administered a harmful laxative to the ill Kuang-tsung in 1620.[144] Another eunuch who was attacked was Liu Ch'ao, who had been involved in "the case of the removal from the palace." He was especially hated by the Tung-lin men because at the height of that crisis in 1620, he had circulated a rumor that Madame Li had committed suicide in humiliation, which for a time aroused widespread vilification of her attackers. Liu was also opposed because he was a special protégé of an anti-Tung-lin grand secretary, Shen Ts'ui, who was driven out of office in 1622 because he allowed Liu Ch'ao and Wei Chung-hsien to inaugurate military training for the palace eunuchs.[145] Liu Ch'ao had subsequently been banished to the palace in Nanking, but in 1623 the censor Sung Shih-hsiang ineffectually attacked him anew for conspiring with Shen Ts'ui and for having some part in the removal of various "good element" officials, including Tsou Yüan-piao.[146]

Wei Chung-hsien, during his rise to power, was specifically and directly denounced in 13 censorial memorials that are noted in the *Shih-lu* chronicles.

The first mention of Wei Chung-hsien in the *Shih-lu* for Hsi-tsung's reign occurs in Yang Lien's denunciation of Madame Li early in the ninth month of 1620. Yang demanded punishment for Wei and another eunuch who together had robbed the imperial treasure chests when Madame Li moved out of the imperial residence hall; and an investigation was promised.[147] Then in 1623 Wei was denounced three times by the censor Chou Tsung-chien, who had earlier warned the emperor to beware of Mistress K'o.[148] Chou's three memorials were principally aimed at Wei's outer-court spokesman, the supervising secretary Kuo Kung, with whom Chou was feuding over the case of Hsiung T'ing-pi.[149] Chou warned that the eunuch and Kuo Kung were conspiring to subvert all honest men in the government. The censor Fang Ta-jen, a fellow townsman of Tso Kuang-tou, joined Chou in this attack, being careful to avoid relying on rumors, a fault for which Chou had been rebuked. Fang's specific denunciation of Wei Chung-hsien was as follows:

Now, as for Wei Chung-hsien's dangerous perversities, I would not presume to memorialize about anything I have not seen with my own eyes. But yesterday I took advantage of supervising the Spring Festival ceremonies at the Chao tomb [i. e., the tomb of Mu-tsung, father and predecessor of Shen-tsung] to tour among the various imperial tombs; and on the road home I happened to pass by the Azure Cloud Monastery in the western hills, where I saw a burial place that [Wei] Chung-hsien is making ready for himself. Not only does it rival the imperial tombs in the grandeur of its design and the excellence of its materials; it perhaps surpasses them in size. In front of the tomb are such animals as lions and elephants carved of beautiful stone, forming rows and ranks no different from the arrangement at the imperial tombs. Moreover, there are two figures of a civil and a military official standing in attendance on left and right, the military figure garbed in armor and the civil figure garbed in court-audience hat and gown. Now, [Wei] Chung-hsien is just a eunuch. It might be possible to countenance his having military personnel in attendance, but how could he have civil ministers wearing court-audience hats and gowns? I cannot imagine what position Chung-hsien hopes someday to occupy! But to exhibit such extravagance now violates propriety and discipline. Because of these things that I have personally seen, I deduce that the rumors I have heard about his dangerous perversities must all be true.[150]

Chou Tsung-chien was rebuked and fined three months' salary for his audacity. Fang Ta-jen apparently escaped unscathed, though in 1625 he was arrested while living at home and was dismissed from the civil service.[151] The response to his memorial of 1623 was merely that it should be sent to "the Ministries and the Censorate" for consideration.

There were no further direct censorial denunciations of Wei Chung-hsien until more than a year had passed. Then, in the sixth month of 1624, the vice censor-in-chief Yang Lien submitted his famous denunciation of Wei's "twenty-four great crimes." When this had no effect except to provoke an edict strictly rebuking Yang, other officials echoed his charges in successive follow-up memorials. The *Ming History* reports that more than 70 such memorials were submitted, but the fragmentary *Shih-lu* entries of this season merely note, in each case very concisely, that denunciations were also submitted by the chief supervising secretary Wei Ta-chung, the censor Liu P'u, the chief supervising secretary Li Ch'un-hua, the Nanking supervising secretary Yang Tung-ch'ao, the censors Chao Ying-ch'i and Yang Yü-k'o, and the supervising secretary Lo Shang-chung.[152] No details of their denunciations are given.

Yang Lien's denunciation of Wei Chung-hsien. Because it is the single most famous censorial memorial of Ming times and perhaps of all Chinese history, Yang Lien's denunciation of Wei Chung-hsien's "twenty-four great crimes" is worth noting in detail.[153] It is a long memorial of almost exactly 4,000 characters, filled with the rhetorical flourishes and the clichés common to all bureaucratic documents of the period, but relatively straightforward and businesslike. Above all, it is passionately indignant. It is dated on the first day of the sixth month, 1624, and begins as follows:

> The vice censor-in-chief of the left, Yang Lien, memorializes concerning the treacherous eunuch's taking advantage of his position to wield imperial authority, his monopolizing power and disrupting administration, his deceiving the ruler and scorning the law, his recognizing no sun and no Heaven, his turning his back on imperial mercy, and his interfering with the ancestral institutions; and earnestly begs for a resolute imperial decision to undertake an investigation so as to rescue the ancestral altar before it is too late.
>
> When the emperor T'ai-tsu first fixed the laws, eunuchs were not permitted to interfere with outer affairs, and in the inner court they were only permitted to engage in such services as sprinkling and sweeping. Violators were to be punished without possibility of pardon. Therefore eunuchs in the palace esteemed caution and obedience, and the following emperors observed the rules without daring to change them. Even though such arrogant and unrestrained persons as Wang Chen and Liu Chin did appear, they were promptly annihilated. Therefore the dynastic prosperity has been perpetuated down to the present.
>
> Who would have imagined that now, with a sagelike intelligence on the throne, anyone would be so outrageous and reckless as to disrupt the court's orderliness, to deny the ruler and give rein to selfishness, to subvert the good elements, to spoil the emperor's reputation for being a Yao or a Shun [sage rulers of antiquity], and to brew inexhaustible disasters for the ancestral altar as has the Eastern Depot chief eunuch, Wei Chung-hsien?
>
> The whole court is intimidated; no one dares denounce him by name. I am actually sick at the prospect. But as supervising secretary of the Office of Scrutiny for War, I personally received the last commands of the former emperor, that I must help your majesty to be a sage ruler like Yao or Shun. His

words still ring in my ears. If, fearing harm, I remained silent now, then I would fail in my determination to be loyal and upright as well as my duty as a guardian of the customs and fundamental laws. And if I turn my back on your majesty's special grace in recalling me from the fields to service, then in the future how shall I be able to look the former emperor in the face in Heaven?

I have carefully gathered together twenty-four items of evidence about his great crimes, and I now present them for the sake of my emperor.

Yang Lien then proceeds to enumerate Wei's major offenses in detail. These can be summarized as follows:

1. Usurping from the Grand Secretariat its privilege to prepare rescripts for imperial consideration, and reporting imperial decisions orally so that their validity is questionable.

2. Inciting the supervising secretary Sun Chieh to denounce the grand secretary Liu I-ching and the minister of personnel Chou Chia-mo, and thus getting rid of them.[154]

3. Being hostile to such loyal and righteous ministers as the minister of rites Sun Shen-hsing and the censor-in-chief Tsou Yüan-piao, and bringing about their removal from office, while attaching himself to and protecting unprincipled sycophants.[155]

4. Being intolerant of, and driving out of service, such upright men as the minister of justice Wang Chi and the minister of works Chung Yü-cheng.[156]

5. Subverting the prestige of the Grand Secretariat by vetoing the court nominations of Sun Shen-hsing and others.

6. Similarly undermining the Ministry of Personnel by blocking the appointments of the men named for its highest posts in court nominations of 1623.

7. Being vindictive, as in removing from office men whose remarks happened to offend him, such as Man Ch'ao-chien, Wen Chen-meng, Hsü Ta-hsiang, and others.[157]

8. Murdering a favorite though lowly imperial concubine while the emperor was visiting outside the palace, and then making the emperor believe she had died of a sudden illness.

9. Forging an imperial order that caused the high-ranking concubine, Madame Chang, to commit suicide after she had become pregnant.

10. Reportedly bringing about the death in infancy of the emperor's first son, born to the empress (another Madame Chang), and thus depriving the emperor of an heir.

11. Murdering Wang An and untold other eunuchs who had given long and faithful service in the palace.

12. Building a tomb for himself that is obviously designed to be an imperial sepulcher.

13. Showering honors and titles upon himself and his relatives.

14. Punishing and terrorizing even imperial in-laws.

15. Putting a man to death on a charge of illegally opening a mine when all he had done was complain that a coal pit was interfering with his ancestral graves.

16. Imprisoning and torturing men to death for the minor offense of trespassing on grazing lands, after they had already been dealt with by proper judicial authorities.

17. Usurping the authority of the Ministry of Personnel over promotions, specifically in blocking the promotion of the supervising secretary Chou Shih-p'u, who had complained about imperial textile manufactures.[158]

18. Removing Liu Ch'ao from his post as warden of the imperial bodyguard's palace prison because he would not be a murderer and a sycophant, thus "clearly demonstrating that the Great Ming laws need not be observed, but the Chung-hsien laws cannot be disregarded."

19. Making the emperor look ridiculous by countermanding his orders, as when Wei Ta-chung was promoted to the position of chief supervising secretary but was then rebuked for undertaking his new duties.[159]

20. Utilizing the Eastern Depot to institute a reign of terror, as when Wang Wen-yen was arrested without any authorization from the Grand Secretariat.

21. Allowing his private retainers to associate with a spy who recently stole into the capital, and in general demonstrating that it is not Peking he intends to defend.

22. Inaugurating military training for a eunuch army in the palace, contrary to the dynastic regulations.

23. Affecting, when he jaunts outside the palace, all the regalia of the imperial entourage; "has he already majestically mounted the imperial carriage?"

24. Arrogantly defying the imperial authority, as when he made no apology and obviously feared no punishment for riding horseback in the imperial presence, in violation of all propriety.

Yang's itemized accusations build up into an ever more forceful warning that Wei Chung-hsien obviously has designs on the throne. At this point, in a very long peroration, Yang Lien pounds and pounds away on this main theme in the most passionate spirit and in terms that any emperor would certainly have found humiliating in the extreme:

Now, Chung-hsien bears responsibility for these twenty-four great crimes. Fearful lest the inner court disclose his villainy, he kills those whom he must kill and replaces those whom he must replace; and the intimate attendants are so awed that they dare not speak. Fearful lest the outer court disclose his villainy, he expels those whom he must expel and imprisons those whom he must imprison; and the outer court likewise just looks on and dares not speak. There are even some fellows of an ignorant and spineless sort who are so intent on gaining wealth and honors that they cling to him like twigs and leaves, or hang about his gates, or pledge themselves to be his patrons, or join him as protégés. They advocate whatever pleases him and attack whatever he dislikes; there is nothing they will not do. The inside proposes, and the outside disposes; the outside calls, and the inside answers. When what should be behind suddenly moves to the front, one's fate hangs in the balance. And if by chance the inner-court villainies are betrayed, then there is always Mistress K'o to make amends for offenses and to gloss over vileness.

Thus throughout the palace all know there is a Chung-hsien, but none know there is an emperor, and throughout the capital all know there is a Chung-hsien, but none know there is an emperor. Even the major and minor officials and functionaries, in their turning toward the sources of power and authority, unconsciously reveal that they do not know there is an emperor but only know there is a Chung-hsien. Whenever they see that there is something within or without that urgently needs to be done, or someone who ought to be called to service, they always say, "We must talk it over with Inside." Or, if someone cannot be employed or something cannot be carried out, then they just say that Inside is unwilling. Whether in the palace or in the government, whether in great matters or in small matters, there is nothing that is not decided solely by Chung-hsien. Even in the handling of documents, it would appear that the emperor is only a name, whereas Chung-hsien is the reality. For example, when Chung-hsien went to Chung-chou, all matters had to be sent to him by night express couriers, and no rescripts could be issued until Chung-hsien had arrived. Alas! The intimate advisers to the throne did not request imperial decisions, but by courier sought edicts from Chung-hsien a hundred miles away. Circumstances having reached this point, is it known that there is an emperor, or that there is no emperor? That there is a sun in the sky, or that there is no sun in the sky?

Yang Lien then suggests that a recent series of strange natural phenomena, including earthquakes, must have been clear warnings from Heaven, and he complains that the emperor, instead of taking heed and punishing Wei Chung-hsien, actually heaped more and more favors on him. Referring again and again to the emperor's inability to protect his own concubines and even his own son, Yang almost jeers at Hsi-tsung in an attempt to arouse his indignation. Finally, he comes to a demand for action:

In the tenth year of T'ai-tsu's Hung-wu era [i. e., 1377], there was one eunuch who, because he had long served in the inner court, carelessly happened to speak about governmental matters. The emperor dismissed him on the very same day and then proclaimed to the host of ministers: "Although it is said that the disasters of Han and T'ang were the crimes of eunuchs, the rulers actually brought them about by erroneously giving eunuchs trust and affection. If eunuchs are not allowed to command troops or take part in administration, even though they might wish to cause trouble, what can they do? Now, although this eunuch has served me for a long time, I cannot be indulgent with him. He absolutely must go, as a warning for the future."

What a magnificent stroke of wisdom! The eunuch just happened to refer to government matters and yet became a warning to the future. In the case of Chung-hsien, who deceives the ruler, recognizes no superior, accumulates evil, and heaps up crimes, how can the lack of a similar decision be borne? I beg that the emperor stiffen up and thunder out, so that Chung-hsien may be taken in fetters before the ancestral temple. Assemble the major and minor civil and military officials, and order the judicial offices to conduct a careful enquiry, checking item by item the precedents from previous reigns for dealing with eunuchs' misbehavior—having relations within and without, usurping the imperial authority, violating the laws of the ancestors, disrupting court affairs, alienating the hearts of the empire, deceiving the ruler, and turning their backs on imperial grace—so as to deal with [Chung-hsien] according to law, and to quiet the righteous anger of spirits and men. As for Mistress K'o, she should be ordered to take up residence outside the palace, so that she may preserve the favor in which she is held but will not be further allowed to spread her poisons in the palace. As for Fu Ying-sheng, Ch'en Chü-kung, and Fu Chi-chiao, they also should be turned over to the judicial offices for trial. Thereafter there should be an announcement to the empire to explain their crimes and to show that the evil at the ruler's side has indeed been cleared away and that the path of intrigue and influence has indeed been blockaded.

If all this is done and still Heaven's blessings do not return and men's hearts are not pleased—if good order within and peace without do not usher in a new epoch of Great Peace—then I request that you behead me as an offering to Chung-hsien.

I realize that once these words come out, Chung-hsien's partisans will of course be unable to tolerate me. Yet I am not afraid. If I should be able to get rid of just Chung-hsien alone, so as not to deprive the emperor of his reputation as a Yao or a Shun, then I should have fulfilled the command of the former emperor and might face the spirits of the imperial ancestors. In the loyal and righteous service of my lifetime, the extraordinary grace conferred by the two prior rulers might be recognized. And if some small recompense is wished, I should even die without regrets.

May your majesty take note of my intense sincerity and promptly order action.

We are told that Wei Chung-hsien, despite all his arrogance and power, was terrified when Yang Lien's memorial was submitted.[160]

But the wonder was that Yang escaped with a mere rebuke—for the time being.

As I have already suggested, the censorial officials of Hsi-tsung's time, active as they were in submitting impeachments, were even more active in submitting counseling and remonstrating memorials in which they made suggestions ranging over the whole spectrum of governmental concerns: the adoption of new policies, the abandonment of old policies, the undertaking of some activities, and the cessation of other activities. Their proposals, and imperial responses to them, are analyzed in Table 12 on the basis of the types of officials from whom the memorials originated, and in Table 13 on the basis of the subjects they touch upon. As was the case with the 1424–34 data discussed in Chapter 4, there is a certain amount of overlapping, since some censorial memorials served dual purposes as impeachments and counselings; and there is not a one-to-one correlation between the totals of Tables 12 and 13, since some proposals touched upon more than one subject category.

Imperial responses to the censorial proposals of 1620–27 followed the pattern of responses to impeachments of the same period. Thus they differ markedly from the responses to censorial memorials of 1424–34. In percentages, the responses to proposals of 1620–27 can be compared to those of 1424–34 as follows:

	1424–34	*1620–27*
Approved	70%	34%
Deliberation ordered	17%	42%
Disapproved, or no action indicated	13%	24%

This comparison reinforces the conclusion derived from the comparison of impeachments in the two periods: it was not that Hsi-tsung was more reliant on ministerial advice than Jen-tsung or Hsüan-tsung, but that the later period's prevalent factionalism created greater doubt about the honesty and validity of censorial proposals than existed between 1424 and 1434.

Other significant variations can be found by comparing the subject categories of the 1620–27 proposals (Table 13) with those of the 1424–34 proposals (Table 6). What strikes the eye first of all is that memorials relating to the personal conduct of the emperor, which can most confidently be labeled remonstrances, constitute a substantial proportion of the memorials tabulated for 1620–27, whereas they were all but nonexistent between 1424 and 1434. Another variation worth noting is the relative importance of military matters in censorial thinking during Hsi-tsung's reign, in comparison to the earlier period. Proposals relating to border defenses and war make up the second largest single subcategory in the tabulations, even though proposals concerning domestic rebellions in Shantung and in the southwest have not been tabulated in this subcategory, but in subcategory C-2: "Banditry, etc." In short, analysis of the subject matter of censorial proposals reflects quite accurately the essential differences in general conditions between the 1424–34 era of conscientious emperors, stability, and peace and the 1620–27 era of imperial irresponsibility and extreme military danger.

Counsel Concerning Imperial Conduct

The officialdom's many frustrations under Shen-tsung, and its anxieties about the sudden illness and death of Kuang-tsung, led to a great sense of relief when the boy Hsi-tsung came safely to the throne. The officials felt that it would now be possible to make a fresh start in government and to bring about a general revival. Censorial officials besieged Hsi-tsung with advice.

"Now that your majesty has ascended the throne," the supervising secretary Wei Ying-chia proclaimed, "Heaven and mankind are alike overjoyed!" Setting a pattern for his censorial colleagues, Wei then proceeded to suggest to the new ruler where his best interests lay: in undertaking an educational program under ministerial tutorship, in making preparations for an early marriage so as to perpetuate the imperial line, in appointing proper men as his senior advisers, and in promptly taking care of governmental business by issuing rescripts in response to memorials.[161]

To be sure, partisan feelings were running high, especially over the "great cases" arising out of Kuang-tsung's illness and death. There were protests that Kuang-tsung's ambitious consort Madame Li was dealt with either too leniently or too harshly.[162] And before long the censor Fang Chen-ju and the supervising secretary Yang Lien were lengthily lecturing Hsi-tsung on the "true facts" of the hotly controversial "case of the removal from the palace," and even of the earlier controversies as far back as "the case of the attack with the club" in 1615.[163] At Yang Lien's urging, Hsi-tsung issued a long proclamation condemning the outrageous behavior of Madame Li after Kuang-tsung's death.[164] The censor Wang Yeh-hao then protested that the emperor, under Yang Lien's influence, was much too vindictive.[165] Then Fang Chen-ju memorialized anew to defend Yang Lien against

Wang's criticisms, deploring the continuing uneasiness about the controversial cases. Fang asked that a special audience be devoted to a discussion in which doubts might be cleared away. The emperor objected to continuing arguments about the matter, which he felt he had clarified authoritatively.[166] But the censor Chia Chi-ch'un would not let the argument rest. He had already protested Madame Li's mistreatment; and now in a memorial he made wild claims that because of the officials' abusiveness Madame Li had hanged herself in humiliation and one of Kuang-tsung's daughters had drowned herself in a well. Ordered to explain his statements, Chia finally admitted they were false and was dismissed from the civil service, not to be recalled until Wei Chung-hsien's rise to power.[167]

Early hopes about the new emperor began to fade rapidly as aspects of his character successively became known. His lack of a proper education caused censorial officials to urge from the very beginning of his reign that he submit to tutoring by responsible civil-service officials.[168] He did so, but as soon as cool weather came he suspended all such activities. The supervising secretary Li Jo-kuei and the censor Kao Hung-t'u protested in vain.[169] Protests continued all through the winter of 1620–21, but equally in vain.[170] Only when spring weather came was the tutoring resumed. A similar recess in the winter of 1621–22 was resignedly overlooked by the remonstrators, but when tutoring was about to be resumed in the second lunar month of 1622 the grand secretary Yeh Hsiang-kao suggested that it be suspended because of the urgency of other governmental business; the Liaotung defenses had just collapsed. The supervising secretary Hou Chen-yang and the censor Chang Chieh argued vigorously against any suspension, and the tutoring did go on.[171] But Hsi-tsung never became an apt pupil; perhaps, as has already been suggested, he remained illiterate. Apparently in the hope of stimulating his interest, the supervising secretary P'eng Ju-nan in 1623 suggested that he be read to from the great historical chronicle *Tzu-chih T'ung-chien,* as well as from the classical works of antiquity that were standard fare; and Hsi-tsung welcomed this idea.[172]

The court officials hoped that marriage might stabilize the young emperor's character and from the beginning of his reign advocated that wedding arrangements be promptly made.[173] A marriage to the daughter of Chang Kuo-chi of Honan, a girl renowned for her beauty, did take place in 1621; and it was generally believed that Madame Chang was a good influence on Hsi-tsung, even if she was unable to prevent his deterioration. When the wedding was approaching, the

Ministry of Revenue wanted to set a limit on ceremonial expenditures, but Hsi-tsung refused any such restraint. The supervising secretary Ch'eng Ming-shu and others protested this and other imperial extravagances, but the emperor haughtily responded, "It is already decided."[174]

Censorial officials continued to protest against Hsi-tsung's increasing extravagance. In 1622 the supervising secretary Chang Yün-ju asked that the emperor's clothing allowance be reduced, so that the savings could be used to help alleviate popular distress. Hsi-tsung was enraged and ordered that Chang be beaten and dismissed from the civil service. Yeh Hsiang-kao and other grand secretaries, who had themselves vainly tried to get a similar reduction, came to Chang's rescue. They pointed out that he had recently served as a county magistrate and was so intimately acquainted with desperate conditions among the people that they naturally preyed on his mind; and if now as a speaking official he were punished for trying to do something about them, the emperor would have to endure widespread public criticism. Hsi-tsung was dissuaded, and Chang suffered only a one-year salary suspension.[175] Later the same year the censor Chiang Jih-ts'ai, then inspecting frontier supplies, asked for economy measures in the palace so that frontier needs might be met without additional impositions on the public; but Hsi-tsung retorted that there was enough economizing in the palace already.[176] When the supervising secretary Yin T'ung-kao proposed a reduction in the manufacture of cloth for imperial use, and when the supervising secretary Lo Shang-chung and the censor Chou Tsung-chien, then inspecting the Court of Imperial Entertainments, asked for less extravagant imperial demands on that catering establishment, none received any satisfaction.[177] In 1623, when the treasury-inspecting supervising secretary Fang Yu-tu remonstrated about excessive costs in the construction of imperial tombs, he was severely rebuked and fined a half-year's salary.[178] Hsi-tsung was well launched on as wasteful a reign as that of his grandfather, Shen-tsung.

As these instances suggest, Hsi-tsung also quickly began to treat critical officials harshly, especially censorial officials. This was one legacy of Shen-tsung's era that was particularly resented, and when Hsi-tsung came to the throne remonstrators were quick to urge him to keep open the "avenues of criticism." The supervising secretary Chou Ch'ao-jui begged that he not allow himself to become indignant about "forthright speech," and the supervising secretary Chou Shih-p'u argued that the five most important principles for him to adopt were to respect Heaven, emulate the ancestors, esteem frugality, feel compassion for the masses, and accept remonstrances.[179] Hsi-tsung commended these sentiments, but in mid-1621 an official of the Supervisorate of Imperial Instruction felt compelled to complain to him that before he had completed his first year on the throne he had already punished more than ten speaking officials. The emperor protested that he had never denied straightforward remonstrances but that censorial officials had recently been biased and antagonistic.[180] Censors persisted in remonstrating about Hsi-tsung's intolerance of criticism from speaking officials, but in vain.[181] When the supervising secretary Lo Shang-chung joined the chorus in 1622, he was rebuked for making a nuisance of himself.[182]

It quickly became apparent that the young emperor was inclined to be arbitrary in a variety of ways. A month after taking the throne, he promoted the vice minister of rites Sun Ju-yu to the position of grand secretary, without rendering even lip service to the tradition that high-ranking officials were appointed or promoted only on the basis of nominations made in court assemblies. The censors Chia Chi-ch'un, An Shen, and T'ien Chen immediately protested. "We beg that the order be revoked," they memorialized, "so that the gate of luck may be closed; thus the basic ground of government may be purified and the canon of promotion may be esteemed." Hsüeh Feng-hsiang, the chief supervising secretary of the Office of Scrutiny for Personnel, threw the prestige of his position behind their argument. But Hsi-tsung was not intimidated. "Remembering his accomplishments," he said of Sun, "I chose him specially. It was my own personal decision. Speaking officials ought not to question my orders."[183]

Such an attitude on the emperor's part was considered shocking. It threatened the whole procedural structure of checks on absolutism, challenged the semi-autonomous, partner-like status of the civil service in government, and opened up possibilities for sycophancy and improper influences in general. Consequently, a storm of protests came from many censors and supervising secretaries, who demanded that important appointments be made only on the basis of court nominations, that the issuance of "palace edicts" be halted, and that the Grand Secretariat reassert its rescript-drafting prerogatives.[184] Hsi-tsung's reliance upon eunuchs to transmit decisions soon began to be noted in these criticisms.[185] When the Nanking censor Wang Yün-ch'eng proclaimed "Palace edicts must not be promulgated, and memorials must not be retained unanswered," his salary was suspended for three years.[186] Though Sun Ju-yu, embarrassed by the controversy over his promotion, repeatedly requested retirement and was finally permitted to leave office early in 1621, memorialists continued to remonstrate about "palace edicts" through 1621 and into 1622. Fuel was added to the controversy and it flared up anew in 1622 and again in early 1624, when the emperor appointed to high offices men listed second in court nominations rather than the first-preference nominees.[187]

Long before 1624, of course, the outer court and even the grand secretaries had lost effective contact with Hsi-tsung. Since 1621 censorial officials had been complaining about the empty ritualism of court audiences and had begged for opportunities to memorialize in person in the emperor's presence, but their pleas had no effect.[188] The emperor was increasingly out of reach of the officialdom, devoting himself only to his carpentry and to other hobbies in the palace; and Wei Chung-hsien was becoming the unchallengeable dictator of the inner court.

The censorial officials became aware early in Hsi-tsung's reign that Mistress K'o's influence over the emperor was a key to his increasing reliance on eunuchs. The censor Wang Hsin-i protested against honors being conferred on both Mistress K'o and Wei Chung-hsien at the beginning of 1621.[189] Soon thereafter—taking advantage of the obvious opportunity afforded by the emperor's marriage—the censors Pi Tso-chou and Liu Lan, the supervising secretary Hsüeh Feng-hsiang, and others began to argue that Mistress K'o's usefulness was at an end and that she should be made to move to a residence outside the palace.[190] A residence was provided for the nursemaid outside, but she continued to have free access to the inner apartments and to wield influence as before. In the tenth month of 1621 the censors Chou Tsung-chien, Hsü Yang-hsien, and Wang Hsin-i and the supervising secretaries Hou Chen-ch'ang, Ni Ssu-hui, and Chu Ch'in-hsiang all protested anew. Ni Ssu-hui urged that Hsi-tsung should "demonstrate his childlike affection at the tomb of his parents rather than toward Mistress K'o, so as to dissipate the sources of the outer court's suspicions and destroy the threat of interference from intimates." Chu Ch'in-hsiang was even more provocative, saying:

If one wishes to scour away the Manchu threat, one must first get rid of the female threat. The Middle Kingdom and the literati represent the Yang force; thus the prospering of the Middle Kingdom derives from the employment of literati. The barbarians and the inner attendants represent the Yin force; thus barbarian conquests derive from the employment of inner attendants. Since the rebellious Manchus began to run wild, administration has depended upon the bright Yang essence, and dark Yin has been suppressed. But then arose the matter of disposing of Mistress K'o. Mistress K'o was

moved out, but then she was summoned back in; and in future she will be
now in and now out. When she is out, she plays with the imperial authority
in such a way as to terrify the villagers; and when she is in, she spreads
around rumors in such a way as to confuse your majesty's hearing. Thus she
corrupts and disorganizes the palace apartments; thus she interferes with
court administration; and thus she fosters the villainous and depraved while
subverting the good and respectable. The Yin force overturns destiny and
deceptively causes your majesty to worry about the Manchus in the east and
disregard the female threat before your eyes. This is what is called not being
able to see well enough even to see one's own eyelashes!

Ni, Chu, and Wang Hsin-i were all demoted three degrees and transferred to provincial posts, and Hsi-tsung made it clear that Mistress
K'o was none of the outer court's business.[191] In 1623, when privileges
already granted to Mistress K'o to secure official titles and emolu-
ments for her relatives were made perpetual, six censors and supervising secretaries protested in succession, but as much in vain as before.[192]

Meantime, censorial officials had begun their direct denunciations
of Wei Chung-hsien, as has been noted above. They also remonstrated
about eunuch influence in more general ways, and in reference to
other specific abuses.[193] The censors Wang Hsin-i and Liu T'ing-tso
and the supervising secretaries P'eng Ju-nan and Hou Shou-tien complained about honors successively showered on Wei Chung-hsien.[194]
The supervising secretaries Yang So-hsiu and Ch'eng Ming-shu both
complained about the size of the palace eunuch staff when in 1623 it
was to be augmented by 2,500 new recruits.[195] The censors Chang
Chieh, P'eng K'un-hua, Sung Shih-hsiang, Liu Chih-feng, Hu Liang-
chi, and Li Ying-sheng all successively protested against military
training of eunuchs in the palace.[196] The supervising secretary Chou
Shih-p'u protested against establishing a dangerous precedent when
in 1623 eunuchs rather than civil officials were sent to the frontier to
distribute gifts to the troops.[197] The censor Wang Ta-nien and the
supervising secretary Hsü Yü-ch'ing separately remonstrated against
accepting impeachments of civil officials submitted by eunuchs.[198]
Wang Ta-nien's criticism was as follows:

There already are those whose function is to submit impeachments, and for
eunuchs to do so is unheard-of. I am afraid that, whereas today they take advantage of imperial favor so as to enhance their prestige, in future they might
arrogate imperial power unto themselves so as to turn the sword of authority
against its giver, your majesty. This threat cannot be allowed to develop.

The supervising secretary Tseng Ju-chao in 1623 asked that eunuchs
be restrained from using the cangue on prisoners, and when Wan

Ching was beaten to death by eunuchs in 1624 after Yang Lien's denunciation of Wei Chung-hsien, the censors P'an Yün-i, Liu T'ing-
tso, and Li Ying-sheng still felt there was some point in submitting
protests, though their remonstrances were as ineffective as had been
all those previously submitted about eunuch influence and abuses.[199]

After Wei Chung-hsien's power was clearly established late in 1624,
censorial remonstrances did not cease altogether. In mid-1625, the supervising secretary Yü T'ing-pi suggested that the emperor would do
well to have personal conferences with his senior civil-service advisers
about important matters, and at about the same time the censor Kao
Hung-t'u, while denouncing the Tung-lin Party, suggested that criminals should be dealt with by the regular judicial agencies rather than
in the imperial bodyguard's palace prison.[200] Though they escaped
with rebukes at the time, both were forced out of office in 1626–27.[201]
In 1626 the chief supervising secretary P'eng Ju-nan urged lenience
in the treatment of criminals and was also rebuked.[202] When eunuch
supervisors were assigned to each of the northern frontier defense
commands in 1626, the censors Mou Chih-hsin and Shih Yu-hsiang
and the supervising secretaries Hsüeh Kuo-kuan, Kuo Ju-an, and
Huang Ch'eng-hao submitted successive memorials of protest.[203] The
emperor immediately dismissed Huang Ch'eng-hao from the civil
service on the ground that he was a leftover Tung-lin partisan, but
no action was taken against the other remonstrators. Mou Chih-hsin
even became grand coordinator of Shansi province the next year.[204]

The censor Chia Chi-ch'un went unpunished in 1625 when he
urged cessation of military training in the palace, but only because
he argued that the training noise might disturb a newborn imperial
son. Hsi-tsung assured Chia that he need not be concerned, since the
guns and drums had already been silenced in the palace.[205] In the
summer of the same year, when the emperor's tutoring sessions were
suspended on the pretext of unseasonably hot weather, the supervising secretary Hu Yung-shun, knowing better than to protest in the
manner of a few years earlier, courteously suggested that the emperor
might do well to study independently during the perfectly justified
recess.[206]

The great majority of remonstrators during Wei Chung-hsien's re-
gime, however, went far beyond the politeness of Chia Chi-ch'un and
Hu Yung-shun. They dedicated themselves to obsequious praises of
Wei, urging only that the emperor trust him ever more wholeheart-
edly. The censor Liang Meng-huan contributed often to this chorus.
In 1626 he credited Wei Chung-hsien with the successful completion

of a palace construction project.[207] In 1627 he even gave Wei full credit for Yüan Ch'ung-huan's successful defense of Ning-yüan and Chin-
chou against the Manchus, crying "His virtue blankets the four cor-
ners of the universe, and his patriotism surpasses any for a hundred
generations!"[208] The censor Cho Mai echoed, "Wei Chung-hsien cher-
ishes the state as if it were his own family and protects it everywhere,
not only at Ning-yüan and Chin-chou!"[209] The prevalent mood is reflected in the following representative *Shih-lu* entry from 1627:

Eighth month, the day *chia-wu*: The censor Liu Mei of the Nanking Honan
Circuit and others memorialized: "The Manchus have been beaten down
at Ning [-yüan] and have thrice been defeated at Chin [-chou]. Their tricks
are exhausted, and our arms are triumphant. This is entirely due to the
military genius of our emperor, which Heaven conferred, and which the
intimately advising palace minister by his purity and sincerity has brought
to flower. When troops are required, troops assemble; and when supplies
are required, supplies abound. In attacking he has firm strategies, and in
defending he leaves no openings. So it is that men's hearts leap up, and
spiritual forces manifest themselves.

"Now, in this quiet interval, he cultivates a solid administration, intelli-
gently confers rewards, and carefully discriminates merit from guilt. He
causes our plans to be complete, our strength to be abundant, our troops
to be well fed, and our horses to be alert—either to drive the Manchus out
and exterminate them or to entice the Manchus in and annihilate them.
Thus the commands to restrain the Manchu bandits and the schemes to
achieve recovery [of Liaotung] may promptly be realized." Acknowledged.[210]

From late in 1625 until the end of Hsi-tsung's reign in 1627, similar
panegyrics poured in from censors, supervising secretaries, and other
officials.[211]

The flattery of Wei Chung-hsien reached its peak in requests for
permission to establish temples in his honor. To establish a temple
to anyone who still lived was a rare honor indeed; but when in 1626
the grand coordinator of Chekiang province, P'an Ju-chen, thought
of this way to win favor, no one else could do anything but follow his
lead. Such proposals were most commonly made by the regional inspector, or jointly by the grand coordinator and regional inspector,
of a province or a frontier defense region.[212] Two salt-control censors
also made such requests, and a ward-inspecting censor passed along
a request from the general citizenry of Peking.[213] One regional inspector varied the routine slightly by asking permission to put up a memorial arch in Wei's honor.[214] And the censor Ni Wen-huan even
asked permission to establish a Wei Chung-hsien temple at his own
home.[215]

Counsel Concerning General Administration

Censorial proposals for 1620–27 in the realm of general administration are principally concerned with two themes: bureaucratic partisanship and economic difficulties.

In general-administration proposals, concern with bureaucratic partisanship is revealed in part by a continuous series of suggestions about ways to assure propriety and to prevent partisan bias in the routine appointment processes of the Ministry of Personnel and the Ministry of War; these include recurrent suggestions that more reliance be placed on guaranteed recommendations.[216] The censor Chang Chieh suggested that appointments would be less suspect if they were based more on public recommendations than on the whims of the Ministry of Personnel.[217] The censor Su Shu and the supervising secretary Liu Hung-hua separately suggested that careful investigation of a nominee's hometown reputation would throw more light on his character traits than did his official dossier.[218] The supervising secretary Chu Ch'in-hsiang urged that when promotions were considered less emphasis should be given to seniority and more to ability.[219] Especially because of past partisan exploitation of the regular evaluations, there were repeated warnings about avoiding bias as the outer evaluations of 1622 and the capital evaluations of 1623 approached.[220] Then, because the Tung-lin Party did unquestionably make use of these evaluations to get rid of many of their enemies, the censor Shih San-wei in 1625 asked that the past evaluations be repudiated, and the emperor in response agreed that anyone responsible for such evaluations who still happened to be in office should be dismissed and that the victims of such evaluations should be recalled to service.[221]

In 1622 the aforementioned establishment of an academy of the Tung-lin type in the capital was promptly denounced by the supervising secretary Chu T'ung-meng primarily because of its partisan implications, and it was ordered closed for that reason.[222] The bitter arguments that followed this action, and general bitterness about the Tung-lin Academy's long relation to court factionalism, led to attacks on academies in general after Wei Chung-hsien came to power. The attack was inaugurated early in 1625 by the probationary censor Chou Wei-ch'ih, who insisted that bureaucratic partisanship should be suppressed and that one means of doing this would be to wipe out all the private academies in the empire. His memorial was referred to "the Ministries," and nothing seems to have come of it.[223] Then the censor Ni Wen-huan urged that the laudatory stone inscriptions that normally adorned academies be destroyed, and this was approved, specifically as a warning against partisanship.[224] Finally, in the eighth month of 1625, the censor Chang Na revived Chou Wei-ch'ih's proposal, and the emperor now ordered that the Tung-lin and other academies be razed.[225] At the end of the year the supervising secretary Li Lu-sheng won approval for his proposal that the sites of private academies be transformed into memorials to the Liaotung dead, and early in 1626 the Nanking censor Hsü Fu-yang again advocated destruction of all academies.[226]

We do not know whether the destruction of private academies was carried out throughout the empire, as Chang Na insisted. For a time Kao P'an-lung's influence with the local authorities saved some of the Tung-lin Academy buildings, but after his suicide in the third month of 1626, everything was confiscated by the government.[227] Late in 1626 the regional inspector of Kiangsi province, Ts'ao Ku, requested permission to sell the lands of private academies in his province and to contribute the proceeds to palace construction expenses. This was approved, and Ts'ao sent in 3,017 taels in 1626 and another 350 taels in 1627.[228] It had been Chang Na's intention that all academy properties should in this way be converted into contributions for palace construction work, but to what extent this was done in areas other than Kiangsi, and how generally academies were actually suppressed, is not clear.

The censorial concern about partisanship was also reflected in a determination, first on the part of the Tung-lin men and then on the part of their enemies, to see that history was correctly written—in other words, that history was written with a favorable bias. Compilation of the *Shih-lu* chronicles for Shen-tsung's long reign was one matter of partisan interest. In 1621, the censor Chou Tsung-chien expressed fears that the chronicles would be incomplete, and urged that all pertinent documents be made available to the Hanlin Academy officials who served as court historiographers.[229] But the *Shen-tsung Shih-lu* was not completed until 1630 and thus did not become a matter of controversy in Hsi-tsung's time.

In any event, there was more intense feeling about the compilation of the *Kuang-tsung Shih-lu,* since the facts about Kuang-tsung's illness and death were matters of hot partisan controversy. When in 1620 Yang Lien expressed interest in having the emperor issue an authoritative account of "the case of the removal from the palace," he was largely motivated by his determination to commit the official historiographers to his interpretation of the incident. The grand supervisor of instruction, Kung Nai, promptly praised Yang's account and asked that an honest record of Kuang-tsung's reign be compiled; and Hsi-tsung thereupon ordered compilation of the *Kuang-tsung Shih-lu* to begin.[230] In early 1622 the censor-in-chief Tsou Yüan-piao complained about the delay in its production; and the censor Hsü Ching-lien, urging that the *Kuang-tsung Shih-lu* be written objectively, proceeded to explain how it should recount the misdeeds of the controversial grand secretary Fang Ts'ung-che.[231] The supervising secretary Fang Yu-tu urged that Hsü's views be given most careful consideration.[232] At the beginning of 1623, the censor Huo Ying pointed out that not all the officials who deserved punishment had actually been punished, and not all who deserved rewards had actually been rewarded; and he expressed the hope that the *Kuang-tsung Shih-lu* would at least give a full record of the facts to compensate for these oversights.[233]

The *Kuang-tsung Shih-lu* was completed in 1623, with Yeh Hsiang-kao as nominal compiler-in-chief; and it was presumably satisfactory to the Tung-lin men who then dominated the outer court. But under Wei Chung-hsien a revision was undertaken. In early 1625 the supervising secretary Huo Wei-hua presented a complete anti-Tung-lin account of all the court controversies beginning with the dispute over "the root of the state" in the 1590's, intended to be a reference for the historiographers.[234] The censor Liu Fang asked that all provincial authorities be ordered to seek out gazetteers and biographical writings that would be of use to the historiographers, and the supervising secretary Yang So-hsiu demanded that all government offices make their records available for historiographic examination.[235] Late in 1626 the censor-in-chief Liu T'ing-yüan objected to delays in completing the revision, as his predecessor Tsou Yüan-piao had objected to delays in preparing the original. Moreover, he reported that the surveillance vice commissioner of Kwangsi province, Ts'ao Hsüeh-ch'üan, had privately compiled and printed his own version of the history of Kuang-tsung's reign. The emperor ordered that Ts'ao be dismissed from the civil service and that his work and its printing blocks be destroyed.[236] The revised *Kuang-tsung Shih-lu* apparently was not completed until after Hsi-tsung's death. But the only version that now survives seems to be yet another revision, and we know nothing about its compilation.[237] In general, it seems to give a Tung-lin interpretation of the dramatic events of 1620.

Huo Wei-hua's memorial of early 1625, and more particularly two proposals by the supervising secretary Yang So-hsiu that soon followed, led to the production of a special historical work devoted to the controversial cases that the Tung-lin Party had been involved in, especially "the three great cases" of 1615 and 1620.[238] Compiled under the general supervision of the grand secretary Ku Ping-ch'ien, this appeared in 1626 with the title *San-ch'ao Yao-tien*, "the canon of the three reigns." It is akin to the "white papers" published by modern governments, in that it presents a currently orthodox anti-Tung-lin interpretation of events under Shen-tsung, Kuang-tsung, and Hsi-tsung.[239] The censors Chia Chi-ch'un and Shih San-wei gave advice about its compilation; and even the old-time censor K'ang P'ei-yang offered his interpretation of earlier controversies and asked that they also be dealt with in the new publication.[240] (K'ang had been aligned with the Grand Secretariat against the "good elements" at the turn of the century in such controversies as "the case of the subversive book" and had lived in retirement since 1609.) Surprisingly, Hsi-tsung (or Wei Chung-hsien) responded to K'ang's memorial angrily, calling him an evil partisan of former times who now sought merely to reinstate himself. Deliberation of his case was ordered, and after three months, when the court proposed that he be deprived of his status as a literatus, the emperor ordered instead that he be sentenced to serve at the frontier as a common soldier.[241]

When the *San-ch'ao Yao-tien* was in preparation, it was ordered, at Chia Chi-ch'un's urging, that all private publications relating to the court controversies be confiscated by the provincial authorities and that henceforth no such books might be published without government approval.[242] After the new work's publication, at the urging of the supervising secretary Yü T'ing-pi, it was ordered that all privately published lists of Tung-lin men, whether friendly or antagonistic, be prohibited, confiscated, and burned, so that the *San-ch'ao Yao-tien* could stand as the sole standard of historical judgment about the Tung-lin Party and the officialdom might cease to bicker any longer about partisanship.[243]

Aside from all these partisan concerns, economic problems loomed largest in censorial officials' thoughts about general administration. The nature of these problems has been sketched at the beginning of this chapter, and their urgency is well indicated in the following censorial memorial of 1623, translated in its entirety as recorded in the *Shih-lu:*

Seventh month, the day *hsin-mao:* The Office of Scrutiny for Works supervising secretary Fang Yu-tu memorialized: "Since troubles erupted east of the Liao River, military needs have swelled to the point of exhausting the empire's resources. For one example, in these five years expenditures from the palace treasury must be reckoned in the tens of millions; and the extraordinary assessments for troop rations that are paid by the people annually come to about 4,850,000 taels—totaling more than 20 million taels in five years. The masses crack their bones, scrape their marrow, and sell their children and wives to make up their payments, and this is repeated year after year.

"I have seen a report from Pi Tzu-yen, the vice minister of revenue in charge of military supplies at Tientsin, calculating that expenses in grain and equivalents for the 110,000 cavalry and infantry troops at Shan-hai-kuan, expenses for horse fodder, expenses for sea-transport labor, salaries for civil and military officials and troops and laborers, and expenses of miscellaneous sorts in all amount to about 4 million taels annually.

"This just refers to the hundred thousand troops at Shan-hai-kuan alone. It does not include 'courtesy payments' to the Mongols, which according to the 1622 precedent amount to 70,000 taels. In addition, in 1619 some 20,000 sea and land forces were added in the Teng-lai area [on the north coast of Shantung] and 14,000 sea and land forces were added at Tientsin. There were 3,300 new troops added in 1620 when the Military-Inspiring Training Division was created in the capital. In 1621, cavalry and infantry troops numbering 9,800 were added at T'ung-chou [just east of Peking, on the Grand Canal]. And in 1622, 10,000 transport troops were added at Mi-yün [between Peking and Shan-hai-kuan], 6,000 new troops were added at Chang-chia-wan [on the Grand Canal just south of T'ung-chou], 8,000 new recruits were added for the 16 gates of the capital, and Mao Wen-lung [operating off the north coast of Korea] had 20,000 seaborne troops. This is a total of more than 91,000 new troops. Except for the rations for the Teng-lai area troops that are paid for out of the extraordinary assessments of that province and the rations of the troops of the Military-Inspiring Training Division and at the 16 gates that are paid for out of the capital granaries, the 900,000 taels that are expended annually for the new troops at these various localities are also not included. Moreover, the several ten thousands of taels in increased rations that were proposed in 1622 for the old-quota troops in the Chi-chen defense command [north of Peking] are not included.

"Where there are armies, there also are expenses for gifts for the troops, expenses for maintaining horses, expenses for repairing boats and carts, and expenses for officers' salaries and miscellaneous costs. For example, the sea transport for Mao Wen-lung alone has already cost 50,000 taels for labor. Every year such expenses exceed 100,000 taels—and this is not included.

"Over and above the 4 million taels for Shan-hai-kuan, the new troops in the various localities annually cost about 1,200,000 taels. Thus the total is about 5,200,000 taels. Even if there should not be the slightest discrepancy in the annual revenues of 4,850,000 taels from extraordinary assessments, there would still be a deficiency of 350,000 taels for the whole Shan-hai-kuan theater. This is impossible!

"Furthermore, as for the extraordinary assessments: 430,000 taels from the Northern Metropolitan Area have been remitted; 448,000 taels in Shantung are retained for troop rations in the Teng-lai area and for buying rice to transport to Tientsin; 719,000 taels in Hukwang, 60,000 taels in Kwangsi, 120,000 taels in Szechwan, and 16,000 taels in Yunnan are all retained for troop rations in Kweichow [because of the southwestern rebellion]. In all, deducting what is thus remitted and retained, the annual extraordinary assessments of 4,850,000 taels are already 1,790,000 taels short. And I have had no time to consider shortages that result from such calamities as floods and droughts.

"The 350,000 taels that are needed in excess of what the extraordinary assessments provide, combined with this shortage of 1,790,000 taels within the extraordinary assessments, gives a total deficiency in the new quota of 2,140,000 taels. However, the old quota called for annual rations for the Liaotung defense command of 520,000 taels. When this is taken into account, then the annual rations deficiency for the whole Shan-hai-kuan theater is actually 1,620,000 taels.

"Are these 1,620,000 taels now to be sought among the people? The people's lives are already difficult. What the empire ordinarily pays in to the national treasury to provide for the rations of the nine frontier regions is about 3,400,000 taels. Now extraordinary assessments for the Liao affair have reached 4,850,000 taels. What is paid in to the national treasury is more than double the ordinary standard. If another 1,620,000 taels were added, then the extraordinary assessments would jump another 30 per cent above the ordinary standard. Can we follow this path without [precipitating] rebellion?

"The Manchus now are loath to bestir themselves and have rested in their lairs for a long while; but without their even having to loose a single arrow in our direction, our empire might fall in ruins!

"I beg for an order that the Ministries of Revenue and of War consult together to see how the present military forces can be supported and how the present deficiencies in income can be made up in such a way that on one hand the state will not be weakened, and on the other hand the people will not be oppressed. Don't wait for rebellion and then start planning!"

The emperor ordered the Ministries of Revenue and of War to give careful consideration and report.[244]

The urgency of meeting the defense costs that are described in Fang Yu-tu's memorial caused censorial officials throughout the early 1620's to plead for economies in other governmental activities. Their complaints about the emperor's personal extravagance have been noted above; but the principal focuses of their economizing efforts were the great construction projects undertaken in and around Peking in Hsi-tsung's time: the construction of tombs for Shen-tsung and Kuang-tsung and, most particularly, the reconstruction of burned-down pavilions and halls in the palace. In 1621, the censor Wang Ta-nien vigorously denounced wasteful expenditures on such projects and criticized the Office of Scrutiny for Works for not keeping a closer check on expenditures.[245] In early 1622, when the Manchu threat reached its peak, the supervising secretaries Ch'en Yin-ts'ung and Chiang Hsi-k'ung successively asked that all such construction projects be suspended so that funds could be made available to strengthen the frontier defenses.[246] They won a very temporary suspension of palace construction, and before the end of the year the supervising secretaries Wang Ch'ing-po and Liu Hung-hua resumed making such requests.[247] When the minister of works seconded their proposals, Hsi-tsung pointed out that work already begun could not be stopped, but agreed that any new construction should be undertaken with hesitance. The censorial struggle for economies in construction work continued, but without effect.[248]

In addition to pleading for such economies, the censorial officials in the early 1620's pleaded rather consistently for reductions in the tax burdens borne by the people. As in the decade 1424–34, they regularly requested tax remissions for areas that had experienced extraordinary natural calamities.[249] In addition, they often asked for cessation of the extraordinary assessments that were intended to pay for the war in Liaotung, and in general they urged that the state find some source of revenues other than further levies on the people at large.[250] In 1623, the supervising secretary Yin T'ung-kao made the Legalistic proposals that supervision be tightened and that punishments be toughened to force local officials to fulfill their tax quotas more regularly; and he complained that provincial grand coordinators and regional inspectors were too lenient in overlooking such failures.[251] In response, the censor Wu Chih-jen pointed out that the people bore a very heavy tax burden, that the tax quotas were unrealistic and should be revised in fairness both to the people and to the officials who were held responsible for fulfilling them, and especially that some device other than land taxes must be relied upon to meet the new defense needs.[252]

To all such appeals for lightening the people's tax load, Hsi-tsung responded without enthusiasm. Late in 1622 he became quite angry at two censors, Yang Hsin-ch'i and Wu Sheng, when they urged the lowering of taxes. Probably with some justification, the emperor objected that officials were not devoting themselves to devising workable plans for meeting the current national emergency, but merely thought to make reputations for themselves by clamoring for lower taxes, regardless of the state's great needs. He rebuked Yang and suspended Wu's salary for three months.[253] On the other hand, when the censor Fang Ying at about the same time proposed that local militias be organized in all areas and paid for by an increase in taxes, Hsi-tsung thought this was a marvelous idea.[254]

After Wei Chung-hsien came to power late in 1624, the censorial officials' attitude toward revenues and expenditures changed perceptibly. Requests for relief in disaster areas were still submitted, and were still in general acted upon—though occasionally in the rescripts there were grumblings that tax arrears must still be recovered even in disaster areas, and that the capital granaries were after all empty, no matter how pitiable conditions might be elsewhere.[255] In 1626 the salt-control censor Lu Shih-k'o even objected to a proposed new increase in salt taxes.[256] For the most part, however, censorial officials in Wei Chung-hsien's time showed little concern for popular distress and great concern for increasing state revenues to pay for Wei's special projects if for nothing else.

Then came complaints that defense costs were too high.[257] There were proposals to increase revenues, and especially to assure more regular and full payments of taxes and to guarantee their delivery to the capital.[258] But the principal aim of all these efforts was really to provide funds for palace construction, which censorial officials of the early 1620's had complained about. Palace construction projects had become the special interest of Wei Chung-hsien, and eagerly supporting such work was the principal way in which censorial officials catered to Wei's whims before building temples in his honor was thought of. Beginning in 1625, censors and supervising secretaries competed with each other and with the officialdom at large in devising ways to save funds that could be diverted to the construction work; and they even made contributions to it from their own personal resources if they could not effect savings in the governmental enterprises they supervised. The censor P'an Yün-i contributed 5,000 taels, the supervising secretary Huo Wei-hua 50,000 taels, the Nanking supervising secretary Kuo Ju-an 4,000 taels, and the censor Hsü Ch'ing-po 1,006 taels.[259] The salt-control censor Lu Shih-k'o arranged for the submission of a grand total of 1,016,386 taels.[260] Various Nanking censors made unspecified contributions from their salaries.[261] The supervising secretary Li Heng-mao proposed that since all of the literati were making salary contributions to the construction work the members of the various Princely Establishments should be required to do so as well, and it was so ordered.[262] The supervising secretary P'an Shih-wen even went so far as to propose that half the grain in all of the empire's local emergency-reserve and ever-normal granaries be sold to provide funds for construction, but he was rebuked for his extremism.[263] In 1626, the Nanking censor-in-chief Hu Tung-chien impeached a former prefect and got him dismissed from the civil service because he had not fulfilled his quota in making contributions.[264]

Proposals about increasing the flow of such contributions poured in endlessly through 1626 and 1627, usually filled with praises of Wei Chung-hsien's construction attainments.[265] The censor Lu Hsien-ming even proposed new construction projects—residences for various princes, each to cost 450,000 taels.[266] Censorial concern for the popular welfare seems to have vanished completely by 1627.

Censorial proposals in the general-administration category also include a substantial number devoted to maintaining and improving the Grand Canal transport of revenues to Peking; not surprisingly, the vast majority of them date from Wei Chung-hsien's era.[267] In 1621 the supervising secretary Wei Fan proposed reviving the old sea-transport system from the Yangtze around the Shantung peninsula.[268]

Among the disasters of the 1620's that necessitated special action was the Manchu conquest of Liaotung, which drove Chinese refugees southward. Especially in 1621 and 1622, censorial officials submitted proposals about means to relieve and resettle the refugees. These officials included T'ao Lang-hsien, the Shantung surveillance commissioner in charge of the Coastal-defense Circuit at Teng-chou; the supervising secretary Huo Wei-hua, the censor Chang Chieh, and the Northern Metropolitan Area regional inspector Chang Shen-yen.[269] Their suggestions were generally approved, including Huo Wei-hua's proposal that able-bodied refugees be used in the army. Later, in 1624, the censor Li Ying-sheng objected to the oppression of Liaotung refugees by local authorities in Shantung.[270]

The most dramatic non-military disaster of the era was an explosion of gunpowder, apparently precipitated by an earthquake, in the fifth month of 1626. The gunpowder was stored in the eunuch-controlled imperial arsenal within the palace, and its detonation reportedly cost 537 lives and destroyed more than 10,930 room-units of housing. Some of the damages were apparently caused by the imperial bodyguard's elephants, which, terrified by the explosion, stampeded through the city.[271] The ward-inspecting censor Li Ts'an-jan submitted the official report of damages.[272] Supervising secretaries and censors, led by Yang So-hsiu and Wang Yeh-hao, asked imperial aid for the victims of the disaster and expressed fears that the explosion may have been touched off by spies.[273] The supervising secretary Yü T'ing-pi supplemented Li Ts'an-jan's report with details of damages done to one of the major gates of the palace, and asked that repairs be undertaken immediately.[274] The supervising secretary P'eng Ju-nan and several censors all asked that because of the calamity punishments of imprisoned criminals be suspended, and even that tax collections be suspended.[275] Punishments were actually suspended for a month.

General personnel administration was a continuing censorial concern throughout Hsi-tsung's reign, entirely aside from its partisan implications. In 1620 the Nanking censor Wang Yün-ch'eng and the supervising secretary Sun Chieh both urged that civil-service vacancies—part of Shen-tsung's legacy—be filled as rapidly as possible, to assure normal administration.[276] Because of continuing shortages of officials, the supervising secretary Wang Ch'ing-po in 1621 proposed that an increased number of doctoral degrees be granted in the civil-service recruitment examinations of 1621–22. When the Ministry of Rites concurred, the emperor approved, but only with the assurance that the increase would be considered an emergency expedient.[277] As a consequence, in 1622 doctoral degrees were won by 409 men, the largest number since 1523. In 1625 the quota dropped back to a more normal 300.[278] At the urging of the censor Li Jih-hsüan, members of the imperial clan were permitted to participate in the civil-service examinations of 1621–22, for the first time in Ming history, though Li's suggestion that a special quota be allocated to them was not approved.[279]

By late 1622 the shortage of officials seems to have turned into a surplus, at least of officials on duty in the capital. Late in that year, the censor Lien Kuo-shih complained of excessive appointments to capital posts; and the supervising secretary Chao Shih-yung and the censor Lu Hsien-ming complained about appointments of supernumerary officials in the capital and proposed means of restricting appointments to the authorized complements for the various agencies.[280] Though supernumerary appointments were temporarily suspended in response to these complaints, the supervising secretary Sun Shao-t'ung complained about them again late in 1623, apparently without any effect. Sun particularly objected because, although supervising secretaries and investigating censors were formerly appointed only every two or three years and only to fill existing vacancies, they were now appointed irregularly and without regard to vacancies, so that supervising secretaries or censors had to wait a year or even two years after appointment for vacancies to occur. He felt that this situation cheapened the censorial offices.[281]

The accumulation of officials in the capital may have resulted, at least in part, from an order prompted by a proposal from the supervising secretary Chou Ch'ao-jui. The order stated that when local officials from all over the empire appeared in Peking at the beginning of

1622 for the outer evaluations, those of special merit should be retained for urgent defense work.[282] The overabundance of capital officials seems to have persisted from 1623 to the very end of Hsi-tsung's reign.

As the officials readily agreed, there was also an overabundance of palace eunuchs. It has already been observed that the supervising secretaries Yang So-hsiu and Ch'eng Ming-shu complained about the size of the eunuch staff when in 1623 it was to be augmented by 2,500 new recruits.[283] This increase followed the recruitment of 3,000 eunuchs in 1621, at which time more than 20,000 candidates made such a clamor around the Ministry of Rites that the supervising secretary Li Jo-kuei demanded that they be dispersed to prevent a riot, and urged that the prohibition against private castration be enforced more rigorously. Hsi-tsung reacted by denouncing all persons who performed castrations in the hope of getting sons or other relatives into the palace service; and he ordered that henceforth such castrators must be charged with murder. The supervising secretary Yin T'ung-kao, however, sympathized with the plight of those candidates who had not been selected for the palace, and suggested that the surplus candidates be assigned to service in the various Princely Establishments throughout the empire.[284]

Other general-administration proposals of this era that deserve mention include: (1) suggestions by the supervising secretaries Chao Shih-yung and Li Ching-po that the state solve its fiscal problems through "creating money," by a greatly expanded production of copper coins, (2) demands by the censors Hsü Ch'ing-po and Yüan Ching that the state restrain members of local gentry families from enclosing public water reservoirs to the disadvantage of poor independent farmers, and (3) the censor Wu Sheng's demand that local civil authorities, rather than specially detailed officers of the imperial bodyguard, be utilized to collect rent arrears from farmers working the estates of the imperial princes.[285]

Counsel Concerning Military Matters

Proposals dealing with all aspects of the Liaotung crisis together with those dealing with the aboriginal rebellion in the southwest make up the largest single concentration of memorials submitted by censorial officials in the years 1620–27. In fact (and naturally under the circumstances) almost all of the memorials in the broad military category relate in some way to these two great military struggles on which the fate of the dynasty depended.

In 1621 and 1622, the successive losses of the far northeastern cities

of Shen-yang, Liao-yang, and Kuang-ning dramatically focused censorial attention on the Manchu threat. And all censorial officials
seemed to have something to say about the progress of the war—not
only the army-inspecting censors and supply-supervising censors at
the front, but censors and supervising secretaries stationed at Peking,
and even those stationed at Nanking, and censors serving as regional
inspectors in provinces far distant from the fighting. All had notions
of how the war could be won.[286] Suffice it to say here that the proposals were highly varied and that they were submitted continuously
until the end of Hsi-tsung's reign.

Censorial officials who had no plans of their own were quick to call
on the Ministry of War to clarify and firm up its plans.[287] Those who
were active at the front impatiently demanded that those in the capital cease giving advice and criticism.[288] In late 1621, when the mutually antagonistic northern commanders Hsiung T'ing-pi and Wang
Hua-chen were bombarding the court with contradictory proposals
about strategies, each had his censorial supporters; and the censor
Hsü Ch'ing-po just wanted them to stop reporting what they intended
to do and to go ahead and do something and then report, so as to preserve some degree of military secrecy.[289] Late in 1622 Hsi-tsung wanted to dismiss two censors and one supervising secretary from the civil
service for disclosing military secrets in their memorials, but he was
dissuaded by the grand secretary Yeh Hsiang-kao.[290] Late in 1625 the
censor Chang Shu urged that all capital and provincial officials be
required to submit their own ideas about defense strategies, but the
emperor said it would be enough if they all conscientiously went
about their prescribed duties.[291]

Great court debates about strategy were held from time to time, but
they do not seem to have been very successful.[292] In the third month
of 1621, when such a court session was convened to consider the loss
of Liao-yang, censorial officials generally became so panicky and so
abusive toward one another, and were so obviously at a loss to know
what ought to be done, that the supervising secretary Huo Shou-tien
finally memorialized that such deliberations were useless.[293]

In the early 1620's military personnel problems were acute. Morale
was shattered and training was ineffective. In early 1621 the censor Li
Chiu-kuan complained that there were only two attitudes prevalent among the frontier forces: either "let things drift" or "trust to
luck."[294] At about the same time, the supervising secretary Chao Shih-
yung deplored the state of China's military training, comparing it
very unfavorably to the Manchu practices.[295] Not much later, the
army-inspecting censor in Liaotung, Fang Chen-ju, reported that mo-

rale was so low that the soldiers were no longer willing to die; and officers at the front made so many requests for sick leave that the supervising secretary Ts'ai Ssu-ch'ung felt it necessary to propose that military officers not be permitted to leave the frontier zone.[296] Consequently, throughout the reign, censorial officials wishing to improve the quality and the morale of the troops offered many proposals: (1) for improving methods in the training divisions in the capital, (2) for extending and improving the military schools of the empire, and (3) for relying more freely on competitive military-service examinations to recruit competent officers.[297]

The need for extraordinary numbers of troops on the Manchu front evoked many controversial discussions about how best to augment the regular frontier garrisons. At first the standard device was to transfer forces from other frontier defense commands to Liaotung, but the other commands could not be drawn upon indefinitely. Besides, the transferred forces had even less zeal for fighting the Manchus than did those of the regular Liaotung command. Their detachments often disintegrated en route, or once arrived they proved to be more troublesome than helpful. In 1621 the supervising secretary Ts'ai Ssu-ch'ung and in 1622 the censor Tung Yü-ch'en complained vehemently about the lack of leadership and discipline in transferred forces.[298] At one point the supervising secretary Wang Chih-tao even argued that it would be preferable to rely on locally recruited Liaotung natives rather than on the transferred forces.[299]

For a time Manchus belonging to tribes that were antagonistic to Nurhaci volunteered their services to the Ming generals in Liaotung. One commander was reported to have accepted as many as 3,000 into his service in early 1621, and some were used in battle.[300] The supervising secretaries Ts'ai Ssu-ch'ung, Hsiao Chi, Ch'en Yin-ts'ung, and others, and several censors, including Wang Yeh-hao and Chiang Tung-ch'ien, repeatedly denounced this practice, feeling that such volunteers could not be trusted and that they formed a dangerous fifth column among the Ming forces.[301] It was finally decided that such volunteers should no longer be accepted into service, but presumably there were few subsequent occasions on which Manchus even offered to serve.

Some aboriginal tribes of south and southwestern China (those not involved in the southwestern rebellion) were called upon to send detachments of soldiers to Liaotung. The desertion rate among them was so high that in 1621 the Hukwang grand coordinator, whose province provided many such forces, urged that the aboriginal detachments be dismissed to return home.[302] The next year, however, the censor Tung Yü-ch'en advocated recruiting new forces among the aborigines for frontier service, and the idea was commended.[303] Apparently such forces continued to be used, for in 1626 the censor Liu Chih-feng felt moved to warn that they should be employed only with the greatest caution.[304]

Higher hopes were held by some—most notably by the frontier grand coordinator Wang Hua-chen—about reliance on Mongol allies, and heavy payments of reverse tribute from the Ming court kept the Mongols at least neutral throughout Hsi-tsung's reign. When Liao-yang fell to the Manchus in early 1621, the Shansi surveillance commissioner Kao Ch'u, who was on special duty in Liaotung as an army-inspecting circuit intendant, retreated with the army westward across the Liao River to Kuang-ning but reported that that bastion was indefensible and proposed abandoning it to the Mongols, who might hold it against the Manchus.[305] In 1622, when Wang Hua-chen and his supporters persisted in thinking that the Mongols were eager to join the war on the Ming side, the censor Hsia Chih-ling warned that the Mongols could not be trusted any more than enlisted Manchus, but thought they might render useful help if they were offered a bounty of 50 taels for each Manchu head they could produce.[306] The censors Huo Ying and Wang Ta-nien warned against China's being lulled into a trusting friendship with the Mongols and urged the strengthening of defenses against them as well as against the Manchus.[307] In 1623, when there were reports of Mongol raids on the frontier, the supervising secretary Chou Chih-kang urged that arrears in payments to the Mongols be made up, to prevent further attacks.[308] In 1626 the censor Li Mou-fang proposed that Wang Hua-chen, then awaiting execution in prison, be given an opportunity to redeem himself by inciting the Mongols to attack the Manchus, as Wang had always advocated doing. Hsi-tsung (that is, Wei Chung-hsien) rejected this idea as being silly.[309] But as late as mid-1627 the supervising secretary Li Lu-sheng still advocated in vain that China rely on the Mongols to crush the Manchus.[310]

The forces that did support the regular frontier garrisons were specially recruited mercenaries. Censorial officials were themselves active in recruiting work, as will be seen in Chapter 6. The idea of using censorial officials as recruiters was apparently first proposed in early 1621 by the supervising secretary Li Ching-po.[311] The suggestion was welcomed at court, especially by the investigating censor Fu Tsung-lung, who patriotically insisted on being allowed to go out to raise troops for Liaotung.[312] When regional inspectors were instructed to take on this additional duty, the supervising secretary Yang Tao-yin expressed grave misgivings. Yang believed that censors would be of little help in such work, and particularly that it reduced the dignity of their offices. The supervising secretary Sun Chieh soon complained that there was excessive recruiting but ineffective training.[313] But the recruiting of mercenaries continued unchecked. Late in 1621 the censor Yü Ho-chung, on duty as an inspector of the Grand Canal operations, proposed that one man be taken from each canal-transport unit to form a special brigade for frontier service, and when his idea was approved he recruited 130 soldiers in this fashion.[314]

Such troop-recruiting activities by censorial and other officials produced the mercenary troops on which the Ming state heavily depended for defense in its last years, but there were many difficulties in the system and many objections to it. As early as 1622, the supervising secretary Chu T'ung-meng complained that the number of new recruits who actually reached the frontier defense forces was far short of the number reportedly dispatched by the recruiters. He urged that personnel-accounting procedures at the frontier be revised and improved so that recruiters could be credited only with recruits actually delivered, and their expense allowances could be adjusted accordingly. It was ordered that the Ministry of War consider the matter.[315] Late that year the investigating censor Ch'en Pao-t'ai complained that troop recruiting was creating as much danger at home as it was providing support at the front, because it encouraged all kinds of adventurers to muster at state expense armed bands called "patriotic volunteers," who turned into bandits and rebels on the slightest pretext. He urged that much stricter controls be imposed on the recruiting activities, and Hsi-tsung approved his suggestion that severe punishments be threatened when anyone undertook to recruit troops without specific government authorization.[316] In mid-1623 the supervising secretary Yang Wei-hsin similarly complained that among the recruits there were many soldiers of fortune addicted to violence and abuses that disrupted the whole military establishment. His complaint was referred to the Ministry of War, and troop-recruiting went on, no doubt without any significant reforms.[317] In a rare editorial observation, the *Shih-lu* at one point comments on this situation as follows:

From the time when troubles first arose in the east, nothing entailed worse calamities than the recruiting of troops. Recruited troops for the most part were made up of village bullies, unable to defend against an enemy but more than able to create disturbances. In all, millions of taels were wasted on them but not a single decent soldier got to the front. The worst of them deserted and became bandits, and both the troublemakers and the starving joined them in rebellion. The heartland had many instances of this.[318]

Problems of supply and equipment at the frontier were immense, and provoked censorial officials to submit proposals about revitalizing military agricultural operations, reforming the horse-supply system, and so on.[319] The supervising secretary Ts'ai Ssu-ch'ung asked for reforms in the techniques of accounting for supplies and equipment at the front.[320] In 1621, the supervising secretary Li Ch'un-hua persuaded Hsi-tsung to divert 100,000 taels of palace-construction funds to Shan-hai-kuan to repair the Great Wall there.[321] In addition, the supervising secretary Hou Chen-yang prompted a decision to divert winter-uniform textiles to Liaotung for the winter of 1621–22 rather than issue them as usual to the training-division troops in the capital, who had to be satisfied with equivalent monetary allowances.[322] By the last months of Hsi-tsung's reign, censorial memorials urging action and reforms indicate that after several years of stability, the supply situation at the front had become precarious, probably because of the steady diversion of state funds into Wei Chung-hsien's construction projects and other schemes.[323]

Since the Chinese had been acquainted with representatives of the early modern West for a century, it is not surprising that censorial memorials of Hsi-tsung's time reveal an interest in using firearms to fight the Manchus. China's own independent developments along this line had long since stagnated, but after the Manchu invasion of Liaotung suggestions were made that Portuguese cannons be obtained from Macao. The leader in this modernizing effort was Hsü Kuang-ch'i (Paul Hsü), a disciple of Matteo Ricci who had helped translate many Western technological works into Chinese and who eventually became the most distinguished Ming protector of the Jesuit mission.[324] Late in 1619 Hsü, as junior supervisor of instruction and concurrently investigating censor, was assigned to train new recruits at T'ung-chou, east of Peking. He requested four modern cannons from Macao, but they never arrived; and Hsü encountered other frustrations as well.[325] Early in 1621 he took sick leave. Before long the censor Fang Chen-ju urged that Hsü be recalled to duty, specifically to supervise an urgent cannon-production project for the Ministry of Works.[326] Deliberation was ordered. In 1622 the supervising secretary Hou Chen-ch'ang and the censors Chang Hsiu-te and Wen Kao-mo successively urged an emergency program of firearms development, and specifically asked that Portuguese help be sought.[327] The censor P'eng K'un-hua memorialized in the same vein in 1623.[328] In consequence of these urgings, Portuguese cannons and even Portuguese gunners were brought into use on the northern frontiers by the supreme commanders Sun Ch'eng-tsung and Yüan Ch'ung-huan in the last years of the reign.

Aside from problems related to defense of the Liaotung front, the censorial officials throughout Hsi-tsung's reign showed great concern about preparing the defenses of the capital and the palace, and about improving the police system of the capital to prevent thievery and disorderliness.[329] They proposed punitive action against small-scale domestic banditry and rebellions, which were apparently becoming common in Hsi-tsung's last years.[330] They submitted proposals about dealing with the Dutch in the Pescadores and the White Lotus rebellion in Shantung.[331] But their major concern in the military realm, aside from the Manchus, was the protracted rebellion of aboriginal tribes in the southwest.

For the most part, proposals concerning the southwestern rebellion were submitted by regional inspectors of the provinces that were directly affected — Kweichow, Szechwan, Hukwang, Yunnan, and Kwangsi.[332] But censors and supervising secretaries on duty in the capital discussed strategies and problems of the southwest as freely as they did those of the Manchu front.[333] One of the solutions often proposed was coordination of defense efforts among the various provinces in which the aboriginal rebels operated.[334] And one of the most constructive proposals advocated building a road from Szechwan south into Yunnan to permit assaults on the rebels from the rear. It was offered in 1623 by the censors Lo Ju-yüan and Fu Tsung-lung and the supervising secretary Yang Tung-ch'ao, and it was revived in 1626 by the censor Yang Fang-sheng.[335] The proposed road was apparently not completed by the end of Hsi-tsung's reign, and its construction may not have been undertaken.

Among the censorial officials most actively interested in military matters was Ts'ai Ssu-ch'ung, who was chief supervising secretary of the Office of Scrutiny for War from the second month of 1621 until the third month of 1622. In little more than one year, according to entries in the *Shih-lu,* Ts'ai submitted 25 major memorials about defense against the Manchus, the southwestern rebellion, military personnel administration, military supplies, and troop-recruiting.[336] He seems to have taken quite seriously the specialized responsibilities of his office, for the *Shih-lu* chronicles of this period do not refer to any memorial from him that pertains to anything other than the military.

Counsel Concerning Judicial Matters

Censorial memorials of 1620–27 that pertain to judicial matters fall generally into three categories: (1) requests that pending judicial action be completed without delay or that sentences be implemented or increased in severity; (2) protests against too harsh sentences; and (3) suggestions about judicial and penal administration in general.

A proposal submitted in 1623 by the supervising secretary Hsü K'o-cheng is representative of many memorials in the first category. Hsü had previously impeached a county official for venality. When the trial results became known, Hsü protested that they were unsatisfactory, particularly since no provision had been made for confiscation of the official's illegal gains. He demanded a more strict inquiry, and Hsi-tsung ordered that it be undertaken.[337] In the same year, the supervising secretaries Ch'eng Ming-shu and Chou Shih-p'u both protested that no action had ever been taken against eunuchs who had previously assaulted and humiliated a civil official.[338] In 1625 the probationary censor Men K'o-hsin complained that Hsiung T'ing-pi's death sentence, rendered in 1622, had not yet been carried out, and thus he finally precipitated Hsiung's execution.[339]

Censorial officials sometimes protested against sentences that they considered too lenient. In 1623, when Cheng Yang-hsing, father of Shen-tsung's favorite consort, was sentenced to live in exile away from the capital, the Nanking censor Ch'en Pi-ch'ien argued that he should have been punished more severely.[340] After Wei Chung-hsien's rise to power, censorial officials sometimes demanded that old Tung-lin enemies who were already out of office should now be deprived of civil-service status entirely, or be forced to pay punitive damages. It was at the urging of the censor Liu Hui, for example, that the relatives of Hsiung T'ing-pi were after his death ruined by demands for damages.[341]

More commonly, censorial officials tried to rectify injustice by defending persons who they thought were wrongfully accused or sentenced. Thus in the early years of Hsi-tsung's reign, the censor Shen Hsün defended the vice minister of war Chang Hao-ming against accusations of murder; the censor Wei Kuang-hsü tried to rectify unjust treatment previously accorded several officials in the 1615 controversy over "the case of the attack with the club"; and a host of censors and supervising secretaries in both Peking and Nanking protested the dismissal from the civil service of the censor Liu Chung-ch'ing, who had offended the emperor by denouncing the grand secretary Liu I-ching.[342] Most such efforts were useless. In one interesting case, a county magistrate in Shantung was accused of fleeing his post during the White Lotus uprising and was proclaimed a traitor and fugitive from justice—until the supervising secretary Kuo Yün-hou cleared his name by demonstrating that he had in fact been killed at his post by the rebels.[343]

After Wei Chung-hsien assumed power, censorial officials occasionally tried ineffectively to defend less controversial persons.[344] But they failed to protest against the major injustices of Wei's regime, including the judicial murders of Yang Lien and other Tung-lin men.

In regard to general judicial and penal administration, censorial officials often recommended reforms in procedures.[345] Both before and during the Wei Chung-hsien era, they regularly asked lenience in punishments, and especially in the use of the dreaded cangue.[346] In 1621 the censor-in-chief Wang Te-wan protested that the Ministry of Justice was holding more than 800 persons accused of serious crimes whose cases had not yet been disposed of, and he begged that many be pardoned.[347] And in 1625 the supervising secretary Chou Chih-kang of the Office of Scrutiny for Justice urged that there be careful reviews of the cases of all prisoners then in custody throughout the empire and that all those who were pardonable be released.[348] Both of these proposals were favorably received by Hsi-tsung.

SOME TENTATIVE EVALUATIONS

At the end of Chapter 4, I concluded that censorial officials in the decade 1424–34 were conscientiously active and responsibly true to their calling, at least in denouncing wayward officials and submitting counsel, though they were somewhat less zealously aggressive than might have been justifiable. What general conclusions can be drawn about censorial service for 1620–27?

First of all, it must be acknowledged that censorial officials under Hsi-tsung were furiously active—far more so than under Jen-tsung and Hsüan-tsung. Whereas Hsüan-tsung often complained that the censorial officials were negligent, Hsi-tsung's principal complaint was that they made too much of a fuss.

It has been noted, however, that both censorial impeachments and proposals were received less favorably by Hsi-tsung than they had been by Jen-tsung and Hsüan-tsung. In Chapter 4, I suggested that under such emperors as Jen-tsung and Hsüan-tsung imperial approval might well be taken as a reliable measure of the validity and appropriateness of a censorial memorial. It would undoubtedly be going too far to suggest that for Hsi-tsung's era the reverse is true—that imperial approval might serve generally to discredit a censorial memorial; but Hsi-tsung's character was such, and general conditions were such, that imperial disapproval certainly cannot be adopted as a measure of the invalidity of a censorial memorial.

Nevertheless, at least the effectiveness of censorial memorials can be measured by imperial approval.* In general, censorial officials could achieve what they wished to achieve only if the emperor approved of their denunciations and proposals. Inasmuch as they failed to win such approval more often than had their predecessors of 1424–34, censorial officials under Hsi-tsung must be judged to have been less effective.

This judgment can be modified significantly when one compares censorial activities in the two periods into which Hsi-tsung's reign can logically be divided: the 50-month early period, continuing into 1624, when the "good elements" dominated the court, and the later period of 34 months when the Wei Chung-hsien faction dominated the court. There is not much difference between the periods in terms of the number of memorials submitted:

	1620–24	*1624–27*
Impeachments		
Number submitted	330	196
Rate per month	6.6	5.8
Proposals		
Number submitted	791	505
Rate per month	15.8	14.9

The slight lessening of activity in Wei Chung-hsien's time seems quite insignificant. But there are very significant differences between the two periods in their patterns of imperial responses to memorials:

	1620–24	*1624–27*
Impeachments		
No action taken	176 (53%)	32 (16%)
Investigation or trial ordered	121 (37%)	47 (24%)
Punitive action directly ordered	33 (10%)	117 (60%)
Total	330	196
Proposals		
Approved	187 (24%)	260 (51%)
Deliberation ordered	365 (46%)	175 (35%)
Disapproved, or no action noted	239 (30%)	70 (14%)
Total	791	505

* To be sure, the real intention of a memorialist in any particular instance might not have been to win imperial approval, or might have been to achieve something that could be achieved without winning imperial approval. An enemy official, for example, might be hounded into retirement by his attackers even though the em-

It is clear that censorial officials received much more direct and favorable responses to their memorials when Wei Chung-hsien was in power than before his ascendancy. No action, the common fate of impeachments submitted while the "good elements" were dominant, became a relatively rare fate later, and the rate of direct approval of impeachments rose dramatically from 10 per cent to 60 per cent. Approvals of proposals rose markedly from 24 per cent to 51 per cent, and disapprovals fell from 30 per cent to 14 per cent. The conclusion must be that censorial memorials were much more effective under Wei Chung-hsien than before his dominance.

From what has already been said, it should be clear why this was so. The officials with whom Wei Chung-hsien packed the censorial agencies after 1624 were content to cater to his whims. With rare exceptions, they did nothing that was likely to offend him. They did not object to his influence over the emperor, they did not object to the honors heaped upon him and his relatives, they did not object to his expenditures on palace adornments, they did not object to the servile flattery of his sycophants, they did not object to his treatment of the officials who had previously opposed him or his favorites. Their memorials were effective in that they easily won his approval, but their service in a larger sense was so ineffective that they only hastened the state toward its destruction.

The censorial officials of the early 1620's were probably no more effective in this larger sense. They failed to make Hsi-tsung a responsible ruler, failed to stem eunuch influence and the rise of Wei Chung-hsien, failed to prevent a succession of military disasters, failed to alleviate the demoralization and oppression of the people at large, and failed to halt the general deterioration of the state. But they did recognize the major problems of their time, and they vigorously warned against the dangers of imperial irresponsibility, of eunuch influence, of bureaucratic partisanship, of the Manchu conquests in Liaotung, of the aboriginal uprising in the southwest, and of general economic distress. At least they tried to affect the course of Chinese history, as their successors did not. Given the circumstances they faced, it is difficult to see how they might have avoided failure.

---

peror disapproved of the accusations; and it might be argued that Yang Lien, in submitting his famous denunciation of Wei Chung-hsien, realized he had no hope of terminating Wei's influence but wished merely to set the record straight for posterity—or possibly that he even courted martyrdom deliberately.

Chapter six

Censorial Distractions and Discipline

Modern students of organization theory might suppose that the effectiveness of a government control system such as that of Ming China would be safeguarded in certain ways. They might expect that the detachment and objectivity of censorial personnel would be guaranteed by denying them any administrative powers and especially any judicial powers. They might also expect that censorial officials would enjoy freedom of action protected by security of tenure and immunity from punishment. What has been said in the preceding chapters, however, clearly indicates that the Chinese did not traditionally share such beliefs and expectations. To understand the effectiveness of the Ming censorial agencies and their special roles in government, one must realize that censorial officials regularly engaged in non-censorial activities and that they were also regularly punished. Exploring this aspect of Ming censorial operations is the purpose of the present chapter.

NON-CENSORIAL ACTIVITIES OF CENSORIAL OFFICIALS

It is very difficult to draw the line between a solely censorial involvement in government and a more substantive involvement of a directive or magisterial sort. In many instances the prescribed surveillance duties of censorial officials could have led them, more or less by accident, into playing something more than surveillance roles. Thus the close relations between the Offices of Scrutiny and the corresponding Ministries could have made it difficult for supervising secretaries to avoid influencing administrative decisions in the Ministries. In addition, since both censors and supervising secretaries participated in the great court assemblies at which policy recommendations were agreed on, even if their sole assignment had been to rectify impropriety, it would have been difficult to exclude them from the policy-formulating process itself. Also, when censors and provincial surveillance commissioners toured the local areas, they could hardly have refrained from giving advice and otherwise influencing local administration so that they became something more than visiting inspectors. No control system could possibly prevent the controllers from taking some part in administration.

But the censorial officials' intrusions into non-surveillance realms were not accidental. To be sure, in all their activities their principal responsibility was essentially a censorial one; but they were expected to be much more than mere observers and critics. The censor-in-chief, as one of the "seven chief ministers" at the capital, was one of the chief executive counselors of the realm. The fact that all of the speaking officials freely offered advice about government policies and operations gave them something akin to legislative powers. And the regional inspector's relations with the grand coordinator and the "three provincial offices" made him somewhat like an adjunct provincial governor with very tangible executive powers. As has been noted, it was sometimes objected that non-censorial responsibilities distracted the censorial officials from their principal duties, which suggests that Ming Chinese did indeed have some uneasiness when censorial and administrative activities were not differentiated. But there seems to have been no thought that censorial officials should be rigidly excluded from executive powers or from non-surveillance activities.

These attitudes about the censorial system were somewhat analogous to Chinese attitudes about the judicial system. It was traditionally expected that magistrates would themselves perform the functions of prosecutors, judges, and juries. Good men by Chinese definition could be expected to perform well all those duties that in the Anglo-Saxon tradition are considered mutually prejudicial. To preserve objectivity—or, more accurately, a sense of propriety—the Chinese relied on Confucian indoctrination through education, more than on organizational and procedural safeguards. At least, there was much more ambivalence about such matters in the Chinese tradition than there is in our own. The principle of separation of powers could be cited when it served a purpose, or it could be ignored. Thus late in 1620, when Hsiung T'ing-pi was under severe censorial attack, it was ordered—at his specific request—that his principal attackers go to Liaotung to investigate the charges against him. Some of Hsiung's friends protested that accusers ought not investigate their own charges, and a supervising secretary who was not involved in the attack was finally sent to investigate.[1] On the other hand, in 1623 the supervising secretary Li Ch'un-yeh impeached certain frontier officials and was ordered to go to investigate the charges. Li suggested that he ought to decline, and the emperor on second thought agreed that sending a different investigator would be convenient. The emperor called on the Offices of Scrutiny to propose someone else for the assignment, but they unanimously nominated Li. So Li undertook the investigation after all.[2]

The expectation that censorial officials would perform tasks that cannot be considered mere surveillance was manifested in both general and specific prescriptions. The most general prescription applied to censors traveling on commission and to provincial surveillance commissioners. It was specifically directed that wherever they toured they should call the attention of local authorities to anything they felt ought to be done, and should make sure it was done.[3] Though they were expected to memorialize about important matters, they were authorized to give immediate decisions about minor matters.[4] It was not just by accident, therefore, that censorial officials on tour served as administrative superiors of the local authorities rather than merely as censorial inspectors.

This general authorization for censorial officials to render decisions and give directions was supplemented by more specific directives that involved them heavily in non-surveillance activities—and most heavily in judicial activities.

Censorial Participation in Judicial Affairs

The Provincial Surveillance Offices were at all times judicial as well as censorial agencies, and their judicial functions seem to have gradually overshadowed their censorial functions as the Ming dynasty grew old. The Censorate was also a judicial as well as a censorial agency, as is indicated by its inclusion—with the Ministry of Justice and the Grand Court of Revision—in the "three judicial offices."

Because they were judicial agencies, the Provincial Surveillance Offices and the Censorate were routinely involved in the ratification of judicial sentences. In general, accused criminals were tried by magistrates of original jurisdiction (probably most commonly by county magistrates), and sentences were then ratified in successive reviews by supervisory agencies in the appropriate hierarchies.[5] Case records involving serious sentences—and at times the prisoners themselves—were eventually sent to the capital for examination by superior offices there. Those coming through Regional Military Commissions or from the Guards and Battalions of the metropolitan areas were sent to the appropriate Chief Military Commissions; those coming through Provincial Administration Offices or from the Prefectures of the metropolitan areas were sent to the Ministry of Justice; and those coming through a Provincial Surveillance Office were sent to the appropriate Circuit in the Censorate. After examination and approval or modification by these agencies, the cases were submitted to the Grand Court of Revision for ratification. If the Grand Court of Revision found no evidence of injustice, it returned a report of approval—or, in very important cases, memorialized for imperial approval and then reported. If it found evidence of injustice, it was empowered to return a case to the original magistrate for retrial, or to transfer it to a different magistrate for retrial, or to request that it be considered by a great court assembly, or in the last resort to request a decision by the emperor.[6]

Five kinds of punishment were prescribed by law: (1) from 10 to 50 strokes of the light bamboo; (2) from 60 to 100 strokes of the heavy bamboo; (3) from 1 to 3 years of temporary banishment coupled with from 60 to 100 strokes of the heavy bamboo; (4) permanent banishment from one's home at a distance of from 2,000 to 3,000 miles *(li)* coupled with 100 strokes of the heavy bamboo; and (5) death, either by strangulation or decapitation.[7] All cases involving the death penalty seem to have been submitted through normal channels to the capital for ratification. In 1393 it was ordered that magistrates at the provincial level could summarily inflict beatings but should submit all other sentences for ratification. In 1439 there was a relaxation of this requirement. Thereafter, apparently only death sentences required ratification of this sort. Sentences of banishment could be ratified at an intermediate stage—in the provinces by Surveillance Offices, and in the metropolitan areas by regional inspectors acting jointly with officials deputed from the Ministry of Justice.[8] However, sentences in cases originating in the capital seem to have always required ratification by the Grand Court of Revision.[9]

Superimposed upon this system of ratification through normal channels was another practice that might be called judicial review. It became customary for the three judicial offices to conduct judicial reviews of all prisoners awaiting punishment in the capital, once every autumn and once every summer. At these times great imperial mercy was shown in reducing and commuting sentences, and the responsible officials had a final opportunity to make sure that injustices were prevented. Similarly, censors, supervising secretaries, and officials of the Ministry of Justice were frequently sent out to conduct judicial reviews for prisoners awaiting punishment in local prisons. Judicial review in the provinces seems to have served partly as a substitute for the ratification otherwise conducted by the Grand Court of Revision, but for the most part it supplemented such routine ratification.[10] As has been noted in Chapter 3, regional inspectors and Surveillance Office circuit intendants were expected to conduct judicial reviews wherever they inspected.

One source indicates that the process of judicial review included five basic steps: (1) inspection of the case record to determine the details from beginning to end; (2) consultation with the senior local official to determine the justification of the sentence; (3) consultation with the official who had been in charge of the original trial, to determine the means of obtaining a confession; (4) consultation with the coroner or police officers and the witnesses to determine the reasons for the original charges; and (5) consultation with and observation of the offender to determine the entire circumstances of his offense.[11]

Surveillance commissioners, investigating censors, and to a lesser extent supervising secretaries all regularly participated in these routine reviews and ratifications of judicial sentences. As was noted in Chapter 3, they also accepted special complaints of injustice submitted by or on behalf of persons who were sentenced; and supervising secretaries handled appeals made as a last resort by striking the Complaint Drum. Such judicial activities must have been a heavy burden at all times on both the Censorate and the Surveillance Offices. It is perhaps noteworthy that all men who were assigned to the Censorate for a probationary period before being given substantive appointments as investigating censors were known as "sentencers" or "regulators of punishments" and were said to have passed the probationary period "regulating the Censorate's criminal cases" to gain experience.[12] It is also noteworthy, as will be shown subsequently, that a number of censors and surveillance commissioners who were removed from office were so disciplined because they "were not versed in punishments." It has repeatedly been observed that the judicial obligations of Surveillance Offices gradually overwhelmed their censorial functions; at times it seemed that the Censorate itself was in similar danger. Thus a chief minister of the Grand Court of Revision once complained to Jen-tsung as follows:

The Censorate is charged with [serving as your majesty's] ears and eyes and [guarding] the fundamental laws; it is employed to remove the evil, to honor the pure, and to clarify injustice. But now it is solely used to adjudicate criminal cases. This violates the dynasty's original intention in establishing "guardians of the customs and fundamental laws."[13]

Since the *Shih-lu* chronicles are devoted principally to matters that received imperial attention, the routine review and ratification processes of the judicial agencies get little attention in them, and it would be impossible on the basis of *Shih-lu* entries to make any fruitful quantitative analyses of such activities. But some entries are illuminating. For example, it is recorded that in 1428 the vice censor-in-chief Ch'en Mien, the assistant censors-in-chief Li Chün and Ling Yen-ju, the investigating censor Miao Jang, and three officials of the Grand Court of Revision were all imprisoned for mismanaging a criminal case. The case involved three battalion commanders who had been found guilty of stealing military provisions and had been sentenced to death. They protested injustice and their case eventually came for review to the Censorate and the Grand Court of Revision. Ch'en Mien and his colleagues changed the sentence to beating with the heavy bamboo. On learning of this, Hsüan-tsung demanded a re-investigation, because it was evident that either the original sentence or the changed sentence was grossly improper. Senior officials of the three judicial offices in the capital took the matter under consideration and reported that the original sentence was appropriate and that the offenders should indeed be put to death. Hsüan-tsung then ordered Ch'en Mien and his fellow reviewers put in prison, but he almost immediately relented and pardoned them.[14]

During the decade 1424–34, great judicial reviews of prisoners in the capital were conducted 20 times.[15] Censorate personnel regularly participated in them, and late in 1424 it was ordered that supervising secretaries should thenceforth take part in them also.[16] The numbers of prisoners involved varied from a few hundred to more than 5,000, according to the frequency with which reviews were held during a given period.[17] The following is a representative *Shih-lu* report of such a judicial review held in 1427:

Seventh month, the day *keng-tzu*: The minister of justice Chin Ch'un, the Censorate's censor-in-chief of the left Liu Kuan, . . . and others made a thorough classification of all minor and major prisoners and memorialized requesting that they be cleared out and disposed of. The emperor inspected it and decreed to Chin Ch'un and the others:

"As for those who rebel, are unfilial, take human life, rob with violence, assemble mobs, thieve, resist arrest, wound others, deliberately burn down public buildings or the residences of officials and people, forge orders, fabricate credentials, and forcibly seize the wives and daughters of respectable families, let them all be dealt with according to the law.

"As for those who steal what they are themselves responsible for guarding, who accept bribes to pervert the law, or who steal government livestock, money, and provisions, recover the things that they have stolen or accepted but excuse them from the death penalty.

"As for those subject to temporary banishment or permanent banishment, or to beating with the light bamboo or with the heavy bamboo, assign them to transport-labor according to the seriousness of their offenses.

"As for laborers and artisans subject to temporary banishment, assign them to transport-labor according to the number of years of banishment.

"As for those who should atone in commutation, let it be as prescribed by law."

In all, 2,465 persons were thus dispatched from prison.[18]

It was in character for Hsüan-tsung to be most cautious about dealing out severe punishments. In 1426 Liu Kuan memorialized for permission to execute 70 fierce bandits and murderers then held in prison. The emperor acknowledged that by law they might not be pardoned, but he ordered that another judicial review be conducted. Liu replied that such reviews had been conducted repeatedly without revealing any possibility of injustice and that the prisoners really deserved to be put to death. Hsüan-tsung finally assented, but when audience had been terminated he nevertheless sent a eunuch to tell Liu that the executions should be suspended and that a full report of the cases should be sent in for his own inspection.[19]

In addition to the general judicial reviews at the capital, censors and supervising secretaries occasionally conducted or took part in reviews of particular cases when specially ordered to do so.[20] Also, on 12 recorded occasions during the years 1424–34, regional inspectors and provincial surveillance commissioners were ordered to conduct special reviews for prisoners held in the provinces. Usually these prisoners were captured bandits, and at times they were quite numerous. There were reviews, for example, of 275 captured bandits in 1433 and of 224 in 1434.[21] The following, from 1434, is a rare example of a case in which the eventual results are given at least in part:

Eleventh month, the day *kuei-mao*: The regional inspector of Chekiang, Wang Hsien, and others memorialized: "In regard to the fierce bandits of Chin-hua, Ch'u-chou, and other localities, we lately received an order to review the facts before executing them, so as to bring to light any who were falsely accused or wrongly imprisoned. Now, together with the three provincial offices, we have reviewed the facts about the fleeing bandits Chou Yin-ching and others, 53 men. Those who confess their crimes are 51 men; those wrongly imprisoned are 2 men."

The emperor ordered the Censorate to instruct Wang Hsien to assemble the officials to review the facts once more and, if there were no other injustices, to carry out executions as previously commanded. Those wrongly imprisoned were to be released forthwith.[22]

The *Shih-lu* chronicles for 1424–34 record the receipt by supervising secretaries of six appeals made at the Complaint Drum.[23] One dramatic exoneration that resulted has been described in Chapter 3. When such appeals were made, and also frequently when impeachment memorials were submitted, investigation and clarification of the facts were entrusted to investigating censors—or, if investigation had to be conducted in the provinces, to regional inspectors acting jointly either with provincial surveillance commissioners or even with officials of all of the three provincial offices. During the period 1424–34 one investigation was entrusted to supervising secretaries and two to Surveillance Offices alone.[24] Counting these and all those in which investigating censors participated, according to entries in the *Shih-lu*, there were 26 such cases between 1424 and 1434, involving more than 63 accused persons. The posts and ranks of persons subjected to censorial investigations are analyzed in Table 14. Only 3 of the 26 cases actually originated with censorial accusations.

Results of these investigations are seldom reported. However, it is clear that they eventually resulted in death penalties for 1 battalion commander, 1 deserted soldier, and 2 civilians; unspecified punishment for more than 3 civilians and 1 investigating censor; demotion for 3 investigating censors and also for 1 vice minister, 5 directors, 2 vice directors, and 7 secretaries, all of Ministry Bureaus; disgrace by demotion to the status of common soldiers for 22 military officers; and imprisonment for 1 military officer.[25] Also, the investigations clearly resulted in the exoneration of 19 accused persons—18 civilians and 1 assistant regional military commissioner.[26]

One *Shih-lu* entry, from 1434, relating to the exoneration of a military officer by censorial investigation is perhaps worth noting in full:

Eighth month, the day *wu-shen*: The Liaotung assistant regional military commissioner Kuang Shun was restored to duty. When Kuang Shun originally went to his post, he traveled in the company of the Guard commanders Wang Hsiang, Chang Jung, and three others—five men. Arriving at Chichou, they separated and spent the night in civilians' homes. Chang Jung became drunk, cut his own throat, and died. His younger brother Chang Yung reported this to Kuang Shun. Kuang Shun, Wang Hsiang, and the others were suspicious about the circumstances. They seized Chang Yung and sent a man to escort him in fetters to the Ministry of Justice, where he stood trial. Chang Yung, hating Kuang Shun for arresting him, falsely accused Kuang Shun of having murdered Chang Jung. Kuang Shun was accordingly arrested and brought to the capital, and he was sentenced to severe punishment for plotting murder. But Kuang Shun's wife complained of injustice, and the legal offices delayed a long time about carrying out the sentence.

The emperor said: "What hatred did Kuang Shun have for Chang Jung? Why did he plot?" He sent the censor Chang Ts'ung and the imperial bodyguard battalion commander Yin Yüan to go to the Chi-chou places where Chang Jung and the others spent the night to investigate the matter. All the members of the family with whom Chang Jung had lodged said that he dreaded going to Liaotung to guard the border; sitting or lying down, he talked ceaselessly about it. Very late, in a drunken state, he cut his own throat. Actually, he was not murdered. Chang Ts'ung and the others returned and reported. The emperor said: "I certainly suspected it had not been plotted by Kuang Shun. If there had not been an investigation, how should the injustice have been cleared up? Now the truth is obtained. Forthwith release Kuang Shun and restore him to duty. Also release Chang Jung's younger brother."[27]

Data for 1620–27 relating to censorial participation in judicial activities of these sorts is much more meager. The *Ming History,* which notes 20 general judicial reviews of capital prisoners for 1424–34, makes no mention of any such reviews in its chronicle of Hsi-tsung's reign. *Shih-lu* entries indicate that requests for such reviews were approved in 1621 and in 1625, but no results are reported.[28] The *Shih-lu* chronicles for 1620–27 do not mention that any complaints were made via the Complaint Drum and they note only seven instances in which the charges made in impeachments were verified by censorial investigations: three by supervising secretaries, and four in the provinces—one by a regional inspector alone, the others made jointly by regional inspectors and grand coordinators. In one of these cases the supervising secretary Chu T'ung-meng investigated charges against the Liaotung supreme commander Hsiung T'ing-pi; his investigation in the end merely rationalized Hsiung's dismissal.[29] In other instances, a grand coordinator was exonerated by a regional inspector's investigation of charges that he had committed thievery, and a vice commissioner of a Salt Distribution Commission was cleared of unspecified charges by a joint investigation by a grand coordinator and a regional inspector.[30] The other charges—against two investigating censors, one grand coordinator, one surveillance vice commissioner, and one county magistrate—were similarly investigated, but the results are not clearly indicated.[31]

The judicial activities so far discussed—judicial reviews, ratification of sentences, and investigation of charges—of course have an appropriate censorial character and do not relate to the general principle that censorial officials were authorized to exercise administrative and magisterial powers. What was distinctly non-censorial about censorial officials' participation in judicial affairs was that they had the right to serve as magistrates of original jurisdiction themselves and even to inflict punishments.

When impeachments were submitted, the accused persons were sometimes pardoned and sometimes subjected to investigation, as has been noted. But it was also common for emperors to order them tried and sentenced, or even to order them punished forthwith. When the punishment that was ordered was demotion in office, dismissal from the service, or the like, it was naturally the Ministry of Personnel or the Ministry of War that carried out the order. But when nonadministrative types of punishments were prescribed, or when trials were ordered, censorial officials were often called on for action. Common practice called for trials or punishments to be carried out by (1) the judicial offices, including the Censorate; (2) the Censorate and the Ministry of Justice; (3) an appropriate regional inspector; (4) an appropriate Surveillance Office; or (5) a specially designated investigating censor not serving as a regional inspector. With such imperial authorization, any censorial official could serve as a magistrate of original jurisdiction and sentence any offender, or could carry out any sentence. The Provincial Surveillance Offices and the Censorate itself even had their own prisons in which accused persons could be confined pending trial or the carrying out of sentence.

Moreover, censorial officials could try, sentence, and punish certain types of offenders even without such specific imperial authorization. Investigating censors on tour in the provinces, and surveillance commissioners as well, were generally authorized to take judicial and punitive action of these sorts on their own authority against any person not having status in the civil or military officialdom and in addition against any civil official on duty outside the capital with grade 6 or lower rank. In the case of all military officers, all capital officials, and all civil officials on duty in the provinces ranking 5b or higher, the censorial officials could only submit impeachments unless they were specifically authorized to take other action.[32] But since the vast majority of civil servants were in the vulnerable group—on duty in the provinces and ranking 6a or lower—the touring censor or surveillance commissioner had significant punitive powers. He could inflict up to 100 blows of the heavy bamboo on civilians and low-ranking civil officials entirely on his own authority, without any need to seek ratification of the sentence at any level. Moreover, beating with the bamboo, though technically one of the lesser punishments, could actually be a very severe one; for the first blow usually drew blood, and application of more than fifty blows was often fatal.[33] Thus anyone who could on his own authority impose 100 blows must have had the real power to send a man to his death. That this power was indeed used is plainly indicated in a proclamation of 1439 that warned censors against "maliciously punishing to please themselves and repeatedly flogging men to death."[34] And it was no doubt with this consideration in mind that Matteo Ricci wrote that the regional inspector was "naturally respected and feared by everyone" because he had "the power to impose capital punishment."[35] That any magistrate had equal power over the citizenry at large was not impressive; it was the censorial official's arbitrary punitive power over other officials that gave him particular prestige.

Specific instances of censorial officials' meting out punishments on their own authority are naturally rarely encountered in the *Shih-lu* chronicles, since they did not require imperial sanction. But a few cases are referred to. It is clear that regional inspectors freely dismissed students from state schools.[36] In 1430, the Kiangsi regional inspector Liu Po-ta had traveling with him a National University student who abused people, and Liu punished him for this offense.[37] The censor Li Li is said to have cruelly punished village elders and others while on troop-purifying duty in 1428.[38] In 1430 the Nanking censor Chang K'ai, in impeaching the Nanking minister and vice minister of justice for gross abuses committed by their subordinates, reported that the subordinate officials and functionaries who were directly responsible had already been seized and tried.[39] In 1434, when the Nanking censor Shu Chi inspected an Office of Produce Levies in the Southern Metropolitan Area, he found that bamboo and lumber accumulated there had been left exposed to the weather, so that much of it had rotted. He impeached various officials of the Ministry of Works for failing to give proper supervision; and he reported that the officials and functionaries of the Office of Produce Levies itself had already been seized and sentenced to punishment, presumably by himself.[40]

In addition to such specific cases, the *Shih-lu* chronicles for 1424–34 include numerous reaffirmations of the general authorization for censorial officials to punish on their own authority. For example, when Wang Lai was given the commission of regional inspector in the Southern Metropolitan Area, he received special instructions to evaluate lesser functionaries there, and the instructions happened to include the words "request a decision from above." Wang protested, saying: "As for removing lesser functionaries who harm the people, I only fear lest it not be done quickly. If it is necessary to submit requests before action can be taken, the people will suffer greatly." Hsüan-tsung promptly amended the instructions to make it clear that Wang could indeed punish on his own authority.[41] But such reaffirmations are not encountered in the *Shih-lu* of 1620–27, and the only seemingly relevant case from Hsi-tsung's time is that of the censor Lin Ju-chu, who had two eunuchs beaten in 1624. For doing so, Lin himself was eventually beaten and dismissed from the civil service.[42]

Instances in which censorial officials were specifically ordered to try persons are analyzed in Table 15 (1424–34) and Table 16 (1620–27). The results of such trials are seldom reported in the *Shih-lu;* but those results that are recorded are itemized in Table 17 (1424–34) and Table 18 (1620–27). The cases that are tabulated include trials conducted by the Censorate alone, or by regional inspectors and Surveillance Offices jointly (common in 1424–34, but no occurrences in 1620–27), or by Surveillance Offices alone (common in 1424–34, but no occurrences in 1620–27), or by regional inspectors and grand coordinators jointly (no occurrences in 1424–34, but common in 1620–27), or very commonly by regional inspectors alone.[43] By no means all of the cases originated in censorial impeachments, nor did censorial officials handle the actual trials of all those they impeached who were ordered tried. However, it is apparent that no category of persons was excluded from censorial trials.

The tabulations do not include trials conducted by the legal offices in general, or by "the Censorate and the Ministry," or by great court assemblies in which censors and also supervising secretaries played some part.[44] They reveal exclusively those cases in which censorial officials—primarily investigating censors—had principal if not sole responsibility for the conduct of trials and the sentencing of offenders.

Table 19 analyzes instances during the period 1424–34 in which censorial officials were specifically ordered to punish persons who had been impeached. The records throw no light on the manner in which these orders were carried out. Whether or not punishments were imposed without formal trials is not wholly clear. The Chinese terminology seems to imply that this was indeed the case, but it is possible that these cases were in no way different from those of persons ordered tried (analyzed in Table 15). The officials concerned were mostly regional inspectors, though in some cases Surveillance Offices were also ordered to punish impeached persons. Comparable entries do not occur in the *Shih-lu* chronicles for 1620–27, except that regional inspectors were regularly ordered to collect punitive damages from persons already convicted and sentenced, or from their relatives. For example, in 1626 the regional inspector Hsü Chi reported on the collection of damages in the case of Ku Ta-chang, a Ministry of Rites official who had been sentenced to death and had committed suicide in prison in 1625. Hsü reported that he had collected 17,500 taels of assessed damages, that 10,365 taels remained to be collected, and that he believed he could make up this deficiency by selling lands belonging to the Ku family. He was ordered to do so promptly.[45]

One of the most complex judicial cases recorded in the *Shih-lu*, showing many different facets of censorial participation in judicial processes, is the following, from 1431:

Eleventh month, the day *i-ch'ou*: Supervising secretaries of the six Offices of Scrutiny, Nien Fu and others, memorialized impeaching the Censorate's censor-in-chief of the right Ku Tso, the vice censor-in-chief of the left Ch'en Mien, the investigating censors Ch'iu Ling and Ch'en Jui, the assistant regional military commissioner Lu Tseng of Hukwang, and the assistant administration commissioner Yü Shih-yüeh for their injustices in punishing innocent men.

Originally, when the prefect Sung Chung of T'ing-chou prefecture in Fukien was journeying homeward, he encountered bandits while passing Huang-chou and was killed. By the time his son Sung Ying reported this to the authorities, the boat in which he traveled had floated to the Huang-shih harbor. Seventeen citizens who lived at the harbor, Ch'en Li and others, broke it up and divided the materials among themselves. When the authorities sent men out to capture the bandits, they found planks from the destroyed boat and forthwith arrested Ch'en Li and the others as bandits. They were sent in fetters to the capital, and the Censorate sentenced them all to the death penalty as bandits.

When Ch'en Li and the others repeatedly complained of injustice, the Censorate directed that a reinvestigation be undertaken in Hukwang. The regional inspector Ch'en Jui and officials of the three provincial offices did not make a thorough investigation but just reported that the men all were indeed bandits.

After Ch'en Li had died in prison, and while the others awaited execution, Ch'en Li's younger brother went so far as to strike the Complaint Drum and appeal for justice. The emperor consequently sent the investigating censor Hu Chih to Hukwang to make personal inquiries and investigations at the site in the company of the senior officials of the three provincial offices. And when Hu Chih returned, he memorialized that Ch'en Li and the others had only broken up the boat among themselves—that actually they were not bandits.

Thereupon supervising secretaries of the six Offices of Scrutiny submitted an impeachment: "Ku Tso and others wrongly sentenced men to the death penalty; Ch'en Jui and others in investigating were not truthful. Their crimes ought to be rectified."

It was decreed that all be pardoned, but the emperor proclaimed to Ku Tso and the others: "The matter is certainly clear. Those who fortunately did not die should be released. As for Ch'en Li, who was guiltless and yet died in prison, are you moved or not? I am alarmed about you!" Ku Tso and the others all knocked their heads.[46]

All persons sent to the Censorate for trial or for punishment were presumably confined in the Censorate's own prison, and those tried by Surveillance Offices were presumably confined in the Surveillance Office prisons. Many other offenders described by the *Shih-lu* merely as "sent to prison" must also have been turned over to the Censorate or the Surveillance Offices, though the Ministry of Justice and the imperial bodyguard also maintained prisons in the capital and both the Provincial Administration Offices and the Regional Military Commissions maintained prisons in the provincial capitals. The *Shih-lu* for 1424–34 refers to five persons who were sent specifically to the Censorate's prison—one chief minister of the Court of State Ceremonial, one military commissioner-in-chief, one assistant military commissioner-in-chief, one regional military commissioner, and one civilian.[47] No such specific mention of the Censorate's prison occurs in the 1620–27 data.

One other aspect of censorial participation in judicial affairs deserves some mention. At least during the years 1424–34, the Censorate was utilized for the preparation and promulgation of warnings and rebukes—either for particular offenders or for the officialdom at large.[48] In 1432, for example, Hsüan-tsung apparently became alarmed at what he considered corruption among Buddhists. He said, "the Buddha originally transformed men so that they became good, but now Buddhists rarely observe the warnings and laws and rarely devote themselves to the ancestral ways." He complained that Buddhists everywhere collected contributions from the people to be wasted on ornate buildings and icons, and he ordered the censor-in-chief Ku Tso to promulgate clarifications of the regulations governing such matters and warnings against violations.[49] In the following year he was annoyed that many of his palace eunuchs were being converted to Buddhism, even to the point of deserting their posts and becoming monks. He assembled the senior eunuchs and lectured them:

There is an ever-constant Way by which a man may establish his character. As a subject he must be loyal, and as a son he must be filial; and a loyal and filial man will naturally enjoy good fortune. Is it necessary to be a vegetarian and to recite the sutras to have good fortune? The Buddha only taught that men should set their minds on goodness. The heavenly palaces and the subterranean prisons that he spoke of, after all, exist only in the mind. If the mind is fixed on good thoughts, that is heaven. If the mind evokes evil thoughts, that is hell. This is why the sutras say, "Buddhahood exists in the mind." Hereafter, you take warning. Just set your minds on goodness; that is true reverence. Any of you who dare to desert and become monks will be put to death with no hope of pardon.

Then he ordered the censor-in-chief to promulgate a general warning to all the local civil and military authorities to keep watch for eunuchs who had shaved their pates and become monks, threatening the death penalty for anyone who gave them protection.[50] The promulgation of such warnings and rebukes is another censorial activity of 1424–34 that has no counterpart in the 1620–27 records.

The foregoing comments about the greater abundance in the years 1424–34 than in the years 1620–27 of *Shih-lu* references to censorial participation in judicial affairs require some explanation. So far as the Surveillance Offices are concerned, the virtual absence in the 1620–27 chronicles of references to their judicial work supports the interpretation already offered: that they had become almost wholly divorced from the censorial system and were devoting themselves to judicial and administrative tasks of such a routine nature that they did not deserve mention in the court chronicles. This is not surprising. But it is somewhat surprising to find that the Censorate proper, judging from the *Shih-lu* chronicles, was so much less active in judicial realms in Hsi-tsung's reign than in Jen-tsung's and Hsüan-tsung's. This apparent change in emphasis can perhaps be explained in part by the fact that the later censors were so much more active in submitting impeachments and remonstrances—and that the court was generally so concerned with dramatic and urgent matters—that such relatively routine matters as the processing of criminal case records and the conduct of judicial reviews just got crowded out of the chronicles, as had not been the case in the more tranquil years of 1424–34. But I nevertheless think that there is no avoiding the conclusion that the Censorate's judicial functions had actually declined in significance between Hsüan-tsung's and Hsi-tsung's times, inasmuch as judicial processes in general had increasingly come to be dominated by palace agencies rather than by civil-service agencies. In Hsi-tsung's time, it was not censorial officials who made the most important arrests and conducted the most important trials, but representatives of the imperial bodyguard and of the eunuch-controlled Eastern Depot in the palace. Although the Censorate remained one of the "three legal offices" and still engaged in judicial work, neither it nor the outer court in general had anything to do with many of the most vital judicial decisions of the era, such as the trials of Wang Wen-yen, Yang Lien, Tso Kuang-tou, and other Tung-lin martyrs. Thus, while the Surveillance Offices were becoming steadily less censorial in nature, the Censorate itself may well have become much more narrowly censorial in its basic orientation.

Censorial Participation in Military Affairs

That censorial officials sometimes took active directive parts in military affairs seems even more anomalous than their participation in judicial affairs.

One of the irregular censorial commissions described in Chapter 2 was the assignment to supervise the progress of military campaigns whenever they were undertaken. The principal duty of army-inspecting censors was to complement the reports of the military commanders proper by reporting on such campaigns as independent observers. This conception of the commission was explicitly cited in the case of the censor Fang Chen-ju, who was army-inspecting censor in Liaotung during the disastrous days of 1621–22. Fang was criticized, along with Hsiung T'ing-pi and Wang Hua-chen, for losing Kuang-ning to the Manchus in 1622, but when his case was reviewed, the legal offices pointed out that his case differed from Hsiung's or Wang's in that it was not his responsibility to direct troops or take part in fighting. Fang was indeed found guilty, and he was eventually sentenced to strangulation, though the sentence was never carried out; but the principal charge brought against him was merely that he had failed to denounce the lack of harmony between the two commanders Hsiung and Wang, to which the Liaotung debacle of 1622 was generally attributed.[51]

Nevertheless, it is abundantly clear that Fang Chen-ju, and even more notably his predecessor Chang Ch'üan, who gave his life in the unsuccessful defense of Liao-yang in 1621, both did in fact play active roles in military planning and even in the command of troops in actual combat.[52] The military defense circuit intendants of the Provincial Surveillance Offices, who proliferated in the last Ming decades, must have had even more regular responsibilities in the direction of military operations. The Shensi surveillance commissioner Kao Ch'u, serving as military defense circuit intendant in Liaotung in 1621, was arrested and tried for his part in the loss of Liao-yang.[53]

Sometimes, too, censorial officials became involved in active military leadership by accident, as in late 1621 when the Szechwan surveillance commissioner Lin Tsai had to take substantive part in the defense of the provincial capital Chengtu while it was besieged by aborigines, at the beginning of the long-drawn-out southwestern rebellion.[54]

But censorial officials played much more regular roles in active military direction than any of these. Between 1424 and 1434 both censors and surveillance commissioners were repeatedly instructed to take the lead in suppressing local and regional banditry. The *Shih-lu* chronicles for the era record 31 specific instances of this sort: 22 involving regional inspectors and surveillance commissioners along with Provincial Administration Offices and Regional Military Commissions, 2 involving only the Surveillance Offices along with the other two provincial offices, and 7 involving specially delegated censors.[55] Often the censorial officials were simply directed to dispatch troops to quell local bandits.[56] Sometimes, too, it was ordered that military suppression be avoided except as a last resort—that the censorial officials should send men, or go themselves, to deliver "soothing edicts" to the offenders. This meant to lecture bandits on the immorality of their lives and the consequences of their misbehavior if they did not desist. Thus in 1433 the vice censor-in-chief Ch'en Mien, having been specially dispatched to collaborate with the regional inspector and the three provincial offices of Kiangsi province in quelling widespread banditry, was able to report that by such peaceful persuasion they had obtained the submission and rehabilitation of 496 families totaling 3,622 persons.[57] On another occasion, when more than 200 murderous bandits were supposedly rehabilitated, their leader soon led a series of new uprisings. It was then ordered that troops be sent to capture the bandits once more, but that only the leader was to be punished; his followers were all to be rehabilitated again.[58]

In some of these instances censorial officials were held responsible for more active participation than just going out to deliver "soothing edicts" or ordering troops into action. Sometimes the regional inspector or the senior officials of the provincial offices were specifically ordered to carry out the suppression of banditry personally.[59] In 1434 the regional inspector of Chekiang province was severely rebuked by Hsüan-tsung for failing to do so, and for passing the blame to a Guard vice commander. Hsüan-tsung said:

I now hear that the censor and also the officials dispatched by the three provincial offices did not personally undertake to direct the capture. Wherever the pursuit led, they passed the days in carousing and paid no attention to the military problem. Not only were the bandits not captured; the citizenry actually had to endure annoyances. Now, to conceal their own faults, they impeach the vice commander T'o Kang.

The emperor threatened the regional inspector and his provincial-office colleagues with the death penalty if they did not promptly do their duty.[60]

The clearest indication of the extent of censorial responsibility in such matters is the case of the investigating censor Chin Lien, who while serving as a regional inspector in the Southern Metropolitan Area in 1431 was ordered to capture some bandits, but who let them escape. Chin was suspended from office until he could redeem himself. He subsequently tracked down the bandit chieftain and brought him as a prisoner to the capital, whereupon he was allowed to resume his censorial post.[61]

There are no entries in the *Shih-lu* for 1620–27 relating to such censorial bandit-catching activities, but, as was previously noted, censorial officials of Hsi-tsung's time were personally active in the recruiting and training of mercenaries for the frontier forces. Investigating censors, supervising secretaries, and surveillance commissioners all participated in this work, especially from 1620 through 1622, though there were complaints about both the propriety and the effectiveness of their doing so.[62] The censor Fu Tsung-lung reportedly trained 5,000 troops; the censor P'an Shih-liang reportedly recruited 5,000; and the censor Yu Shih-jen claimed to have recruited and trained more than 8,000.[63] The supervising secretary Ming Shih-yü and the censor Li Ta were ordered tried late in 1621 for inciting riots and rebellions by their recruiting efforts.[64]

The most notorious troop-recruiter of the 1620's was the censor Yu Shih-jen. Yu was sent out in mid-1621 to recruit troops in the Huai River region of the Southern Metropolitan Area, and because he and friends of his boasted of his great military abilities he was specially given certificates with which he could grant 30 officers' appointments on his own authority. He conferred these appointments upon old friends and with them swaggered about the towns while two ne'er-do-wells who had won his confidence busied themselves with his recruiting and training duties. Of the more than 8,000 troops that he supposedly recruited, none ever reached Liaotung. When a local rebellion erupted, his whole force was routed. Investigation revealed that he and his cronies for more than a year had, in the words of the *Shih-lu*, "just sat around wasting taels by the hundreds of thousands." Yu was repeatedly denounced, repeatedly imprisoned, and finally in 1626 was sent off into frontier service as a common soldier.[65] Because one of his impeachers called him a Tung-lin partisan in 1625 to make certain he would be punished, his name appears on many of the Tung-lin blacklists.[66] But there is no good evidence to associate him with the Tung-lin group, and it might be hoped that he was not a typical censorial troop-recruiter.

These troop-recruiting activities in the 1620's may be considered, in a limited sense, later counterparts of the troop-purifying commissions that kept many censorial officials busy between 1424 and 1434. Though troop-purifying censors and surveillance commissioners in Hsüan-tsung's time were apparently only intended to maintain censorial surveillance over the filling of vacancies in the hereditary troops and over the recovering of deserters, some *Shih-lu* entries suggest that they played directive roles in these processes, and it is clear that some censors (such as the notorious Li Li referred to in Chapter 3 and earlier in this chapter) grossly abused their authority, impressing people into military service without proper grounds and entirely on their own authority.[67]

Censorial Participation in Other Non-surveillance Activities

Among other realms in which censorial officials played roles that do not seem appropriate to their censorial status was the issuance of relief in areas suffering from natural disasters. That censorial officials requested the amelioration of disaster conditions has been noted, especially in Chapter 4; but in addition they often actively directed it, at least in the years 1424–34. Regional inspectors and Provincial Surveillance Offices were most commonly involved in such activities, and it is apparent that they often issued government grain in relief on their own authority, without waiting for specific imperial authorization.[68] Finally, in 1434, Hsüan-tsung sent an order to all grand coordinators, regional inspectors, and provincial offices that included a general authorization for such direct action, saying: "In localities that have suffered calamities, where people are in want of food, immediately dispatch officials to distribute grain in relief, from local government granaries. Do not sit idly by and watch the people suffer."[69]

In both the earlier and the later period supervising secretaries of the Offices of Scrutiny were commonly used as messengers in certain rather ceremonial circumstances. Whenever enfeoffment warrants were issued to the wives and heirs of imperial clansmen, who lived scattered throughout the provinces, the assignments to deliver and present the warrants went more commonly to supervising secretaries than to any other group of officials (and such assignments must have kept the Offices of Scrutiny short-handed at times for extended periods).[70] Censors were rarely so assigned.[71] A supervising secretary was also among the officials who were sent out to all areas of the empire in 1621 to make public announcement of Hsi-tsung's marriage.[72] Supervising secretaries were also sent as envoys carrying messages to foreign rulers. In 1425 it was reported that the supervising secretary Fu An had returned from a mission to a Mongol khan that had kept him out of China for more than 20 years. (Ironically, the Ministry of Personnel bureaucratically insisted that, since it had been impossible for him to have merit ratings while absent, it was now impossible for him to be reappointed in the officialdom; but Hsüan-tsung impatiently ordered that the ordinary rules should be waived in his case.)[73] The supervising secretaries Yang Tao-yin, Chou Hung-mo, and Wang Meng-yin all went on separate diplomatic missions to Korea during the 1620's.[74]

Less frequently, censors and supervising secretaries were specially assigned to such miscellaneous tasks as directing campaigns to exterminate locusts, distributing gifts and rewards to the armed forces, purchasing sacrificial animals for imperial ceremonies, collecting and destroying paper money that was no longer fit for circulation, gathering lumber and other materials for state construction projects, and even designing, repairing, and constructing temples and palaces.[75]

The use of censorial officials in these miscellaneous tasks, however irregular, could only have distracted them from the performance of their principal, strictly censorial functions: to maintain objective and disinterested surveillance over the operations of government, and in consequence to impeach wayward officials and propose changes in policies and practices. At least to a modern student, doing this work well seems demanding enough without occasionally being called on to serve as a judge, a military commander, a bandit-catcher, a locust-exterminator, a messenger, or any other temporary agent that an emperor happened to need.

THE DISCIPLINING OF CENSORIAL OFFICIALS

Far more distracting than any of these assignments to non-censorial tasks, no doubt, was the ever-present prospect of discipline or punishment, either for deeds done or for deeds neglected. One Ming writer said, "of the inner and outer posts, none are more difficult than those of the guardians of the customs and fundamental laws, and none are more dangerous than those of the guardians of the customs and fundamental laws."[76] Analysis of the punishments of censors, supervising secretaries, and surveillance commissioners during the periods 1424–34 and 1620–27 supports this contention decisively.

There was no pretense that the situation was otherwise in Ming times—no pretense that censorial officials benefitted from or should benefit from guaranteed tenure or immunity from punishment. They were a carefully selected group, and they were given certain special privileges and powers. It was not an illogical corollary to this that they were held to a higher standard of conduct than were officials in general, and the consequences of failing to measure up to high expectations were severe. At least for censors and surveillance commissioners, the general rule was that for committing any offense a censorial official would be punished three degrees more severely than any other official; and for an offense involving the acceptance of bribes the punishment would be still more severe.[77] In an equally general admonition, the Ming regulations specified that if a surveillance official should fail to make known the good that he saw, or fail to initiate punitive action against the evil that he saw, he must be given 100 blows of the heavy bamboo and then be exiled to a malarious district.[78] Although supervising secretaries of the Offices of Scrutiny were not singled out in such threatening regulations, the same threatening atmosphere surrounded them. Emperors regularly paid lip-service to the notion that remonstrators should not be punished for speaking their minds; thus Hsi-tsung once magnanimously decided not to punish a censor who had offended him "since after all he is a speaking official."[79] But Ming emperors usually acted on a different premise, which was stated explicit in an edict of Hsi-tsung's time: "The responsibility of speaking officials is to speak out; if what they say is not proper, then they fail their responsibility."[80] "To fail one's responsibility" in Chinese also happens, not by accident, to mean "to lose one's job." Such was the general understanding: that speaking officials unavoidably ran risks. One supervising secretary himself in a memorial of 1607 accepted it quite plainly. "There are only two ways for the court to deal with the Censorate and the Offices of Scrutiny," he wrote. "If what they say is proper, then act upon it. If what they say is not proper, then punish them."[81]

Many special offenses for which censorial officials could be punished are spelled out in the Ming regulations. In Chapter 3 it was noted that regional inspectors and surveillance commissioners on tour were subject to special restrictions—about what personnel and baggage might accompany them, about their behavior toward other officials, and so forth. In submitting memorials, censorial officials were also held accountable for what they said, in more ways than whether or not it was deemed proper by the emperor. In the case of an impeachment, for example, it was required that they clearly set forth the evidence, complete with pertinent dates, and that they not engage

in vague phraseology, careless accusations, slanderous gossip, or trifling complaints.[82] They were also held accountable for the accuracy
of what they said; for the Ming dynasty, like the Yüan, did not honor
the old T'ang and Sung practice of allowing censorial officials to impeach or otherwise memorialize on the basis of hearsay evidence. One
sixteenth-century censor-in-chief tried to persuade the emperor Mu-
tsung that the Ming system did indeed permit hearsay evidence, but
the Ming regulations gave the censorial officials no refuge of this sort,
and the historical record abounds with evidence to the contrary.[83]
The founding emperor, T'ai-tsu, established the Ming pattern by
once demoting a censor who had denounced someone on the basis
of what he had heard "in the street."[84] Hsüan-tsung once demoted
a censor because he memorialized untruthfully, and in the 1620's censors and supervising secretaries were repeatedly rebuked for relying
on hearsay evidence.[85]

Who censored the censors? Almost anyone could. For valid cause,
any official or officer could impeach any censorial official; as has been
noted repeatedly, the censorial establishment in no way monopolized
impeachment powers. In cases of injustice, any citizen could lodge a
complaint against a surveillance commissioner with a regional inspector or could complain about the Censorate itself by striking the
Complaint Drum at the palace gate. Moreover, it was specifically prescribed that the censorial officials should keep close watch over each
other. Regional inspectors were encouraged to check on the performance of provincial surveillance commissioners; and regional inspectors in turn were to be watched closely by Surveillance Offices, by
grand coordinators, and by other censors on commission in the same
territories.[86] And censors of the Honan Circuit had the special prescribed responsibility of maintaining surveillance over all activities
of the Censorate itself.

Censorial officials were also subject to the same evaluation procedures that they subjected other civil officials to. At regular intervals,
and especially when they completed prescribed terms of office, they
were evaluated by their administrative superiors: surveillance vice
commissioners and assistant surveillance commissioners by the surveillance commissioners, supervising secretaries and left and right supervising secretaries by the chief supervising secretaries of their respective Offices of Scrutiny, and investigating censors by the Honan
Circuit and the censor-in-chief. On the basis of these evaluations, and
after further consideration by the Ministry of Personnel, they were
either promoted or demoted. The only special qualification in this
regard was that investigating censors, because of their status as "ears

and eyes" of the emperor, could not be promoted or demoted without explicit imperial consent.[87]

Investigating censors were also subjected to special evaluations whenever they returned from the provinces after extended commissions, especially as regional inspectors; and officials of the Surveillance Offices were similarly evaluated on returning from duty in the circuits to which they were assigned.[88] The elaborate reports required of such touring inspectors (which were discussed in Chapter 3) were particularly designed to provide data for these evaluations.[89] For example, it was specified that, aside from fulfilling his routine duties with propriety, a censorial inspector must carry out to completion at least 70 per cent of all his special instructions or be impeached for inadequacy.[90] Evaluators also took into consideration the expense accounts that inspectors submitted for audit when they returned from touring.[91] Such special evaluations of censorial officials seem to have become lax in the long reign of Shen-tsung, but in the 1620's there was a stiffening of the regulations.[92] In 1623 Chao Nan-hsing, then censor-in-chief, urged that the final reports of regional inspectors not only should be processed by the Honan Circuit before being considered by the censor-in-chief, but should be seen and commented on by the senior investigating censor of every other circuit.[93] It was the censor-in-chief Kao P'an-lung's impeachment of Ts'ui Ch'eng-hsiu in 1624, when he returned to the Censorate from a commission in the Huai River region, that drove Ts'ui to seek help from Wei Chung-hsien and thus finally brought Wei into open dominance at court.[94]

In previous chapters it has been pointed out that censorial officials —especially investigating censors and supervising secretaries—enjoyed a notable independence of action in that they could submit memorials directly to the throne and were in general considered representatives of the throne rather than of their own administrative superiors. However, the fact that censors-in-chief and chief supervising secretaries did have powers to discipline them through evaluations and impeachments was not an insignificant restraint on their freedom. The case of the censor-in-chief Liu Kuan, to be discussed below, indicates that in practice investigating censors were sometimes thoroughly submissive to strong leadership within the Censorate. And most of all, of course, all censorial officials were unprotected from the disciplinary and punitive powers of the emperors.

Censorial Punishments in the Years 1424–34

Judging from the number and kinds of complaints made about them, censorial personnel in general had a rather bad reputation in the 1420's and 1430's. Surveillance officials in particular were thought to be lax, arbitrary, susceptible to bribery and flattery, and more concerned about their own personal safety and advancement than about fulfilling their heavy responsibilities. It is noteworthy that the imposition of significant restrictions on eligibility for censorial appointments began in this era. In 1425 Jen-tsung suggested that henceforth censors should be selected only from among men who had experience in other governmental posts, and in 1428 Hsüan-tsung initiated the practice of making newly appointed investigating censors serve probationary periods before being confirmed in their posts.[95] Restrictions such as these were direct reactions to censorial shortcomings of the time.

The general attitude toward censorial officials is suggested in a complaint submitted in 1425 by an official of the Shansi Provincial Administration Office:

The court sends out censors ... to evaluate the worthiness or unworthiness of the local authorities. For the most part, the censors pay no attention to facts. [Local authorities] who are pure and incorrupt, capable, humble, just, upright, affable, lenient, generous, and not good at subservience are abruptly judged inadequate to their duties and are removed. Those who are venal, coarse, common, vile, incapable of fostering and caring for the people, but good at subservience and artful in attendance are abruptly judged to measure up to their duties and are advanced. The worthy and the unworthy are confusedly mixed up, and the way of justice does not prevail.[96]

The same judgment was made in 1432 by K'uang Chung, reportedly the best prefect Soochow had in the Ming period.[97] He made this general denunciation of the conduct of censors on commission in the provinces:

Recently censors on commission in every locality have often violated propriety and exceeded their authority. Among the prefects of the various prefectures, there are of course some who, being self-seeking, dull, stupid, venal, or cruel, dread impeachment. In meeting censors they fawn and flatter, do obeisance and kneel down, willingly submitting to curses and insults. As for those among them who uphold the law, discipline themselves, and refuse to flatter and bow, [the censors] seize upon petty faults and become arrogant. Thus they bring it about that the worthy and honorable cannot enjoy their posts while the evil and sycophantic prosper.[98]

The emperors themselves were full of complaints in the same vein. On one occasion Jen-tsung lamented that most censors did not measure up to their duties.[99] At another time he was even driven to making threats:

Censors are the ears and eyes of the court. They ought to purify their hearts and rectify themselves so as to stimulate the fundamental principles. But in recent years their venal and vile habits have been most extreme. Hereafter ... if they remain venal and vile, they will be punished without mercy.[100]

Hsüan-tsung, though generally tolerant and moderate, was vigorously outspoken about censorial ineptness and corruption. He complained: "In recent years licentiousness and corruption have prevailed in all the agencies of the capital, and those responsible for the customs and fundamental laws not only have been unable to take corrective action against it but have actually joined happily in it. If this is what they do, what shall the state rely upon?"[101] And he went on complaining, in one instance saying:

Censors of every Circuit are still sunk in their long accustomed corruption. They connive and consort with inferiors. Some presume upon the public law to get harsh and cruel revenge for private resentments, and some honor private feelings and recklessly disregard public law, without care or dread.[102]

Hsüan-tsung warned the censor-in-chief Ku Tso to be very careful, lest the censors "take advantage of you and make a fool of you."[103] He said that censors tolerated and even promoted general corruption for their own profit, and that they actively undermined discipline instead of upholding it.[104] He deplored abuses in the judicial system and censorial roles in them. People took complaints to their local magistrates, who in return for bribes took no action or punished the innocent complainers. Then the people complained to the provincial offices and the regional inspectors, only to find right and wrong turned topsy-turvy and in some cases to suffer long confinement for their pains. Then the people flocked to the capital to seek justice, and were usually cast in jail for going out of regular channels. In recent years, the emperor said, multitudes of farmers had entered the capital daily to complain of injustice.[105] On another occasion he said:

Guardians of the customs and fundamental laws must first of all observe the law; only then can they use the law to regulate others. Now many censors are frivolous and young; they do not discipline themselves either with propriety or law. They enjoy men's flattery. If [local officials] fail to welcome or escort them, they abruptly cause trouble, imposing insults and humiliations. Thus the outer officials are themselves unable to maintain propriety and the law, and flattery becomes the custom.[106]

Such being the general feeling about the censorial personnel of the 1420's and 1430's, it is not surprising that censorial officials were repeatedly punished in consequence of evaluations and impeachments.

Table 20 analyzes all such instances reported in the *Shih-lu* chronicles, by category of officials and by type of punishment; and Table 21
lists the reasons that are most commonly cited for such disciplinary
action, venality heading the list.

The most significant disciplinary action of the era was a great
purge of the Peking and Nanking Censorates instituted by Hsüan-
tsung in 1428, terminating the regime of Liu Kuan as censor-in-chief
and beginning the regime of Ku Tso as censor-in-chief. And the primary focus of discontent with the Censorate was Liu Kuan himself.

Liu Kuan became administrative head of the Censorate under
Ch'eng-tsu and remained so after the accession of Jen-tsung and then
Hsüan-tsung.[107] Then in the sixth month of 1428 Hsüan-tsung suddenly commissioned him to supervise activity along the Grand Canal,
and he left the capital.[108] Nine days later Ku Tso, then serving as
transmission commissioner of the Office of Transmission, was promoted to the post of censor-in-chief of the right, and after only two more
days Ku was ordered to start weeding out inadequate investigating
censors.[109] The first results of this purge appeared in the eighth
month, as will be shown below; and in the ninth month Liu Kuan
was denounced.[110] The *Shih-lu* for 1428 records this event as follows:

Ninth month, the day *keng-ch'en*: The Honan Circuit investigating censor
Chang Hsün-li and others memorialized an impeachment: "The junior
guardian of the heir apparent and concurrent censor-in-chief of the left in
charge of the Censorate's affairs, Liu Kuan, presumes upon imperial favor
by toying with the law, and he goes to great excess in villainy and fraud. He
has associated intimately with the venal, evil, and shameless censor Yen K'ai
and others in committing deeds of great corruption. Also, he has gone about
with Bureau directors and various Ministry secretaries such as Hsü Hsing
and Wang Jun, singing, dancing, carousing, and sporting obscenely without
restraint. Also, each time officials have been commissioned to attend to affairs and tour outside, he has first required five taels of silver of them, calling
it 'departure-sanction silver'; and when they have returned he has required
another five taels of them, calling it 'completion-sanction silver.' When Feng
Pen and other local bullies of Chia-hsing Prefecture were guilty of murder
and were imprisoned pending judicial review, Liu Kuan accepted bribes
and permitted them to escape. He has also given free rein to his son Liu Fu,
who has opened a wine shop, enticed prostitutes into unrestricted lewdness,
stolen and made use of utensils that had been confiscated by the state, and
connived with the clerk An Chung to commit wrongs of many sorts. Now,
Liu Kuan's duty is to be in general charge of discipline, and he ranks among
the great honorific dignitaries. However, observing neither propriety nor the
law, he commits villainy and violates the rules. His punishment ought to be
rightly fixed so as to purify the fundamental principles."

The emperor said: "We also are aware of this. However, because he is an official of long standing during successive reigns, We have just patiently endured it, hoping he would be able to reform. Yet he has not reformed but has become increasingly reckless in his aims. We recently sent him to tour and inspect the Grand Canal and gave orders to Ku Tso in his place; it was not without intent." Then he ordered the various great ministers to deliberate.

Now the junior preceptor and minister of personnel Chien I and others all spoke out requesting that the censors' impeachment be complied with. Thereupon it was ordered that the Ministry of Justice should send men to arrest Liu Kuan.[111]

Nineteen days later Liu Kuan was brought to the capital and, on Hsüan-tsung's orders, was shown the impeachment lodged by the censors. Liu said in his own defense:

I have successively served the emperor T'ai-tsu, the emperor T'ai-tsung [i.e., Ch'eng-tsu], and the emperor Jen-tsung in successive offices up to censor-in-chief of the left honorifically entitled junior guardian of the heir apparent, with two salaries paid. Your majesty succeeded to the throne and constantly conferred gifts upon me, and day and night I have diligently thought and schemed to make recompense. Now the censor-in-chief of the right, Ku Tso, seeks my punishment and, as their master, has ordered the censors of every Circuit to submit impeachments. He has also compelled the clerk An Chung to indicate falsely that I received bribes and committed other crimes. I humbly hope that your majesty will sympathetically investigate the circumstances and clearly distinguish them so that there will be no injustice.[112]

To this the emperor replied that many officials had secretly memorialized about Liu's offenses and that Liu had not been punished previously only because of his long service. He added, "Now does he still wish to gloss over his faults?" Then he sent out some of the secret memorials for Liu's perusal. They revealed that, in all, he had accepted more than 1,000 taels of silver in "selling criminal cases." Liu confessed. The legal offices demanded that he be beheaded in accordance with the law, and he was sent to the palace prison of the imperial bodyguard.[113] There he apparently remained until the seventh month of 1429, when the death penalty was revoked. His son Liu Fu was sent in disgrace to serve as a soldier in Liaotung, and Liu Kuan was ordered to live with his son in exile.[114] Hsüan-tsung explained that, although Liu Kuan was evil in the extreme, he still could not bring himself to punish him more severely.[115]

In summing up the case, the *Shih-lu* makes clear that Liu Kuan had repeatedly befriended and abetted rich and influential gentry members whom he had first known while serving as a prefect; that in return for heavy bribes he had aided them to escape severe punishments for murder, theft, and other offenses; that he led a group of censors and other capital officials devoted to the "sale of criminal cases"; and that his son Liu Fu was even more corrupt than he was. Liu Fu took bribes that are said to have equalled his father's and through his father got murderers released. Liu Fu was venal and cruel; he shrank from nothing. Moreover, it is said that the censors of all the Circuits obeyed Liu Fu's instructions even though he himself apparently had no official capacity at all.

Persons of his time seem to have seen Liu Kuan as the symbol of governmental corruption. When Hsüan-tsung once lamented the seeming increase of avarice and foulness among officials and asked the grand secretaries Yang Shih-ch'i and Yang Jung who was the worst, Yang Jung unhesitatingly named Liu. It was this revelation that prompted the emperor to send Liu out to tour the Grand Canal; and it was on the recommendation of these two counselors that Ku Tso was given charge of the Censorate.[116] Liu Kuan and his son are also said to have been the worst offenders among those who caroused with prostitutes.[117] The *Shih-lu* notes that when Liu was sentenced "public opinion" was greatly pleased.[118] As late as 1432, when it was requested that the guardians of the customs and fundamental laws evaluate local officials to weed out the unworthy, Hsüan-tsung said: "Let it be so. If We had not dismissed Liu Kuan, how could the guardians of the customs and fundamental laws be respected?"[119] It is also said that after Liu Kuan, censors-in-chief were not carelessly appointed.[120]

The purge of investigating censors that Ku Tso was ordered to undertake had its first results in the eighth month of 1428, when Ku reported the results of his first survey of the Censorate's personnel. Eleven censors, he said, had foul reputations for extreme avarice and shamelessness. These 11 included Liu Kuan's special crony Yen K'ai. Also denounced in this category was the Censorate's office manager Tuan K'ai. Eight other censors were avaricious and unlawful; 7 others did not thoroughly understand governmental principles, as was the case also with the Censorate's chief clerk Chao Pin; 1 censor was not versed in the rules of correspondence; 3 were old and ill. Ku said that these 30 investigating censors, as well as two other Censorate officials (who are not included in my tabulations), ought to be got rid of. Hsüan-tsung decreed that the 19 censors who were avaricious, as well as the office manager, should be sent in disgrace to serve as lesser functionaries in the various Liaotung garrisons; and that all the other men whom Ku Tso had denounced should be degraded to the level of county clerks, except that the three old and ill censors should be dismissed from the civil service entirely.[121]

Six of the censors who were disgraced at this time were absent on commissions. In the fifth month of 1429, when they had returned to Peking and were to be sent off to Liaotung, they submitted a complaint of injustice. Hsüan-tsung promptly changed their sentences for the worse: he ordered that they be sent to serve as common soldiers in Liaotung, rather than as lesser functionaries. Moreover, he angrily added that others already sent should also be so treated.[122]

In the seventh month of 1429 Ku Tso reported that Yen K'ai had escaped from his garrison in Liaotung and had returned to the capital. He took up his old habits, making false accusations and extorting bribes; moreover, he was a serious threat to Ku's own life. It was ordered that the imperial bodyguard capture him, and more than a year later Yen was tried and sentenced to death.[123]

At the beginning of 1429 Hsüan-tsung ordered that the Nanking Censorate be purged as Ku Tso had purged the Peking Censorate.[124] Soon the vice censor-in-chief Shao Ch'i, senior Censorate official at Nanking, reported that he found 3 investigating censors who were avaricious and shameless, 6 who did not understand governmental principles, 3 who were not versed in correspondence, and 1 who had already been convicted of bribery. The emperor ordered that all 13 men be demoted according to regulations.[125] The posts to which they were demoted are not specified.

These instances did not terminate the purge of censors, which was a continuing matter. In the eleventh month of 1428, for example, Hsüan-tsung reminded Ku Tso that the weeding-out process in Peking was not complete.[126] Disciplinary action remained frequent even through 1431. But there were no more mass denunciations; subsequent action concerned individual censors.

In addition to Yen K'ai, one other censorial official of this era was put to death. This was the investigating censor Chao Yen. Chao had been sent to purify troops in Honan and had beaten to death nine innocent village elders. He was imprisoned late in 1428 pending judicial review of his death sentence. His old friend and associate, Chang Hsün-li, the same censor who shortly before had played a leading role in the impeachment of Liu Kuan, one day summoned Chao out of prison for a brief visit. While they were drinking together, Chao seized the opportunity to escape. In 1431 he was finally recaptured and was then beheaded. Meanwhile Chang had been imprisoned for his negligence and had died of illness in prison.[127] (In my tabulations, Chao Yen is counted as having been put to death but not as having been imprisoned; in general, only the final disposition of an offender as recorded in the *Shih-lu* is tabulated.)

One other censorial official died in apparent consequence of disciplinary action during this period. This was the Nanking vice censor-in-chief Hsia Ti, who in 1425 was impeached by the censor Ho Ch'u-ying and others for permitting bribery and for beating to death a local tax collector while expediting tax matters in the Southern Metropolitan Area. Even though at least part of the accusation was known to be false and though Ho was plainly motivated by personal hatred, Hsia was sent in disgrace to serve as a postal-service runner. It is reported that he promptly died of exasperation.[128]

One vice censor-in-chief, named Hu I, had an especially troubled career. In 1428 he was impeached for neglect while supervising the transport of rations from the Kwangtung-Kwangsi region to Annam. He may have been imprisoned briefly but was soon pardoned and restored to duty.[129] Then in 1431 he was accused of abuses while supervising a state lumbering project in Szechwan—he was said to use government lumber and workers for private purposes, to force merchants to sell goods at less than the true value, and the like. The Ministry of Justice demanded that he be beheaded, but the emperor sentenced him instead to exile in Liaotung.[130] Even this sentence was not fulfilled, however. Instead, he performed punitive labor in commutation and was about to be restored to office when the emperor intervened on the ground that he was no longer fit to serve in a censorial capacity. He was demoted and sent away from the capital to become administration vice commissioner of Fukien province.[131]

Aside from Chao Yen's friend Chang Hsün-li, the four investigating censors whose imprisonments are noted in the *Shih-lu* chronicles of this era included Li Shih-mien, the Hanlin official who offended Jen-tsung in 1425 by suggesting that the emperor should not consort with his concubines during the official mourning period. He was transferred to the position of censor, and almost immediately thereafter was cast into prison; he was finally released late in 1426 by Hsüan-tsung. Another censor punished by imprisonment was Wang Hsün, who was sent to prison in 1425 for failing to denounce corruption.[132] Chao Pen was imprisoned in 1434 because while serving as regional inspector of Honan province he was rude to an imperial prince.[133] No more is heard of either of these two offenders in the *Shih-lu*.

The only other censor imprisoned in this era was Chang Chün. Early in the decade a citizen of Chekiang province accused four members of one family of having committed murders and of having broken the law by dealing with foreigners. Chang, a censor of the Chekiang Circuit, instructed the appropriate county magistrate to arrest the accused persons and send them to the Censorate for trial. The magistrate sent one man, but the other three had gone into hiding and could not be found. Chang imprisoned the one accused offender and delayed trying him until the other three could be captured. In 1430, after four years had thus passed, relatives brought the case to the emperor's attention. Hsüan-tsung decided that Chang's conduct of the case was inexcusable and had him thrown into prison.[134] However, Chang was subsequently allowed to redeem himself by doing punitive labor and was restored to office; and in 1434 he even became an assistant censor-in-chief.[135]

Since the *Shih-lu* makes no mention at all of the imprisonment of the investigating censor Ch'en Tso from 1431 to 1435 (discussed in Chapter 4), his case is not included in my tabulations here. Obviously, however, it cannot be overlooked as an important part of the factual record. Ch'en's suggestions that Hsüan-tsung pay more attention to his literary studies were not necessarily meant to be the insults that the emperor interpreted them to be. But Ch'en was imprisoned for a long time, and several members of his family suffered imprisonment with him. His father even died in prison. The treatment of Ch'en must therefore be reckoned one of Hsüan-tsung's more arbitrary and harsh acts.

It is said that displaying censors in the portable pillories called cangues began in the fifth month of 1428 when three investigating censors and five other capital officials were punished in this way for licentiousness, drunkenness, and flagrant neglect of their duties. One of these men was Yen K'ai, who was later disgraced and then put to death.[136]

Accepting bribes was the most common offense for which censors were punished, but the cases recorded in the *Shih-lu* include many other offenses. For example, the censor Ho Ching got into trouble on behalf of a relative. While marketing for vegetables, the relative had become incensed when one vendor would not accept his paper money because of its ragged condition. As a result, Ho gave the vendor 20 blows of the light bamboo, from which he subsequently died. For his unjustified act, Ho was given 100 blows and was then sent in disgrace to serve as a soldier.[137]

As Table 20 indicates, in the period 1424–34 supervising secretaries and surveillance commissioners were disciplined far more rarely than were censors. Eighteen of the 39 supervising secretaries who were disciplined were punished in the single-year reign of Jen-tsung, 13 being demoted simultaneously at the very beginning of his reign for being inattentive to their duties.[138] Thereafter supervising secretaries were disciplined only at rare intervals, and there were no notorious cases in the Offices of Scrutiny comparable to those that shook the Censorate. One supervising secretary was "punished" (no specific result indicated) because he failed to have Hsüan-tsung confirm an edict delivered by a eunuch.[139] In 1427 the supervising secretary Chang P'an was demoted to the post of assistant subprefectural magistrate because he reported that he was ill and not fit to be an intimate attendant upon the emperor.[140] Ch'en Hsiang used the seal and forged the signature of a colleague on some documents and was sent in disgrace to serve as a menial worker in a state salt manufactory.[141] Li Fang was demoted to the post of county vice magistrate because he complained to the emperor about petty matters in the governmental offices so much that Hsüan-tsung decided he was just a busybody.[142] Other instances of supervising secretaries' being disciplined are no more dramatic or significant than these examples.

Officials of Surveillance Offices may have been disciplined more often than Table 20 indicates, since their cases need not all have attracted sufficient imperial attention to justify being noted in the *Shih-lu*. But even those instances that are noted in the *Shih-lu* seem distinctly routine. Three surveillance commissioners were denounced for misdeeds committed during their previous assignments as investigating censors. One was the surveillance vice commissioner Li Lun of Kiangsi province, discovered in 1430 to have been an intimate crony of Liu Kuan's son Fu, in whose company he dissipated, slept with harlots, and took bribes for alleviating punishments. He was sent in disgrace to serve as a soldier at the Liaotung frontier.[143] Another was the assistant surveillance commissioner Chao Ch'un of Honan province, who during his previous service as a regional inspector had accepted bribes and moreover had married a woman of his jurisdiction in violation of censorial prohibitions. Even though an amnesty had been declared, he was dismissed from the civil service.[144] The surveillance vice commissioner Li Su of Fukien province was impeached at the same time for having had immoral relations with a woman and then marrying her, during his service as a regional inspector. By the time his arrest was ordered, however, he had already died.[145] In 1424 one surveillance vice commissioner, Chao Wei, was degraded by being made a county clerk as a punishment for wrongs done while serving as a supervising secretary.[146]

One of the more interesting reasons for removing an official from a censorial post in this era was cited in the case of the surveillance commissioner Ch'en Lien of Szechwan province. The Ministry of Personnel reported that Ch'en was such a Confucian that upholding the fundamental laws was not his forte. The Chinese have traditionally used the term *Ju*—which has the original meaning "weakling"—to identify the Confucian school of thinkers as distinguished from Legalists, Taoists, Buddhists, and others. The implication seems to be that Ch'en was too scholarly and genteel, and probably too lacking in sternness, to do well as a judicial official. At the Ministry's request, he was transferred to the post of Nanking transmission commissioner with the special added responsibility of supervising the National University at Nanking.[147]

When demoted during this period, both investigating censors and surveillance commissioners were most commonly demoted to county magistracies—during the early years, often in Annam. Many investigating censors were also demoted to prefectural judgeships. Supervising secretaries, if demoted, most commonly became county vice magistrates or assistant magistrates of subprefectures.

Despite his great lenience toward others, Hsüan-tsung very rarely pardoned censorial officials when they were denounced and was very rarely satisfied merely to rebuke a censorial offender. Among those few whom he refused to punish was the reformist censor-in-chief Ku Tso, who was so stern and austere that he was called "Sit-alone Ku" and even after a century was still recalled as a model of censorial awesomeness.[148] In 1431 Ku was only mildly reproved when the Censorate unjustly sentenced the censor Chou An to strangulation on the basis of an accusation later proved false. (Chou's accuser was a man whom Chou himself had arrested and committed to trial.)[149] That this occurred was, perhaps, an indication that Ku was somewhat overzealous in purging the Censorate of undesirables. Late the same year Ku and some of his associates were rebuked when seventeen men whom the Censorate had convicted of murder and banditry—one of whom had died in prison—were found to be innocent.[150]

Ku Tso himself was not entirely immune to charges of venality. Soon after he took office in the Censorate a lesser functionary impeached him, saying that he accepted money from servants provided for him by the state and secretly released them to go home. Hsüan-tsung showed this complaint to Yang Shih-ch'i. The grand secretary said it was probably true—that because salaries were insufficient for officials in the capital they took fees from servants and released them, thus stretching their funds enough to cover their expenses. All capital officials did this, said Yang; he did it himself. The emperor, exclaiming "The court ministers are as poor as this!" became angry at the accuser and notified Ku Tso that he himself should punish the man. Ku summoned his accuser and merely urged that he change his ways. It is said that on hearing of this Hsüan-tsung was more pleased than ever with Ku.[151]

Censorial Punishments in the Years 1620–27

The punishments given to censorial officials in the years 1620–27, as recorded in the *Shih-lu* chronicles of Hsi-tsung's reign, are analyzed in Tables 22 and 23. There are some remarkable contrasts between these data and the comparable data from 1424–34, and some even more remarkable contrasts between the punishments given during the era of Tung-lin ascendance and those given during Wei Chung-hsien's open dominance.

On the face of the matter, and contrary to what one would properly expect, it would appear that censorial officials did not suffer more grievously in Hsi-tsung's era of partisan strife and eunuch terrorism than under Jen-tsung and Hsüan-tsung. To be sure, 10 censorial officials were put to death in the later period as against only 2 in the earlier period. But the *Shih-lu* for 1620–27 indicate an overall total of only 209 instances of disciplinary action as against 238 for 1424–34. And what is most impressive is that only 6 men were degraded by being sent away as lesser functionaries or frontier soldiers under Hsi-tsung as against 45 under Jen-tsung and Hsüan-tsung. Since being degraded or disgraced in this fashion must have been thought more punitive than demotion, removal from office, or even dismissal from the civil service, the tabulations could suggest that Hsüan-tsung's reign was more terroristic than Hsi-tsung's, despite the praise generally accorded Hsüan-tsung and the universal execration of Wei Chung-hsien by historians.

This impression can be modified by several considerations. For one thing, I am less confident of the completeness of my 1620–27 data than of my 1424–34 data. This is largely because the *Shih-lu* for 1624, the year with the greatest censorial upheavals in Hsi-tsung's reign, have been so mutilated that only a skeleton remains.[152] Some instances of censorial disciplining in that year have therefore probably eluded my tabulation, although all famous cases are included. Also, the *Shih-lu* do not give any details about the 235 capital officials who were rated unfavorably in the capital evaluations of 1623 and were ordered removed from office or retired or demoted.[153] Some investigating censors and supervising secretaries must have been in this large group. Finally, although I am sure that the 1424–34 *Shih-lu* do not record all disciplinary actions against surveillance commissioners, I am certain that my 1620–27 data in this category are much more incomplete. If all these probable omissions could be rectified, I expect that my tabulations for 1620–27 would show a larger total of disciplinary actions than could be counted for 1424–34. However, the number of severe punishments—death penalties and disgracings— would not be changed significantly if at all.

Another consideration that may alter the first impression given by my tabulations is that some officials who were promoted from posts as investigating censors and supervising secretaries in the 1620's were actually being disciplined rather than rewarded. As was pointed out in Chapter 2, and as the censor-in-chief Chao Nan-hsing lamented in 1623, by late Ming times almost any post in the capital was considered preferable to almost any post in the provinces.[154] Thus Wang Hui-t'u, after protesting vigorously that his promotion to assistant surveillance commissioner (5a) in 1626 was unfair, was permitted to resume his former office of investigating censor (presumably 7a) in 1627.[155] And the investigating censor Chang Chieh, an enemy of the Tung-lin partisans who got rid of him in early 1624 by having him promoted to surveillance vice commissioner (4a), indignantly refused to go to his new post and in 1625 gratefully accepted his reappointment as a censor by Wei Chung-hsien.[156] Consequently, my tabulations should perhaps include as disciplinary actions all of the 38 instances in which investigating censors were promoted into provincial offices during the 1620's, and the 22 instances in which supervising secretaries were similarly promoted. Moreover, since censorial offices also seem to have been prized more than most other capital offices, it would probably not be much of a distortion to count as disciplinary actions the 99 and 48 respective instances when censors and supervising secretaries were promoted to non-censorial offices in the capital— especially in those most common cases when they were promoted as supernumerary officials of such agencies as the Court of the Imperial Stud. This also, however, would not increase the number of relatively severe punishments meted out to censorial officials in Hsi-tsung's time.

My tabulation is more seriously distorted by another characteristic

of personnel disciplining under Hsi-tsung. That is, persons were
often disciplined long after committing the offenses by which their
eventual disciplining was justified. For example, the vice censor-in-
chief Feng Ts'ung-wu went into voluntary retirement in 1622 when
he and Tsou Yüan-piao were denounced for conducting academy discussions in the capital. Then late in 1624, after Wei Chung-hsien
came into open dominance at court, he was punished by being dismissed from the civil service and made a civilian.[157] Thus by the time
he was disciplined he was no longer an active censorial official. Yang
Lien, Tso Kuang-tou, and others who were put to death were also no
longer active censorial officials when the final action in their series of
punishments—the only action counted in my tabulations—was taken.
I have unhesitatingly counted former censors and former supervising
secretaries in my tabulations, even though I am thereby forced to include a few men who were out of office long before Hsi-tsung's time.
But I have not included instances of the punishment of former censorial officials if they held non-censorial posts following their censorial service, even though they may have been punished principally
for what they had done as censorial officials. The kind of problem
presented by such cases is illustrated by the career of Chao Nan-hsing,
one of the most venerable Tung-lin heroes, who was dismissed from
the civil service in 1593, became a famous academy lecturer, and was
reinstated in the civil service in 1621.[158] From late 1622 until late
1623 he served as censor-in-chief, and he played a major role in ousting Tung-lin enemies from office in the capital evaluations. Then
from late 1623 on he served as minister of personnel until, in collaboration with the new censor-in-chief Kao P'an-lung, he proposed disciplinary action against the venal censor Ts'ui Ch'eng-hsiu and thus
precipitated the baring of Wei Chung-hsien's palace power. Late in
1624 he left office in voluntary retirement in protest against Wei's
interventions in government. Thereafter he was dismissed from the
civil service and then sent in disgrace to serve as a common soldier at
the frontier, where he eventually died in exile. It would be impossible
to determine with any precision whether Chao was eventually punished for what he did as censor-in-chief, or for what he did as minister
of personnel, or even because he inspired a much more general and
vague vindictiveness. In Chao's case and in many others like his, I
have felt I had no choice but to exclude the victims from my censorial tabulations; and for this reason above all I fear my tabulation
seriously understates the real extent of censorial disciplining in the
1620's.

As the foregoing intimates, the real difference between the data of 1424–34 and of 1620–27 lies in the fact that, whereas the disciplining of censorial officials in Hsüan-tsung's time was a rather isolated element of severity in a general atmosphere of moderation, the disciplining of censorial officials in 1620–27—and specifically in the era of Wei Chung-hsien's dominance—was representative of a widespread terrorism. It would be impossible to estimate the total of those who died as a result of Wei's dictatorship, but one contemporary source that lists his civil-service victims gives these totals, by categories:[159]

Cruelly murdered	16
Unjustly beheaded	1
Beaten to death	2
Committed suicide	3
Banished to guard the frontier	15
Sent to labor on the Great Wall	3
Dismissed from the service	225
Imprisoned	6
Removed from office	20
Driven into retirement	68
Took leave of absence	6
Total	365

It is noteworthy that of the 22 men who are identified as having died as Wei's victims, 13 had been active censorial officials. Moreover, of 309 men listed on the principal blacklist of Tung-lin partisans issued in Wei's time (including men active in any court controversies from the 1590's into the 1620's) at least 93 are identifiable as censors or supervising secretaries.[160] Yet another Tung-lin roll, which lists men in categories according to the types of agencies they served in, names 76 investigating censors and supervising secretaries in the largest single category of Tung-lin partisans; and of 57 Tung-lin men listed in another large category, "the Ministries and the Censorate" (apparently intended to include only ministers and censors-in-chief), 29 are identifiable as censors-in-chief, or onetime investigating censors or supervising secretaries.[161] Thus, as prominent leaders of the partisan movements that came to be labeled Tung-lin, censorial officials suffered in perhaps disproportionately large numbers when punishments were meted out by Wei Chung-hsien, or by Tung-lin opponents under his patronage. But the disciplining of censorial officials was nevertheless just part of a more general punitive endeavor—as was not the case during the years 1424–34.

This essential difference between the two periods is also reflected in a comparison between reasons cited for censorial disciplining during the years 1620–27 (Table 23) and those cited during the years 1424–34 (Table 21). Under Jen-tsung and Hsüan-tsung censorial officials were punished principally for unfitness, either personal or professional. But this was no longer the case in Hsi-tsung's time, when censorial officials were swept up in great tides of partisan cannibalism, partly of their own making, but whose effects and consequences they could not control or avert. As Table 23 clearly indicates, the censorial officials of 1620–27 were punished, not for being unfit by 1424–34 standards, but for being imprudent—for offending people who, sooner or later, were able to retaliate. Hsüan-tsung's general complaints that censors were corrupt and derelict in their duty had their counterparts later in general laments by censorial officials themselves, by other officials, and especially by Hsi-tsung that censors and supervising secretaries talked too much, or were too biased, or sought too zealously to dominate decision-making.[162] "Don't harass me!" and "Stop trying to outdo one another!" were now common responses to censorial memorials.[163]

Table 22 reveals far more striking disparities between censorial punishments given while the Tung-lin men were dominant at court and those given under Wei Chung-hsien's regime, than between those of the whole period 1620–27 and those of the earlier period 1424–34. Though some Tung-lin men were notoriously vengeful and vindictive, they were satisfied to have their censorial opponents demoted, or "promoted out" in the sense described above, or at worst removed from office. And when they themselves gave offense, their high-placed champions—particularly including the grand secretary Yeh Hsiang-kao—were influential enough to ward off severe punishments. The record of censorial discipline prior to Wei Chung-hsien's ascendance in 1424, consequently, shows remarkable moderation.

The two most severe punishments of the early 1620's were beatings in court administered to the investigating censors Cheng Tsung-chou in 1620 and Lin Ju-chu in 1624. Both were considered Tung-lin partisans; they were not punished at the instigation of Tung-lin men. Cheng was beaten because he offended Hsi-tsung in demanding punishment of the eunuch physician Ts'ui Wen-sheng for his mistreatment of the ailing Kuang-tsung.[164] Cheng was eventually dismissed from the service as a Tung-lin partisan in 1625.[165] As was noted in Chapter 5, Lin Ju-chu offended Wei Chung-hsien in mid-1624 by beating two eunuchs. Knowing his action would be revenged, he fled;

as a result, the residence of his patron, the grand secretary Yeh Hsiang-kao, was surrounded by a eunuch military detachment, and Yeh left office in humiliation. Lin then gave himself up, was beaten in court, and thereafter was further punished by dismissal from the civil service.[166]

The only other relatively severe censorial punishments of the Tung-lin era were dismissals from the service. One instance involved the long-time Tung-lin antagonist Yao Tsung-wen. For bringing about the removal of Hsiung T'ing-pi from command in Liaotung in 1620, Yao was suspended from his post as supervising secretary and in 1621 was made a civilian. Although Yao later returned to service under Wei Chung-hsien and in 1627 became grand coordinator of Hukwang province, his removal in 1621 was not particularly a Tung-lin achievement, for the Tung-lin group at that early time was not yet championing Hsiung T'ing-pi. One of Yao's accusers, in fact, was the censor Chang Chieh, already referred to as a Tung-lin enemy.[167] Other cases that had no clear relation to Tung-lin partisan interests involved the troop-recruiting censors Ming Shih-chü and Li Ta, and the surveillance vice commissioner Wu Jui-cheng of Honan province, who was dismissed from the service in 1621 for leaving his post without permission when a local rebellion occurred.[168] Ming and Li had both voluntarily gone to Szechwan in 1621 to recruit south-western aborigines for military service in Liaotung. When the aborigines started a rebellion, the two censors were arrested and tried on a charge of having provoked the revolt. The trial proved that charge false, but they were convicted of serious indiscretions. In 1623, in consequence, they were made civilians.[169]

Liu Ch'ung-ch'ing, a probationary investigating censor awaiting assignment, was dismissed from the civil service in 1621 for presumptuously impeaching the grand secretary Liu I-ching, apparently attributing Liaotung military reverses to him. According to the *Shih-lu*, all the censors and supervising secretaries of both Peking and Nanking and finally hosts of high-ranking officials of both cities and even Liu I-ching himself memorialized in Liu Ch'ung-ch'ing's defense, but in vain. Finally, however, late in 1622, he was reinstated in his former post. He served again under Wei Chung-hsien but in 1627 was ordered to retire on a charge of being a partisan of Yang Lien.[170] However, there is no reason to think him either a Tung-lin partisan or a Tung-lin opponent in 1621. Certainly, his dismissal was not the Tung-lin group's doing.

The dismissal of Chia Chi-ch'un is the only one in this group that was a controversial issue involving the Tung-lin men, though the Tung-lin leaders by no means were united against him. Chia, as a censor, vehemently protested Yang Lien's and Tso Kuang-tou's impolite treatment of Madame Li, Kuang-tsung's consort, in "the case of the removal from the palace" in 1620. Finally in 1621 he confessed that he had spread false rumors about the case, and he was made a civilian. Though Yang and Tso attacked him, he was defended or recommended for recall by the grand secretary Yeh Hsiang-kao and by other Tung-lin men, even Chou Tsung-chien and Yüan Hua-chung, who eventually were tortured to death in the same prison as Yang and Tso and are almost equally renowned as Tung-lin martyrs. Chia Chi-ch'un's dismissal in 1621 clearly seems to have been insisted upon by Hsi-tsung himself. Chia was finally recalled to office by Wei Chung-hsien, and he encouraged Wei to promulgate the anti-Tung-lin interpretation of the "three great cases" of 1615 and 1620.[171]

Some other censorial officials narrowly escaped severe punishment in the early 1620's. The supervising secretary Sun Chieh antagonized Hsi-tsung in late 1620 by attacking the minister of justice Huang K'o-tsan too insistently, and the emperor ordered that a court assembly be convened to sentence Sun. But the grand secretary Liu I-ching soothed the emperor, and the assembly was canceled.[172] And in 1622 the supervising secretary Chang Yün-ju was ordered beaten and was sent in disgrace to serve as a soldier at the frontier when he proposed a reduction in the emperor's clothing allowance. The grand secretary Yeh Hsiang-kao intervened and got the sentence reduced to a one-year's salary suspension.[173] In neither case was the Tung-lin group the accuser.

In short, the Tung-lin men did not advocate severe punishments for their enemies in the censorial establishment, and severe punishments were seldom resorted to at all when the Tung-lin men dominated the government. As often as not, they were even then the victims of punishment rather than its instigators.

The most commonly given punishment of this period was the salary suspension—for three months, or six months, or a year, or an even longer period. The investigating censors Chang Shen-yen and Kao Hung-t'u were both fined two years' salaries in 1621 for provocatively defending a colleague whom Hsi-tsung had rebuked; and a few months later the Nanking censor Wang Yün-ch'eng had his salary suspended for three years when he remonstrated about eunuch control over the issuance of imperial edicts.[174] Hsi-tsung also resorted frequently to rebukes rather than to punishments, sometimes because of the soothing influence of such advisers as Yeh Hsiang-kao, and sometimes in frustrated realization that he could not punish everybody. Thus in 1622 all of the supervising secretaries on duty in all six of the Offices of Scrutiny joined in a combined denunciation of the anti-Tung-lin grand secretary Shen Ts'ui, whom Hsi-tsung admired. The emperor was enraged but let the critics off with a rebuke simply because, as the *Shih-lu* explicitly state, "they were so numerous they could not all be tried."[175] In all, Hsi-tsung rebuked censorial officials on 43 occasions from 1620 into mid-1624.

In the second period of Hsi-tsung's reign, when such moderating influences as Yeh Hsiang-kao had been removed and Wei Chung-hsien unrestrainedly dominated the court, the disciplining of censorial officials became notably more vicious, as Table 22 clearly indicates. Though censors and supervising secretaries who mildly displeased Wei were occasionally merely rebuked (26 times), not a single censorial official who was punished in Wei's time escaped with anything so light as a salary suspension. Rather than to fine, Wei preferred to demote; rather than to demote, he preferred to remove from office; and rather than to remove from office, he preferred to dismiss from the service. For anyone whom he considered a real enemy, of course, even dismissal was not enough.

Wei Chung-hsien's failure to assess fines should not suggest that he totally renounced monetary penalties. One of his favorite tactics was to ruin someone by imposing punitive damages—often in addition to some more severe punishment, and sometimes even posthumously. Punitive damages were nominally not damages; they allegedly were bribery profits, which had to be recovered by the state. For example, almost all of the Tung-lin men who were arrested upon being implicated in the forged confession produced after the trial and judicial murder of Wang Wen-yen, in 1625, were charged with having accepted bribes from the Liaotung commander Hsiung T'ing-pi, and recovery was ordered. Efforts to make such collections were continued, if necessary, until the property of all known relatives of the victim had been liquidated. One of the most extreme cases of this sort involved the onetime censor-in-chief and later minister of personnel Chang Wen-ta, who had been a leading Tung-lin partisan since the early 1600's and was a central figure in "the case of the attack with the club" in 1615. Chang went home on extended leave in 1623 and in 1625 was dismissed from the service along with most other Tung-lin leaders. In his case punitive damages of 100,000 taels were assessed, technically to be used for troop-recruiting costs. When Chang died in 1626 still owing most of this huge sum, the grand coordinator of his home province got permission by special grace to reduce the requirement to 50,000 taels; but even so Chang's family was ruined in efforts to make up what was owed.[176]

Although most of Wei Chung-hsien's punishments were directed at the Tung-lin men, these were not his only censorial victims. The only longtime Tung-lin opponent who was finally punished by Wei's order was the former censor K'ang P'ei-yang, referred to in Chapter 5. K'ang had been a bitter opponent of the Tung-lin group in the early 1600's but had been in retirement since 1609. In 1625, when Wei was having partisan history rewritten, K'ang submitted his own interpretation of the very early controversies and asked that it be added to the compilation. He was upbraided for his partisan bias and was ordered tried. When the judicial offices proposed that he be deprived of civil-service status, an edict increased his punishment to serving as a common soldier at the frontier. It is not clear whether he actually served.[177]

Ten censors and supervising secretaries were impeached under Chuang-lieh-ti and were officially labeled eunuch partisans and oppressors of the Tung-lin "good elements," although they were actually dismissed from the civil service by Wei Chung-hsien himself. These were the ten: (1) The censor Shih San-wei, appointed in 1625. He demanded the execution of Hsiung T'ing-pi, denounced Ku Hsien-ch'eng and Chao Nan-hsing, and was himself punished in 1626 because of improper proposals and personnel recommendations.[178] (2) The supervising secretary Huang Ch'eng-hao, son of a man who had opposed the "good elements" in the 1590's. He was appointed in 1625, tried to clear his father of prior Tung-lin opprobrium, impeached some Tung-lin men, and was himself denounced as a Tung-lin partisan and punished in 1626 when he objected to eunuchs being sent to supervise the frontier forces.[179] (3) The Nanking censor Hsü Fu-yang, appointed in 1625. He impeached some Tung-lin men, and was himself punished in 1626 on a charge of bribery.[180] (4) The censor Wang Yeh-hao, appointed in 1620. He was reappointed in 1623 and 1625 (why he was then out of office is not clear). He asked lenience in punishments and in tax collections in 1626, then was punished when the Ministry of Personnel nominated him for promotion.[181] (5) The Nanking censor Liang K'o-shun, appointed in 1625. He impeached some Tung-lin men, proposed ways to stimulate tax collections, and was punished in 1626 for partisanship.[182] (6) The censor Liu Chih-tai, appointed in 1622. As regional inspector of Chekiang, he collected punitive damages from Tung-lin men and was punished in 1627 for partisanship.[183] (7) The censor Ch'en I-jui, appointed in 1625. He impeached Tung-lin men and was punished in 1627 for making partisan criticisms.[184] (8) The censor Ho Tsao, appointed in 1620. He was recalled in 1625, and impeached Tung-lin men. He was punished in 1627 when impeached by a eunuch after opposing the eunuch's proposal that civilians handle Grand Canal transport service.[185] (9) The supervising secretary Yeh Yu-sheng, appointed in 1625. He impeached the former grand secretary Liu I-ching and other Tung-lin men, and was punished in 1627 for being a long-time partisan.[186] (10) The supervising secretary Yü T'ing-pi, appointed in 1625. He impeached Tung-lin men, objected to continued circulation of private lists of "good elements" heroes, and was punished in 1627 as a partisan.[187]

In most of these cases, the reasons given for eventually dismissing the men from the civil service are not clarified in the *Shih-lu* beyond the indications given above. Many of the men were punished just when they were being nominated for promotions or assignments to commissions. It would almost appear that their dismissals were merely Wei Chung-hsien's whims of the moment.

Three other censorial officials who were blacklisted as eunuch partisans by Hsi-tsung's successor were also punished by Wei. In the tenth month of 1624, the censor Ch'en Chiu-ch'ou, on instructions from one of Wei's agents, attacked the minister of personnel Chao Nan-hsing and the supervising secretary Wei Ta-chung and thus brought about a mass exodus of Tung-lin leaders from the capital and the emergence of Wei Chung-hsien into open dominance at court. But Ch'en was at the same time demoted three degrees and transferred to an unspecified provincial post, on a charge of wrangling in court.[188] In 1625 the supervising secretary Chang Wei-i was ordered demoted one degree and transferred to a provincial post because of his impropriety in impeaching a grand coordinator, but he was defended by Wei's henchman Ts'ui Ch'eng-hsiu and was eventually restored and successively promoted.[189] The censor T'ien Ching-hsin, who formed part of Ts'ui Ch'eng-hsiu's claque and who repeatedly denounced Tung-lin men, was forced to retire in 1627 when he was nominated for a commission and insistently declined to undertake it.[190]

Instances like these were oddities of the Wei Chung-hsien era. They suggest in part that Wei and his chief associates were somewhat fickle patrons and in part that the enemies of the eunuch partisans who gained power under Chuang-lieh-ti were not wholly reasonable in distinguishing Wei's supporters from his victims.[191]

The most ill-treated of Wei Chung-hsien's censorial victims were, of course, "good elements" who had long associations with the Tung-lin movement or who had otherwise offended Wei and earned Tung-lin labels. In addition to K'ang P'ei-yang (mentioned above) these included five men whom Wei sentenced to serve as common soldiers at the frontier: (1) The former censor Hsü Chin-fang, active in the controversies of the early 1600's but out of active service since about 1613. He was denounced in 1625, was assessed punitive damages in 1626, and was further sentenced to frontier duty in 1627.[192] (2) The censor Chang Shen-yen, active in controversies over the "great cases" of 1620. He was denounced and sentenced in 1626.[193] (3) The supervising secretary Mao Shih-lung, who led the censorial attack on Hsiung T'ing-pi's accuser Yao Tsung-wen, and praised Yang Lien in regard to the "great cases" of 1620. He repeatedly criticized Wei Chung-hsien and was removed from office in 1621 for feuding with Shao Fu-chung, who eventually became one of Wei's protégés. He was not recalled despite recommendations by the grand secretary Yeh Hsiang-kao and others, was dismissed from the civil service late in 1624, and was then sentenced to frontier service in 1625 when implicated in the forged confession of Wang Wen-yen. But apparently he escaped arrest even before he was sent to the frontier, successfully remained a fugitive until after Hsi-tsung's death and Wei Chung-hsien's fall from power, and was then recalled to service and eventually promoted to the post of assistant censor-in-chief.[194] (4) The censor Yu Shih-jen, the notoriously corrupt troop-recruiter discussed previously. His abuses were denounced and investigated from 1622 on, but he was not sentenced until 1626. Apparently he was considered a Tung-lin man only because he was punished in Wei's era.[195] (5) The Nanking assistant censor-in-chief Hsiung Ming-yü, an active Tung-lin supporter since Shen-tsung's time. He was repeatedly recommended by Tung-lin men, was removed from office early in 1625 for protesting the punishment of Yu Shih-jen, then was implicated in the forged confession of Wang Wen-yen and was dismissed from the civil service. In 1626 he was sentenced to frontier service; but he was eventually recalled to duty under Chuang-lieh-ti.[196]

Two censorial officials were sentenced to death in Wei Chung-hsien's time without actually being put to death, and in both cases the available records give no clue as to what saved them from joining the Tung-lin marytrs. One was the oft-mentioned censor Fang

Chen-ju, who was regional inspector and army-inspecting censor in Liaotung when the Ming defense forces were swept back to the Great Wall in early 1622. Fang was subjected to repeated accusations and investigations in the court's prolonged attempt to fix responsibility for the Liaotung debacle. In mid-1625 he was finally sent to the Ministry of Justice to be sentenced and to have punitive damages assessed. In the twelfth month of that year the recommendations of a court assembly that had been convened to consider his case were reported to the emperor. What specific sentence the assembly proposed is not clear, but Wei Chung-hsien felt that it was insufficiently harsh. An edict was issued rebuking the judicial authorities and ordering them to reconsider the case so as to arrive at a more severe punishment. Finally, in early 1626, a sentence of strangulation was approved. Fang nevertheless survived to give further service under Hsi-tsung's successor.[197]

The supervising secretary Hui Shih-yang was also sentenced to death but not executed. Hui first gained notoriety by his activity in the "red pills" controversy in 1620. He attacked the grand secretaries Fang Ts'ung-che and Shen Ts'ui, opposed military training for palace eunuchs, blamed the minister of war Chang Hao-ming rather than the supreme commander Hsiung T'ing-pi for the Liaotung troubles, and in general was consistently on the Tung-lin side throughout the series of controversies that enlivened the early 1620's. He apparently left office in 1624. Then early in 1625, in consequence of the trial of Wang Wen-yen and in the same edict that sent Yang Lien and many other Tung-lin men to prison, he was dismissed from the civil service and ordered to be tried by the judicial authorities of his home province, Shensi. Subsequently he was transferred to the palace prison of the imperial bodyguard, and in the second month of 1626 he was sentenced to death.[198] Like Fang Chen-ju, he somehow survived to give service again under Chuang-lieh-ti. His pedigree as one of the anti–Wei Chung-hsien "good elements" of the 1620's is nearly flawless, and what he did is abundantly recorded both in the *Shih-lu* and in other sources on the partisan controversies, including the biographies of his friends and enemies. But he himself has no biography in the standard collections that extol the "good elements" champions; and what seems an awkward, embarrassed silence covers his later life. This appears to be entirely because in the end he betrayed his "good elements" reputation by accepting service briefly under both the rebel Li Tzu-ch'eng and the conquering Manchus, who shared in destroying the Ming dynasty.[199]

Of the censorial officials who died because of Wei Chung-hsien's orders, two were somewhat isolated cases. One, Wu Yü-chung, was appointed an investigating censor in 1625, after Wei Chung-hsien had come to power. Almost immediately he denounced Wei's protégé the grand secretary Ting Shao-shih, whom he blamed for bringing about the long-delayed execution of Hsiung T'ing-pi. Since Wu was a Hukwang fellow-townsman of Hsiung, it was easy for Wei to justify punishing him for partisan bias. Wu was sentenced to 100 blows of the heavy bamboo and dismissal from the civil service, but he did not survive his beating.[200] The other, the censor Hsia Chih-ling, had earned Wei's enmity as early as 1622 by criticizing the Liaotung adventurer Mao Wen-lung, whom Wei admired, and especially by punishing some offensive eunuchs while serving as a ward-inspecting censor in Peking. Hsia was dismissed from the civil service early in 1625 at the instigation of Wei's chief censorial agent, Ts'ui Ch'eng-hsiu, and then in the ninth month was impeached again by the censor Ni Wen-huan for being a partisan of Hsiung T'ing-pi. He was then arrested and imprisoned, and he died of prison tortures before the end of the year.[201]

The most celebrated Tung-lin martyrs, and the most mourned of Wei Chung-hsien's victims, were 13 men who died in two groups: the "six heroes" of 1625 and the "seven heroes" of 1626. All but one died after enduring tortures in the palace prison of the imperial bodyguard, which was wholly dominated by Wei Chung-hsien; the thirteenth committed suicide rather than be arrested. Nine of the 13 had recently been active censorial officials.

The "six heroes" of 1625 were all implicated in the forged confession of Wang Wen-yen, presented at court in the third month of that year, and it was immediately ordered that all six be imprisoned and tried in the palace prison on charges of having taken bribes from the Liaotung commander Hsiung T'ing-pi (who was also in prison). Beginning in the sixth month, all were subjected to tortures intended to force confessions from them, and none survived more than a few weeks. The only non-censorial official among them was a Ministry of Justice official, Ku Ta-chang, who had long defended Hsiung T'ing-pi and who had often enraged Wei Chung-hsien in other ways. Ku finally committed suicide in the palace prison rather than endure any further tortures. Even Ku, though he had no censorial background and was still nominally a ministry official, was actually on special detached service as surveillance vice commissioner of Shensi province when he was arrested.[202]

Of the five active censorial officials in the group, the two most famous were Yang Lien and Tso Kuang-tou, who were quickly immortalized in the folklore of Chinese heroism. The five were: (1) Yang Lien, a doctoral graduate of 1607 who was active in the Tung-lin Academy while serving as a county magistrate in the vicinity. He became one of the most aggressive Tung-lin political activists at court after being appointed a supervising secretary in 1619. He was the most active controversialist in the "great cases" of 1620, went home on sick leave early in 1621, was recalled in 1622 as a chief supervising secretary, and became assistant censor-in-chief in 1623 and then vice censor-in-chief in early 1624. Throughout his censorial career, he insistently supported Tung-lin men and opposed their enemies, and it was he who provoked the eventual Tung-lin disaster by openly denouncing Wei Chung-hsien. He was dismissed from the civil service on a charge of partisanship late in 1624, and was living at home while Wei prepared for more drastic action.[203] (2) Tso Kuang-tou, who was appointed an investigating censor in 1619. Though not as aggressively partisan as Yang Lien, Tso befriended Yang and gave him close support in the "great cases" of 1620. Early in 1624, after a brief interlude of service in the Grand Court of Revision, he was made assistant censor-in-chief. He quickly antagonized two men who were soon to become Wei Chung-hsien's chief henchmen—Juan Ta-ch'eng and Fu K'uei. Tso also gave Yang Lien help and encouragement in drafting the famous denunciation of Wei. Like Yang, he was made a civilian late in 1624 on charges of partisanship. In 1625 he and Yang were thrown in the palace prison on the same day, endured identical tortures, and died of torture on the same day in the seventh month.[204] (3) Wei Ta-chung, a one-time student at the Tung-lin Academy under Kao P'an-lung. Wei became a supervising secretary in 1621, and was perhaps an even more aggressively partisan Tung-lin spokesman than Yang Lien. He befriended Wang Wen-yen, attacked the grand secretaries Fang Ts'ung-che and Shen Ts'ui, and came to be hated by the eunuch supporters Fu K'uei and Juan Ta-ch'eng. He joined in denouncing Wei Chung-hsien after Yang's attack in mid-1624 and was removed from office late that year when Yang and Tso were dismissed from the service. He died in prison on the same day as Yang and Tso.[205] (4) Yüan Hua-chung, who served as an investigating censor from 1620 on. He denounced Fang Ts'ung-che, complained about the growing influence of eunuchs, joined in the denunciation of Wei Chung-hsien after Yang's attack in 1624, and also denounced Ts'ui Ch'eng-hsiu. Like Wei Ta-chung, he was removed from his office late in 1624.[206] (5) Chou Ch'ao-jui, one of the most daring and provocative remonstrators of Hsi-tsung's reign. Chou served as supervising secretary from 1620 on. He argued against the young emperor's inclination to avoid studying and his unwillingness to tolerate criticism. He also defended Hsiung T'ing-pi, and he attacked Shen Ts'ui and others whom Wei Chung-hsien favored. Unlike others in this group, he was apparently still on duty in 1625 when he was arrested in consequence of Wang Wen-yen's trial.[207]

The "seven heroes" of 1626, four of whom were censorial officials, were all men of the rich southeastern provinces around the mouth of the Yangtze. All but one were already out of office early in 1626 when they were denounced in a mass impeachment by the eunuch Li Shih, obviously at the instigation of Wei Chung-hsien.[208] All but one were tortured to death later in the year in the same palace prison where Yang Lien and the others had died the year before. One of the non-censors in this second group of martyrs was the grand coordinator Chou Ch'i-yüan of the Soochow region, a Tung-lin partisan since the early 1600's who had seen service as a censor and as a surveillance commissioner but now was only nominally a censor-in-chief.[209] Another was the Hanlin official Miao Ch'ang-ch'i, a longtime friend of Yang Lien who had probably helped draft Yang's denunciation of Wei Chung-hsien.[210] The third was Chou Shun-ch'ang, a Ministry of Personnel official who had been in retirement since 1622. Though known as an honest and upright man, Chou had never been associated with any great Tung-lin causes; but he ostentatiously befriended Wei Ta-chung when Wei was escorted under arrest through Soochow in 1625, and at the same time openly cursed and calumniated Wei Chung-hsien in the presence of the generally dreaded mounted guardsmen of the imperial bodyguard who were escorting Wei Ta-chung. Chou was consequently included in Li Shih's impeachment, which accused the seven victims of plotting together for partisan and subversive purposes. When mounted guardsmen arrived to arrest Chou Shun-ch'ang, the people of Soochow rose up in his defense in one of the most dramatic confrontations of the oppressed and their oppressors in Ming history. They killed at least one and perhaps two imperial guardsmen and endangered and humiliated both the new grand coordinator Mao I-lu and the regional inspector Hsü Chi, but without preventing Chou's arrest and eventual death.[211]

The four active censorial officials among the "seven heroes" of 1626 were: (1) Kao P'an-lung, one of the founders of the Tung-lin Academy. Kao had been a patron of Yang Lien since 1608–9 and had helped secure the dominance of the Tung-lin men in the early 1620's. He doomed himself in 1624 when, as censor-in-chief, he collaborated with the minister of personnel Chao Nan-hsing in disciplining the venal censor Ts'ui Ch'eng-hsiu, making Ts'ui a viciously vengeful supporter of Wei Chung-hsien. When he was implicated in the partisan machinations of Wei and his henchmen following Yang Lien's attack in mid-1624, Kao went home in voluntary retirement. He was dismissed from the civil service late in 1625; and in 1626, when he learned that his arrest had been ordered, he drowned himself at home before his captors arrived.[212] (2) Chou Tsung-chien, appointed an investigating censor in 1620. Chou was a very independent-minded man and was repeatedly at odds with the more vindictive Tung-lin partisans such as Wei Ta-chung. But he won Tung-lin respect and confidence by honoring the memory of the Tung-lin founder Ku Hsien-ch'eng, by supporting Hsiung T'ing-pi, by attacking Shen Ts'ui, by remonstrating against military training of palace eunuchs, and especially by being among the earliest denouncers of Mistress K'o and Wei Chung-hsien. He also participated actively in the academy discussions in Peking sponsored by Tsou Yüan-piao and Feng Ts'ung-wu. He had been living at home in mourning since early 1624 when he was arrested in 1626.[213] (3) Li Ying-sheng, a censor from 1622 on, who became one of the most outspoken critics of Wei Chung-hsien in 1624. He denounced Wei for sponsoring military training for eunuchs, for placing his sycophants in office, and for abusive use of the cangue on prisoners. He had even prepared a comprehensive impeachment of Wei prior to Yang Lien's attack, but a brother persuaded him not to submit it. After Yang's attack on Wei, Li joined vigorously in the chorus of Yang's supporters. He also antagonized Ts'ui Ch'eng-hsiu by refusing to intercede on his behalf when Ts'ui was disciplined by Kao P'an-lung. Early in 1625 he was impeached and dismissed from the civil service.[214] (4) Huang Tsun-su, best remembered as father of the great scholar and historian Huang Tsung-hsi.[215] Huang was appointed an investigating censor in 1622 and became a close associate of Yang Lien, Tso Kuang-tou, and other Tung-lin men, though he was known for his prudence and caution. He thought that it was unwise for Tsou Yüan-piao and Feng Ts'ung-wu to organize an academy in the capital, and he advised Yang Lien not to submit his 1624 denunciation of Wei Chung-hsien because he considered it ill-timed. After Yang's attack Huang advised him to leave the capital, saying: "Every day that you are at court is one more day when Wei Chung-hsien is ill at ease, so that state affairs will be increasingly disrupted. It would be best for you to leave, so that the disaster may be somewhat moderated."[216] But Yang procrastinated, and the situation did worsen. Finally, when the grand secretary Yeh Hsiang-kao was humiliated and the censor Lin Ju-chu was beaten, Huang did speak out angrily against eunuch oppression. Like Li Ying-sheng, he was impeached and dismissed from the civil service early in 1625 and was living at home when arrested in 1626.[217]

What all these victims endured in prison was nominally only interrogation, supposedly intended to wring confessions from them. At least in Yang Lien's and Tso Kuang-tou's cases, the interrogations were scheduled every five days. They normally involved a variety of tortures, principally 40 blows with a willow or elm rod some five feet long and about as thick as a man's little finger, which sliced the flesh almost like a knife. It was applied to the bare buttocks while the victim was held with ropes so that he could neither turn to the side nor flex his legs; his wrists were bound in a small hand-stock and his arms were weighted down with iron manacles. A normal interrogation session also included up to 100 squeezings with a finger-press and up to 50 jerks by jailors holding one's arms and legs and pulling in opposite directions. Moreover, the interrogation sessions became more frequent, until at least Yang and Tso had to endure them daily. Confessions were unavailing; the real intention was that the victims should not survive.[218]

Friends and relatives of the victims were allowed to visit them on certain days, but only by paying large fees to the jailors. Tso's sons paid fees of this sort totaling 530 taels. To permit complete surveillance by the jailors, the victim and his visitor were always required to kneel ten feet apart and to speak in loud voices, without resorting to any local dialects that the watching jailors could not understand.[219] Through such visitations, news of what was happening in the palace prison steadily leaked to the outside.

Tso Kuang-tou was also able to send notes to his sons from prison, and these were preserved for at least a century in his family, and eventually were reproduced in a biography compiled by his great grandson. To whatever extent Tso was representative of his fellow victims, they give us a moving glimpse into the sufferings, the stoic resignation, and the loyal frustrations of the Tung-lin martyrs, as in the following excerpts:

I have been an honest official and have no private fortune to leave you; I leave only a reputation. I have now endured a hundred kinds of tortures. I can neither live nor die. Moreover, there is no medicine to take, and inside

here it is oppressively hot. It is unspeakable misery. Misery! . . . Those who
have no silver are beaten, but those who have silver are also beaten. I cannot
endure it; I cannot suffer any more. . . . By now my pain and distress are
extreme. I can no longer even walk a step. In the middle of the night the
pain gets still worse. If I want water to drink, none is at hand. Death! Death!
Only thus can I make recompense to the emperor and to the two imperial
ancestors. . . . My silver is long ago exhausted, my strength long ago spent.
After the agony of thirty blows comes only more agony. After the pain comes
only more pain. What remains of my life will be paid out under the rod.
But you, my beloved son—you must in all things be prudent and not do anything rash lest calamity extend to the whole family, for the misfortune could
be unfathomable. . . .

By now I am thoroughly done in. My thirst is agonizing, and day and night
my blood flows out like a stream. . . . Let me exhort you insistently not to
forget that today I again need 200 taels of silver; if there is one tael less, I
immediately die! My pain and suffering are beyond description. My body
has been transformed into an inhuman lump without any whole flesh. . . .
On the twenty-third I need 200 more taels of "interrogation silver." I know
that you out there will exhaust every possibility and entreat everyone. If
there is no help I shall not last long. I barely have one mouthful of breath
left. Perhaps there is no point in saving me. . . .

Every bone in my body seems broken, and my flesh is bloodlogged. . . . This
loyal heart came to be at odds with powerful villains and brought about this
sore calamity. All sorts of punishments I have willingly endured. Since I
have already argued at the risk of my life, why need I shrink from running
against the spear and dying? My body belongs to my ruler-father. I am lucky
I shall not die in the arms of my wife and children; for I have found the
proper place to die! I only regret that this blood-filled heart has not been
able to make recompense to my ruler, and that my aged parents cannot once
again see my face. This will be my remorse in Hades! . . .

My misery is extreme; my pain is extreme. Why do I live on? Why do I
cling to life? Death! . . . My misery is extreme, my filth is extreme, my disgrace is extreme, my pain is extreme. There is nothing left for me to do but
cry out to Heaven. Crying out to Heaven and getting no answer, I can only
submit to Heaven. How can I any longer cling to these dregs of my life?[220]

Tso Kuang-tou's death in prison did not save his family from further calamities after all. Punitive damages of 20,000 taels were demanded, and attempts to collect this sum implicated not only his immediate family but relatives on his mother's and his wife's sides.[221]
His brother Tso Kuang-ch'i was put to death. His eighty-year-old
father fell ill of anxiety and became almost wholly paralyzed, and his
mother grieved to death. His sons and brothers, one second cousin,
eleven nephews, and one grand-nephew were all imprisoned at one
time or another until the punitive damages were fully paid.[222]
Similar punitive damages were assessed on other victims and their
families, at least including Wei Ta-chung, Chou Tsung-chien, and

Huang Tsun-su. Because he had always been poor, Yang Lien's relatives apparently escaped such persecution. It is reported that after Yang's death his two sons had to beg food to maintain his wife and his mother.[223]

Thus, notwithstanding all its prestige and all its powers to harass emperors and bureaucrats alike, the Ming censorial establishment in the last resort was powerless to protect itself from tyrannical oppression.

Chapter seven

Censorship and the Traditional State System

All evaluations of traditional China's censorial system have tended toward polar extremes; the system has been extravagantly praised and extravagantly denounced. Some see it as a bureaucratic restraint upon monarchical despotism and sometimes even endow it with a certain democratic force, whereas others see it without qualification as an instrument of monarchical despotism. Therefore, a comment on the system's role in Ming government and Ming history in general is perhaps an appropriate conclusion to this study.

Admirers of the system generally echo Matteo Ricci, who, as was noted in Chapter 1, called the Ming censorial officials "a source of wonder to outsiders and a good example for imitation," and who commended "their courage and frankness."[1] A nineteenth-century observer, reporting somewhat inaccurately about "the public censorate, the officers of which are appointed to oversee the affairs of the whole empire, and are allowed to reprove the sovereign, or any of his officers, without being liable to punishment," concluded with the following encomium: "Such an institution as this, where the expression of public opinion is generally suppressed, is certainly of great value, and indicates the wisdom of those statesmen who established, and the magnanimity of those rulers who endure it."[2] Others, following the lead of Sun Yat-sen, founder of the modern Republic of China, have even claimed that the censorial system "was by nature an institution apart from the Emperor" and that at times it was "practically the final authority in the empire."[3] Lin Yutang, who has idealized many facets of the Chinese tradition for American readers, has written that the censorial system "fulfils in the ancient Chinese monarchy the function of public criticism usually fulfilled by the modern press," and he says that the system was rooted in "an essentially democratic principle of government." He adds:

The imperial censors were in a true sense the equivalents of modern publicists; their impeachments and petitions may be regarded as expressing the voice of the people, or as we say in ancient China, they were the "eyes and ears of the Emperor." ... True, the Chinese state was an absolute monarchy, and we had no electorates and no Houses of Parliament. Any semblance of a modern machinery of self-government was lacking. Nevertheless Chinese scholars and philosophers from the very earliest days went upon the assumption that government was based on the good-will of the people, and when a government had lost that, it was doomed to collapse. When this happened, we said that the "Heaven's decree" had passed from one ruling house to another, but this so-called decree or will of Heaven could only be ascertained from the opinions of the people. ... This philosophic principle became established as a popular notion throughout the history of China, as embodied in the principle that when the "avenues of expression" (of the people's opinion) are free, the government is regarded as good, and when these "avenues of expression" are blocked, so that the Emperor has no way of finding out the true conditions and opinions of the people, the government is doomed to failure. ...

The strange thing is, when the conduct of a government is bad enough to call for outspoken and fearless criticism, there were always censors or other officials indignant enough about the state of affairs to risk all the penalties for themselves. ...[4]

The contemporary American scholar Richard L. Walker has been even more admiring:

As an element which aided very greatly in the stability and continuity of Chinese political institutions, the Control system is eminently worth study by Western political scientists. It does not have to prove its efficacy as an independent organ of government; it did that over a thousand years ago. That is a part of its nature as it has existed. The Censoral system of the Chinese might even be studied by Occidental scholars with the end in view of including its best features in their own political institutions. For example, with an independent Censoral body in the United States the legislative bodies would not have to devote their valuable time to committee investigations of their own members and would be able in consequence to produce more carefully planned legislation. With a vigorous Control body in existence government jobs would be less open to criticism as nests for lazy people.[5]

The idealistic interpretations of the censorial system as a defender of the people's rights against tyrants badly need correctives, and there has been no lack of them, some even verging on cynicism. Samuel Wells Williams, the most influential nineteenth-century interpreter of China to Americans, tried to be fair in his usual Christian way.

He noted that "the existence of such a body [as the Censorate] and the publication of its memorials, can hardly fail to rectify misconduct to some degree, and check maladministration before it results in widespread evil." He also said that "the suspension or disgrace of censors for their freedom of speech is a common occurrence, and among the forty or fifty persons who have this privilege a few are to be found who do not hesitate to lift up their voice against what they deem to be wrong." However, he could not resist adding that "in a despotic government this [censors' freedom to speak out] is little else than a fiction of state, for the fear of offending the imperial ear, and consequent disgrace, will usually prove stronger than the consciousness of right or the desires of a public fame and martyrdom for the sake of principle." As regards the Censorate in general Williams observed that "a close examination of its real operations and influence and the character of its members may excite more contempt than respect."[6] The Britisher Sir Robert Hart, who eventually had a distinguished career as an official of the nineteenth-century Chinese empire and who probably understood its government better than any other modern Westerner, said early in his acquaintance with China that the censorial officials "contributed to the corruption of officials and did not hear the people's anger."[7] The great sociologist Max Weber, while recognizing that Chinese emperors could be reprimanded by speaking officials, emphasized that Chinese government included "a thorough spy system in the form of so-called censors."[8] At the extreme of cynicism is the following commentary by an early nineteenth-century observer:

In investigating the principles on which the government of China preserves its power over the people, we find two prominent points,—a system of strict *surveillance,* and a system of universal, mutual *responsibility.* . . . The system of surveillance, and the mutual liability to punishment, operate . . . by means of *fear,* to deter men from offering resistance to government; and this fear is at the same time fortified by the habit of submission, arising out of the peaceable character of the people, and their mental debasement. Thus, with a state of society we might almost say ripe for rebellion, the people are nevertheless effectually kept in check, by a government acting on the baneful and debasing principle of surveillance and universal responsibility.[9]

Both the idealizers and the debunkers could substantiate their interpretations with the data presented in the foregoing chapters. It is possible to think of the censorial system either as a tool with which emperors kept their officials submissive or as a check on the emperors themselves. The choice depends on whether one is more impressed by the aspect of censorial operations that derived from the "surveillance officials" tradition or by the aspect that derived from the "speaking officials" tradition. It also depends on whether one aspect or the other happens to be dramatically manifest in the period under study. As we have repeatedly seen, both elements were present in the system; and they could not be expected to stay in a perpetual equilibrium.

One would suppose that the dual functions of the censorial system would have fluctuated in importance and prominence with the differing personalities of the emperors. As Lin Yutang suggests, "When an emperor was good, he had very little need of censors, and when he was bad, the work of putting him on the right road was a thankless task, like the reforming of drunkards."[10] It might be expected that a harsh and oppressive ruler would have provoked censorial officials into dramatic remonstrances, and that a mild and benevolent ruler would have provoked little remonstrance, thus allowing censorial officials to concentrate on surveillance and impeachment. But there are of course two sides to this coin. For it is likely that the ruler who most provoked remonstrances was most adept at using the censorial officials for intensive surveillance over the officialdom and at frightening them into withholding their criticism of himself; and it is likely that the mild ruler would have urged moderation of censorial surveillance and invited criticism of his own laxity.

Neither type of ruler dominates my study, and perhaps neither often existed. The rulers I have dealt with are more complicated persons. Hsüan-tsung was strong, capable, and conscientious—one might almost say harsh but benevolent. Hsi-tsung was inattentive, ineffectual, and susceptible to improper influences—one might almost say mild but oppressive. And the censorial responses to them were equally complicated. The censorial officials were clearly afraid to remonstrate with Hsüan-tsung even about those of his policies that might have deserved criticism, but in their impeachments of officials they often went to excesses that the emperor himself felt impelled to restrain or moderate. They were not his tool, nor were they his antagonists. Under Hsi-tsung, the censorial officials viciously attacked enemies in the officialdom, but at the same time they protested dramatically against the emperor's laxity, wastefulness, and favoritism, though only until Wei Chung-hsien came to power and protests became hopelessly dangerous. They were clearly not Hsi-tsung's tool; they annoyed and irritated him at every turn. But they served Wei Chung-hsien as submissively as he could have wished.

The existence of the censorial institutions was not in itself a guarantee that vigilant surveillance would be maintained, either over the officialdom or over the ruler; and it was certainly not a guarantee that censorial impeachments and remonstrances would effectively check government irregularities at any given time. The effectiveness of any important censorial action always depended upon the ruler's reaction to it, and this was in turn shaped by the total political environment of the time. On the other hand, the vigor of censorial action depended upon the personalities of the censorial officials, and particularly upon their conscious or unconscious appraisal of the total political environment. Of their motivations we can naturally say very little. Our evidence suggests that they were in some cases corrupt, in some cases vindictively partisan, in some cases doggedly dedicated, and in some cases willing to court martyrdom for principle. As a group they were probably not significantly more honest and courageous than their colleagues in the other civil service agencies, and no less so. As for their accomplishments, the particulars from the prior chapters need not be repeated here. They caused many persons to suffer from their personnel evaluations and impeachments, they corrected or ameliorated many injustices, they brought about the adoption or modification or termination of many policies and practices, and they often gave rulers cause to reconsider their decisions. On the other hand, they committed injustices of their own, they unreasonably harassed their personal or partisan enemies, they kept silent when the evidence suggests they should have spoken out, and they let themselves be intimidated by the corrupt censor-in-chief Liu Kuan in the 1420's and by the domineering eunuch Wei Chung-hsien in the 1620's. However their accomplishments may be evaluated, it is clear that the censorial officials were far from being optimally effective, either as checks against bureaucratic malfeasance or as checks against monarchical aberrations.

However, as Samuel Wells Williams suggested in the comments cited on p. 289, the censorial institutions in traditional China did at least serve as a deterrent to irregularities in government, and this was perhaps their most significant service. The political scientist Herman Finer has stressed this point in writing about controls wielded by modern parliaments over the executive:

We do not mean that parliaments have, or pretend to have, or ought to have, the power of continuous intervention in administration and positive participation in the operation of the law. They do not, in fact, do more than act as the judge and the corrector of the Cabinet and its administrative assistants. We could show, further, that it is almost impossible to do more than this. . . .

It is not always necessary for parliaments or any controlling body to *intervene*. Their mere presence is sufficient to establish a standard of behaviour for Ministers. Kant said that the value of the social-contract theory was not in its historical truth, but that it set a standard by which rulers and ruled might judge of governments. Similarly with control over the Executive: we must give due credit to the influence of the simple presence of Parliament, to the "silent rhetoric of a look." However, this is not all; nor is it enough.[11]

Just so, the mere presence of the censorial institutions in China no doubt had a substantial deterrent or preventive effect—though this was not all it did, nor was it in any sense enough. As an official of the Yüan dynasty once said, in more colorful language than Finer's: "The Censorate is like a sleeping tiger. Even when it does not bite, men still dread its tigerishness."[12] For ruler and ruled alike, the potential "tigerishness" of the censorial institutions in China could not have failed to exert a cautionary influence, whether beneficial or detrimental.

In any event, to think of the Chinese censorial system as being in any way involved in a tug-of-war between the emperor and the people would be grossly misleading. As has been noted, Lin Yutang is fond of suggesting that traditional China was in certain ways democratic. He compares censorial activities to "public criticism" as expressed in the modern press. For what I have called "avenues of criticism" (a traditional informal designation of the censorial institutions) he uses the term "avenues of expression (of the people's opinion)," and he curiously suggests that the traditional Chinese designation for censors as specialized surveillance officials, "the eyes and ears of the Emperor," means that the censorial officials "may be regarded as expressing the voice of the people." Although he holds back from saying so explicitly, Lin intimates that at least in Ming times the Chinese people and the officialdom (naturally excluding "bad" officials who became puppets of the ruler) were natural allies against tyrannical emperors and their eunuch henchmen, and that the censorial officials were the spokesmen or shock troops for an alliance between the people and the officialdom. In creating this impression, Lin not only emphasizes the "speaking officials" tradition to the point of obscuring the "surveillance officials" tradition; he also misrepresents the nature of the traditional Chinese state system in its totality.

The controversial modern scholar Karl A. Wittfogel distorts the traditional state system at the opposite extreme. In a series of works about what he calls "hydraulic societies" and "Oriental despotisms,"

Wittfogel has built some notions of Max Weber's into an elaborate edifice of interpretation that traces the autocratic and bureaucratic characteristics of the Chinese state, among others, back to an original and continuing need for centralized management of irrigation projects.[13] He creates the impression that in traditional times Chinese rulers and their bureaucrats (excluding occasional "good" rulers and officials whose benevolent inclinations did not alter the characteristic imbalance) were natural allies in oppressing the people at large, and that the bureaucrats ("men of the apparatus," like the administrative class in a modern totalitarian regime) were themselves as victimized by "total social control," "total terror," and "total submission" as were the people, so that the ruler-controlled state apparatus functioned always in the ruler's interest. The China specialist F. W. Mote, in a general criticism of Wittfogel's view of a static despotism in traditional China, concedes that special circumstances did indeed create a reign of terror in Ming China.[14] And a modern Chinese scholar who calls himself Ting I, in an impassioned book about "government-by-secret police" in Ming times, has catalogued all the eunuch interferences and brutalities that lent an aura of terror to the Ming state.[15]

None of these discussions of despotism in traditional China takes any significant note of the censorial system. To the best of my knowledge, Wittfogel, unlike Max Weber, does not even mention the surveillance and impeachment functions of the censorial institutions, though they presumably could be interpreted in support of his general thesis about Chinese despotism.[16] He does, however, make some observations about the function of criticism in "hydraulic" states generally:

Bureaucratic criticism is vital to the proper functioning of complex administration, but it is voiced either behind closed doors or in publications accessible only to a limited number of educated persons, who are usually members of the ruling group. In both cases, the people's problems are viewed essentially from the standpoint of a more or less rationally conceived government interest.

Wielding total power, the masters of the hydraulic state can readily maintain the ruler's publicity optimum. Under socially undifferentiated conditions, the government's (frequently the sovereign's) voice drowns out all criticism except as it may appear in such inconsequential media as popular tales and songs. More differentiated conditions provide additional outlets in secondary religions and philosophies, in popular short stories, novels, and plays. But even these media remain significantly feeble. In contrast to the independent writers who, under Western absolutism, challenged not only the excesses but the foundations of the despotic order, the critics of hydraulic society have in almost every case complained only of the misdeeds of individual officials or of the evils of specific governmental acts. Apart from mystics who teach total withdrawal from the world, these critics aim ultimately at regenerating a system of total power, whose fundamental desirability they do not doubt.[17]

Perhaps even more pertinently, he adds:

Throughout the hydraulic world serious-minded rulers attended to their managerial and judicial duties conscientiously, and honest officials strove to prevent fiscal and judicial oppression. Courageous functionaries insisted on what they considered proper policies, although by doing so they opposed the wishes of powerful superiors, and occasionally even of the sovereign himself.

But those who pursue such a course clash with the interest of the vast self-indulgent and scheming ruling group; and history shows that only a handful of unusually community-minded (ethically "possessed") persons were so disposed. Furthermore, even this pathetically small number of "good" men was not completely aware of how slanted the ruler's optimum was, which they recommended. Confucius' gentleman bureaucrat, the ideal ruler of the *Bhagavad-gita,* and the "just" statesmen of the ancient Roman or Islamic Near East all try to be fair within the framework of a society which takes the patterns of despotic power, revenue, and prestige for granted.[18]

Although censorial remonstrances were not voiced "behind closed doors" and censorial remonstrators were not a "pathetically small number," Wittfogel's remarks in these passages presumably serve to dispose of China's "speaking officials" tradition. At least, I find no other reference to it in his work.

This is obviously not the place for a thorough evaluation of Wittfogel's theories, even as they are applicable to China. Suffice it to say that, in general, I am not in full sympathy with his view that "replacing myth by reality, we may truthfully say that hydraulic despotism is benevolent in form and oppressive in content," insofar as China is concerned.[19] But he has provided a useful antidote to the sentimentalism that sees democracy at work in the Chinese censorial system, and he has usefully called attention to the intimidation and terror that undeniably existed in the Chinese state system as a whole. Most of all, he clearly sees that the fundamental polarity in traditional China was not between the people and the officials on one side and the emperor on the other, but was between the people on one side, and on the other a ruling Establishment, so to speak, comprising both the emperor and the officialdom.

One vital error that Wittfogel makes, it seems to me, is failing to take adequate note of the interdependence or co-dependence of emperor and officialdom in the traditional Chinese state, which created a persistent tension within the ruling Establishment and which made it impossible for the Establishment to be a monolithic juggernaut of oppression. The China historian Joseph R. Levenson has described the situation with balance and clarity and, in my view, with a much truer ring.[20] He speaks of the officialdom's "conflict-collaboration with the emperor in manipulating the state,"[21] and describes the foundations of this conflict-collaboration as follows:

We have observed that a genuinely Confucian concern about satisfying the *min*, the people, carried no implications of 'democracy', Caesarist or otherwise. On the contrary, it was essentially Confucian to reject majority rule, with all its air of impersonal, mathematical abstraction. But if the strongest in numbers were not to rule, the strongest in power would, and brute power was no more congenial to Confucianists than impersonal number. Still, individuals, unlike faceless masses, have moral possibilities, so Confucianists had attached themselves to emperors. While a dynasty worked, they covered its monarchs with a veneer of morality; this would gloss over (to their emotional and the monarch's political advantage) the actual basis of rule, sheer power. When Confucianists hypocritically, or even slavishly, ascribed morality to an emperor, they seemed indeed his creatures. But this very morality, or the assumption that he required it and that they could judge it, was the mark of their independence—co-dependence, to put it a little lower.[22]

Levenson also appropriately points out that the Chinese officialdom's commitment to Confucian morality above all differentiated it clearly from "the professional bureaucracy of experts which joined the European princes on their modern rise to power."[23] Thus it was not a "modern bureaucracy" in Weberian terms, and China could not become a modern state so long as the conflict-collaboration between Confucian officials and the emperor persisted.[24] Thus, too, despite the impression Wittfogel gives, it is clear that "the minister *was* a person, not a thing—not a cog in a bureaucratic wheel that kept on turning, whatever the Legalist dynasty that generated the power."[25] As Levenson puts it:

This was the tension between companions, Chinese monarch and Chinese bureaucracy, which only the Taiping Rebellion (1850–64) finally began to resolve. Until that beginning of the post-traditional era, the monarchy, standing for central power, worked against the bureaucracy's private aggrandizement, while Confucian bureaucracy, resisting such pressures, interpreted them as the monarch's moves to make the *t'ien-hsia* [the empire] private, and thus to fail in moral concern for the public well-being.[26]

In short, traditional Chinese emperors and officials alike were dependent upon and subordinate to an ideology or a system that we call Confucianism, which permitted the ruling Establishment to deal with the people in an arrogant manner but required it to be benevolently paternalistic. Therefore, the official's loyalty to his ruler was always conditioned by his higher loyalty to the system, and the ruler's despotism was always restrained ultimately through his being legitimated by the system. To be sure, as Wittfogel points out, the officials almost never criticized the system itself. Naturally not. But this was not because they dared not criticize a system that gave rulers terroristic powers; it was because the officials were themselves committed first of all to the system and because their own status and self-esteem depended upon it.

Viewing the censorial system in this light, one must conclude that censorial officials in their roles as surveillance agents and impeachers cannot be seen as secret police-like tools of despotic oppression; nor in their roles as remonstrators can they be seen as potential revolutionaries. Neither representatives of the imperial will nor representatives of the majority will, they were spokesmen for the general will —that is to say, guardians of the Confucian governmental heritage handed down from the past. In this manner alone can their prestige and their influence be accounted for.

It follows, then, that the censorial system was intended to be a bulwark of the traditionalism that characterized Chinese government throughout imperial times. I believe that my analyses of the censorial activities of 1424–34 and 1620–27 show that the system actually served as such a bulwark. It did initiate changes—changes in personnel and changes in policies. But the changes it advocated were all well within the tradition. Conversely, it was a brake on change that was not traditionally justifiable.

This does not mean, necessarily, that the censorial institution served to suppress initiative and creativity on the part of either rulers or officials. It was certainly not intended that it should do so, and censorial officials in practice—except by their failures to perform properly—do not seem to have got in the way of Hsüan-tsung in his progress as a vigorous and creative ruler. Similarly, as has been noted in Chapter 5, censorial officials put no obstacles in the way of Hsü Kuang-ch'i, who wanted to introduce Western-style cannons into the fighting with the Manchus; instead, they actively encouraged him and men like him. Of course, at any time a particular censorial official might have judged matters in an excessively conservative way; and the whole censorial system could have easily reacted in an excessively conservative way to a particular problem. But the system was not committed to extreme conservatism and to a static condition of affairs.

My work does suggest, however, that the censorial system frustrated the effective functioning of the government under certain conditions. I have pointed out in Chapter 5 that the period of strong leadership by the grand secretary Chang Chü-cheng in the 1570's and early 1580's was followed by a long period (that included most of Shen-tsung's reign and the whole reigns of Kuang-tsung and Hsi-tsung) in which the censorial officials were much more clamorously outspoken than was the case in the 1420's and 1430's. They actually dominated political life at the court with their criticisms and proposals. A corollary of this, as was noted in Chapter 6, is that censorial officials under Hsüan-tsung had been criticized principally for their unfitness and inactivity, whereas under Hsi-tsung they were criticized—by their own censorial colleagues, by other officials, and by the emperor—principally for talking too much and seeking too zealously to dominate decision-making. Hsi-tsung's own repeated cries of "Don't harass me!" and "Stop trying to outdo one another!" contrast markedly with Hsüan-tsung's manifest displeasure with the censorial officials for their failure to keep him fully informed.

The injurious effect of censorial clamor in the late Ming years is observable in the case of Hsiung T'ing-pi, who served twice as supreme commander of Liaotung military affairs when the Manchus were pressing hard against the Ming empire's northeastern frontier. Both his tours of duty ended in his failure and dismissal, and during both Hsiung was harassed unmercifully by court critics and especially by censorial critics, who forced him again and again to send memorials explaining and defending his policies and who even convened great court assemblies at which panicky malcontents of all sorts discoursed lengthily on his tactical errors and strategic miscalculations.[27] A grand secretary complained that censorial memorials criticizing Hsiung finally accumulated into a veritable mountain of paper.[28] With the whole censorial establishment looking over his shoulder (but from a safe distance) and offering advice and criticism in such fashion, no military commander could have been expected to function effectively in the field.

Hsiung's was by no means an isolated case. Beginning in the 1590's, the history of the great court controversies involving the Tung-lin partisans abounds with instances of grand secretaries' being similarly hounded and frustrated.[29] As early as 1608 a grand secretary likened the censorial clamor to the "squawkings of birds and beasts."[30] Hsi-tsung obviously came to share this sentiment. The result was that high-ranking officials, and especially grand secretaries, continuously had to defend themselves against attacks and had to submit repeated resignations to salve their wounded self-esteem and to obtain expressions of confidence from the emperor. Shen I-kuan, who served as a grand secretary from 1594 to late 1606 and was one of the principal targets of Tung-lin abuse, is reported to have submitted his resignation 80 times.[31] And the great Grand Secretariat patron of the Tung-lin partisans, Yeh Hsiang-kao, apparently submitted his resignation 33 times in 1624 before it was accepted.[32] The champion resigner may well have been Li T'ing-chi, who served as a grand secretary from 1607 into 1612 and who, like Shen I-kuan, was repeatedly criticized by Tung-lin partisans. Li finally left office after having submitted his resignation more than 120 times.[33]

Li T'ing-chi's case illustrates the fact that harassment and humiliation of high-ranking officials were not the only consequences of the censorial clamor. Not only was Li harassed; he was effectively prevented from performing his duties. When he was first appointed to the Grand Secretariat he repeatedly declined the office because of censorial disapproval, and after less than a year on duty he began staying home to avoid provoking attacks, his resignation having already been offered and rejected many times. When censorial attacks still did not cease, he sought refuge in a deserted temple. Finally, after more than a full year of total isolation, during which he continued to be subjected to censorial criticisms, he abandoned the area of the capital entirely and departed for his home in the far southern province of Fukien, without having imperial permission to do so. Only then, retroactively, was his resignation at last accepted. Having been nominally a member of the Grand Secretariat for more than five years, he had actually performed the duties of his office for only nine months.[34]

In retiring from office when criticized, Li T'ing-chi was merely doing what had come to be expected. How and when the custom originated is not at all clear, but by the beginning of the seventeenth century it was considered essential that any civil servant, when impeached by a censorial official, withdraw from the performance of his duty pending exoneration. C. Alvarez Semedo, the early seventeenth-century European commentator on China, reported this as an established procedure. Writing in general about impeachment memorials submitted by either censors or supervising secretaries, he noted:

Assoone [sic] as this *Memoriall* . . . is published, presently the Magistrate, or other person, against whom it is framed, is obliged to do two things, whether it be with, or against his will, (which is more ordinary.) The *first* is, that he give in a *Memoriall,* not in his own defence, (for to excuse himself were to shew little humility,) but he must say therein, that the *Tauli* [censor] hath great reason; that he hath committed a great errour, and is in fault, and doth deserve to have a penace laid upon him, and that with all subjection, he will submit to any punishment, that shall be imposed. The *second* is, that he presently retire himselfe, and leave the *Tribunall,* and so all Acts of Justice are suspended, so that he neither giveth audience, nor endeth any suite, untill the King have answered his petition, and declared his pleasure thereon....[35]

Similarly, after commenting on the regional inspector's power to inflict punishments on lesser officials on his own authority and initiative, Semedo wrote: "Concerning the greater *Mandarines,* if there be cause, he is to give in *Memorialls,* and they are from thence forward suspended from the function of their Offices, till the Kings answer come from Court."[36]

Throughout the long history of the Tung-lin controversies, emperors regularly had to cajole sulking ministers, offended by censorial criticisms, into terminating their self-imposed suspensions and resuming their duties. Hsi-tsung, in his earliest years on the throne, repeatedly complained that his ministers were so sensitive to criticism that he could not even persuade them to open their gates; they insistently claimed to be ill and demanded leaves of absence.[37] In 1620 he protested that of all the major central-government agencies only the Censorate and the Ministry of War had senior officials on duty; all other high-ranking officials were sulking at home, expecting leaves of absence. He ordered all Ministry ministers and vice ministers to appear for duty immediately and to withdraw their requests for leave. He insisted that thenceforth when any high-ranking official was criticized, he must submit an explanatory memorial but must remain on duty, and that any who falsely pleaded illness and sought leaves of absence would be punished.[38] His anger had little effect. The custom persisted, and in 1623 a censor even impeached some senior officials because when they were denounced they did *not* withdraw from office.[39]

The consequences of all this seem predictable. As the supervising secretary Mao Shih-lung was provoked to say, "The critics outnumber the actors!"[40] Administrative officials were increasingly intimidated by the censorial clamor, partisan cliques used censorial impeachers to rid the government of their enemies, and the state apparatus stagnated. Inactive and unresponsive to the real needs of the time, the Ming government drifted almost helplessly. Later Chinese commentators have suggested that epidemic "mouth-and-tongue disease" in Hsi-tsung's time clearly foreshadowed the collapse of the dynasty.[41] As I have had occasion to write elsewhere:

Too often in the late Ming years, consequently, the censorial system served neither as an instrument of bureaucratic control over the monarch nor as an instrument of monarchical control over the bureaucracy, but as a lash with which a sadly fragmented officialdom indulged in paralyzing self-flagellation.[42]

This is no doubt too harsh a judgment. For the trouble was not rooted in the nature of the censorial system itself, but in the nature of the Ming state system as a whole. The different censorial performances under Hsüan-tsung and Hsi-tsung, respectively, suggest that the traditionalism defended by Ming censorial officials required above all else a firm hand at the helm and required that this hand be the emperor's. It can be speculated that so long as an emperor was vigorous and clearly in command much could be forgiven him; at least the government functioned. And for officials to display initiative and creativity under such circumstances—that is, within the broad framework of centralized control by a strong emperor—was commendable and fruitful. But when emperors who were inattentive and unresponsive came to the throne, then censorial alertness to danger was greatly heightened; and, since the Ming system did not provide a way for any other hand to take the helm legitimately, initiative and creativity on the part of any senior official—however necessary, and however effective—inevitably suggested usurpation. Inasmuch as the censorial institution was most particularly the defender of the traditional way of government, the censorial officials could only be expected to struggle against any aggressive leadership not emanating from or controlled by the throne.

Thus, for an emperor to rely on eunuchs was not in itself objectionable, so long as the emperor was strong; and for a grand secretary to wield great power was not in itself objectionable, so long as his emperor was strong. But when an emperor was weak, then the emergence of power in any other quarter was dangerous and intolerable. It is no wonder that, under such ineffective emperors as Shen-tsung and Hsi-tsung, censorial officials focused their attention more and more closely on the court to the exclusion of almost everything else and lent themselves to a rampant partisan cannibalism within the bureaucracy. Nothing could go right unless the emperor was firmly in control. Without a strong emperor, it was unavoidable that the censorial officials merely contributed to chaos and stagnation, since they could not properly be silent.

On balance, then, what can one say in general about the Ming censorial system? The system was highly organized in several echelons with differentiated functions. It was staffed with experienced civil servants, but they were not elder statesmen, and, though carefully selected, they were not career-long censorial officials. They had well-developed techniques for informing themselves about government activities, and they vigorously impeached members of the bureaucracy, freely proposed changes in government policies and practices, and on occasion dramatically remonstrated with emperors whose conduct they disapproved of. Sometimes they were cowed and inactive; sometimes they were arrogant and intimidating. They did not characteristically serve as agents of imperial oppression and terrorization of the people and the officialdom, nor did they characteristically serve as agents of popular or bureaucratic resistance to imperial domination. Most characteristically, they were spokesmen for and defenders of a traditionalism to which the emperors, the officialdom, and the people at large were equally committed and which no one seriously challenged. In this capacity, they cautioned and harassed emperors and officials alike, and, within limits imposed by the power structure and the ideology to which they were wed, they could and did mitigate oppression, injustice, and malfeasance, sometimes at great cost to themselves. Sometimes, too, under weak rulers who could not properly manage the state, their harassment tended to immobilize the government, to their own and everyone else's dissatisfaction. For good or ill, they were an influential and essential element in the imperial Chinese system, and perhaps never more so than in the Ming period.

Appendix Tables

Appendix Tables

TABLE 1

Geographical Origins of Appointees

Native province	% of China's population	Exam. quota	Sample A[a]	Sample B[b]	Sample C[c]
South China	49%	55%	187 (53%)	53 (44%)	72 (59%)
So. Metro. Area .	18		49	9	16
Kiangsi	10		46	8	18
Chekiang	8		48	21	26
Hukwang	7		27	7	4
Kwangtung . . .	3		3	4	4
Fukien	3		14	4	4
North China	41%	35%	148 (42%)	65 (53%)[d]	42 (34%)
Shantung	9		30	16	8
Shansi	9		16	5	3
Honan	9		40	17	13
Shensi	7		22	7	8
No. Metro. Area .	7		40	19	10
West China	10%	10%	16 (5%)[e]	4 (3%)	9 (7%)
Szechwan	5		13	4	5
Yunnan	2		2	0	3
Kwangsi	2		0	0	1
Kweichow . . .	1		0	0	0
TOTALS			351	123	123

[a] Sample A: 351 ministers and censors-in-chief identified by native places. SOURCE: Huang Ta-hua, "Ming Ch'i-ch'ing K'ao-lüeh," in the *K'ai-ming Er-shih-wu-shih Pu-pien*, VI, 8571–8578.
[b] Sample B: 123 supervising secretaries appointed to the Office of Scrutiny for Rites between 1368 and 1530. SOURCE: *Li-k'o Chi-shih-chung Shih-chi.*
[c] Sample C: 123 investigating censors appointed in 1425–35. SOURCE: *Lan-t'ai Fa-chien Lu*, ch. 7.
[d] Includes one man from Liaotung.   [e] Includes one man from Annam.

TABLE 2

Censorial Impeachments of Civil Officials, by Ranks, 1424–34

Ranks of accused	Times denounced	No action	Investigated or tried	Demoted	Otherwise punished
2a, b	20	6	3	9	2
3a, b	37	15	5	9	8
4a, b	39	10	10	11	8
5a, b	43	9	4	17	13
6a, b	18	1	—	12	5
7a, b	75	3	3	63	6
8a, b	2	1	—	1	—
9a, b	6	—	—	1	5
Not clear	21+	5+	6+	2+	8+
TOTALS	261+	50+	31+	125+	55+

TABLE 3

Censorial Impeachments of Civil Officials, by Duty Categories, 1424–34

Category	Times denounced	No action	Investigated or tried	Demoted	Otherwise punished
Capital officials	155	23	13	91	28
Provincial officials . . .	85	22	12	32	19
Not clear	21+	5+	6+	2+	8+
TOTALS	261+	50+	31+	125+	55+

TABLE 4

Censorial Impeachments of Military Officers, by Ranks, 1424–34

Ranks of accused	Times denounced	No action	Investigated or tried	Demoted	Otherwise punished
Nobles	41+	26+	3	1	11
1a, b	23	12	4	—	7
2a, b	36	8	7	1	20
3a, b	50	7	3	6	34
4a, b	5	1	—	—	4
5a, b	19	—	3	—	16
6a, b	9	2	—	—	7
Not clear	215+	1+	—	1	213+
TOTALS	398+	57+	20	9	312+

TABLE 5

Censorial Proposals and Responses to Them, 1424–34

Initiated by	Total submitted	Approved	Deliberated	Disapproved	No action
Censors	178	129	28	13	8
Supervising secretaries . .	18	10	4	3	1
Surveillance Offices officials	47	32	9	2	4
Censors and surveillance commissioners jointly . .	7	4	—	—	3
Censors and supervising secretaries jointly	1	1	—	—	—
TOTALS	251	176	41	18	16
Percentages	*100%*	*70%*	*16%*	*7%*	*7%*

TABLE 6

Censorial Proposals and Responses, by Subject Categories, 1424–34

Subject category	Total proposals	Approved	Deliber- ated	Dis- approved	No action
Imperial conduct: total	5	3	—	1	1
General	3	1	—	1	1
Reliance on eunuchs	2	2	—	—	—
General administration: total . . .	147	105	25	10	7
Miscellaneous	33	24	3	5	1
Disaster relief	29	20	4	—	5
Personnel matters	28	23	3	2	—
Waterways, transport, etc.	16	9	7	—	—
Taxes, land use, etc.	32	23	6	2	1
Schools, examinations	9	6	2	1	—
Military matters: total	88	63	14	3	8
Miscellaneous	11	10	1	—	—
Banditry, etc.	29	18	2	3	6
Border defenses, war	13	9	3	—	1
Troop recruitment, morale . . .	16	12	4	—	—
Selection and use of officers . . .	4	3	1	—	—
Supplies	15	11	3	—	1
Judicial matters: total	57	37	13	6	1
TOTALS	297	208	52	20	17
Percentages	*100%*	*70%*	*17%*	*7%*	*6%*

TABLE 7

Responses to Censorate Memorials Under Liu Kuan and Ku Tso

Memorials	Responses	
	Under Liu Kuan	Under Ku Tso
Impeachments submitted by censors: total	83	116
No action	11 (13%)	18 (15.5%)
Investigation or trial	16 (19%)	17 (14.5%)
Demotion or other punishment	56 (68%)	81 (70%)
Proposals submitted by censors: total	70	108
Approved	54 (77%)	75 (70%)
Deliberated	6 (8.5%)	22 (20%)
Disapproved	6 (8.5%)	7 (6%)
No action	4 (6%)	4 (4%)

TABLE 8

Censorial Impeachments of Civil Officials, by Ranks, 1620–27

Ranks of accused	Times denounced	No action	Investigated or tried	Demoted	Otherwise punished
2a, b[a]	268	172	49	42	5
3a, b	77	26	5	45	1
4a, b	66	12	19	33	2
5a, b	65	12	18	33	2
6a, b	30	7	9	13	1
7a, b	90	21	26	40	3
8a, b	1	—	1	—	—
9a, b	—	—	—	—	—
Not clear . . .	94+	25+	49+	18	2
TOTALS . . .	691+	275+	176+	224	16

[a] Includes grand secretaries, supreme commanders, and grand coordinators.

TABLE 9

Censorial Impeachments of Civil Officials, by Duty Categories, 1620–27

Category	Times denounced	No action	Investigated or tried	Demoted	Otherwise punished
Capital officials	428	192	65	164	7
Provincial officials . . .	169	58	62	42	7
Not clear	94+	25+	49+	18	2
TOTALS	691+	275+	176+	224	16

TABLE 10

Censorial Impeachments of Military Officers, by Ranks, 1620–27

Ranks of accused	Times denounced	No action	Investigated or tried	Demoted	Otherwise punished
Nobles	4	—	—	4	—
1a, b	1	1	—	—	—
2a, b	11	—	3	8	—
3a, b	4	1	—	3	—
4a, b	—	—	—	—	—
5a, b	—	—	—	—	—
6a, b	—	—	—	—	—
Tactical commanders[a] . . .	59	6	12	39	2
Not clear	93+	6+	30+	46+	11+
TOTALS	172+	14+	45+	100+	13+

[a] Ranks not cited.

TABLE 11

Censorial Impeachments of Miscellaneous Persons, 1620–27

The accused	Times denounced	No action	Investigated or tried	Demoted	Otherwise punished
Imperial clansmen	1	—	1	—	—
Imperial in-laws	4	1	—	2	1
Palace women	2	2	—	—	—
Eunuchs	38+	27+	5+	1	5
Students	15	1	5	—	9
Relatives of officials	3	3	—	—	—
Relative of a eunuch	1	1	—	—	—
Merchant	1	—	1	—	—
Common people	2+	—	1+	—	1
TOTALS	67+	35+	13+	3	16

TABLE 12

Censorial Proposals and Responses to Them, 1620–27

Initiated by	Total submitted	Approved	Deliberated	Disapproved	No action
Censors	674	235	275	75	89
Supervising secretaries .	603	210	259	71	63
Surveillance Office officials	4	—	—	2	2
Censors and supervising secretaries jointly . . .	15	2	6	6	1
TOTALS	1296	447	540	154	155
Percentages	*100%*	*34%*	*42%*	*12%*	*12%*

TABLE 13

Censorial Proposals and Responses, by Subject Categories, 1620–27

Subject category	Total proposals	Approved	Deliber- ated	Dis- approved	No action
Imperial conduct: total	217	46	19	75	77
General	133	15	16	55	47
Reliance on eunuchs	84	31	3	20	30
General administration: total .	681	268	261	75	77
Miscellaneous	151	58	48	16	29
Disaster relief	42	10	25	5	2
Personnel matters	231	99	82	23	27
Waterways, transport, etc. . .	30	14	14	2	—
Taxes, land use, etc.	112	39	55	12	6
Schools, examinations	34	16	13	2	3
Government expenditures . .	53	21	16	11	5
Partisanship	28	11	8	4	5
Military matters: total	616	181	360	34	41
Miscellaneous	49	12	33	1	3
Banditry, etc.	107	37	63	2	5
Border defenses, war	223	60	129	18	16
Troop recruitment, morale .	80	27	43	2	8
Selection and use of officers .	51	13	30	4	4
Supplies	106	32	62	7	5
Judicial matters: total	56	17	13	21	5
TOTALS	1570	512	653	205	200
Percentages	*100%*	*32%*	*42%*	*13%*	*13%*

TABLE 14

Persons Specially Investigated by Censorial Officials, 1424–34

Posts and ranks	Numbers investigated
Civil-service personnel	
Vice minister (3a)	1
Director of Ministry Bureau (5a)	5
Vice director of Ministry Bureau (5b)	2
Secretary of Ministry Bureau (6a)	7
Investigating censor (7a)	4
Military-service personnel	
Marquis	1
Commissioner-in-chief (1a)	2
Regional commissioner (2a)	5
Assistant regional commissioner (3a)	3
Battalion commander (5a)	5
Company commander (6a)	1
Battalion judge (6b)	1
Guard granary vice director (?)	1
Unspecified	2+
Others	
Prince	1
Civilians	21+
Unspecified	1+
TOTAL	63+

TABLE 15

Persons Ordered Tried by Censorial Officials, 1424–34

Posts and ranks	Numbers tried
Civil-service personnel	
Provincial administration commissioner (2b)	2
Vice minister (3a)	1
Provincial surveillance commissioner (3a)	1
Ass't provincial administration commissioner (4b)	1
Ass't provincial surveillance commissioner (5a)	1
Princely Establishment administrator (5a)	1
Ministry Bureau director (5a)	1
Ministry Bureau vice director (5b)	1
Court of Imperial Entertainments ass't minister (6b)	1
Investigating censor (7a)	2
Prefectural judge (7a)	1
Supervising secretary (7b)	1
County magistrate (7b)	1
County vice magistrate (8a)	1
Unspecified local authorities	1+
Military-service personnel	
Marquis	1
Ass't commissioner-in-chief (2a)	1
Regional commissioner (2a)	3
Regional vice commissioner (2b)	3
Ass't regional commissioner (3a)	4
Guard commander (3a)	9
Battalion commander (5a)	1
Guard judge (5b)	1
Company commander (6a)	2
Unspecified military officers	4+
Other persons	
Central Buddhist Registry clerk (nominal rank 8b)	1
Eunuch	1+
Civilians	43+
TOTAL	91+

TABLE 16

Persons Ordered Tried by Censorial Officials, 1620–27

Posts and ranks	Numbers tried
Civil-service personnel	
Minister (2a)	1
Grand coordinator (2a)	1
Censor-in-chief (2a)	1
Provincial administration commissioner (2b)	1
Provincial administration vice commissioner (3b) . . .	1
Ass't censor-in-chief (4a)	1
Ass't provincial surveillance commissioner (5a)	1
Ministry Bureau director (5a)	1
Seal Office vice director (5b)	1
Supervisorate of Imperial Instruction mentor (5b) . .	1
Ass't prefect (6a)	1
Chief supervising secretary (7a)	1
Investigating censor (7a)	4
County magistrate (7a)	2
Supervising secretary (7b)	1
Unspecified	4
Military-service personnel	
Ass't commissioner-in-chief (2a)	1
Regional commissioner (2a)	6
Ass't regional commissioner (3a)	1
Tactical commanders (ranks not clear)	21
Other persons	
County school instructor	1
Student	3
Unspecified	4
TOTAL	60

TABLE 17

Recorded Results of Censorial Trials, 1424–34

Year	Persons sentenced	Sentences	Results
1424	Court of Imperial Entertainments ass't minister	*unknown*	Dismissed from service
1425	Civilians	Beheading	Disgraced[a]
1425	Ass't military commissioner-in-chief	Banishment	Retired
1425	Supervising secretary	*unknown*	Disgraced
1426	Soldier	Beheading	Released
1426	Regional military vice commissioner	Beheading	Beheaded
1426	22+ civilians and civil officials	Death	Various[b]
1427	Company commander	Beheading	Beheaded
1428	Ass't regional military commissioner	Disgrace	Demoted
1429	Provincial military commissioner	Banishment	"Atoned"
1429	Ass't regional military commissioner	Disgrace	Pardoned
1430	Guard ass't commander	Beheading	Beheaded
1430	Guard granary officer	Strangling	Strangled
1430	Civilian	*unknown*	Beheaded
1430	Guard commander	Beheading	Beheaded
1430	Investigating censor	Beating, labor	Disgraced
1431	County vice magistrate	Banishment	Banished
1431	Investigating censor	Strangling	Released
1431	Battalion commander	Beheading	Beheaded
1431	17 civilians	Death	Released
1432	Guard judge	Labor	Put at labor
1433	Regional military vice commissioner	Beheading	Disgraced
1433	Vice minister	Strangling	Disgraced
1434	Provincial surveillance commissioner	*unknown*	Put at labor, then retired

SOURCE: JTSL 2B.6b–7b; HTSL 10.7b–8a, 11.9a, 12.11a–b, 14.10b, 16.6b–7b, 19.8a, 26.13a, 42.6a–b, 57.6b, 67.2a–b, 67.8b–9a, 68.2b, 68.8a–b, 68.11b–12a, 75.9a, 81.2b, 83.8b, 84.16b–17a, 89.7b–8a, 107.12a, 107.12b, 110.6b–7a, 112.5a.

[a] "Disgraced" means assigned to serve as a soldier or a lesser functionary, usually at the frontier and apparently in perpetuity.

[b] Two were put to death, 13+ put at labor, and 7 released.

TABLE 18

Recorded Results of Censorial Trials, 1620–27

Year	Persons sentenced	Sentences	Results
1626	Military tactical commander	*unknown*	Beaten
1626	Seal Office vice director	Disgrace	Disgraced
1626	Assistant censor-in-chief	Disgrace	Disgraced
1626	Provin. admin. vice commissioner	Disgrace	Disgraced
1626	Civil official	Disgrace	Disgraced
1626	Four men	Banishment	Banished
1627	Investigating censor	Disgrace	Disgraced
1627	Military tactical commander	Beheading	Pardoned

SOURCE: STSL 64.17a, 66.7b–8a, 68.36a, 73.13b, 75.18a–b, 76.1b–2a.

TABLE 19

Persons Ordered Punished by Censorial Officials, 1424–34

Posts and ranks	Numbers punished
Civil-service personnel	
Provincial administration commissioner (2b)	1
Provincial administration vice commissioner (3b) . .	2
Pasturage Office director (3b)	1
Provincial surveillance vice commissioner (4a)	1
Prefect (4a)	2
Provincial ass't administration commissioner (4b) . .	5
Provincial ass't surveillance commissioner (5a)	1
Vice prefect (5a)	3
Princely Establishment administrator (5a)	1
Subprefecture magistrate (5b)	1
Ministry Bureau vice director (5b)	1
Ministry Bureau secretary (6a)	1
Subprefecture ass't magistrate (7b)	1
Court of Imp. Sacrifices ceremonial usher (9a)	1
Prefecture collator (?)	1
Military-service personnel	
Regional commissioner (2a)	7
Ass't regional commissioner (3a)	1
Guard commander (3a)	15
Guard vice commander (3b)	2
Battalion commander (5a)	8+
Battalion vice commander (5b)	1
Guard judge (5b)	1
Company commander (6a)	3
Unspecified	259+
Other persons	
Eunuchs	2
Aboriginal chieftain	1
TOTAL	323+

TABLE 20

Disciplinary Action Against Censorial Officials, by Disposition, 1424–34

Action taken	Censors-in-chief			Investigating censors			Supervising secretaries			Surveillance commissioners		
	L	K	Total	L	K	Total	L	K	Total	L	K	Total
Put to death	—	—	—	—	2	2[a]	—	—	—	—	—	—
Imprisoned	—	—	—	2	3[b]	5	—	—	—	—	—	—
Disgraced[c]	—	2	2[d]	1	35	36	5	1	6	—	1	1
Punitive labor	—	—	—	—	6	6	—	1	1	—	—	—
Placed in cangue	—	—	—	3	—	3	—	—	—	—	—	—
Dismissed from service	—	—	—	3	6	9	1	—	1	4	4	8
Demoted, transferred	—	1	1[e]	20	59[f]	79	29	1	30	24	5	29
Fined	—	—	—	—	1	1	—	—	—	1	1	2
Tried, "punished"[g]	—	—	—	—	5	5	—	1	1	3	4	7
TOTALS	—	3	3	29	118	147	35	4	39	33	16	49

NOTE: All categories are mutually exclusive. "L" stands for era of Liu Kuan. "K" stands for era of Ku Tso.

[a] Includes 1 man put to death after being subjected to imprisonment and escaping, and 1 man put to death after he was disgraced by being sent to guard the frontier, and then escaping.

[b] Includes 1 man who fell ill and died in prison.

[c] Includes persons sentenced to serve as lesser functionaries or sent to guard the frontiers as common soldiers.

[d] Includes the censor-in-chief Liu Kuan, who though not personally sentenced to banishment as a soldier, was ordered to live in exile with his banished son.

[e] Includes 1 man demoted after doing punitive labor.

[f] Includes 2 men demoted after doing punitive labor, and 1 man who made a commutation payment in rice, was thereafter demoted, and who was eventually restored to his censorial office.

[g] Final results not clear.

TABLE 21

Stated Reasons for Which Censorial Officials Were Disciplined, 1424–34

Reasons specified	Censors	Supervising secretaries	Surveillance commissioners
Venality	45	2	21
Improper personal conduct	37	12	8
Inadequacy	38	5	18
Uninformed about responsibilities . .	25	—	6
Negligence, irresponsibility	15	12	11
Injustice, false accusations	14	2	3
Miscellaneous	20	3	3

NOTE: Categories are not mutually exclusive.

TABLE 22

Disciplinary Action Against Censorial Officials, by Disposition, 1620–27

Action taken	Censors-in-chief			Investigating censors			Supervising secretaries			Surveillance commissioners		
	A	B	Total	A	B	Total	A	B	Total	A	B	Total
Put to death	—	2	2	—	6	6	—	2	2	—	—	—
Imprisoned	—	—	—	—	1	1[a]	—	—	—	—	—	—
Disgraced[b]	—	1	1	—	4	4	—	1	1	—	—	—
Beaten	—	—	—	1	—	1	—	—	—	—	—	—
Dismissed from service	—	3	3[c]	4[d]	43	47	2	26[e]	28	1	4	5
Removed from office	—	—	—	1	15	16	2	3	5	2	4	6
Demoted, transferred	—	—	—	12	3	15	9	2	11	6	8	14
Fined	—	—	—	25	—	25	15	—	15	1	—	1
TOTALS	—	6	6	43	72	115	28	34	62	10	16	26

NOTE: All categories are mutually exclusive. "*A*" stands for era prior to Wei Chung-hsien's dominance. "*B*" stands for era of Wei Chung-hsien's dominance.
[a] Finally sentenced to strangulation but not actually executed.
[b] All sentenced to guard the frontier as common soldiers.
[c] Includes 1 man who later committed suicide rather than face arrest and torture.
[d] Includes 1 man dismissed from the service after being beaten.
[e] Includes 1 man who was later sentenced to death but was not actually executed.

TABLE 23

Stated Reasons for Which Censorial Officials Were Disciplined, 1620–27

Reasons specified	Censors			Supervising secretaries			Surveillance commissioners		
	A	B	Total	A	B	Total	A	B	Total
Partisanship	18	58	76	10	29	39	—	5	5
Offensive remonstrance	13	1	14	13	3	16	1	—	1
Offensive impeachment	21	7	28	17	5	22	—	—	—
Offensive personnel recommendation	5	16	21	—	2	2	—	—	—
Venality	4	10	14	1	5	6	5	2	7
Inadequacy, negligence, etc.	5	8	13	6	2	8	8	4	12
Miscellaneous	2	—	2	—	4	4	3	—	3

NOTE: Categories are not mutually exclusive. "*A*" stands for era prior to Wei Chung-hsien's dominance. "*B*" stands for era of Wei Chung-hsien's dominance.

Notes

Notes

Abbreviations used in the Notes are listed on page 385
of the Bibliography, which gives complete authors'
names, titles, and publication data for all works cited.

Chapter one

1. Ricci, *China in the 16th Century*, p. 49.
2. Latourette, *The Chinese*, pp. 546, 523.
3. Kracke, "The Art of Government," p. 321.
4. MS 73.4b; HTT 28; MHY 33.2a.
5. The most useful general history of the censorial system in Chinese is Kao, *Yü-shih Chih-tu*. A 1947 newspaper article by Nieh, "Chien-ch'a Chih-tu," is a highly perceptive short summary, but unfortunately it is not easily accessible. Wist, *Das Chinesische Zensorat*, is the only general history in a Western language but is very brief and is derived largely from Kao's work. A background survey is included in Walker, "The Control System."
6. Yü, "Chien-ch'a Chih-tu"; and a series of articles by T'ang Chi-ho in *Hsin She-hui K'o-hsüeh Chi-k'an*, vol. I, no. 1 (1934), pp. 67–74; *She-hui K'o-hsüeh Ts'ung-k'an*, vol. I, no. 2 (1934), pp. 153–62; *She-hui K'o-hsüeh Lun-ts'ung*, vol. I, no. 2 (1934), pp. 207–13; and *Chung-shan Wen-hua Chiao-yü-kuan Chi-k'an*, no. 2 (1935), pp. 517–25.
7. Tang, "The Censorial Institution"; Li Hsiung-fei, *Les Censeurs*.
8. For example, Tang and Li both report, for the entirety of the 268-year Ch'ing dynasty, a total of 464 "reporting and advising" memorials and 223 impeachment memorials by censorial officials. The incompleteness of these data can be suggested by comparing them with statistics given in following chapters of the present work, which reveal that in the decade 1424–34 alone, in the Ming dynasty, comparable censorial officials submitted 204 "reporting and advising" memorials and 210 impeachment memorials and that in the still shorter Ming period 1620–27 the totals were 1292 and 524, respectively. Since even these Ming dynasty data are themselves somewhat selective, as will be shown, the selectivity of the Ch'ing dynasty data used by Tang and Li clearly renders them all but useless for significant analysis.
9. Feifel, *Po Chü-i*.
10. *Lun-yü* 15.15; trans. by Waley, *Analects*, p. 196.
11. A much fuller discussion of the ideological foundations of Chinese censorship can be found in Hucker, "Confucianism and the Censorial System."
12. *Lun-yü* 12.16; trans. by Waley, *Analects*, p. 167.
13. *Mencius* 4.2.9; trans. by Legge, *The Chinese Classics*, II, 321.

14. Kao, *Yü-shih Chih-tu*, p. 43.
15. *Lun-yü* 14.23; trans. by Creel, *Confucius*, p. 160.
16. *Li-chi* 54.6a; trans. by Legge in *Sacred Books of the East*, p. 345.
17. *Hsiao-ching*, ch. 15. I know it is doubtful that Confucius said all the things that are attributed to him in such works as *Li-chi* and *Hsiao-ching*. The belief that these were valid attributions, however, made them part of the intellectual baggage of all traditional Chinese, which is the only aspect of the matter that concerns us here.
18. E.g., see *Han Fei Tzu* 5.1a, 4.4a–7b; trans. by Liao, *The Complete Works of Han Fei Tzu*, I, 106–12, 135.
19. Cf. Mote, "Confucian Eremitism," pp. 202–40.
20. For the history of the censorial institutions, see Kao, *Yü-shih Chih-tu*. General material is also available in *Li-tai Chih-kuan Piao*, I, 473–537. More detailed information can of course be found in primary sources pertaining to specific historical periods. Many important primary materials are indicated in Kao, *Yü-shih Chih-tu*, and in *Li-tai Chih-kuan Piao*. Chief supplementary sources that I have used for the early periods of censorial history include the following. For the Han dynasties: Wang Yü-ch'üan, "Central Government of the Former Han"; Chavannes, trans., *Memoires historiques*, II, 513–33; and Sah, "The Impact of Hanfeism." For the T'ang dynasty: Rotours. trans., *Le Traité des examens* and *Traité des fonctionnaires*; and Pulleyblank, *The Rebellion of An Lu-shan*. For the Sung dynasty: Kracke, *Civil Service*, chap. 3; *Sung-shih*, ch. 164; and *Sung Hui-yao Kao*, Chih-kuan section, ch. 17.
21. Naito, *Shina Shigakushi*, pp. 26–27; Tung Tso-pin, *The Ancient Chinese Civilization*, p. 11; Han, *Chinese Historiography*, p. 2.
22. Naito, *Shina Shigakushi*, p. 7; Creel, *Birth of China*, pp. 139–40; Watson, *Ssu-ma Ch'ien*, p. 70. The Shang term *shih* certainly could not have denoted "a hand holding a fountain pen enscribing characters," as Han (*Chinese Historiography*, p. 2) has rendered Leon Wieger's interpretation.
23. Watson, *Ssu-ma Chien*, p. 71. "Recorders" of the Chou dynasty are mentioned not merely in the Chou-li, but in the *Tso-chuan* and *Li-chi* and even in the *Shu-ching*.
24. Han, *Chinese Historiography*, p. 2.
25. Watson, *Ssu-ma Chien*, p. 74.
26. This aspect of censorial history has been badly confused in the historical literature. Because the traditional title for censors, *yü-shih,* originally denoted "royal recorder," there has been a tendency to assume that the censor's function grew out of the historian's function. Thus Walker ("The Control System," p. 7) has written: "As recorders of the acts of the Emperors, the *Yü-shih* soon expanded their activity to include insuring that the Emperor did no wrongs for them to record; and before the end of Chou times . . . this had developed into the additional power of seeing that the ministers committed no errors." Cf. Hsieh, *Government of China*, p. 87. Another version of the same idea appears in Linebarger, etc., *Far Eastern Governments*, p. 52: "The Chinese term for censor, *yü-shih,* originally designated an imperial historian whose duty it was to record the speeches and deeds of the emperors. In so doing the historian inevitably accepted the responsibility of criticizing the ruler for improper speech or for his misconduct.

The role of *yü-shih* was later extended to include criticism of the conduct of all officials, whatever their grade."

This interpretation of censorial origins derives in part from the functional continuity that clearly related early historians to later bureaucratic remonstrators. Chou recorders, and later Chinese historians as well, did function partly as critics of the rulers and other powerful persons. The traditional notion that Confucius compiled the *Ch'un Ch'iu* ("Spring and Autumn Annals") for the moralistic purpose of assigning credit and blame supports this concept of the historian's role. Moreover, the Chou recorder "was close to the ruler, acting often as adviser and moral counselor." (Watson, *Ssu-ma Ch'ien*, p. 74.) That historians of all periods did use their writing as a check on the powerful is abundantly documented. See, for instance, the case of Ts'ui Chu in *Tso-chuan*, under the 25th year of Duke Hsiang (cf. Han, *Chinese Historiography*, p. 5), and p. 240 of Hucker, "Su-chou." It is also clear that "to the history-minded Confucian ruler" of the imperial age "the reputation Confucian historians might give him if he violated the accepted code was not a slight consideration." (Kracke, *Civil Service*, p. 29.) It would seem quite justifiable, therefore, to say that in the Chinese tradition historians and remonstrators "exemplified the same ideal in two distinct ways." (Han, *Chinese Historiography*, p. 4.) And I am sure that Chinese censors of much later ages, after censors had assumed specialized remonstrance functions in addition to surveillance functions, did while remonstrating draw inspiration from the examples of the Chou recorders whose title they bore.

The difficulty with this history-by-etymology lies in the fact that Ch'in and Han *yü-shih* do not seem to have been significantly concerned with remonstrance. They may indeed have engaged occasionally in remonstrance, as was every official's wont, but their prescribed and characteristic function as *yü-shih* was to provide disciplinary surveillance over the bureaucrats. Remonstrance with the emperor was the special function of the separate speaking officials; the censors proper—the *yü-shih*—were surveillance officials, instruments of monarchical control over the officialdom at large. See Wang Yü-ch'üan, "Central Government of the Former Han," pp. 147ff., 160–61; Sah, "The Impact of Hanfeism," p. 96. It is not without reason that one modern authority has described the *yü-shih ta-fu* or censor-in-chief of Han times as "Grand Judge and Director of Police of the State." (Balazs, trans., *Le Traité juridique*, p. 188.) It has recently even been suggested that the Han emperors, under the influence of still prevalent Legalist notions, created the Censorate to serve as a kind of built-in political opposition to the grand councilor or prime minister, to prevent his encroaching upon imperial authority. (Sah, "The Impact of Hanfeism.")

The common supposition that Han censors exercised remonstrance functions, and thus might be linked functionally to Chou historians, seems based on the fact that Han palace censors had a duty station within the palace. This Censorate outpost in the palace was maintained for centuries, until rulers of the Sui dynasty (581–618) abolished it. Thus we find Hsieh (*Government of China*, p. 88) saying, "The Sui emperors deprived the censor of the right to correct the emperor and made it his special duty to censure officials. From that time on, he became a spy on the mandarins and 'eyes and ears' of the sovereign. His original duty of recording the speech and acts of the emperor was given to another office . . . ." Walker ("The Control System," p. 8) has even claimed that in the centuries prior to the Sui era censors "were members of the Inner Court and became the formulators of imperial policy rather than mere advisors to the Emperor" and, still more extravagantly, that "the Censors, and not the Emperor, were held responsible for all affairs . . . ." Even the great modern Chinese historian Ch'ien Mu (Cheng-chih Te-shih, pp. 59–62) has assumed that the palace censors of the pre-Sui period were essentially critics of the emperor—that the Censorate was a tool wielded by the prime minister against the emperor rather than one wielded by the emperor against the officialdom.

These are stimulating hypotheses, but I can find no evidence to support them. Although palace censors may have informed on emperors surreptitiously for the benefit of prime ministers and occasionally did exercise the general privilege of remonstrance, I know of no grounds for contending that their specially prescribed functions normally, principally, or characteristically included direct criticism of the emperor. Before as well as after the Sui era, censors in general were surveillance officials; and pre-Sui palace censors in particular were expected merely "to supervise the Imperial attendants and the palace ladies." (Wang Yü-ch'üan, "Central Government of the Former Han," p. 150.) When the Sui emperors abolished the palace outpost of the Censorate they saved their intimate attendants from annoying surveillance but they did not terminate remonstrance, since remonstrance was the special prerogative of the totally separate speaking officials.

27. Kracke, Civil Service, p. 35.

28. CMMYL 48.41b–42a.

29. Sung Hui-yao Kao, Chih-kuan section, 17.16a–b.

30. See Rotours, trans., Traité des fonctionnaires, II, 656–80; Rotours, "Les Grands Fonctionnaires"; and Ch'ien Mu, Cheng-chih Te-shih, pp. 59–62.

31. Kracke, Civil Service, pp. 50–53; Ch'ien Mu, Cheng-chih Te-shih, pp. 62–64.

32. One Sung source, Pao's Tsou-i, 3.47b, ascribes to judicial intendants the ordinary, and clearly censorial, function of scrutinizing the conduct of all local officials. For a brief period, fiscal intendants were even known by the designation an-ch'a shih—a term with specific surveillance denotations. See Li Tao, T'ung-chien Ch'ang-pien, 141.3b.

33. Sung Hui-yao Kao, Chih-kuan section, 17.9b. Cf. Li Ch'ih, Shih-ch'ao Kang-yao, 10A.6a.

34. Sung Hui-yao Kao, Chih-kuan section, 17.9b–10a.

35. Ibid., 17.11a–b. Cf. Li Ch'ih, Shih-ch'ao Kang-yao, 10B.3a.

36. Sung Hui-yao Kao, Hsüan-chü section, 27.10a.

37. For general surveys of the history of speaking officials, see Li-tai Chih-kuan Piao, ch. 19; Kao, Yü-shih Chih-tu, ch. 3; and WHTK, ch. 50, pp. 458–61.

38. Rotours, trans., Traité des fonctionnaires, I, 143–47, 151–52, 187. Cf. Waley, Po Chü-i, pp. 41–43; Feifel, Po Chü-i, pp. 30–33; and William Hung, Tu Fu, p. 24.

39. Rotours, trans., Traité des fonctionnaires, I, 147–49, 180–87.

40. Kao, *Yü-shih Chih-tu*, pp. 54–56; Kracke, *Civil Service*, pp. 33–37; Ch'ien Mu, *Cheng-chih Te-shih*, pp. 59–62.

41. Rotours, trans., *Traité des fonctionnaires*, I, 147–49; Kao, *Yü-shih Chih-tu*, pp. 42–54. Cf. Ku Yen-wu, *Jih-chih Lu*, vol. IV, pp. 6–7 (ch. 9); and Wu Han, *Chu Yüan-chang Chuan*, pp. 236–38.

42. Ch'ien Mu, *Cheng-chih Te-shih*, pp. 59–62.

43. See Feifel, *Po Chü-i*, pp. 36–37.

44. Su Shih, *Tung-p'o Tsou-i*, 1.23a ff. Su's memorial is of particular interest because it reveals his attitude toward the service expected of the Censorate and the Bureau of Remonstrance. He considered that the state's gravest problem was to maintain a proper balance between forces favoring centralization and those favoring decentralization. Overcentralization made it possible for evil ministers to gain imperial favor and usurp the authority proper to the sovereign, while extreme decentralization permitted regional authorities to become strong enough to do so. The Sung government, Su thought, tended toward centralization and was thus susceptible to the abuses of cunning men in high places. He said that he could not presume to explain entirely the measures that the dynastic founders had instituted to prevent overcentralization and its dangers, but he added:

"However, in regard to the single matter of their employment of a Censorate and a Bureau of Remonstrance, this is the sages' perfect preventive plan. Successively considering [history from] Ch'in and Han and on to the Five Dynasties period [907–60], there were undoubtedly several hundred men who met their deaths because they remonstrated; but from the Chien-lung era [960–62] on, no critics have ever been punished. Even though they were reproved, they have forthwith been granted extraordinary promotions. Being permitted to make use of hearsay evidence, they have not been intimidated by high rank or prestige and have paid no attention to the honorable or humble [status of those criticized]. When their criticisms extended to the imperial person, the emperors have shown disturbance; when [they spoke of] matters concerning state policies, the grand councilors have expected trouble. Thus in the time of Jen-tsung (reigned 1022–1063) public opinion ridiculed the grand councilors, (saying) that they merely accepted and enacted the criticisms of the Censorate and the Bureau of Remonstrance, and that's all.

"How should the profound intentions of the sages be thought of? The Censorate's and the Bureau of Remonstrance's criticisms are not necessarily all to be thought worthy and are not necessarily all to be approved. But it is necessary to foster their ardent spirit . . . , since it will check the rise of evil ministers, thus preventing the abuses of centralization. When evil ministers first arise they can be checked by the Censorate and the Bureau of Remonstrance with ease; but after they have reached full stature military forces are not sufficient to restrain them. At present the laws and decrees are stern and strict; the dynastic government is pure and bright. There are no evil ministers. Nevertheless, one keeps a cat to get rid of mice; one cannot, because there happen to be no mice, keep a non-catching cat. One keeps a dog to guard against villains; one cannot, because there happen to be no villains, keep a non-barking dog. Is it possible for your majesty not to remember the intentions of the ancestors in establishing these officials or [fail] on behalf of posterity to maintain protection just in case? [In maintaining] the dynastic principles, what is greater than this?" *Tung-p'o Tsou-i,* 1.23b–24a. Parts of Su's memorial are given in free translation in Lin, *The Gay Genius,* pp. 118–23.

45. Rotours, trans., *Traité des fonctionnaires,* I, 304–5.

46. Sun Feng-chi, *Chih-kuan Fen-chi,* 14.24b; *Li-tai Chih-kuan Piao,* 18.512. Cf. Kracke, *Civil Service,* p. 31.

47. Hung Mai, *Jung-chai Sui-pi,* book IV, 11.8a.

48. Kracke, *Civil Service,* p. 37.

49. See comments by Su Shih in the memorial cited in note 44 above. Feifel says that the T'ang poet Po Chü-i, while serving as a "reminder" (*shih-i*), "enjoyed legal immunity." "Unless the emperor had good reason to suspect slander or deliberate vengeance, he did not call to task a censor who, in good faith, had overstepped himself in the zealous pursuit of his duty. This was the rule at any rate." (*Po Chü-i,* p. 38.) So far as I am aware there was no such law, though certainly censorial immunity from punishment was an accepted ideal.

50. Feifel, *Po Chü-i,* p. 186.

51. Kao, *Yü-shih Chih-tu,* p. 13.

52. *Sung Hui-yao Kao,* Chih-kuan section, 17.9b–10a.

53. *Ibid.,* 17.3a–4a, 31b, 34b–35a. Cf. *Li-tai Chih-kuan Piao,* 18.510–11.

54. *Yüan-shih,* chs. 85–91; Ratchnevsky, *Un Code des Yuan, passim.*

55. *Yüan-shih* 86.27b–31a; Ko, *Hsin Yüan-shih,* 57.1a–8b; Ratchnevsky, *Un Code des Yuan,* pp. 153–54, 161–62, 169–70, 175, 177–80; *Yüan Tien-chang,* chs. 5–6. Also see Hucker, "The Yüan Contribution."

56. *Yüan Tien-chang* 5.1b, 7a, and 9b–10a; and 6.2a.

57. *Ibid.,* 5.9b–10a; 6.8a–9a, 12b–14a, 22b–23b; and 2.4a–6a.

58. *Yüan-shih* 88.8b; Ko, *Hsin Yüan-shih,* 59.6b–7a; Ratchnevsky, *Un Code des Yuan,* p. 186, note 1.

59. *Yüan-shih* 6.15b.

60. The general Yüan policy was that the heads of all government units, even down to the county level, had to be Mongols or other non-Chinese whose loyalty to the Mongols could be trusted absolutely. See Ratchnevsky, *Un Code des Yuan,* pp. xxvff. My presumption that Mongols were numerous even among lesser officials of the various Censorates is based upon the statement in *Yüan-shih* 86.29b that in 1286 when 18 new positions as investigating censors were authorized for the Chiang-nan branch Censorate 14 were reserved for Mongols.

61. *Yüan-shih* 128.11a ff.

62. *Ibid.,* 85.1a–2a; Howorth, *History of the Mongols,* I, 311, 316.

63. For a general survey of the Censorate's history since Ming times, see Hucker, "The Traditional Chinese Censorate."

64. On the Ch'ing Censorate, see Li Hsiung-fei, *Les Censeurs;* Tang, "The Censorial Institution"; Wist, *Das Chinesische Zensorat,* pp. 36–45; Hsieh Pao Chao, *Government of China,* pp. 87–98; Mayers, *The Chinese Government,* pp. 23–24; Brunnert and Hagelstrom, *Present-Day Political Organization,* pp. 75–79.

65. For general data on censorial institutions in twentieth century China, see Tung, *Political Institutions,* especially pp. 97, 121–22, 188, 210–11, 272, 297–99.

66. On the Control Yüan, see Ch'ien Tuan-sheng, *Government and Politics*, pp. 262-77; Linebarger, *The China of Chiang K'ai-shek*, pp. 313-24; Tsao, *Constitutional Structure*, pp. 188-203; Siu, *Le Pouvoir de contrôle*; *China Yearbook 1957-58*, pp. 128-38; Chen, "Impeachments of the Control Yüan," pp. 331-66 and 515-42. In probably the most impressive achievement of its history, the Control Yüan in 1957-58 impeached and brought about the resignation of Premier O. K. Yui and his whole cabinet. See the *New York Times*, Dec. 24, 1957, p. 2; Jan. 10, 1958, p. 3; Jan. 21, 1958, p. 7; Feb. 15, 1958, p. 8; and July 1, 1958, p. 10.

67. See Hucker, "The Traditional Chinese Censorate," pp. 1053ff.; Ginsburg and Stahnke, "Genesis of the People's Procuratorate"; Linebarger, etc., *Far Eastern Governments*, p. 249; and Barnett, *Communist China*, p. 51.

Chapter two

1. I have already described the state and society of Ming times, at some length but not technically, in *The Traditional Chinese State*, and have provided a technical description of the whole Ming government apparatus in "Governmental Organization." The following brief discussion of the societal and institutional background for Ming censorial operations is based principally upon research reported on in these earlier monographic studies, and my English renderings of the Chinese names of agencies and offices are in accord with the usages set forth in the latter study.

2. An excellent study of civil-service recruitment in Ming times and its relation to social mobility in general is Ho, *The Ladder of Success*.

3. Grimm, *Erziehung und Politik,* is a thorough modern study of the entire educational system in Ming times.

4. Though all these services were theoretically civil-service agencies, the officials of such agencies as the Directorate of Astronomy, the Imperial Academy of Medicine, and the Music and Dance Office were normally not civil servants in the ordinary Ming sense but were permanently assigned and were usually hereditary professional specialists.

5. Hucker "Governmental Organization," pp. 64-66; TMHT 80.1834.

6. Ch'ien Mu, *Kuo-shih Ta-kang*, pp. 476-77. Cf. Wu Han, *Chu Yüan-chang Chuan*; Mote, *The Poet Kao Ch'i*; Ku Chieh-kang, "Literary Persecution"; and Mote, "Chinese Despotism."

7. Yeh Tzu-ch'i, *Ts'ao-mu-tzu*, cited in Ch'ien Mu, *Kuo-shih Ta-kang*, pp. 476-77.

8. Ch'ien Mu, *Kuo-shih Ta-kang*, p. 481.

9. The following discussion is based primarily on Hucker, *The Traditional Chinese State*, pp. 10-12, 55-58. Also see MS 74.24a-32a; Ting, *T'e-wu Cheng-chih*; and Crawford, *"Eunuch Power."*

10. A history of judicial abuses by the Embroidered-uniform Guard (*chin-i wei*) is included in MS 95; and Ting, *T'e-wu Cheng-chih*, provides a thorough analysis of its collaboration with eunuchs for terroristic purposes.

11. See Tout, *Collected Papers*, III, chap. 7: "The English Civil Service in the Fourteenth Century," especially p. 202.

12. E.g., see Hucker, "The Tung-lin Movement."

13. *Ibid.*, pp. 136ff. Cf. de Bary, "Chinese Despotism," p. 175; and Ch'ien Mu, *Cheng-chih Te-shih*, pp. 79–85.

14. The following discussion of the organizational development of the Ming Censorate is generally based on MS 73.4b–6a and 75.4a–b; TMHT 2.30–32, 3.61–62, and especially ch. 209–11; MHY 33.1a–3a; MSK 55.1a–4a; CMMYL 48.4b–5a; MSHU 65.1300-02; TWL 27.3a, 10b, 15b, and 26a–27a; *Ku-chin T'u-shu Chi-ch'eng*, Kuan-ch'ang section, 335.1a ff.; HTK ch. 54; HTT ch. 28; HTC ch. 135; Kao, *Yü-shih Chih-tu*, pp. 43ff.; Yü, "Chien-ch'a Chih-tu," pp. 213ff.; Mano, "Mindai Tosatsuin"; and Mano, "Kobucho no Tosatsuin." Cf. Hucker, "The Traditional Chinese Censorate."

15. MS 2.16a, 72.4a–11a.

16. MS 2.16b, 73.4b–6a; TTSL 131.10b. Cf. the various sources cited in note 14 above.

The episode of the so-called "abolition" of the Censorate in the fifth month of 1380 and its reorganization in the tenth month of 1382, despite clear and categorical statements with dates in the basic source, TTSL, is confused in several of the secondary sources. Confusion probably stems from the fact that during the period between the "abolition" and the reorganization of the Censorate there are numerous references to active censors in TTSL. All references there to current censorial activities, however, give the designation investigating censor (*chien-ch'a yü-shih*) or simply censor (*yü-shih*). The only references to censors-in-chief or vice censors-in-chief that I have located speak clearly in the past tense of "the former" censor-in-chief and vice censor-in-chief An Jan, who was removed from office in 1380. See TTSL 136.5a, 138.8a. I find no occurrence of the title associate censor; and I find only two occurrences of the term Tribunal of Censors, one referring back to An Jan's career and the other referring back to the year 1375. During the "abolition" period, moreover, there is frequent use of the designation Court of Surveillance (*ch'a-yüan*) in contexts suggesting that this was the current designation of the central censorial institution staffed by investigating censors. E.g., see TTSL 143.1b and 9b, 147.15b. In a narrow literal sense, it may have been quite accurate to say that in 1380 the Tribunal of Censors was abolished; for the Court of Surveillance, though subordinate to it, was probably always considered a separate entity. In just this way, after the reorganization of 1382, the investigating censors' Circuits were part of the Censorate in a broad sense but were still thought of as independent agencies, so that there were sometimes references to "the Censorate *and* the Circuits."

17. The designation Chief Surveillance Office (*tu ch'a-yüan*) is sometimes rendered "All-examining Court" (suggesting the hyphenation *tu-ch'a yüan*). Although grammatically possible, this rendering does not accurately convey the sense of the Chinese term. The separate Circuits were spoken of as the various *ch'a-yüan*, and in popular parlance even individual censors were referred to as *ch'a-yüan*. The term *tu ch'a-yüan*, then, clearly meant chief or superior *ch'a-yüan*.

18. *Yüan Tien-chang* 82.1b and chs. 5 and 6 *passim*, especially 5.5b and 9a, 6.4a and 7b ff.

19. TMHT 12.280.

20. TMHT 210.4179.

21. Wang Shih-chen, *Yen-chou Shih-liao,* 2.21b; Wang Shih-chen, *Yen-shan-t'ang Pieh-chi,* 52.2a–3a; *Kao, Yü-shih Chih-tu,* pp. 43–44; CMMYL 48.5a; MHY 34.3a–b; *Li-tai Chih-kuan Piao* 18.518.

22. As early as 1409, Ch'eng-tsu ordered a skeleton Censorate staff sent to Peking for detached or auxiliary *(hsing-tsai)* duty. See MS 158.2b–4b. When Peking was named principal capital in 1421, the designation "auxiliary" was removed from all the offices there including the Censorate, and the staffs left in Nanking—now mere skeleton staffs in their turn—were differentiated by being called, for example, the Nanking Ministry of Rites. See MS 72.10b–11a. A Nanking Censorate thus came into formal existence, though apparently not until 1424. It was only then that special appointments as Nanking censors-in-chief, etc., began to be recorded. Prior to 1424 the Peking and Nanking Censorates seem to have shared one body of personnel. See Wang Shih-chen, *Yen-shan-t'ang Pieh-chi,* 55.1a–6a, 62.1a–4a, 62.14a–17a.

In general, the terminological differentiation between, for example, "the Ministry of Rites" and "the Nanking Ministry of Rites" persisted as a standard usage from 1421 to the end of the dynasty. But the period from 1425 to 1441 was exceptional in this regard. The pre-1421 usage was then restored, in the unfulfilled expectation that the actual seat of government would be moved back to Nanking. See MS 72.10b–11a. Documents of this relatively brief period are consequently somewhat confusing, since they generally apply the unqualified term "Censorate" to the skeletal auxiliary Censorate at Nanking and by "Auxiliary Censorate" actually denote the full-bodied Censorate at Peking that was exercising empire-wide responsibilities. For the sake of simplicity, this deviation will be ignored in the present study. Unless qualified, the names of all central-government agencies will denote those that existed until 1421 at Nanking and thereafter at Peking, and the prefix "Nanking" will consistently denote the auxiliary agencies in Nanking after 1421.

23. One of the original 12 Circuits to which investigating censors were assigned, the Peiping Circuit, was retitled the Peking (Pei-ching) Circuit in 1403 and was finally abolished in 1421, when Peking became the official seat of government. In the same year 3 new Circuits were created, for Kweichow, Yunnan, and Chiao-chih (Annam). In 1435 the Chiao-chih Circuit was discontinued, leaving a total of 13.

Occasional reference is made in some documents to a Metropolitan Circuit *(ching-chi tao).* TMHT 7.147–50, for example, states that 4 ungraded lesser functionaries were normally assigned to the Metropolitan Circuit. In Ch'ing times (1644–1912) the Censorate did include a Metropolitan Circuit with status comparable to that of any other Circuit. See *Ch'ing-shih Kao,* 115.3b–6a. But in Ming times "Metropolitan Circuit" was an unofficial designation for investigating censors of all the regular Circuits who, collectively, were commissioned to check records in the capital agencies. No investigating censor was ever appointed principally to the Metropolitan Circuit.

24. Hui-ti (1398–1402) gave the Censorate its ancient designation *yü-shih fu,* retitled censors-in-chief *yü-shih ta-fu,* and grouped investigating censors into two Courts *(yüan),* one of the left and one of the right, rather than in Circuits. But his innovations did not last beyond his own short reign.

TWL 27.10b states that in Hui-ti's time investigating censors were re-titled principal censors (? *cheng yü-shih*) and that subsequently all the var-ious *yü-shih* were redesignated as reminders (*shih-i*) and omissioners (*pu-ch'üeh*)—the old titles of remonstrators. MS 73.14b–15a confirms that re-minders and omissioners were indeed reestablished at this time but indi-cates that they were officials of the Office of Transmission. MS 74.13a also mentions the "additional establishment" at this time of such remonstrance posts in its discussion of supervising secretaries. I find no support, however, for the contention that censors were given such titles.

The next substantial change in Censorate titles did not occur until the very end of the dynasty, when the rebel Li Tzu-ch'eng captured Peking and set up a dynasty of his own that lasted for a brief interval until invading Manchus destroyed it. Li retained the designation Chief Surveillance Office, but for all its censors he resurrected the old Han term "straight-pointing commissioner" (*chih-chih shih*), and censors-in-chief became "chief straight-pointing commissioners" (*tu chih-chih shih*). See Li Wen-chih, *Wan Ming Min-pien,* pp. 137 and 211.

There exists an apparently unexplainable assertion that in the fourth month of the year 1425 there was established a Peking branch (*hsing*) Cen-sorate. See JTSL 9A.4b:

"There was established a Peking branch Censorate and, subordinate to it, a Registry, a Record Office, a General Services Office, a Prison Office, and four Circuits: Lu-lung, Heng-nan [both designations of regions in modern Hopei or Chihli province], I-pei [in modern Shansi province], and Kuang-p'ing [in modern Hopei or Chihli province]. There were established one vice censor-in-chief of the right (6a), one record clerk (8a), *ssu-shou* (3a) [?]; one assistant censor-in-chief of the left (4a), *shou-ling kuan* [cf. note 29 be-low]—one registrar (6a), one record clerk (8a), one office manager and one prison superintendent (both 9b)—and the various Circuits' investigating cen-sors, three in each (all 8a)."

Clearly, the entry is garbled. The modern Academia Sinica editor Huang Chang-chien (in *Chiao-k'an Chi,* p. 143), collating various extant copies of JTSL, reconstructs the latter portion of the entry to read: "There were established one vice censor-in-chief of the right (3a), one assistant censor-in-chief of the left (4a), *shou-ling kuan*—one registrar (6a), one record clerk (8a), one office manager and one prison superintendent (both 9b)—and the various Circuits' investigating censors, three in each (all 7a)." So corrected, the entry is understandable. However, except for a corroborative and ob-viously derivative statement merely that "a Peking branch Censorate was established," in MS 8.6a, I find no confirmation of this entry in other sources and know of no way to account for it in JTSL.

It was only in the preceding month that Jen-tsung ordered the designa-tion "auxiliary" (*hsing-tsai*) restored to the various Peking offices (MS 8.5b). Thus it is tempting to believe that the designation "branch" (*hsing*) here should be read as the equivalent of "auxiliary" and that these statements refer to the formal redesignation of the Peking Censorate in compliance with the order of the previous month. This temptation is strengthened by the fact that the *Shih-lu* for this period does not refer to a *hsing-tsai* Censor-ate until the very day on which it is said that the *hsing* Censorate was established. Then the *Shih-lu* record that I Ch'ien was named vice censor-in-chief of the right for the *hsing-tsai* Censorate (JTSL 9A.4a). Thereafter no other individual is specifically identified with the *hsing-tsai* Censorate until the seventh month of the year, although in the interval I Ch'ien is so identified three times (JTSL 9A.5b; HTSL 3.10b–11b, 13b) and the *hsing-tsai* Censorate itself is referred to on two other occasions (JTSL 9A.6a, HTSL 3.14a). When in the seventh month other individuals were so identified for the first time, they were investigating censors being promoted and appointed (HTSL 4.3b–4a).

Censors-in-chief in Peking at this time were Liu Kuan and Hsiang Pao. During the interval concerned, Hsiang is not mentioned at all in the chronicles; his name does not occur until the ninth month, when he was identified with the *hsing-tsai* Censorate. Liu's name, however, occurs twice during the seventh month without being specifically identified with the *hsing-tsai* Censorate (HTSL 4.9a, 12a-b), though in the latter case the context associates him with activities of the *hsing-tsai* Censorate. Finally, in the succeeding intercalated month, he is identified with it specifically. Inasmuch as I Ch'ien in the seventh month was transferred out of his Censorate post to become a provincial administration commissioner (HTSL 3.13b), it might therefore seem possible that until the seventh month the Peking Censorate (*hsing-tsai*) was in fact the *hsing* Censorate referred to, organized as noted under a vice censor-in-chief, namely I Ch'ien, and that the full-scale *hsing-tsai* Censorate came into being only after that time.

Other considerations, however, seem to render this possibility clearly improbable. That Liu Kuan before the ninth month is not specifically identified with the *hsing-tsai* Censorate is in itself of little significance. To call the Peking offices "auxiliary" ones at this time was unrealistic to start with; and because most entries in the *Shih-lu* relate to the Peking offices, the compilers did not consistently follow the cumbersome practice of using the *hsing-tsai* prefixes for them but, rather, often made a more realistic and less unwieldy distinction by referring, for example, to "the Censorate" and "the Nanking Censorate," as I do throughout this study for the sake of simplicity. Besides, if the designations *hsing* and *hsing-tsai* refer to one Peking Censorate under I Ch'ien's leadership, the status of Liu Kuan and Hsiang Pao apparently cannot be accounted for. Both seem to have been in Peking, and that they were even nominally associated with the Nanking Censorate appears unlikely, since at this time Tu Chih was censor-in-chief of the right for the Nanking Censorate (JTSL 3B.9b), and in addition the Nanking minister of war Chang Pen may still have exercised the "concurrent charge of the Nanking Censorate's affairs" to which he was assigned in the eighth month of the preceding year (JTSL 1B.3a) and which he exercised at least as late as the second month of 1425 (JTSL 7A.5a). Finally, when for the seventh month of 1425 there are recorded promotions and appointments of *hsing-tsai* investigating censors, the Circuits with which they are identified are the Shensi, Fukien, Shansi, Kweichow, and Szechwan Circuits—not those provided for in the establishment of the *hsing* Censorate. On the other hand, the existence in fact of a *hsing* Censorate under I Ch'ien in addition to the *hsing-tsai* Censorate under Liu Kuan and Hsiang Pao seems equally unlikely; for neither the *hsing* Censorate itself nor any of its Circuits is identified by name elsewhere in the *Shih-lu* for the reigns of Jen-tsung and Hsüan-tsung or in any other material I have seen, except for the brief MS notice already mentioned.

In short, I cannot believe that a Peking branch (*hsing*) Censorate ever actually existed.

25. Censors-in-chief were commonly referred to as the executive officials (*t'ang-shang kuan*) of the Censorate. Both prescribed offices were not always filled. Although they were of the same rank, the censor-in-chief of the left was normally understood to be senior to his counterpart of the right.

26. The censors-in-chief, vice censors-in-chief, and assistant censors-in-chief were collectively known as the principal officials (*cheng-kuan*) of the Censorate. See *Ku-chin T'u-shu Chi-ch'eng*, Kuan-ch'ang section, 335.1a–b.

27. The post of chief clerk was discontinued in 1570.

28. The Censorate's General Services Office was established in 1383, with 4 office managers. At an unspecified later time the number was reduced to 2.

29. The term *shou-ling-kuan* was a collective designation for certain members of the administrative staffs of Ming offices who might be considered supervisors of the clerical force. HTT 28.1297 indicates that only the registrar and chief clerk were so designated in the Censorate; but *Ku-chin T'u-shu Chi-ch'eng*, Kuan-ch'ang section, 335.1a–b suggests that *shou-ling kuan* was a collective designation for the registrar, chief clerk, office manager, record clerk, and collator. In referring to the Yüan dynasty, Ratchnevsky has explained the term as a general designation for officials acting as *chef des employés du bureau d'un office* and indicates that it denoted registrars and chief clerks most commonly (*Un Code des Yuan*, p. 39, note 7).

30. Originally there were 6 prison superintendents. In 1529, 3 posts were discontinued; in 1581 the number was reduced to 2; and finally it was further reduced to 1 at an unspecified time. See MS 73.1a–b and *Ku-chin T'u-shu Chi-ch'eng*, Kuan-ch'ang section, 335.1a–b. Some sources state that the prison superintendent, rather than having rank 9b, was an ungraded lesser functionary. See MSHU 65.1301, TWL 27.26a–27a.

31. TMHT 7.147–50 indicates that this number included 31 functionaries (2 *tu-li*, 6 *ling-shih,* and 23 *tien-li*) assigned to the Censorate's administrative superiors; 2 *ssu-li* and 7 *tien-li* assigned to the Record Office; 6 *yü-tien* assigned to the Prison Office; and variable numbers of *shu-li* and *tien-li* distributed among the Circuits. The total does not include various *shu-li* and *jen-li* who were attached to censors on commission. TWL 27.26a–27a states that the number of ungraded lesser functionaries assigned to the Censorate was 332. Information on the 250 students is from TWL 27.26a–27a. MS 69.12a states that of National University students who served as novices in the various capital offices, 14 served as copyists in the Censorate itself, 42 accompanied censors on inspection tours, and 178 assisted censors in checking records. This makes a total of 234.

32. MS 70.4b.

33. During the fifteenth century censors-in-chief and vice and assistant censors-in-chief of the left as well as of the right were sometimes appointed in the Nanking Censorate. See Wang Shih-chen, *Yen-shan-t'ang Pieh-chi,* 53.1a–6a, 62.1a–4a, 14a–17a.

34. Originally each Nanking Circuit consisted of 3 investigating censors.

After the period 1567–72 even the lesser numbers of 2 or 3 were not always complete; frequently one censor was assigned to the duties of several Circuits. See MS 75.4a–b; *Ku-chin T'u-shu Chi-ch'eng,* Kuan-ch'ang section, 335.1b.

35. TMHT 7.173–74.

36. See, for example, STSL 8.23b–24a.

37. HTK 54.3287; HTC 135.4075.

38. MS 73.1b; TMHT 209.4155; CMMYL 48.26a–27a; TWL 27.12b.

39. MHY 34.8b.

40. Wang Shih-chen, *Yen-chou Shih-liao,* 2.21a–22b; Wang Shih-chen, *Yen-shan-t'ang Pieh-chi,* 52.2a–3a.

41. MS 2.17a, 74.11a–13a; TTSL 132.2b–3a; HTK 52.3263.

42. For the reconstitution of omissioners and reminders, see MS 74.11a–13a, 73.13b–15a. Several admonishing officials, including admonishers (*ssu-chien*), existed throughout the dynasty in the Supervisorate of Imperial Instruction, but they were concerned only with the education of the heir apparent. See MS 73.17a–19b.

The late Ming rebel Li Tzu-ch'eng, in his governmental reorganization, changed all supervising secretaries to grand remonstrators. See Li Wen-chih, *Wan Ming Min-pien,* pp. 137 and 213.

43. For general discussions of the Ming supervising secretaries, see MS 74.11a–13a; TMHT ch. 213, 2.46–47, and 3.71; Kao, *Yü-shih Chih-tu,* pp. 58–61; CMMYL ch. 25; MHY 37.1a–b; HTK 52.3261; Yü, "Chien-ch'a Chih-tu," pp. 226–28.

44. MHY 37.1a, citing the Ming scholar Wang Ch'i, states categorically that the title of supervising secretary was established in 1367 but does not indicate that any appointments were made until 1373. MS 74.11a–13a gives the impression, without specifically saying so, that the offices did not exist until 1373.

45. MHY 37.1a–b, citing the Ming scholar Wang Ch'i.

46. TMHT 3.71.

47. For general information about the development of Provincial Surveillance Offices in Ming times, see MS 75.11a–15b; TMHT 4.77–78; MSHU 66.1323–24; MSK 57.7a–8a; CMMYL 48.49a–b; HTK 60.3344–45; HTC 136.4078.

48. TTSL 131.10b, 136.1b–2a.

49. TMHT 7.193 indicates that each office had a variable staff of *shu-li, tien-li,* and *ch'eng-fa* lesser functionaries. T'ao, *Kiangsi Fu-i Ch'uan-shu,* reports that the clerical staff of the Kiangsi Surveillance Office late in the sixteenth century included 3 copyists (*shu-shou*), 5 doormen (*men-tzu*), 20 lictors (*chao-li*), 3 archivists (*chia-ko-k'u k'u-tzu*), 2 guards (*p'u-ping*), and 2 runners *(tsou-pao-fu).*

50. Chang Hsüan, *Hsi-yüan Wen-chien Lu,* 93.2a–b.

51. Wang Shih-chen, *Yen-chou Shih-liao,* 2.21b; Wang Shih-chen, *Yen-shan-t'ang Pieh-chi,* 52.2b; CMMYL 48.5a.

52. Chang Hsüan, *Hsi-yüan Wen-chien Lu,* 93.2a–b.

53. These abbreviations included *k'o-tao* ("the Offices of Scrutiny and the Circuits"), *t'ai-sheng* ("The Censorate and the Secretariat," an allusion

to the earlier status of supervising secretaries as subordinate officials of the Secretariat), and *t'ai-chien* ("the Censorate and the remonstrators").

54. For evidence of the Ch'ing incorporation of supervising secretaries in the Censorate, see *Ch'ing-shih Kao* 115.3b–6a; Kao, *Yü-shih Chih-tu*, pp. 62–71; Hsieh Pao Chao, *Government of China*, pp. 87–98; and Li Hsiung-fei, *Les Censeurs*. For evidence of rivalries between Ming censors and supervising secretaries, see Yü, "Chien-ch'a Chih-tu," p. 229.

55. TMHT 209.4153.

56. Lü K'un, *Shih-cheng Lu*, 1.53b–55a.

57. *Ibid.*, 6.42a–43a. Cf. CMMYL 48.49a–b.

58. This code was called *hsien-kang*, literally denoting "fundamental laws and regulatory principles." The meaning might perhaps be rendered conveniently as "fundamental surveillance principles." The code was drawn up by the Censorate and presented to T'ai-tsu in 1371. The emperor personally revised it and then promulgated it to all governmental organs. A new edition was promulgated in 1393, a complete revision in 1439, and "clarifications" (*shen-ming*) in 1527 and again at an unspecified later date. The *hsien-kang* of 1439 and its subsequent clarifications are reproduced in TMHT ch. 210. Cf. TTSL 60.6b–7a; MHY 33.2b; *Ku-chin T'u-shu Chi-ch'eng*, Kuan-ch'ang section, 335.2a; MS 97.12a; CMMYL 48.30b–31a, 33b, and 35b.

A similar term common in documents referring to censorial activities is *kang-chi*, which suggests "disciplinary principles." It frequently occurs in the expression "disciplinary principles of the court" or "disciplinary principles of the dynasty" (*ch'ao-t'ing kang-chi*), which censors were expected to uphold. E.g., see MS 73.4b.

59. See *Yüan Tien-chang* ch. 5 and 6 *passim*, especially 5.5b, 9a, 6.4a, 7b, 8b, 9a–b, 12b–14a, and 16a.

60. For characteristic instances of the Censorate's transmitting orders to Surveillance Offices, see MHY 33.4a; HTSL 73.9b–10a, 74.6b, 79.6a–b, 83.8a, 84.15a, 89.8a–9a, 93.2a, 100.4b–5a, 101.8b, 110.14b–15a.

61. For evidence that Surveillance Office correspondence was routed through the Censorate, see TMHT 76.1778–79. For mention of the Surveillance Offices' reports to the Censorate, see TMHT 214.4287–88; HTSL 91.10b.

62. Lü K'un, *Shih-cheng Lu*, 6.42a–43a, 51a–52a.

63. For example, see Boxer, ed., *South China*, pp. 154 and 298; and Semedo, *The Monarchy of China*, p. 130.

64. Lü K'un, *Shih-cheng Lu*, 1.53b–55b.

65. CMMYL 48.49a–b.

66. E.g., see Hsieh Pao Chao, *Government of China*, p. 300 ("judicial commissioner").

67. CMMYL 48.6a–7a; MHY 33.5b–6a; *Ku-chin T'u-shu Chi-ch'eng*, Kuan-ch'ang section, 335.3b.

68. CMMYL 48.6a–7a.

69. E.g., see CMMYL 48.6a and 45a; MHY 33.3b, 4b, and 6a; Kao, *Yü-shih Chih-tu*, pp. 44–45; HTK 54.3287; TMHT 209.4177–78.

70. MS 71.7b–9b; TMHT 209.4177–78, 213.4242–43; Kao, *Yü-shih Chih-tu*, pp. 44–45; HTK 36.3169; *Ku-chin T'u-shu Chi-ch'eng*, Kuan-ch'ang section, 335.3b; Yü, "Chien-ch'a Chih-tu," pp. 215, 227–38.

71. MS 72.6b–7a.

72. MHY 33.3b; Yü, "Chien-ch'a Chih-tu," p. 215; HTK 54.3287. This rule was restated in 1439. See TMHT 209.4177.

73. MS 71.7b–9b.

74. The modern scholar Yü ("Chien-ch'a Chih-tu," pp. 215–18) has made a statistical study of 209 investigating censors, representing all Ming periods, whose biographies are given in the *Ming History* and comparable sources. His analysis reveals that 180 of the 209 had first entered the civil service by way of the doctoral degree. My own supplementary tabulations suggest a steadily growing reliance on the doctorate as a prerequisite to censorial appointments. For example, of 123 men whose biographies are given in an extant register of appointees to the Office of Scrutiny for Rites, 104 entered the service by way of the doctoral degree; and of the 19 non-doctors who are listed as having served in that Office of Scrutiny none was appointed after the reign of Ching-ti (1449–57). See *Li-k'o Chi-shih-chung Shih-chi, passim.*

My tabulations from JTSL and HTSL reveal that in 1424–34 more than one third of recorded appointments at the lower censorial levels went to non-doctors—106 of 311 investigating censors and 37 of 117 supervising secretaries. Since 77 of the censors and 54 of the supervising secretaries received their appointments after having served in other offices, their degree status is not indicated. Among these must have been additional non-doctors, so that the actual proportion of non-doctors among these 1424–34 appointees was well above one third. (All of the identified non-doctors were graduates of the National University except for 2 censors who were appointed directly from "civilian" status and 4 supervising secretaries who were the sons of former high-ranking officials and inherited their positions.)

The increase in the number of doctors among censorial personnel between the 1400's and the 1600's cannot be demonstrated by tabulations based on KTSL and STSL. By the 1620's no investigating censors or supervising secretaries were being appointed unless they had experience in non-censorial agencies. Their *Shih-lu* appointment notices consequently indicate their prior offices rather than their degree status. But other tabulations are highly suggestive. *Ching-kuan K'ao-ch'a* is a biographical register of 137 relatively high-ranking officials of various sorts who served during the late sixteenth and early seventeenth centuries, of whom not a single man originally entered the civil service through other means than passing the doctoral examinations. Being ultimately of high rank, these men are not necessarily representative. My own tabulations concerning men involved in a great partisan struggle of the last Ming half-century are probably more relevant to the present issue. Of 341 civil servants of all levels who are named on blacklists issued by one faction or the other, and whose entry status is known, all but 34 held doctoral degrees. See my article "The Tung-lin Movement," p. 159. Moreover, in checking 18 different versions of such blacklists involving a total of 1,106 names, I have found only 9 identifiable non-doctors (all licentiates) who served as investigating censors or supervising secretaries.

Such evidence convinces me that non-doctors among censorial appointees, though relatively common in early Ming times, had in practice as well as in theory become a great rarity in the latter part of the dynasty.

75. JTSL 10.1a–b; MHY 33.4b.

76. In reference to the 1435 order, see CMMYL 48.6a–7a; MHY 33.5b–6a; *Ku-chin T'u-shu Chi-ch'eng,* Kuan-ch'ang section, 335.3b.

77. TMHT 209.4177–78. Among the offices which, at one time or another, were declared acceptable preparation for appointments as investigating censors were local instructorships in Confucian schools; messengers of the Mesenger Office; erudites in the Hanlin Academy, the Court of Imperial Sacrifices, and the National University; judges in the Chief Military Commissions, Regional Military Commissions, and Defense Commands; judges in Provincial Administration Offices; drafters of the Central Drafting Office; office managers in the Censorate, the Ministries, and the Grand Court of Revision; judges in the Grand Court of Revision; registrars, chief clerks, record clerks, and collators in Provincial Administration Offices; and Bureau vice directors and secretaries in the various Ministries.

78. MHY 37.5b.

79. Of 311 censors and 117 supervising secretaries appointed in 1424–34, only 110 censors and 60 supervising secretaries were selected from among experienced officials—approximately only one third of the censors and one half of the supervising secretaries. In the late Ming period 1620–27, on the other hand, all of the 178 Censorate and 87 Office of Scrutiny appointees were men who had already served in other offices.

These data, based on KTSL and STSL, are supported by analysis of *Ching-kuan K'ao-ch'a.* Among the 66 censorial appointments noted in that late Ming register of 137 officials, there is not a single case in which the censorial appointment was a first appointment.

In this connection, special mention should be made of the role of Hanlin bachelors (*shu-chi-shih*) in censorial appointments. In the *Ching-kuan K'ao-ch'a* data, 4 of the 27 censors and 6 of the 39 supervising secretaries had served previously only as Hanlin bachelors. In the data for 1620–27 from the *Shih-lu,* 3 of 178 censors and 7 of 87 supervising secretaries were appointed from status as Hanlin bachelors. In the data for 1424–34, 33 of 311 censors and 6 of 117 supervising secretaries were former Hanlin bachelors. In all cases, I have counted such appointees as having government experience prior to their censorial appointments, even though the Hanlin bachelorship was not a functional administrative position. Hanlin bachelors were new doctoral graduates assigned to the Hanlin Academy for a period of advanced study and observation of governmental operations.

80. MHY 37.6b–7b. Cf. TMHT 5.95.

81. The only extensive biographical register of Ming censors is *Lan-t'ai Fa-chien Lu,* which includes career data on censors appointed from the beginning of the dynasty to 1612. Its entries, however, are incomplete and often inaccurate in comparison with the *Shih-lu;* moreover, it gives no information about censors' ages at time of appointment.

Li-k'o Chi-shih-chung Shih-chi (see note 74 above), a biographical register of 123 men who served as supervising secretaries in the Office of Scrutiny for Rites from the beginning of the dynasty into the middle of the sixteenth century, notes ages at appointment of 77 supervising secretaries who were appointed directly from doctoral status, without having held intervening positions; and the average age at appointment was 36 years. The entries also suggest that there was an average delay of about 2½ years between the granting of the doctoral degree and the first appointment. The average age on attaining the doctoral degree, then, was 33 or 34.

Ching-kuan K'ao-ch'a (see note 74 above), a career register of 137 officials of all sorts who served in the late sixteenth and early seventeenth centuries, suggests a marked difference—that the average age at which these officials attained the doctoral degree was 22 or 23. Also, nearly all of the registrants received their first official appointments either before the end of the year in which they won doctoral degrees or in the following year. The early age at which they seem to have become doctors, therefore, was not counterbalanced by a long wait before they received appointments.

Unfortunately, the *Ching-kuan K'ao-ch'a* data are questionable. The work is a register of officials who were subject to a great personnel evaluation in 1623. All of the registrants had by 1623 attained relatively high rank in the agencies of the central government. They may therefore have been an unusually precocious group, and the average age at which they won their doctoral degrees would probably be somewhat lower than that of all examination graduates of their time. A more troublesome doubt arises from the fact that although dates of obtaining doctoral degrees are clearly noted in the register, dates of birth are not recorded. Every dossier merely includes the age at the time of writing. I have assumed that 1623 is the date of compilation, and I have calculated doctoral ages accordingly. However, on checking such data against well-established biographical information about some famous men in the register, I find the presumed 1623 ages to be wildly inaccurate, some too high and some too low; and no pattern emerges that leads to a possibility that the age recorded in each instance refers to some career achievement dated other than in 1623—attaining doctoral degrees, or attaining their first appointments, or first being appointed to their current 1623 positions. Pending clarification of this confusion, I have no choice but to place no reliance whatever on my tabulations concerning doctoral ages of the registrants.

82. HTSL 46.6a; TMHT 209.4177. MS 73.5a states that acting censors were appointed even as early as the reign of T'ai-tsu.

83. TMHT 209.4177.

84. *Ibid.* Six-month probationers were called *wen-hsing* or *li-hsing,* both terms having striking judicial denotations—"sentencers" or "punishment-regulators" might be appropriate renderings. Acting appointments were called *shih-chih,* substantive appointments *shih-shou.*

85. See *Ching-kuan K'ao-ch'a, passim.*

86. MS 71.7b–9b.

87. E.g., see CMMYL 48.6a–7a, MHY 33.5b–6a, *Ku-chin T'u-shu Chi-ch'eng,* Kuan-ch'ang section, 335.3b. A guaranteed recommendation meant that the recommender was subject to punishment if the man recommended violated the law.

88. Chang Hsüan, *Hsi-yüan Wen-chien Lu,* 93.2b–3b.

89. MS 70.5b–6a, TMHT 77.1800. Cf. Ho, *The Ladder of Success,* p. 187. For examination quota purposes, lines were not drawn precisely along provincial boundaries, but in general the provinces were grouped into regions as indicated in Table 1. What I call "West China" was actually

labeled "the middle" region. The population figures used as a basis for
the percentages in Table 1 are those of 1578, as modified by van der Sprenkel
in his article, "Population Statistics."

90. MS 71.7b–9b.

91. TMHT 12.280–81.

92. In the case of supervising secretaries who are registered in *Li-k'o
Chi-shih-chung Shih-chi*, dates of appointment and severance are clearly
indicated in 28 instances. The average tenure in these instances was between 5 and 6 years.

In the case of 27 censors and 39 supervising secretaries registered in
Ching-kuan K'ao-ch'a, tenure was as follows:

Term	Censors	Supervising Secretaries
Less than 4 years	7	23
4–6 years	3	15
7 or more years	17	1

The relative brevity of supervising secretaries' tenure in these instances
is offset by the fact that in most cases tenure was cut short by promotions
to positions of left or right or chief supervising secretaries, so that total
tenure within the Offices of Scrutiny was in fact much longer than is indicated here.

My tabulations in JTSL and HTSL reveal that in the decade 1424–34,
48 censors, 14 supervising secretaries, and 8 Surveillance Office officials were
promoted for the specific reason that they had completed nine years of satisfactory service in their positions. This was, in fact, the reason most commonly given for all such promotions. I do not have comparable data for the
period 1620–27, since the *Shih-lu* for that era do not record reasons for
promotions.

The highest-ranking capital officials, including the senior officials of the
Censorate, differed from the mass of civil-service personnel in not having
specified terms of office. In general, their terms were relatively short. Otto
van der Sprenkel, working with tables given in MS chs. 111–12, has found
that the average length of service of one of the "seven chief ministers"
(*ch'i-ch'ing*)—the ministers of Ministries and the censor-in-chief—was only
31 months in any one of these offices, and the average service of censors-in-
chief was below this level, at only 29 months. Of the 125 men who served
as censor-in-chief in Ming times, only 11 served more than 6 years, and only
33 served more than 3 years. Twenty-four served no longer than 6 months.
See van der Sprenkel, "High Officials," especially p. 92.

93. Of the 125 men who served as highest-ranking censors-in-chief during
the whole of the Ming era, 31 moved directly into this office from status as
vice censor-in-chief. See van der Sprenkel, "High Officials," p. 103. My own
tabulations based on the *Shih-lu* show that of 20 men who served as censor-
in-chief, vice censor-in-chief, or assistant censor-in-chief in 1424–34, 6 at one
time or another had been investigating censors, 3 had seen service as supervising secretaries, and 3 had served in Surveillance Offices. Forty-three
men occupied these senior Censorate offices in 1620–27. Thirteen of them
had once been investigating censors, 16 had once been supervising secretaries, and 5 had once served in Surveillance Offices.

94. Van der Sprenkel, "High Officials," pp. 112–14, suggests that continuity and cumulative expertise were characteristic of the central government as a whole.

95. Personnel statistics relating to surveillance commissioners clearly reflect the growing separation of the Surveillance Offices from the other censorial agencies that was characteristic of the Ming period. The *Shih-lu* for 1424–34 record 112 appointments of surveillance commissioners from outside offices. Eighty-two of these new appointees came from the ranks of the investigating censors, and another 11 came from the ranks of the supervising secretaries. Furthermore, of 28 surveillance commissioners who were promoted to outside offices during the period, 3 went into the senior offices of the Censorate. In the early Ming pattern of relationships, then, it was considered normal for an investigating censor on completion of his tenure to be promoted into a Surveillance Office, and from there he might be promoted back again into the Censorate. But the statistics for the period 1620–27 reveal an entirely different pattern. During this period 496 Surveillance Office appointments from outside offices are recorded—a quadrupling of the 1424–34 number. Incidentally, this reflects the great proliferation of Surveillance Office branches. Only 17 of the 496 appointees were former censors, and only 13 were former supervising secretaries. Moreover, of 339 recorded promotions of surveillance commissioners out of Surveillance Offices, not a single one involved the promotion of a surveillance commissioner into the Censorate.

As the Surveillance Offices' censorial functions declined and their administrative functions flourished, the Surveillance Offices became more and more closely related to the Provincial Administration Offices and the regular administrative hierarchy in general. Whereas only 1 new surveillance commissioner during the 1424–34 period had formerly been an administration commissioner and only 3 had formerly been prefects, in 1620–27 an astonishing total of 222 of the 496 new appointees were former administration commissioners, and 172 were former prefects. Moreover, of the 339 surveillance commissioners who were promoted to outside offices in 1620–27, 307 were promoted to Administration Offices, whereas only 11 in 28 had been so promoted in 1424–34. In late Ming times, therefore, the career pattern censor to surveillance commissioner to censor-in-chief no longer existed. The pattern now led from assistant surveillance commissioner (5a) to assistant administration commissioner (4b), then to surveillance vice commissioner (4a), then to administration vice commissioner (3b), then to surveillance commissioner (3a), and finally to administration commissioner (2b)—with the principal variant that prefects (4a) might step onto the ladder at midpoint by being transferred to the post of surveillance vice commissioner. There could hardly be clearer evidence of the amalgamation of the Surveillance Offices into the regular administrative hierarchy.

In the case of censors and supervising secretaries, the prospects for subsequent careers changed correspondingly. In 1424–34 the overwhelming number of recorded promotions sent censors out into the Provincial Surveillance Offices (82 out of 124); and supervising secretaries were promoted to the Surveillance Offices (11 out of 80) or to prefectships (10) or to county magistracies (33). But in 1620–27 both censors and supervising secretaries characteristically were promoted into other positions in the capital. Of 139 censors promoted out of the Censorate during this period, 65 were appointed vice ministers of the Court of the Imperial Stud and 32 were appointed assistant ministers of the Grand Court of Revision. Of 70 supervising secretaries promoted out of the Offices of Scrutiny, 45 were appointed to vice ministerships or assistant ministerships in the Grand Court of Revision, the Court of the Imperial Stud, or the Court of Imperial Sacrifice. Almost all of these appointments were to supernumerary positions—particularly those in the Court of the Imperial Stud. They were sinecures, providing status and salaries for deserving officials until responsible court positions of adequate ranks became available to them. Many censors and supervising secretaries who were promoted to such positions actually continued to perform their censorial duties. E.g., see STSL 82.21b–23a.

96. STSL 70.13b–14a, 78.3b (the case of Wang Hui-t'u). For data on the "annual provincial transfers" (*nien-li wai-chuan*) in general, see STSL 62.10b, 70.14a–b.

It is commonly understood that the civil-service ranks that are assigned to governmental posts in such sources as TMHT and the MS treatise on government organization were the ranks of the men who served in the posts—in other words, that the rank of the man and the rank of the post corresponded. My researches indicate that this was not always the case.

In Ming times the general rule was that civil-service officials could not be promoted more than two degrees (*teng*) at a time. See MS 72.9b. Presumably this prohibited a promotion from grade 5b, for example, to anything higher than 4b. In special cases, officials were promoted more than two degrees at a time, but these were considered, and labeled, extraordinary (*ch'ao*) promotions. E.g., see *Ku-chin T'u-shu Chi-ch'eng*, Kuan-ch'ang section, 335.1b. Yet I have encountered numerous instances of investigating censors' being promoted, presumably from rank 7a, to much higher-ranking positions—4b, 4a, and so on—without there being any indication that the promotions were considered extraordinary. E.g., see HTSL 110.13a–b, 111.13b–14a; STSL 72.26b. The late Ming promotions of censors and supervising secretaries to vice ministerships in the Court of the Imperial Stud were promotions of this sort, since such vice ministerships carried rank 4a.

This sort of thing would seem to make sense only if officials could have been promoted in rank without actually changing positions, so that an investigating censor, for example, might have risen into the 6th or 5th rank while remaining in his censorial position. I have found no general regulation relating to such cases, but I have found numerous evidences that they occurred. Some typical examples: An administration commissioner (2b) was promoted to the salary of rank 2a without changing his position. See HTSL 58.1b. A surveillance commissioner (3a) was promoted to the salary of rank 2a and an assistant surveillance commissioner (5a) was promoted to the salary of rank 4a, both without changing positions. See HTSL 111.13b–14a, 42.7a–b. A chief supervising secretary (7a) was promoted to the rank of vice minister of the Court of Imperial Sacrifices (4a) without being transferred from his responsibilities in the Offices of Scrutiny. See STSL 78.6a. Another chief supervising secretary (7a) was even promoted to the rank of vice censor-in-chief (3a) and still remained on duty in the Offices of Scrutiny. See STSL 82.21b–23a (the case of Yang So-hsiu).

Perhaps the ranks that are regularly ascribed to particular posts must be considered merely to be base ranks for appointees, who might enjoy several increases in rank before completing their tenure in the offices in question.

97. MS 158.2b–4b; *Ku-chin T'u-shu Chi-ch'eng*, Kuan-ch'ang section, 353.8a–9a.

98. MS 180.13a–15b.

99. MS 244.1a–11a, KTSL and STSL, *passim*. Cf. biographical notice in Hummel, *Eminent Chinese*.

100. MS 241.14a–16b; *Ching-kuan K'ao-ch'a*, vol. I, pp. 19a–20a; STSL 45.1a.

Chapter three

1. TMHT 4.77–78. Cf. the subsequent discussion in the text of the distribution of Surveillance Office personnel in circuit intendancies.

2. See Fairbank and Teng, "Types and Uses of Ch'ing Documents," especially p. 71 (under *T'ang-pao*); and Sun, trans., *Ch'ing Administrative Terms*, pp. 71–72 (under *Ti-ch'ao*). The term most commonly used in Ming times was *Ti-pao*.

3. E.g., in 1590 the investigating censor Ching Chou-shih submitted a memorial provoked by another censor's memorial, which he had read in the *Ti-pao*. See Shen Pang, *Wan-shu Tsa-chi*, p. 87.

4. TMHT 211.4219–21, 213.4241; MSHU 56.1094–95.

5. MSHU 56.1094–95.

6. TMHT 211.4220.

7. See HTSL 40.10b, for the former; STSL 3.26a, for the latter.

8. HTSL 28.15b.

9. TMHT 211.4219–21, 213.4242.

10. TMHT 80.1834, 213.4240.

11. MS 75.11a–12b.

12. See Hucker, "Governmental Organization," pp. 54–55; MS 75.13b–15b; HTK 60.3344–45; TMHT 210.4207–10. The Military Defense Circuits itemized in TMHT 128 are far more numerous than the circuits itemized in MS.

Each vice commissioner and assistant commissioner was assigned to a particular branch office or Circuit for a term of one year. During the year he was expected to be actively on tour in his jurisdiction from the beginning of the second month to the end of the fifth month and again from the beginning of the seventh month to the end of the eleventh month. See TMHT 210.4201; CMMYL 48.35b–37a.

Every Surveillance Office official was required to make detailed reports of his various activities. The chief report was an annual one generally comparable to the reports required of regional inspectors, which are discussed in detail subsequently in the text; but there were supplementary reports of an annual and even a quarterly sort. See TMHT 211.4214–15.

13. MS 75.12b–13a.

14. MS 75.15b.

15. For the tax remission question, see HTSL 31.8a; for the silk problem, see HTSL 16.8b; for the residence question, see HTSL 14.6a–b.

16. HTSL 69.8b–9a.

17. As early as 1371, investigating censors and officials of the Provincial Surveillance Offices were ordered to tour all localities for the special purpose of recommending worthy officials. See TMHT 13.320. In 1377, censors were sent out to "tour and investigate" the prefectures and counties (the term *hsün-an* being the same later used to designate regional inspectors). See MS 2.14a–b; MHY 34.1a–b. Real systematization of the practice of commissions presumably did not occur until after 1382, when the Circuits were first established and the number of investigating censors was apparently increased. By 1390 at the latest, regional inspectors were a standard feature of the censorial system, for seals were cut for them in that year. See MS 73.5b. By 1393, too, censors seem to have been sent out often to make arrests and conduct trials, to conduct judicial reviews, and to check records. See TMHT 209.4153–54. On the origin of *hsün-an* commissions, cf. Mano, "Mindai Tosatsuin," pp. 208–09.

18. TMHT 210.4179; *Ku-chin T'u-shu Chi-ch'eng*, Kuan-ch'ang section, 335.1a–b. Commissions (*ch'ai-ch'ien*) were graded as follows:

Major (*ta*): Checking records in the capital, supervising schools, regional inspectors (with a few exceptions), and inspecting military training divisions in the capital.

Ordinary (*chung*): Regional inspectors of Liaotung, Kansu, and Hsüan-ta on the northern frontier; purifying troops, salt control, inspecting granaries, inspecting the frontier passes, supervising tax transport, supervising trade in tea and horses, and inspecting the Court of Imperial Entertainments. Supervising the branding of horses and military agricultural projects were ordinary commissions when assigned separately, major when assigned concurrently.

Minor (*hsiao*): Inspecting garrisons at the gates of the palace, etc.

19. See the 1593 memorial by Sun Pi-yang in CMMYL 48.37a–39b; cf. TMHT 210.4181–82. Seniority applied in all cases of assignments to commissions except that censors whose places of origin were in the northern provinces were excused from assignments in the far southern and southwestern provinces and southerners were similarly excused from assignments to the northern frontier areas.

20. See the memorial by Chao Nan-hsing in STSL 28.13a–b. In late Ming times, one tour as regional inspector in Yunnan province was allowed to count as two commissions because service in that far southwestern province was so distasteful. See STSL 31.9a. In 1622 the Yunnan, Kweichow, and Liaotung commissions had already temporarily been ordered to count for double credit because of arduous conditions in those war-torn areas. See STSL 21.27b–28a.

21. TMHT 210.4179–80.

22. TMHT 210.4179.

23. E.g., see STSL 40.5a–b.

24. TMHT 210.4179–80, 211.4225; *Ku-chin T'u-shu Chi-ch'eng*, kuan-ch'ang section, 335.1b.

25. HTSL 20.15b–16a, 20.18a.

26. TMHT 210.4183–84. The Chinese term is *ch'ing-chün* or, in a fuller version, *ch'ing-li chün-wu,* "purifying and adjusting the troop ranks."

27. A detailed description of the history of "troop-purification" in Ming times is given in MS 92.1a–4b. Rules governing the conscription process and the recovery of deserters were increased from 8 to 19 items in 1428 and to 22 in 1429. See HTSL 36.1a–3b, 57.3a–6b. Cf. MSHU 70.1412, HTK 13.2892–93.

28. HTSL 109.1a–b.   29. HTSL 56.11b–12a.

30. HTSL 13.12a–b.   31. HTSL 36.1a–3b.

32. TMHT 211.4228.

33. On the late Ming military decline, see Li Wen-chih, *Wan Ming Min-pien,* p. 2; Li Kuang-t'ao, "Chi Ming-chi"; STSL 4.9b.

34. MS 76.4b–6a, 89.1b–11a. Semedo reported on late Ming military training at the local level in the following supercilious fashion (*The Monarchy of China,* p. 100):

"... But in truth this exercise of theirs is the most ridiculous thing in the world: For dividing their men into squadrons, part feign themselves to be enemies, and part *Chinesses.* ... One part cometh, as it were, a farre off to warre with the other; then they send out spies, and send away messengers to the *Mandarines* (who are sitting not farre of under a *Canopie,* or *Pavilion* of silke) giving them notice, that they are in such a place, and the enemie in such a place; then the *Chinesses* send out a partie against them, who encountering knock their *Swords* and *Lances* one against the others, just as plaiers do upon a stage; and this, or very little more is all they do." I do not know what kinds of military training contemporary Europeans were generally accustomed to, but it seems to me that what Semedo describes could be interpreted as a relatively modern sort of training in field maneuvers.

35. E.g., see HTSL 56.8b–9a, 77.3a.

36. TMHT 210.4182–83, 211.4228, 213.4263 (*hsün ching-ying*). In 1620 it was reported that three-year terms for inspectors of the training divisions ought to be reinstated, but no such action seems to have been taken. See KTSL 3.26a.

37. STSL 27.14b–15a, 28.28b–29b, 28.29b–31b, 30.10a–13a, 30.24a–25a, 30.31a–32b, 31.9a–11a, 34.2b, 37.34a–36b. For some other censorial memorials proposing reforms in the training divisions, see STSL 2.45b–46a, 14.20a–b, 19.19b–20b, 27.22a–23a, 32.6a–7a, 41.2a, 51.25b–27b, 65.36a–b, 66.1a, 74.34a–35b, 75.15a–b. On "flying stones," see STSL 30.24a–25a.

38. KTSL 4.9a–b.

39. TMHT 210.4185–86; MS 73.2b (*hsün-kuan yü-shih*).

40. E.g., see KTSL 4.14b–15b; STSL 21.12a–13a, 22.2b–3b, 57.21a–b, 58.21a, 59.9b, 61.19a–b, 62.20a, 63.41b–42a, 63.42a, 66.2b, 71.6a, 79.30a–b, 81.6a–7a.

41. TMHT 210.4190; MS 73.2b (*chien-chün yü-shih*).

42. E.g., see KTSL 3.22a; STSL 7.9b, 8.1a, 54.28b.

43. MS 248.10b–13a; *Chiang-nan T'ung-chih,* 156.11b.

44. STSL 4.38b–39a, 5.33b–34b, 7.11b–12a, 7.17a–18a, 7.27a, 8.1a, 8.5b–7a, 10.9a–b, 10.29b–30a, 11.20b–21b, 12.14a, 13.16b–17a, 13.23a–b, 13.28b, 14.8a, 14.9b–10b, 14.16b, 14.28a–b, 15.16a.

45. STSL 37.29a–31a.

46. MS 291.2a–3b; STSL 3.15a–16b, 5.7b–9a.

47. E.g., see HTSL 51.7b–8a, 110.15a–b.

48. Li Wen-chih, *Wan Ming Min-pien, passim*; Ray Huang, *The Grand Canal*, pp. 102ff.

49. Liaotung expenditure recorded by Li Wen-chih, *Wan Ming Min-pien,* p. 1.

50. E.g., see HTSL 51.7b–8a, 75.7b–8a, 78.5b, 100.4b–5a, 110.15a–b.

51. For mention of this commission in the Nanking Censorate, see TMHT 211.4226 (*t'un-t'ien yü-shih*); for mention of it in the metropolitan Censorate, see TMHT 210.4183; CMMYL 48.43a; MS 73.2b, 74.6a.

52. TMHT 210.4183 (*yin-ma yü-shih*). Another commission, *hsün-ch'ing,* to which both censors and supervising secretaries were assigned, also had to do with horse breeding, the harvesting and storage of fodder, etc. See TMHT 210.4186–87. Cf. STSL 9.22b–23b, 31.1a–b, 61.19b–20a.

53. E.g., see STSL 1.18b, 81.31a–b.

54. KTSL 1.20b (*tu-hsiang yü-shih*).

55. STSL 19.30a–b. Cf. STSL 23.16a, 27.27a, 33.13a–22b, 54.14b–15b, 54.27a–b, 59.38b, 60.22a–b, 74.26a–b, 77.1b–2a, 78.9b–10b, 81.4a–b.

56. For mention of surveillance over guard salaries and supplies in the capitals, see TMHT 213.4258; STSL 56.11b–12a. For surveillance over palace guard units, see TMHT 210.4187 (*hsün-shih huang-ch'eng yü-shih*). Cf. STSL 62.22a–b, 66.6b, 66.9b. For some of the abuses practiced by the guards of the palace gates, see HTSL 89.6b–7a. It was apparently common for anyone who did not submit to a search to be beaten by the guards, and it seems that cooks of the Court of Imperial Entertainments were regularly waylaid when they delivered foodstuffs to the palace.

57. On the complex system of canal transport under the Ming dynasty, see Ray Huang, *The Grand Canal,* and Wu Chi-hua, *Hai-yün chi Yün-ho.* At the beginning of the dynasty, as in Yüan times, grain was shipped from South China by sea around the Shantung peninsula to the Peking area. The Grand Canal system was opened for operation in 1415, and thereafter the sea route was not used. In its early operation the transport system was largely operated by corvée labor, but after 1474 it was almost totally the responsibility of the military service.

58. TMHT 211.4225 (*ts'ao-chiang yü-shih*).

59. TMHT 211.4225–26 (*hsün-chiang yü-shih*).

60. TMHT 211.4226. Cf. STSL 72.17a–b, 81.32a–b.

61. TMHT 210.4185 (*tsan-yün yü-shih*). These loading expediters were apparently no longer being commissioned in the 1620's, although the commission had originally been intended to be a regular one and still existed as late as 1578.

62. TMHT 209.4156; Ray Huang, *The Grand Canal,* pp. 43ff.

63. TMHT 210.4184; MHY 34.2b–3a; CMMYL 48.42b–43a (*hsün-ho yü-shih*).

64. E.g., see STSL 10.7a, 51.19b, 62.22b, 69.11a–b, 75.19a–b (*hsün-ts'ao yü-shih* or *chi-shih-chung*).

65. For mention of the 2 granary-inspecting censors, see TMHT 210.4185 (*hsün-ts'ang yü-shih*). Cf. STSL 1.18b, 14.23a, 28.14b, 60.19a. For mention of the storehouse-inspecting censors, see TMHT 210.4187 (*hsün-k'u yü-shih* or *chi-shih-chung*). By the 1620's this commission had come to be monopolized

by supervising secretaries. E.g., see STSL 6.11a, 21.24a, 22.16b, 23.4a, 24.25a, 29.21b, 51.20b, 51.31b, 55.1a. Similarly, the Nanking Censorate was responsible for keeping watch over the imperial treasury in the auxiliary capital. See TMHT 211.4227.

66. STSL 64.7b.

67. Ray Huang, *The Grand Canal*, p. 62.

68. TMHT 210.4184; MS 73.2a–b; MHY 34.2b–3a; CMMYL 48.24b–43b *(hsün-yen yü-shih)*. For some typical activities of salt-control censors, see STSL 36.8b–10a, 67.19b–20a, 77.15b, 81.34a.

69. TMHT 210.4188, 211.4227 *(chien-k'o yü-shih)*.

70. TMHT 210.4185 *(hsün-ch'a-ma yü-shih)*. Cf. STSL 6.19b, 21.30b.

71. E.g., see HTSL 58.2a; KTSL 2.26b; STSL 4.17a–b, 10.14b–15a, 13.12b, 16.12b, 22.21a–b, 32.7b, 36.10a, 56.6b–7a.

72. TMHT 210.4186 *(hsün Kuang-lu-ssu yü-shih* or *chi-shih-chung)*. For representative activities of such inspectors, see HTSL 108.10b–11a; KTSL 2.13b–14a; STSL 7.2a–b, 23.1a–7a, 34.22a–23a, 74.36b.

73. TMHT 211.4227–28.

74. TMHT 210.4182; MHY 33.6b; MS 73.2a, 69.12b–18a *(t'i-hsüeh yü-shih)*.

75. TMHT 210.4179.

76. STSL 24.3a. For some representative activities of the education intendants, see STSL 32.2a, 77.23a.

77. E.g., see STSL 42.7b–8a, 43.15a.

78. For mention of regional inspectors serving as proctors, see TMHT 210.4201. For mention of censors proctoring in the metropolitan areas, see TMHT 210.4189, 211.4228. E.g., see STSL 82.2b.

79. TMHT 210.4189, 213.4242. E.g., see STSL 50.17a, 51.13b.

80. TMHT 210.4189. Cf. STSL 21.15b.

81. TMHT 210.4187–88, 211.4227–28 *(hsün-ch'eng yü-shih)*. Cf. Shen Pang, *Wan-shu Tsa-chi*, pp. 86ff. for data on the residence rosters kept by the Ward-inspecting censors.

82. CMMYL 48.40a–41b. For some representative activities of Ward-inspecting censors, see STSL 4.26b, 12.33a, 31.16b, 32.22b, 68.27b–28a, 75.17a–b.

83. Ricci, *China in the 16th Century*, p. 53.

84. Semedo, *The Monarchy of China*, p. 129. I have omitted the abundant italics of the English translator.

85. Boxer, *South China*, pp. 6, 11. Ricci and other European visitors to Ming China identified the regional inspector by some variant of the Chinese term *ch'a-yüan*, "surveillance office," which had come to be a popular designation for all investigating censors: e.g., Cia-yuen, Cha Juen, Chaem, Chacins. Boxer (p. 6, note 4) states that *ch'a-yüan* was an "abbreviation of *tu-ch'a-yüan*," but that was not the case at all. Cf. the discussion of these terms in notes 16 and 17 to Chapter 2.

86. For the traditional Ming view of regional inspectors, see MS 73.2a–b.

87. MS 2.14a–b; MHY 34.1a–b. Cf. Mano, "Mindai Tosatsuin no Seiritsu," pp. 208–09.

88. MS 75.15a.

89. Mano ("Kobucho no Tosatsuin," pp. 212–13) makes much of an entry in TTSL for the eleventh month of 1382 recording an order that the newly

reorganized *tu ch'a-yüan* promulgate to all Provincial Surveillance Offices an inspection manual called *Hsün-an Shih-i* (TTSL 150.4b–5a). Though the term *hsün-an* is that used to designate regional inspectors, there is no reference to regional inspectors per se in the manual as abstracted in TTSL. Indeed, just one day previously the emperor had ordered Regional Military Commissions to check on whether or not the Provincial Surveillance Offices were doing their jobs (TTSL 150.4a)—a task one would expect him to assign to regional inspectors had they been available. I find no specific references to regional-inspecting investigating censors in TTSL of this era.

90. MS 73.2a–b; TMHT 210.4179. The modern scholar Yü Teng, relying on a work called *Fang-yü Chi-yao T'u* that I am not familiar with, erroneously includes in an enumeration of regional inspectors such other commissions as inspecting military training divisions in the capital, inspecting granaries, salt control, checking records, and inspecting military agricultural projects. He thus obtains a total of 11 "regional inspectors" assigned to the Northern Metropolitan Area and 9 assigned to the Southern Metropolitan Area. Moreover, Yü's enumeration of regional inspectors proper, without such additions, still does not correspond entirely to that indicated in my sources. See Yü, "Chien-ch'a Chih-tu," pp. 223–24. But assignments of regional inspectors recorded in the *Shih-lu* for as late as 1620–27 correspond precisely with the commissions listed in MS and TMHT.

91. The term of a regional inspector could be extended in unusual circumstances. In 1432, when the censor Teng Ch'i completed his term as regional inspector in the Su-chou area, a crowd of more than 2,000 village elders reportedly called on the grand coordinator of the region to praise his service and ask that he be appointed for a second year. When this request was relayed to the throne the emperor approved it. See HTSL 86.7b–8a. The censor-in-chief Chao Nan-hsing complained in 1623 that in the final years of Shen-tsung's reign some regional inspectors served three years or even five years before being replaced, since the emperor refused to make decisions on assignments and the censors could not leave their posts without being relieved by replacements. See STSL 28.13a–b.

92. MS 73.2b.

93. TMHT 210.4197–99, 211.4224.

94. MHY 34.8b.

95. TMHT 210.4190–4201 (*Ch'u-hsün Shih-i,* issued in 1393 and reissued with substantial emendations in 1439; these incorporate the *Hsien-kang,* "fundamental laws and regulatory principles"; see note 58 to Chapter 2); 211.4221–24 (*Fu-an T'ung-li*).

96. STSL 33.25b.

97. TMHT 210.4190ff. Cf. Mano, "Kobucho no Tosatsuin," pp. 221–26.

98. TMHT 211.4211–14.

99. HTSL 59.6a–b.

100. TMHT 210.4201; CMMYL 48.44a–b. In general, the regional inspector was expected to fulfill all special instructions left unfulfilled by his predecessor as well as those he himself received; but he could leave for his replacement all special instructions received in the last two months of his term. See TMHT 211.4211.

101. TMHT 210.4194. MS 69.12a indicates that 42 National University

students were normally sent on tour with censors; these could have been distributed two to a regional inspector, there being 21 such commissions. One
specific case suggests that censors on record-checking tours also might have
been regularly assisted by 10 National University students. See HTSL
81.5a–b.

102. T'ao, *Kiangsi Fu-i Ch'üan-shu.*
103. TMHT 210.4194; MHY 34.6b; CMMYL 48.35b–37a.
104. TMHT 210.4190–91, 4194. I have found no specific prohibition
against such marriages in the Ming regulations, but at least two censors were
denounced for marrying women of their jurisdictions. See HTSL 46.13a–b.
In the Yüan dynasty the prohibition was explicit. See *Yüan Tien-chang*
6.5a–6a.

105. TMHT 210.4196.	106. HTSL 88.8a–b.
107. STSL 37.36b.	108. STSL 51.23b.
109. HTSL 35.8b.	110. HTSL 48.4a.
111. KTSL 2.13a.	112. HTSL 9.2a–b.
113. STSL 74.37b.	114. STSL 16.23b–24a.
115. HTSL 78.1b.	116. STSL 2.39a–40b.
117. KTSL 1.30a.	118. HTSL 102.1b–2a.
119. STSL 8.26b.	

120. Yeh, *Shui-tung Jih-chi,* 33.11b–12a.
121. TMHT 210.4197.
122. TMHT 209.4165–75, HTK ch. 54.
123. See the itemized regulations for the different Offices of Scrutiny in
TMHT 213.4243–57.
124. The general regulations about personnel evaluations are to be found
in TMHT chs. 12 and 13. Cf. MS 71.12a–15b, 72.9a–10a. For the special censorial role in these processes, see TMHT 209.4176–77, 210.4199–4200,
213.4240; MS 75.9a–11a and 19b–20b; MHY 33.5b, 37.5b; CMMYL 25.4b–5a,
48.1b; HTK ch. 54; MSHU chs. 65 and 66. Cf. Hucker, "Governmental Organization," pp. 15–16.
125. TMHT 213.4244.
126. Ricci, *China in the 16th Century,* pp. 56–57.
127. For some reports on evaluations, see HTSL 61.4a–5a, 98.1b–2a,
105.1b; STSL 2.50b–51a, 13.13a–b, 13.13b–14a, 13.21b–22a, 13.26a, 25.8b–9b,
25.10b, 25.19a–b, 26.1b, 26.6a, 26.7b, 26.21b–22a, 26.27a–b, 50.14b, 52.16b,
63.34a, 64.3a–b.
128. TMHT 210.4200.
129. E.g., see HTSL 1.13a.
130. E.g., see HTSL 2.7b, 5.6a, 12.2a, 13.10b, 27.11a, 68.3b–4a, 96.3a–b.
131. TMHT 13.321.
132. TMHT 211.4217.
133. HTSL 100.8b.
134. TMHT 209.4155, 212.4229 and 4230–31.
135. TMHT 80.1833.
136. HTSL 53.12b–13a.
137. E.g., see Kracke, *Civil Service,* pp. 33–34. The Chinese term is *teng-wen ku.*
138. TMHT 213.4241.

139. TMHT 211.4216–17.
140. HTSL 73.8b–9a. Cf. HTSL 28.15a–b; CMMYL 25.3b–4a.
141. HTSL 16.6b–7b. For a few other cases involving the Complaint Drum, see HTSL 28.17a, 60.3a–b, 84.16b–17a. I have not found references to the Complaint Drum in the *Shih-lu* chronicles for 1620–27, but I have seen no positive evidence that its use had been discontinued by that time.
142. The regulations governing the work of the Offices of Scrutiny are given in TMHT 213. Cf. MS 74.11a–13a; MSHU 66.1316–17; MHY 37.1a–9a; CMMYL ch. 25; HTK 52.3261–63.
143. TTSL 165.3a. Cf. Hucker, "Governmental Organization," p. 28, especially note 54.
144. E.g., see KTSL 4.22a–b.
145. CMMYL 25.3b. Cf. MHY 37.2b.
146. HTSL 51.7b.
147. For Wang's veto, see STSL 2.5a. For Lo's veto of Han's nomination, see STSL 29.23b–24a.
148. MHY 37.6a.
149. TMHT 213.4240. Cf. HTSL 19.4b, 66.12b; MHY 37.6a.
150. TMHT 213.4239.
151. TMHT 213.4241; CMMYL 25.4b; MHY 37.5b.
152. E.g., see STSL 22.20b–21a, noting a three-day time limit.
153. CMMYL 25.5a–6a.
154. STSL 23.1a–b.
155. The special regulations for each of the Offices of Scrutiny are to be found in TMHT 213.4243–57.
Time limits in accordance with standards established in general regulations were imposed on all officials traveling on duty, so as to prevent their going out of the way to visit their homes, etc. The maximum allowances for one-way trips to or from Peking that were fixed in 1575 for censors assigned to commissions were as follows:

Chen-ting and the Hsüan-ta area (Northern Metropolitan Area)	35 days
The Nanking, Su-chou, Sung-chiang area	70 days
The Huai-an and Feng-yang area (Southern Metropolitan Area)	65 days
Chekiang and Kiangsi	90 days
Hukwang	90 days
Fukien	97 days
Honan and the Ho-tung area (Northern Metropolitan Area)	58 days
Shensi	75 days
Kansu	85 days
Shansi and Shantung	53 days
Szechwan	145 days
Kwangtung and Kwangsi	128 days
Yunnan	125 days
Kweichow	135 days
Liaotung	66 days

See TMHT 210.4180–81. These time limits no doubt permitted relatively leisurely and dignified journeying. Government correspondence could be transmitted much more rapidly. The subsequent Ch'ing dynasty expected that dispatches could be carried from Canton, the capital of Kwangtung province, to Peking, for example, in 56 days by relay runners or in 32 days by horsemen, or from the capital of Shansi province in 12 days by relay runners and 6 days by horsemen. See Fairbank and Teng, "Transmission of Ch'ing Documents," especially pp. 23ff.

156. These registered documents or "tallies" (*k'an-ho*) were instituted in 1382. A full description of their use is provided in TTSL 141.3a–b. Cf. Wang Yi-t'ung, *Official Relations,* pp. 37–38. On early use of chirographs in the West, see Chrimes, *Administrative History of Mediaeval England,* pp. 13–14.

157. See TMHT 210.4201–10. The Ming practice of checking records (*chao-shua wen-chüan,* or abbreviated as *shua-chüan*), was patterned closely after that of the Yüan dynasty. For details of the Yüan system, see *Yüan Tien-chang* 6.19a ff. Cf. Ratchnevsky, *Un Code des Yuan,* p. 40, note 5.

158. The original regulation called for record-checking censors to be commissioned for one-, two-, or three-year terms. In 1473 a three-year term was regularized. From 1533 to 1549 regional inspectors concurrently handled record-checking duties. Then the former system was reinstated. For a short time after 1560 checking records was the concurrent responsibility of troop-purifying censors. By the 1570's it was again the concurrent responsibility of regional inspectors. See TMHT 210.4206–07, 4210.

159. Record-checking censors, or regional inspectors concurrently handling this duty, were specifically required to make periodic inventories and inspections of the weapons assigned to each local military garrison throughout the empire. See TMHT 193.3904.

160. E.g., see STSL 24.25a, 61.32b, 65.45b, 70.12a, 77.11a. The Chinese term that I render Metropolitan Circuit is *Ching-chi tao.*

161. TMHT 210.4180.   162. MS 69.12a.

163. HTSL 81.5a–b.   164. TMHT 210.4194.

165. TMHT 210.4201–02.

166. In case of delays, the clerical functionaries who were immediately responsible were subject to beating with the bamboo to a maximum of 40 blows, according to the number of instances; their supervising officials were subject to 30 blows. For errors, the functionaries might receive a maximum of 50 blows, and again the punishment for their overseers was reduced one degree—to 40 blows. In all cases, the senior official of the agency was himself likely to be fined a maximum of three months' salary. More serious offenses, involving willful evasions of the law, were dealt with more severely according to the particular circumstances. See *Ta Ming Lü,* 3.19b–21b.

167. TMHT 210.4202–03.

168. HTSL 95.11b–12a.

Chapter four

1. TMHT 209.4176. Memorials were to be submitted under seal only when the subject matter was "secret and urgent."

2. MHY 33.13b–15a.

3. Brief catalogues of outstanding Ming impeachments and remonstrances are provided in Yü, "Chien-ch'a Chih-tu."

4. MS 180.5a–6a.

5. MS 9, *passim*. The history of Annamese relations with China throughout the dynasty is given in MS 321.

6. MS 8.1a–6b, 9.2a–3b, 118.16b–21a.

7. MS 8 and 9, *passim*.   8. JTSL 9B.4b.

9. MS 9.10b.   10. HTSL 59.3a–4a.

11. See Franke, "Yü Ch'ien."   12. MS 8.5a.

13. E.g., see MS 74.26b, 9.3b–4a, 9.5a; JTSL 2B.6b; HTSL 42.11a–b, 58.1b.

14. E.g., see MS 9.1b, 8a; JTSL 4A.1b, 9A.5b; HTSL 2.2b–3a, 85.2b.

15. HTSL 85.2b–3b.

16. MS 74.31b, 304.1a–2a.

17. MS 8.1a–2b; Wang Shih-chen, *Yen-shan-t'ang Pieh-chi*, 31.6a–7a.

18. JTSL 4A.9a–b.

19. JTSL 9A.3b–4a.

20. E.g., see JTSL 4A.2a–b, 5A.5a–b, 6A.1b; MS 8.4a, 8.5a–b, 94.18b–19a.

21. MS 164.4a–5b; JTSL 7B.2a, 8A.4b–5b.

22. MS 163.1a–4a.

23. MS 8.6b.

24. MS 9.1a–b; Wang Shih-chen, *Yen-shan-t'ang Pieh-chi*, 31.7a–9a.

25. E.g., see HTSL 41.7b–8a.   26. E.g., see HTSL 41.7b–8a.

27. HTSL 18.11b.   28. MS 9.5a, 9.10a.

29. MS 9.5a–b.   30. HTSL 64.2a–b.

31. See Castonnet des Fosses, *La Chine sous les Ming*, p. 21.

32. MS 94.18b–20b.

33. MS 8 and 9, *passim*.

34. MS 163.1a–4a. It is interesting that the *Shih-lu* chronicles of this period, compiled under the direction of Yang Shih-ch'i while the events were still fresh in memory, gloss over the facts of Li Shih-mien's case almost completely, probably in an effort not to besmirch the reputations of the two emperors. Thus, for the fifth month of 1425, there is merely the statement that Li was demoted "because he spoke out about affairs"; and, for the tenth month of 1426, there is the strange report that Li, having originally been demoted for speaking out about affairs, had been sent to prison several days after Jen-tsung's death by "those in control of affairs" and now was released and restored to office because Hsüan-tsung "learned of his literary scholarship." See JTSL 10.3b; HTSL 22.9b. Cf. Ku Chieh-kang, "Literary Persecution," pp. 270–71.

35. E.g., see HTSL 9.12a, 52.4a, 62.2b.

36. For the case of Chang Shan, see HTSL 34.5a. For the case of Yüan Ch'i, see HTSL 85.2b.

37. MS 148. Cf. Grimm, "Das Neiko der Ming-zeit."

38. For mention of the outer evaluations, see HTSL 24.1b, 61.4a–5a, 98.1b–2a. For the reminders to regional inspectors, see JTSL 1B.5a–b; HTSL 5.9b–10a, 13.8a, 63.2a–b, 66.2a, 68.10a–b, 73.4b–6a, 88.1a–4b, 94.2b–3b, 94.5a, 98.4a–5a, 101.8a.

39. JTSL 4A.9a–b.   40. HTSL 24.1b, 61.4a–5a.

41. HTSL 98.1b–2a.   42. HTSL 66.10a–b.

43. HTSL 98.4a–5a.   44. HTSL 40.10b–11a.

45. HTSL 8.11b.

46. HTSL 15.16b. Cf. CMMYL 48.45b; MHY 33.5a.

47. HTSL 37.6a.
48. HTSL 51.15b.
49. For the impeachment of 12,729 officials, see HTSL 95.11b–12a. The reference is to the censor Lo Ch'üan's 1432 report of the results of a great record checking in the Peking agencies (mentioned in Chapter 3). As for the 12,729 persons who were denounced, no punitive action seems to have been taken. The emperor merely ordered that the matter be investigated thoroughly. The overwhelming majority of the accused persons could only have been lesser functionaries. In my tabulations in the text, I take account of this item only by adding 1+ to both the "Civil officials" and the "Others" categories.

For the impeachment of 530 officials, see HTSL 58.2a. Reference here is to an impeachment submitted in 1429 by a censor in conjunction with an official of the Ministry of Revenue. Of the 530 officials and functionaries who were denounced, the emperor ordered that those accused of actual fraud should be tried by the judicial authorities and that others whose records were merely not in order should be fined half their annual salaries. In this case, as in the prior one, I have merely added 1+ to both the "Civil officials" and the "Others" categories in my tabulation.

If both mass impeachments were given full value in my tabulation, it would appear as follows:

Civil officials	261+
Military officers	398+
Others	13,274+
Total	13,933+

50. HTSL 43.4a, 46.8a–b.
51. HTSL 69.6b–7a, 72.7a.
52. HTSL 10.6b–7a, 12.11b. P'ei was vice minister of a so-called Peking Branch Ministry (*Pei-ching hsing-pu*), which was a consolidated general-administration agency that served Peking when it was auxiliary capital from 1403 through 1420. It existed again from 1425 to 1428, apparently in preparation for the anticipated movement of the national capital back to Nanking, which never occurred. See MS 72.6a ff.
53. HTSL 78.1b.
54. HTSL 103.8a–b.
55. See Ch'en Huai's biography in MS 155.11b–12b.
56. HTSL 16.13a.
57. HTSL 66.5b–6a.
58. HTSL 76.17a–b.
59. HTSL 78.4a–b.
60. HTSL 79.6b–8a.
61. HTSL 79.13a–b.
62. HTSL 104.4b–5a.
63. HTSL 108.13a–b.
64. See Ku Ying-tsu's biography in MS 144.9b.
65. For mention of Ku's commission as regional commander, see HTSL 6.14b, 15a. For the order that he explain his actions, see HTSL 9.12a.
66. HTSL 27.13a, 29.4b–5a.
67. HTSL 34.3a–b.
68. HTSL 42.12a.
69. HTSL 58.11a.
70. HTSL 64.14b–15a.
71. HTSL 65.9a.
72. HTSL 66.9a–b.
73. HTSL 101.3a.
74. HTSL 21.1b–2a.

75. HTSL 59.13b. This entry is not wholly clear, and I have been unable to find any corroborative detail in any other source.

76. JTSL 4A.8a–b.   77. HTSL 76.10a–b.
78. HTSL 85.2a.   79. HTSL 96.9a–b.
80. HTSL 87.8b–9a, 91.6a.   81. HTSL 84.12a.

82. MS 162.4b–6a. In 1418, as an assistant administration commissioner of Honan province, Ch'en Tso had protested against moving the capital from Nanking to Peking, and Ch'eng-tsu had dismissed him from the service in disgrace. He had been recommended and recalled to service as a censor in 1426. After his release from prison in 1431 he resumed duty as a censor but promptly got into trouble anew and was again imprisoned. Then he was released in a general amnesty and gave long service in the Nanking Censorate and the Fukien Provincial Surveillance Office until his ultimate retirement and death.

83. HTSL 104.1a–b.   84. HTSL 110.9a.
85. JTSL 4B.5b.   86. HTSL 2.2b–3a.
87. JTSL 5A.3a.   88. HTSL 30.10a.
89. HTSL 89.6a.   90. HTSL 96.6b–7a.
91. HTSL 3.10b–11b.   92. HTSL 30.2a–b.
93. HTSL 100.1b–2a.   94. HTSL 78.5b.
95. HTSL 78.2a.

96. HTSL 66.8b–9a. For a somewhat similar proposal in 1432, see HTSL 91.4b–5a.

97. HTSL 14.2b–3a. The amnesty referred to is presumably that proclaimed when Hsüan-tsung took the throne in the sixth month of 1425. See MS 9.1b.

98. HTSL 18.4b–5a.   99. HTSL 44.7b–8a.
100. HTSL 94.10b.   101. HTSL 66.3b–4a.
102. HTSL 70.2a–b.   103. HTSL 57.13b–14a.

104. E.g., see HTSL 41.12a–b, 57.10a–b, 76.7a, 82.4a–b, 82.10b–11a, 91.9a.

105. HTSL 66.11a.   106. HTSL 31.5b–6a.
107. JTSL 2C.11b.   108. HTSL 113.4b–5a.
109. HTSL 21.9a.

110. For the memorial urging revitalization of garrison schools, see HTSL 73.11b. For the one urging reorganization of community schools, see HTSL 79.6b–8a.

111. HTSL 53.5a–6a.   112. HTSL 15.8a.
113. JTSL 5A.3a–4a.   114. HTSL 9.3b–4a.
115. HTSL 24.9b.   116. HTSL 28.5a, 44.3a–b.
117. HTSL 54.3b.   118. HTSL 72.10a.
119. HTSL 58.9a–b.   120. HTSL 62.7b–8a.
121. HTSL 107.11b.

122. HTSL 36.10a. Cf. Hucker, "Confucianism and the Censorial System," p. 205. I have not found any record of the results of the deliberation that was ordered in response to Liu Kuan's proposal.

123. E.g., see HTSL 41.13b, 103.8a, 104.10a–b.

124. For the proposal about city walls, see JTSL 4A.9b; for the one about Kwangtung forts, see HTSL 87.1a–b; for Police Offices, see HTSL 44.6b, 53.8a, 59.14b, 72.11a–b; for soldiers' horse-tending duties, see HTSL 19.2a–b,

69.1b; for the proposal about improving troop training, see JTSL 2C.13b–14a; for the one recommending more physicians, see HTSL 71.2a; for the proposal about judicial procedures, see HTSL 73.6a.

125. HTSL 58.9b.

126. HTSL 58.10a.

127. E.g., see HTSL 14.3a–b, 71.6a, 72.8a–b, 81.3a–b.

128. For the traditional Chinese distinction between "true criminals rating the death penalty" (*cheng-fan ssu-tsui*) and "secondary criminals rating the death penalty" (*tsa-fan ssu-tsui*), see Sun, E., *Ch'ing Administrative Terms*, p. 271.

129. HTSL 50.7a.

130. HTSL 50.7b–9a.

131. E.g., see HTSL 53.10b–11a. The term for "transporting tiles" is *yün chuan*.

132. HTSL 14.3a–b.	133. HTSL 53.10b–11a.
134. HTSL 46.4a–b.	135. HTSL 53.5a–6a.
136. E.g., see HTSL 47.12b–13a.	137. HTSL 54.6b.

138. JTSL 5A.2b–3a. Cf. HTSL 28.11b–12a.

139. HTSL 89.9b.

140. MS 164.6b–7b. The *Ming-shih* comments on Huang Tse's protest, "Although the emperor commended it, alas, he was unable to profit by it."

141. HTSL 85.2b–3b.

Chapter five

1. For data on Chang Chü-cheng and China in his time, see his biography in MS 213.14a–25a; and also Chu, *Chang Chü-cheng*; Liang, *The Single-whip Method*; CSPM, ch. 61; and Meng, *Ming-tai Shih, pp.* 268–80.

2. MS 22.10b.

3. See CSPM, ch. 62–64.

4. For general information about the Manchu challenge to an eventual conquest of China, see Hsiao, *Ch'ing-tai T'ung-shih*; Michael, *The Origin of Manchu Rule*; and Hummel, *Eminent Chinese,* especially its biographical entry for Nurhaci.

5. See Michael, *The Origin of Manchu Rule*.

6. See the biographies of Hsiung T'ing-pi in MS 259.7a–24b; Tsou, *Ch'i Chen Yeh-sheng*, 6.12a–13b; Hummel, *Eminent Chinese*, I, 308.

7. For information on Yüan Ying-t'ai, see MS 259.4b–7a; Hummel, *Eminent Chinese,* II, 957.

8. Wang Hua-chen's biography is combined with that of Hsiung T'ing-pi in MS 259.7a–24b; cf. Hummel, *Eminent Chinese,* II, 823.

9. See Hummel, *Eminent Chinese,* I, 567–68; and Li Kuang-t'ao, "Mao Wen-lung." Mao Wen-lung continued to harass the Manchus from north Korea and an island refuge off the Korean coast until 1629, when the supreme commander Yüan Ch'ung-huan had him put to death for insubordination.

10. See Sun Ch'eng-tsung's biographies in MS 250.1a–14b and Hummel, *Eminent Chinese,* II, 670–71.

11. See Yüan Ch'ung-huan's biographies in MS 259.24b–39a and Hummel, *Eminent Chinese*, II, 954–55.

12. See CSPM, ch. 69.

13. CSPM, ch. 70.

14. See Chang T'ien-tse, *Sino-Portuguese Trade*, especially pp. 124–28.

15. See MS 22, *passim*.

16. Li Wen-chih, *Wan Ming Min-pien*, p. 1.

17. STSL 1.1b–2a.

18. Li Wen-chih, *Wan Ming Min-pien*, pp. 1–2.

19. *Ibid.*, p. 22, for discussion of normal annual revenue.

20. *Ibid.*, pp. 17–18.

21. Ray Huang, *The Grand Canal*, pp. 127ff.

22. Li Wen-chih, *Wan Ming Min-pien*, pp. 20–24. Cf. Wu Chao-ts'ui, *Shui-chih Shih*, I, 140–41.

23. See Li Wen-chih, *Wan Ming Min-pien*, pp. 1–14; Wang Te-chao, *Cheng-chih Yü She-hui*.

24. Li Wen-chih, *Wan Ming Min-pien*, is an excellent modern study of the late Ming rebellions. Also see the biographies of Li Tzu-ch'eng and Chang Hsien-chung in Hummel, *Eminent Chinese*.

25. There is available an abundant literature in Chinese concerning late Ming political struggles. The discussion that follows is based largely on a variety of standard sources written soon after the events, which include: Wen Ping (1609–69), *Hsien-po Chih-shih*; Wu Ying-chi (1594–1645), *Tung-lin Pen-mo*; Liu Hsin-hsüeh (1599–1674), *Ssu-ch'ao Ta-cheng Lu*; Ku Ling (wrote in the 1640's), *San-ch'ao Ta-i Lu*; and Chiang P'ing-chieh, *Tung-lin shih-mo*. The last item is reproduced verbatim as ch. 66 of CSPM, which also has good accounts of the partisan struggles in chs. 61, 65, 67, 68, and 71. Biographies of most of the leading figures of the era can be found in MS. Brief biographical data on many Tung-lin partisans can be found in Li Yen, *Tung-lin-tang*; and a standard biographical source is Ch'en, *Tung-lin Lieh-chuan*. The most comprehensive modern study of the partisan struggles is Hsieh Kuo-chen, *Tang-she Yün-tung K'ao*. Especially for the philosophical background of the partisan struggle, see Busch, "The Tung-lin Academy." Especially for its political aspects, see Hucker, "The Tung-lin Movement," from which the present text borrows extensively.

26. Some of these controversies are discussed briefly in Lin Yutang, *The Press and Public Opinion*, pp. 64–68.

27. The basic source on the history of the Tung-lin Academy is *Tung-lin Shu-yüan Chih*. The standard source on the Tung-lin and other Ming philosophers is Huang Tsung-hsi, *Ming-ju Hsüeh-an*; for the Tung-lin group, see chs. 58–61. Also see Sheng, *Shu-yüan Chih-tu*, pp. 87ff. Cf. Busch, "The Tung-lin Academy," and Hucker, "The Tung-lin Movement."

28. See Ku Hsien-ch'eng's biography in MS 231.1a–5a.

29. MS 218.17a. See Fang Ts'ung-che's biography in MS 218.14a–20b.

30. See the biographies of Wang Chih-ts'ai in MS 244.25a–30b and Hummel, *Eminent Chinese*, II, 812.

31. See Kao P'an-lung's biography in MS 243.15b–19b.

32. MS 218.15a–b, 16b; Li Wen-chih, *Wan Ming Min-pien*, p. 10, note 1.

33. See Yang Lien's biographies in Hummel, *Eminent Chinese*, II, 892–

93; MS 244.1a–11a; Chiang, *Tung-lin Shih-mo,* 38ff.; and Ch'en, *Tung-lin Lieh-chuan,* 3.1a–3a.

34. See Tso Kuang-tou's biographies in MS 244.11a–15a and in Tso, *Nien-p'u.*

35. See Wang Wen-yen's biographies in Ch'en, *Tung-lin Lieh-chuan,* 3.7b–8a; Chin, *Sung-t'ien Lü-pi,* 22.24a–25b; and *Chiang-nan T'ung-chih,* 160.30b.

36. See Yü Yü-li's biography in MS 236.17b–19a.

37. See Li San-ts'ai's biography in MS 232.17b–19a.

38. For data on these two controversial episodes, especially see Wen, *Hsien-po Chih-shih,* pp. 131ff.; CSPM, ch. 68; Tso, *Nien-p'u,* 1.11a ff.

39. See Tsou Yüan-piao's biography in MS 243.5b–11a; and Chao Nan-hsing's biography in MS 243.1a–5b.

40. See Yen Hsiang-kao's biography in MS 240.1a–9a.

41. See Feng Ts'ung-wu's biography in MS 243.19b–21a.

42. See Wei Chung-hsien's biographies in MS 305.18a–28a and Hummel, *Eminent Chinese,* II, 846–47. Cf. CSPM, ch. 71. Though Wei seems to have been his original surname, he took the name Li Chin-chung ("offer loyalty") on entering the palace. After 1620 he resumed the surname Wei and was given a new personal name by the emperor, Chung-hsien, literally denoting "loyal and worthy."

43. KTSL 1.8a–9b (Wei referred to both as Li Chin-chung and as Wei Chin-chung).

44. See Ting, *T'e-wu Cheng-chih, passim.*

45. This was Li Shih, eunuch supervisor of textile manufacturing in Soochow and Hangchow in 1621, whom the Tung-lin partisan Huang Tsun-su apparently tried to cultivate as a potential rival of Wei. Subsequently, however, Li was partly responsible for the arrests of many Tung-lin men. See Wen, *Hsien-po Chih-shih,* pp. 186–87; MS 245.12a–15b.

46. Tso, *Nien-p'u,* 1.32b–33b; MS 245.3a–5a.

47. Huang Tsung-hsi, *Ming-ju Hsüeh-an,* ch. 61 (part 12, p. 18). Cf. MS 245.12a–15b.

48. MS 240.1a–9a; STSL 43.7b.

49. MS 245.18b–20a.

50. MS 240.1a–9a; Chiang, *Tung-lin Shih-mo,* p. 42; STSL 43.13a.

51. Versions of at least eight such lists are extant, chief of which is *Tung-lin Tang-jen Pang,* a list of 309 names that is reproduced in Ch'en, *Tung-lin Lieh-chuan.* See Hucker, "The Tung-lin Movement," note 90 (p. 375).

52. See MS 306.28a–29a.

53. For Wei Kuang-wei, see MS 306.11b–14a.

54. See MS 306.15b–18a; *Shun-t'ien-fu Chih,* 107.19b–21a.

55. For dramatic eyewitness accounts of a popular uprising that was provoked by the arrest of one of these men, Chou Shun-ch'ang, see Hucker, "Su-chou."

56. MS 305.22b.

57. Data concerning censorial activities in 1620–27 would probably be even more strikingly impressive were it not for the fact that the *Shih-lu* chronicles for the whole year 1624, a most turbulent year, are fragmentary. The standard *Shih-lu* edition, photolithographed in 1940, supplements the

chronicles for this year with footnote-like addenda, mostly reproduced from the *Liang-ch'ao Ts'ung-hsin Lu* by the late Ming author Shen Kuo-yüan. To maintain consistency in my data, I have not incorporated material from these addenda into any of my tabulations. The *Shih-lu* chronicles for the sixth month of 1627 (*chüan* 80) are wholly missing. It has long been supposed that the records for 1624 and 1627 were mutilated by Feng Ch'üan, a grand secretary under Wei Chung-hsien who could have had opportunities to tamper with them early in the Manchu regime. See Hummel, *Eminent Chinese*, I, 240–41; and Franke, "Literary Sources," p. 14.

58. For purposes of this analysis, I have utilized not merely the *Hsi-tsung Shih-lu* (STSL), but the *Kuang-tsung Shih-lu* (KTSL) as well. Despite its title, *Kuang-tsung Shih-lu* deals with the first months of Hsi-tsung's reign and not at all with Kuang-tsung's one-month reign, which is dealt with at the very end of *Shen-tsung Shih-lu*. This ironic situation stems from the unique circumstances of the rapid transition from Shen-tsung to Kuang-tsung and then to Hsi-tsung. When Kuang-tsung took the throne on the first day of the eighth month of the forty-eighth year of Wan-li (Shen-tsung's era-name), it was proclaimed, in accordance with the traditional practice, that the next New Year's Day would inaugurate the first year of a new era, to be called T'ai-ch'ang. When Kuang-tsung died on the first day of the ninth month, the beginning of his T'ai-ch'ang era was still four months in the future. A great court assembly was convened to find a solution for this unprecedented dilemma. It was finally agreed that the forty-eighth year of Wan-li should be terminated at the end of its eighth month and that the ninth through twelfth months of that year should constitute an abbreviated first and only year of the T'ai-ch'ang era, so that Hsi-tsung's era, called T'ien-ch'i, could begin with 1621 rather than be delayed until 1622. The *Kuang-tsung Shih-lu* deals with the T'ai-ch'ang era rather than with Kuang-tsung's actual reign. Thus it begins with the ninth month of 1620, its first entry announcing Kuang-tsung's death. *Hsi-tsung Shih-lu* begins with the first month of 1621, when Hsi-tsung had already been on the throne for four months.

59. STSL 13.21b–22a, 26a.

60. STSL 13.13a–b.

61. STSL 26.1b.

62. TMHT 13.320–23 spells out successive authorizations for censors of various sorts to submit recommendations.

63. E.g., see HTSL 66.3b–4a.   64. STSL 2.47a.

65. TMHT 13.321.   66. STSL 32.5a–b.

67. E.g., see STSL 32.14b–15b, 38.6a.   68. STSL 51.19b–20b.

69. STSL 54.1b.   70. STSL 54.12b–13a, 70.14a–b.

71. KTSL 1.19b. Both Li K'o-shao and Ts'ui Wen-sheng were themselves repeatedly impeached at this time. See KTSL 1.7b–8a, 1.8a, 1.21a–b, 2.8b; STSL 19.9b.

72. KTSL 1.22a.

73. KTSL 1.31a.

74. KTSL 2.7a–b, 4.3b.

75. STSL 41.9a. In Wei Chung-hsien's regime, Fang Ts'ung-che did not respond to urgings that he return to duty, though his critics were purged.

Fang died in 1628. See MS 218.14a–20b. Hui Shih-yang was removed from the civil-service rolls in 1625 and in 1626 was even sentenced to death; but he apparently escaped that punishment and eventually served the rebel Li Tsu-ch'eng. See Hsü, *Hsiao-t'ien Chi-nien*, 1.26a. Wei Ying-chia remained active at court into 1623 but left office not later than 1625. At the end of that year he was denounced by the old Tung-lin enemy Chi Shih-chiao and deliberation of the case was ordered (STSL 61.2a). I am not certain what Wei's fate was. He appears on the major blacklists of Tung-lin men, but some sources consider him a "eunuch partisan," apparently because he criticized Hsiung T'ing-pi, whom Tung-lin men generally defended. For criticizing Hsiung, Wei was demoted out of the Offices of Scrutiny into a lowly provincial office in 1621, but in 1622 he was recalled to his former post. See STSL 5.33a, 20.21b.

76. KTSL 4.28a–29a.

77. For Mao Shih-lung's attack, see STSL 6.16b.

78. STSL 6.23b. For Chia Chi-ch'un's dismissal early in 1621, see STSL 2.52b.

79. STSL 10.15a–b. 80. STSL 18.18b–20a, 20a–b.

81. MS 306.23b–24a. 82. MS 306.38a–40a.

83. STSL 21.10b–11a, 27.5b–6a, 22.14a–b, 22.17b.

84. STSL 22.14a–b.

85. STSL 26.4a, 32.19a, 39.8a.

86. See Hsiung T'ing-pi's biography in MS 259.7a–24b.

87. KTSL 1.25b.

88. KTSL 1.26b–27b.

89. KTSL 1.33b

90. KTSL 2.19b–22a. Cf. MS 259.10b–11a.

91. STSL 2.49a–b.

92. STSL 3.13a, 3.18b, 4.10b.

93. See Chou Tsung-chien's biography in MS 245.7b–11b.

94. STSL 4.10b, 5.33a.

95. KTSL 3.13a–b, 3.14b; STSL 2.55a–b, 3.31a, 5.33a.

96. STSL 10.12b–13b, 12.4a.

97. For Hsi-tsung's response, see MS 259.19b–20a. For the attacks on Chang, see STSL 13.6b–7b.

98. STSL 14.2b–3a.

99. STSL 14.9b–10a.

100. For Chou's defense of Hsiung, see STSL 15.9b. For Chiang's defense, see STSL 15.21a. For Ho's defense, see STSL 16.2b–3a.

101. STSL 16.18a–19a.

102. MS 259.21a. This MS biography of Hsiung T'ing-pi states categorically that Hsiung caused Wang Wen-yen to use 40,000 taels to bribe the palace eunuchs on Hsiung's behalf but that he was rebuffed and Wei Chunghsien swore to see to it that Hsiung was beheaded. This is essentially the charge on which Wang Wen-yen was later tortured to death, and that eventually implicated Yang Lien, Tso Kaung-tou, and other Tung-lin men. But the textual commentary *Ming-shih K'ao-cheng Chün-i* by Wang Sung-yü (appended to the Po-na ed. of MS) insists (26.6b–7b) that the bribery story was concocted by eunuch partisans as a device to trap Yang Lien and that

there is every evidence that Hsiung T'ing-pi was in no way corrupt. It suggests that Wang Wen-yen's vigorous efforts to save Hsiung naturally lent some credence to the story when it appeared.

103. STSL 18.1b–2b, 18.12a–b, 19.5b–6a, 19.29b–30a.

104. STSL 25.10a–b, 37.17b–18a.

105. See Chang Hao-ming's biography in MS 257.1a–3b. Chang finally died at the age of eighty-five in 1635 when domestic rebels sacked his home town.

106. STSL 22.29a.

107. STSL 22.19b–20a.

108. STSL 26.4b–5a, 26.14a–15a, 26.28a–30a, 26.31b–32b, 27.5a–6b, 27.9b–10a, 27.28a–29b, 28.8a, 28.39b–40a.

109. STSL 46.1b, 54.9b–10a, 56.20b.

110. STSL 57.25b–26b, 57.26b–27a.

111. MS 259.21b.

112. MS 259.18b.

113. See STSL 13.7b, 17.22a–b, 19.38a, 22.12a–b, 22.20b–21a, 23.22b–23a, 27.23a–24b, 27.29b–30a, 28.12b–13a, 28.17b, 31.8a, 39.18a, 40.1a–b, 40.5a, 50.3b–4b, 53.31b–33a, 54.1a, 54.9b, 56.16a, 57.20b, 29.19b, 60.8b, 61.36a, 79.23b.

114. See Wen, *Hsien-po Chih-shih*, pp. 142ff.; MS 305.20b (in Wei Chung-hsien's biography); MS 245.5a–6b (Wei Ta-chung's biography); Tso, *Nien-p'u*, 1.30a–31a.

115. Tso, *Nien-p'u*, 1.30a–31a.

116. STSL 41.6b–7a.

117. STSL 41.9a–b, 9b–10a.

118. STSL 41.10b. See also Yüan Hua-chung's biography in MS 244.21b–23a.

119. STSL 46.1b; MS 306.15b–18a.

120. STSL 47.3a, 4b.

121. STSL 47.6b.

122. STSL 49.1b–2a.

123. Chiang, *Tung-lin Shih-mo*, p. 43.

124. Wang's rearrest and death are noted in STSL 49.3a, 53.5a.

125. MS 306.22b. Cf. STSL 65.31b–32a, 72.21a–b, 77.22a, 81.18a.

126. E.g., see STSL 55.10b, 55.14b–15a, 56.16b–17a, 57.20b, 58.16a–b, 61.15a–b, 61.18b–19a, 65.14b.

127. MS 305.24a.

128. Attacks on Yeh are recorded in STSL 55.10b, 57.20b, 57.24b–25a. For mention of his death, see MS 240.1a–9a.

129. STSL 68.1a–b, 2b–3a, 3a–b, 26a–b, 28a–b. Cf. Feng Ch'üan's biographies in *Shun-t'ien-fu Chih*, 105.31a–33a; and in Hummel, *Eminent Chinese*, I, 240–41.

130. STSL 68.25b–26a, 26a, 29b–30b, 32b. Cf. Wang Shao-hui's biography in MS 306.28a–29a.

131. See Ts'ui Ch'eng-hsiu's biographies in MS 306.15b–18a and *Shun-t'ien-fu Chih*, 107.19b–21a.

132. STSL 17.8b.

133. STSL 3.5a.

134. E.g., see STSL 2.3a, 2.16a, 2.21a, 2.37b, 12.14a, 19.5b–6a, 19.7a, 29.21b, 31.8b, 32.11b–14a, 33.31a–b, 33.35b, 78.6a–b.

135. KTSL 3.7a–b.   136. STSL 13.30b.

137. STSL 32.23a–24b.   138. STSL 62.9b.

139. STSL 18.11b, 23.13a, 23.21b, 25.30a–31a.

140. STSL 76.4b; MS 300.25b.

141. KTSL 1.8a–9b.

142. STSL 10.6b.

143. For the impeachment of the stone masons, see STSL 12.30b. For the impeachment of the grand secretary's son, see STSL 27.4b–5a. For the impeachment of the Kweichow students, see STSL 33.31a–b. For the impeachment of the merchant, see STSL 67.25b–26a.

144. KTSL 1.8a, 2.8b; STSL 19.9b.

145. See Shen Ts'ui's biography in MS 218.20b–22b. Cf. STSL 15.3a–4a, 15.13b, 15.20b, 17.9a, 17.20b, 18.12a–b.

146. STSL 29.6a–b.

147. KTSL 1.8a–9b. Wei Chung-hsien here seems to be referred to as two persons, Li Chin-chung and Wei Chin-chung. This probably reflects some confusion deriving from Wei's changing his name (see note 42 above). In response to Yang's memorial, Hsi-tsung responded that there was already a decision about Li Chin-chung and his associate Liu Hsün, but he asked that an investigation be made into the matter of Wei Chin-chung—which suggests that this name meant nothing to him.

148. STSL 10.1a–b.

149. STSL 26.4b–5a, 26.28a–30a, 27.5a–6b.

150. STSL 27.28a–29b, especially 28b–29a. Throughout, Wei Chung-hsien is referred to as Wei Chin-chung.

151. Li Yen, *Tung-lin-tang*, pp. 119–20. Cf. STSL 61.27a–b, 68.36a.

152. The mention of 70 denunciations is from MS 305.21a. Authors are from STSL 43.8a–b, 43.8b, 43.14a, 44.6a, 45.1b.

153. STSL 43.1a–2b gives an abstract, as does Wen, *Hsien-po Chih-shih*, pp. 144ff. An abstract in English is given in Backhouse and Bland, *Annals and Memoirs*, pp. 68–72. What follows in my text is translated from the memorial as reproduced in Yang Lien's collected works, *Yang Ta-hung Chi*, pp. 1–7.

154. Liu I-ching joined Fang Ts'ung-che in the Grand Secretariat under Kuang-tsung and became a vigorous defender of the "good elements" when they were endangered by their remonstrances over "the case of the removal from the palace" and other matters. He insisted that Wei Chung-hsien and other eunuchs be punished for their thefts in the palace in 1620 and subsequently insisted that Mistress K'o be sent out of the palace. Attacked repeatedly by Sun Chieh and others late in 1621, he begged for retirement and finally was released from duty early in 1622. Wei Chung-hsien subsequently had him dismissed from the civil service. In 1628 he was recalled to duty but apparently did not serve. He died in 1635. See his biography in MS 240.9a–13a. Chou Chia-mo was vigorously active, along with Yang Lien and Tso Kuang-tou, in getting first Madame Cheng and then Madame Li to move out of the imperial residence hall in 1620 during Kuang-tsung's illness and after his death. He was responsible for recalling many Tung-lin men to

office in 1620–21 and protected many "good elements" from imperial wrath. When denounced by Sun Chieh at the end of 1621, he also asked for retirement, and his request was eventually granted. Late in 1625 he was dismissed from the civil service on charges of conspiring with the eunuch Wang An. In 1628 he was recalled to duty as Nanking minister of personnel, and he died in 1629. See his biography in MS 241.1a–3b. For Sun Chieh's attack on Liu and Chou, see STSL 11.11b–12a.

155. Sun Shen-hsing, like Tsou Yüan-piao a long-time champion of the "good elements" who had lectured at the Tung-lin Academy, was recalled from retirement early in Hsi-tsung's reign. Because of differences over the "great cases" of 1620, he feuded with Fang Ts'ung-che and then with Huang K'o-tsan and left office on sick leave in 1622. Tung-lin men subsequently nominated him for the post of grand secretary, but his appointment was blocked by Wei Chung-hsien. In the time of Wei's dominance, Sun was first dismissed from the civil service and then sentenced to frontier military service as a common soldier. Before this sentence could be carried out, Chuang-lieh-ti came to the throne and Sun was exonerated. Though repeatedly recommended and recalled, Sun did not respond until 1635, when he accepted an appointment as grand secretary but died upon reaching the capital. See his biography in MS 243.11a–15a.

156. Both Wang Chi and Chung Yü-chung were aligned with "good elements" at court as early as "the case of the root of the state" in the 1590's, and both were removed from office in 1622–23 largely because of bad relations with the anti-Tung-lin grand secretary Shen Ts'ui. See their biographies in MS 241.11b–14a, 241.17a–19a.

157. Man Ch'ao-chien, an official of the Court of the Imperial Stud, spoke out in 1622 about the removal of "good elements" and the rise of eunuch influence and was dismissed from the civil service. He was recalled to duty under Chuang-lieh-ti but died before resuming service. See his biography in MS 246.1a–3b. Wen Chen-meng, scion of one of the most distinguished literati families of Soochow, won first place in the doctoral examination of 1622. Appointed to a post in the Hanlin Academy, he also remonstrated about current irregularities and was dismissed from the service. Recalled to duty under Chuang-lieh-ti, he rose to become a grand secretary but was eventually driven out of office again by a late Ming partisan clique. See his biography in MS 251.17b–21b. In 1623, Hsü Ta-hsiang, as vice director of the Bureau of Honors in the Ministry of Personnel, approved a request for posthumous honors for an official just at a time when Hsi-tsung happened to think such honors were being awarded excessively. He was demoted and transferred to a provincial post. Because he happened to be set upon and robbed by a gang of eunuchs, he went home in indignation. He was recalled to duty in the Ministry of Personnel under Chuang-lieh-ti. See his biography in MS 234.23a–24a.

158. Chou Shih-p'u was one of the most ardent remonstrators in the Offices of Scrutiny in 1621–23. He repeatedly demanded action to curtail eunuch abuses, objected to using eunuchs in frontier service, and warned against the military training of eunuchs in the palace. When his promotion was blocked (in late 1623?) he requested sick leave and went home. He was recalled to duty under Chuang-lieh-ti but eventually offended the new em-

peror by his obstinacy and was dismissed from the service. He committed
suicide in 1642 when the rebel Li Tzu-ch'eng captured his home town. See
his biography in MS 264.5a–5b.

159. As soon as Wei Ta-chung was promoted, he engaged in a feud with
Fu K'uei and was rebuked for taking up his new duties before the accusations against him had been dealt with. See Chiang, *Tung-lin Shih-mo,* pp.
41–42.

160. MS 305.20b–21a.

161. KTSL 1.19b.

162. KTSL 1.2b, 1.5a, 1.36b–38a.

163. KTSL 4.1b–2b, 4.5a–7b.

164. KTSL 4.9b–12a.

165. KTSL 4.12b–13a.

166. STSL 1.15b–16a.

167. STSL 2.52b.

168. E.g., see KTSL 1.25a, 2.11b–12a.

169. KTSL 3.6a–b.

170. KTSL 3.12b, 4.4b–5a; STSL 1.3b–4a, 2.3b, 2.7b–8a.

171. STSL 14.25b.

172. STSL 25.6b.

173. KTSL 1.19b, 3.23b–24a, 4.1b–2b.

174. STSL 2.51b–52a.

175. STSL 17.9b.

176. STSL 19.30a–b.

177. STSL 21.20a–b, 23.6a–7a.

178. STSL 26.11a–b.

179. For Chou Ch'ao-jui's plea, see KTSL 1.31b. For the five principles
mentioned by Chou Shih-p'u, see STSL 1.4b–5a.

180. STSL 7.3b–4a.

181. STSL 7.30b–31a, 10.2a–3a, 13.23a, 17.7b–8a. Cf. Yeh Hsiang-kao's defense of speaking officials' privilege to speak out, in STSL 17.16b–17a.

182. STSL 17.11b.

183. KTSL 2.17b–18a.

184. KTSL 3.10b–11a, 3.15b–16a, 3.16a–b, 3.17a–18a; STSL 1.5b–6a, 1.9b–
10a, 2.3b–4a, 2.12b–13b, 8.4b.

185. KTSL 3.16a–b, 4.21a; STSL 1.9b–10a, 3.3b–4a, 25.25a–26a.

186. STSL 8.4b.

187. STSL 16.20a, 39.8a.

188. HTSL 1.10b, 2.4a–b, 2.12b–13b, 21.16a, 39.11a.

189. STSL 1.25b–26a.

190. STSL 6.24b–25b.

191. STSL 10.1a–b, 10.2a–3a.

192. STSL 31.28a–30a.

193. For examples of general remonstrances about eunuch influence, see
KTSL 2.22b–23b, 4.2b–3a; STSL 2.6a–b, 3.3b–4a, 9.12a–b, 33.6a–8b.

194. STSL 1.25b–26a, 40.6a, 41.5b–6a, 41.11a–b.

195. STSL 30.15b–16a, 30.16a–b.

196. STSL 5.1b–2a, 29.5a–b, 29.6a–b, 30.22b–23a, 32.2b–3a, 40.6b.

197. STSL 26.23b–24a.

198. STSL 8.12a, 37.19a–20b.

199. Tseng's request is noted in STSL 31.15a–b. For the protests of P'an,
Liu, and Li, see STSL 44.1a, 44.3a, 44.3a–b.

200. For Yü's proposal, see STSL 54.22a–23a. For Kao's, see STSL 55.6a–
7a.

201. See STSL 73.27a–b, 81.7a.

202. STSL 66.29b–30a.

203. STSL 64.16a, 65.46b–47a, 71.4a.

204. STSL 76.29a.   205. STSL 59.8a.
206. STSL 54.29a–b.   207. STSL 72.21a–b.
208. STSL 81.18a.   209. STSL 81.30b.
210. STSL 82.1b.

211. See STSL 61.27a–b, 77.11a–b, 81.35b–36a, 81.36b, 82.1b–2b, 82.2b, 82.23b–24b.

212. STSL 75.22b, 75.22b–23a, 76.9b–10a, 76.25b, 77.22a, 79.27b–28a, 79.35b, 81.15b, 82.16b, 82.28a, 82.31b, 82.32a.

213. For the salt-control censors' request, see STSL 81.9b. For the one from the Peking citizenry, see STSL 79.8a.

214. STSL 81.18a–b.

215. STSL 74.26b–27a.

216. E.g., see STSL 1.5a–b, 2.11a, 2.14a–15a, 2.32b–33a, 15.11b–12a, 23.22b, 34.4b–5a, 51.18a–b, 52.6b–7b, 53.31a–b, 53.39a–40a, 54.7b–8a, 54.8a–b, 54.21a–22a, 55.9a–b, 57.11a–12a, 60.19a–20a, 61.23b–24a.

217. STSL 2.21a–b.

218. STSL 2.16b–17a.

219. STSL 2.12a.

220. STSL 12.24b, 13.1a, 22.30b, 23.15a–b, 23.21b, 26.1a–b.

221. STSL 56.18b–19a.   222. STSL 21.10b–11a.
223. STSL 53.27b.   224. STSL 56.8b–9a.

225. STSL 57.7a–8a.

226. For Li's proposal, see STSL 61.30a–b. For Hsü's proposal, see STSL 63.24a–26a.

227. *Tung-lin Shu-yüan Chih*, 1.2b–3a. This work reproduces (14.8b–9b) an official report on the confiscation written by the magistrate of Wusih County, Wu Ta-p'u. It is dated in the fifth month of 1626 and reports that the tax register showed a valuation of 581 taels for the academy's land.

228. STSL 72.20b, 78.25a.

229. STSL 3.4a–5a.

230. KTSL 4.25a.

231. For Tsou's complaint about delay, see STSL 16.26b–27a. For Hsü's recommendations, see STSL 18.15a–16a.

232. STSL 19.5b.

233. STSL 27.35a–36b.

234. For Liu's request, see STSL 53.10a–16b. For Yang's demand, see STSL 46.1a.

235. STSL 53.8a.

236. STSL 70.27a.

237. See Franke, "Literary Sources," p. 14.

238. For Yang's proposals, see STSL 54.16b, 55.34a.

239. See Franke, "Literary Sources," p. 40.

240. For the advice given by Chia and Shih, see STSL 58.10a–12a, 61.17a–b. For K'ang's interpretation, see STSL 56.17b–18a. Cf. K'ang P'ei-yang's biographies in *Chi-nan-fu Chih* 52.27b–29a; and *Ling-hsien Chih* 19.14b–15b.

241. STSL 59.10b–11a. K'ang's biographers (see note 240 above) make no mention of this incident. It is possible he never served his sentence. He is reported to have died in 1632 at the age of eighty-one.

242. STSL 58.10a–12a.

243. STSL 65.31a–b.

244. STSL 31.3a–4b.

245. STSL 1.20b–21a.

246. STSL 13.27a, 15.26b–27b.

247. STSL 21.14a–b, 22.21a–22a.

248. E.g., see STSL 26.11a–b, 35.34b–35b, 42.7a–b.

249. E.g., see KTSL 1.28a, 1.30a, 1.32b, 2.9a; STSL 2.46a–47a, 6.10b–11a, 8.13b, 10.11a, 18.24b, 20.23b, 34.18b–19a.

250. For examples of requests that extraordinary assessments stop, see KTSL 2.12a–b, 3.14a; STSL 1.16b–17b; 2.3b–4a, 4.2a, 17.24a–b, 22.13a–b. For memorials urging the use of other sources of revenue, see KTSL 3.3a–4a; STSL 1.2b.

251. STSL 31.5a–b.

252. STSL 35.38a–40a.

253. STSL 21.20b, 24.15a–b.

254. STSL 21.14b–15a.

255. For examples of requests for relief that were acted upon, see STSL 58.3a–b, 61.14b–15a, 61.35a, 68.20b, 69.21b, 73.12b–13a, 75.7b–8a. For examples of grumblings about capital conditions, see STSL 67.24b, 75.1b.

256. STSL 67.19b–20a.

257. STSL 54.17b, 66.30a–b, 67.2b–3a, 78.24a–b.

258. STSL 56.11b–12a, 65.12b–13a, 71.9a, 74.32a–33a, 74.36b, 78.11a, 81.31a–b.

259. P'an's contribution is noted in STSL 55.18b; Huo's is noted in STSL 55.34b; Kuo's is noted in STSL 57.20b; and Hsü's is noted in STSL 68.21b.

260. STSL 57.24a, 67.18a.

261. STSL 56.2a.

262. STSL 56.13b.

263. STSL 57.22a.

264. STSL 71.15a–b.

265. E.g., see STSL 55.34b, 56.5b, 56.6b–7a, 56.15a, 58.22b, 61.27b, 65.2b–3a, 67.19b, 74.19a, 76.2a, 76.33a–b, 77.11a–b.

266. STSL 69.6b–7b.

267. E.g., see STSL 2.38b–39a, 50.6a, 51.28a–b, 55.36b–37a, 56.15b–16a, 58.13a–b, 58.13b–14a, 58.14a–15b, 59.38b, 62.22b, 63.4b, 64.8a–b, 69.11a–b, 69.17b–18a, 71.10a–b, 75.19a–b.

268. STSL 1.10a. Though no action was taken at this time, Chuang-lieh-ti revived the sea-transport system in the 1630's to supplement canal transport.

269. STSL 5.18a–19a, 5.23a–b, 14.7a, 16.12a–b.

270. STSL 39.9a.

271. STSL 66.6b–7a. Cf. Hucker, "Su-chou," pp. 254–55; and a special one-*chüan* work devoted to the catastrophe, called *T'ien-pien Ti-ch'ao*, which is reproduced in the collectanea *Chieh-yüeh Shan-fang Hui-ch'ao*, *Chih-hai*, and *Tse-ku-chai Ch'ung-ch'ao*.

272. STSL 66.7a.

273. STSL 66.6b–7a.

274. STSL 66.9b.

275. STSL 66.13b–14a, 66.29b–30a.

276. KTSL 4.16a, 4.16a–b.

277. STSL 4.30b.

278. See HTK 35.

279. STSL 6.6a–b, 6.19a.

280. For Lien's complaint, see STSL 21.16a–b. For the proposals by Chao and Lu, see STSL 21.17a–18b, 24.20b.

281. STSL 35.32b–34b.
282. STSL 13.26a.
283. STSL 30.15b–16a, 30.16a–b.
284. STSL 1.6a–b.
285. For the suggestion about coining money, see STSL 7.29a–b. For the demands about reservoirs, see STSL 67.17a–b, 67.18b–19b. For the demand about rent collectors, see STSL 30.30b.
286. See KTSL 1.30b, 4.14b–15b, 4.18b–19a; STSL 2.40b–41a, 2.41a–b, 3.23b–25a, 4.17b–19a, 4.38a–b, 6.27b–28a, 7.17a–18a, 9.20b–22a, 21.12a–13a, 22.2b–3b, 27.10b–11a, 31.17a–18a, *et passim.*
287. STSL 3.21a–b, 14.6a.
288. KTSL 3.21b–22a; STSL 11.20b–21b.
289. For examples of Hsiung's and Wang's supporters, see STSL 13.9a–11a. For Hsü's request about secrecy, see STSL 8.32b.
290. STSL 24.24a–25a.
291. STSL 58.23b.
292. E.g., see STSL 3.25a–b, 13.9a–11a.
293. STSL 3.25a–b.
294. STSL 4.12a–b.
295. STSL 1.25a.
296. For Fang's report on low morale, see STSL 10.29b–30a. For Ts'ai's proposal about officers, see STSL 11.20a–b.
297. For examples of memorials about improving training methods, see STSL 11.4a–b, 28.29b–31b, 37.34a–36b. For proposals about military schools, see KTSL 4.37a; STSL 21.21a–b. For proposals about relying on examinations, see STSL 8.2a, 19.22a.

298. STSL 7.8b–9a, 16.23a.	299. STSL 2.23a–24a.
300. STSL 2.19a–20b.	301. STSL 2.19a–20b, 5.5b–6a.
302. KTSL 1.35b.	303. STSL 16.9a–b.
304. STSL 63.34b.	305. STSL 4.17a–b.
306. STSL 19.14a.	307. STSL 24.2b, 24.7b.
308. STSL 30.28a.	309. STSL 63.6a–7a.
310. STSL 79.14b–17a.	311. STSL 4.9a–b.
312. STSL 4.16b–17a.	313. STSL 7.15a–16a, 11.1a–b.
314. STSL 11.7a.	315. STSL 16.5b.
316. STSL 24.13b–14b.	317. STSL 29.18a.
318. STSL 4.9b.	

319. For examples of proposals about military agricultural operations, see KTSL 2.14a–15b; STSL 51.21b–22b. For examples of proposals about reforming the horse-supply system, see STSL 7.27a–b, 11.17b–18a.
320. STSL 6.11a–b.
321. STSL 4.24a.
322. STSL 10.16b–17a.
323. E.g., see STSL 74.26a–b, 77.1b–2a, 78.9b–10b, 81.9b–10a, 81.36b.
324. See Hsü Kuang-ch'i's biographies in MS 251.15a–17b and Hummel, *Eminent Chinese,* I, 316–19. Cf. Dunne, *Generation of Giants,* pp. 157ff.; and Boxer, "Portuguese Military Expeditions."
325. KTSL 1.34a–35a.
326. STSL 4.4a–5b.

327. STSL 14.27b–28a, 21.7a, 24.27a–b.
328. STSL 29.4a–b.
329. For some proposals about capital defenses, see STSL 1.12a–13a, 2.21b–22a, 10.14b–15a, 62.17a–18a, 63.3a–4a. For suggestions about improving the police system, see STSL 2.55b–56a, 12.33a, 30.17a–b.
330. STSL 55.23a, 65.11b, 67.2a.
331. For proposals about dealing with the Dutch, see STSL 32.23a–24b, 37.36b, 38.5b. For those about the rebellion, see STSL 18.4b–5a, 18.5a, 21.2a, 21.20b, 22.28b, 23.17b–18a, 23.18a–b, 24.9a–b, 25.11b–13a, 51.19b–20b, 51.31a.
332. For proposals from the Kweichow regional inspector, see STSL 11.13b–14a, 38.6a–b, 52.24b. For those from the Szechwan inspector, see STSL 11.23a–b, 25.13a–15a, 55.37a. For those from the Hukwang inspector, see STSL 17.14a–b, 73.4a–b. For those from the Yunnan inspector, see STSL 37.22a–23a, 53.28a, 77.10b. For those from the Kwangsi inspector, see STSL 28.12b–13a.
333. E.g., see STSL 12.8a, 19.38a, 25.18b, 27.23a–24b, 40.4a, 54.6b–7b, 65.37a–38a, 74.1b–2b.
334. STSL 13.2a–4b, 24.3a, 24.23a–b, 74.1b–2b.
335. STSL 37.22a–23a, 67.9b–10a.
336. STSL 2.19a–20b, 2.40b–41a, 2.46a–47a, 2.50b–51a, 3.21a–b, 3.23b–25a, 5.5b–6a, 5.15a–b, 5.32a–33a, 6.11a–b, 6.18a, 6.27b–28a, 7.8b–9a, 7.19b–20a, 7.31a–32a, 8.4a–b, 9.4b–5b, 11.13b–14a, 11.14b–15b, 11.20a–b, 13.15b–16a, 14.2b–3a, 14.18a–19b, 14.23a, 15.2b–3a, 15.3a–4a.
337. STSL 29.21a–b.
338. STSL 30.16a–b, 30.19a–b.
339. STSL 54.9b–10a.
340. STSL 26.5a–b.
341. STSL 74.11a–b. Cf. STSL 73.27b.
342. For Shen's defense of Chang, see STSL 2.24b. For Wei's attempt to rectify the injustices of 1615, see STSL 2.34a–b. For the protests over the dismissal of Liu Chung-ch'ing, see STSL 5.7b. For some similar cases, see STSL 5.35a–b, 11.9b, 12.1b, 16.2a–b, 19.24a, 32.14a–b, 39.8b, 47.3a.
343. STSL 18.3a–b.
344. STSL 51.16b, 54.18a, 57.1a, 64.29a–b.
345. E.g., see KTSL 4.25b–26b; STSL 6.26a–b, 18.8b, 21.28a–b, 29.24a–b.
346. STSL 22.1a, 31.15a–b, 42.4a, 42.5a, 55.6a–7a, 66.13b–14a, 66.29b–30a.
347. STSL 5.4a–5a.
348. STSL 54.10a.

Chapter six

1. KTSL 2.19b–22a, 3.16a.
2. STSL 26.11a.
3. TMHT 210.4191ff.
4. MS 73.2b. Cf. CMMYL 48.1b; MHY 34.1a–b.
5. Judicial processes of the Ming period in general are succinctly described in MS 94. Cf. MS 93, 95. Unfortunately, there is not yet available a good modern study of the Ming judiciary; and I have been unable to clarify some of its aspects, even some that pertain directly to the censorial agencies.

6. TMHT 214.4283ff. Cf. MS 73.15a–17a, 94.1a ff.

7. MS 93.4a–b.

8. MS 94.1a ff.; TMHT 177.3606, 211.4217.

9. E.g., see TMHT 214.4267, 4283–84. Cf. MS 94.

10. MS 94; TMHT 211.4218–19; CMMYL 48.1a–2a; MSHU 65; HTK 54. The Chinese term that I render "judicial review" is *shen-lu.*

11. Ying et al., *Shen-lu Shu-lüeh,* p. 18a.

12. MS 73.5a.   13. HTSL 26.14a.

14. HTSL 46.3a.   15. MS 8–9, *passim.*

16. JTSL 3B.3b–4a. Cf. STSL 10.16a.

17. For an example of "a few hundred" cases reviewed, see HTSL 31.2a. For the mention of 5,000, see HTSL 99.10a.

18. HTSL 29.5a.

19. HTSL 19.4b.

20. E.g., see HTSL 54.1b–2a, 68.8a–b.

21. Mention of the 275 can be found in HTSL 103.7b–8a, mention of the 224 in HTSL 109.9a–b.

22. HTSL 114.7b.

23. HTSL 16.6b–7b, 17.9b, 28.17a, 28.15a–b, 73.8b–9a, 84.16b–17a.

24. For the investigation entrusted to supervising secretaries, see HTSL 59.12a–b. For the one entrusted to Surveillance Offices alone, see HTSL 62.2b, 73.9b–10a.

25. Sources of these data are as follows: For the battalion commander, HTSL 37.8a–9a. For the deserted soldier, HTSL 90.7a. For the 2 civilians, HTSL 30.2b. For the 3+ civilians, JTSL 10.2a, HTSL 28.17a. For the single investigating censor, HTSL 71.3a–b. For the 3 investigating censors, the vice minister, 5 directors, 2 vice directors, and 7 secretaries, HTSL 59.12a–b, 98.2a, 99.6a–b. For the 22 military officers, HTSL 37.8a–9a. And for the single military officer, HTSL 104.2b–3a. This last entry probably refers to a eunuch. The *Shih-lu* passage does not clearly identify the person. It states that the emperor "pardoned the crimes of the Szechwan regional military commissioners Kung Chü and Chao Liang but sent Hsing An to prison." The entry is dated in the eighth month of 1433. The men had been impeached for failure in a campaign against rebellious aborigines, and at Hsüan-tsung's command the regional inspector had investigated the facts. He reported that Hsing An, leading the campaign, was in fact guilty of cowardice, but that Kung Chü and Chao Liang had both fought valiant rear-guard actions when abandoned by their leader. But who was Hsing An? The character used here for his surname ("to punish") is an uncommon surname, and I have found no other mention of the officer apparently referred to. But in the fourth month of the same year Hsüan-tsung had specially ordered several capital officials to go to Szechwan to help supervise pacification of the area. See HTSL 101.11a–b. Among these was a eunuch with the homophonous name Hsing An but with a different character ("to flourish") for the surname. I find no subsequent reference to him in the *Shih-lu* of this period, and it seems plausible that he was indeed the Hsing An sent to prison at this time. Franke has observed that the *Shih-lu* edition that I use "has false characters on nearly every page" ("Literary Sources," p. 12), and I cannot but share this opinion.

26. HTSL 28.17a, 84.16b–17a, 112.1b.

27. HTSL 112.1b.

28. That these requests were approved is indicated in STSL 4.4a–5a, 54.10a.

29. KTSL 2.19b–22a, 3.16a; STSL 2.49a–b.

30. For the exoneration of the grand coordinator, see STSL 36.26a–b. For the clearing of charges against the vice commissioner, see STSL 60.1a–b.

31. STSL 13.18a, 26.11a, 29.3a–b, 42.9a.

32. TMHT 211.4217, 210.4200.

33. Boxer, ed., *South China*, pp. 178–79.

34. TMHT 210.4196.

35. Ricci, *China in the Sixteenth Century*, p. 53.

36. E.g., see HTSL 25.3a–b, 35.8b.

37. HTSL 69.9a–b.   38. HTSL 59.3a–4a, 89.2b.

39. HTSL 69.6b–7a.   40. HTSL 110.5a.

41. MS 172.5a. Cf. MHY 34.2b. For similar reaffirmations of or references to the general authorization, see HTSL 46.4a–b, 67.9a, 71.2a–b.

42. STSL 43.13a.

43. For examples of trials conducted jointly by regional inspectors and Surveillance Offices, see HTSL 60.1a, 68.5b, 71.10b, 103.14a. For examples of those conducted by Surveillance Offices alone, see HTSL 83.8a. For examples of trials conducted jointly by regional inspectors and grand coordinators, see STSL 32.15b, 52.37b–38a, 63.21a–22a.

44. For some entries of these sorts, see HTSL 34.3a–b, 42.11a–b, 42.12a, 43.20b–21a, 64.14b–15a, 65.4b–5a, 68.8a–b, 84.16a–b, 85.8b–9a, 95.9a–b; KTSL 1.26b–27b, 1.36b, 4.8a–b, 4.28a–29a; STSL 2.44a–45a, 11.2a, 12.8a, 12.8a–b, 16.18a–19a, 25.30a–31a, 26.4b–5a, 65.43b.

45. STSL 65.7a. For some similar entries, see STSL 68.36a, 69.4a.

46. HTSL 84.16b–17a.

47. HTSL 13.9a, 22.2b, 54.1b–2a, 84.1b, 104.4b–5a.

48. E.g., see HTSL 43.5b–6a, 53.12b–13a, 89.9b, 103.8b–9a.

49. HTSL 88.5b.

50. HTSL 98.9a–b.

51. STSL 39.7b, 59.31b, 64.15a–b.

52. See Fang Chen-ju's biography in MS 248.10b–13a and STSL 3.15a–16b, 5.7b–9a. Cf. the biography of Hsiung T'ing-pi in MS 259.7a–24b.

53. STSL 4.17a–b, 4.26a, 7.2a, 14.2b–3a, 54.1a.

54. STSL 10.17a.

55. For examples of bandit-suppression orders given to inspectors, commissioners, and Administration Offices, see HTSL 27.14a–b, 79.10a–b, 109.12a. For those involving only the three provincial offices, see HTSL 29.9a, 98.8b. For those involving specially delegated censors, see HTSL 34.8a–b, 87.5b–6a, 98.8a–b, 101.11a–b, 103.6a–b, 104.10a–b, 105.2b.

56. E.g., HTSL 79.8b.   57. HTSL 103.6a–b.

58. HTSL 104.10a–b.   59. E.g., see HTSL 98.8b, 101.9a.

60. HTSL 110.13b–14a.   61. HTSL 87.5b–6a.

62. For examples of censorial officials' recruiting of mercenaries, see KTSL 3.25b–26a; STSL 2.3a, 4.32b, 4.35b–36a, 7.18b–19a. For the complaints, see STSL 7.15a–16a, 13.15b.

63. STSL 8.16a, 9.1b, 11.13a–b.
64. STSL 12.8a.
65. STSL 6.4a–b. Cf. STSL 11.13a–b, 15.4b–5a, 19.7b–8a, 19.37b–38a, 21.24a, 22.16a–b, 25.32b–33a, 26.11a, 33.20a–b, 52.33a–b, 55.42a, 73.27b.
66. Li Yen, *Tung-lin-tang,* p. 33.
67. HTSL 89.2b, 89.3a–b.
68. E.g., see HTSL 53.5a, 87.11a, 99.10a.
69. HTSL 113.12b–13a.
70. E.g., see HTSL 26.7b, 55.8b, 59.1a, 93.4a–b; KTSL 3.20a–b; STSL 5.30b–31a, 22.34b–35b, 30.14a–b, 67.13b–14a.
71. See HTSL 40.7b, 96.10b.
72. STSL 4.39a–b.
73. HTSL 4.10b.
74. STSL 2.1a, 6.5b, 7.9b–10a, 59.31a, 71.4a–6a.
75. For examples of censorial officials sent to direct locust exterminating, see HTSL 55.12b, 65.10a, 104.4b, 111.10a–b. For examples of those sent to distribute rewards to the armies, see HTSL 4.2b, 21.7a; KTSL 2.26b; STSL 1.17b, 4.38b–39a, 5.33b–34b, 7.11b–12a, 7.27a. For examples of those sent to purchase sacrificial animals, see JTSL 9B.4b, HTSL 5.4a. For examples of those sent to destroy old paper money, see HTSL 44.11b–12a, 67.6a–b. For examples of those sent to gather construction materials, see HTSL 43.5b, 63.6b, 79.12a. For examples of those who participated in construction projects directly, see KTSL 3.4a–b; STSL 3.18b, 22.2a.
76. *Ming Nan-ching Tu-ch'a yüan T'iao-yüeh,* cited in Yü, "Chien-ch'a Chih-tu," p. 225.
77. TMHT 209.4154. Cf. MS 73.2b–3a; CMMYL 48.2a; MSHU 65.1302.
78. TMHT 209.4155.
79. STSL 22.28b–29a.
80. STSL 55.45a.
81. Chang Hsüan, *Hsi-yüan Wen-chien Lu,* 93.8a.
82. TMHT 209.4176, 210.4200; MS 73.2b–3a; MSHU 65.1302; CMMYL 48.2a.
83. For the attempt to persuade Mu-tsung that hearsay evidence was acceptable, see CMMYL 48.20b (memorial by Chao Chen-chi).
84. MHY 33.2a–b.
85. For the demotion by Hsüan-tsung, see HTSL 89.6a. For examples of rebukes from the 1620's, see KTSL 1.22a; STSL 5.6a, 26.28a–30a, 58.24a, 60.8b, 68.26a–b.
86. TMHT 209.4176; CMMYL 48.33b, 48.50a.
87. TMHT 12.280.
88. MS 73.2b–3a; TMHT 209.4154, 211.4211; MHY 33.6a, 34.3a–4a; CMMYL 48.2a, 5a, 44a–b; MSHU 65.1300–02.
89. The detailed regulations concerning evaluations upon returning from commissions appear in TMHT 211.4211–15.
90. TMHT 210.4201; MHY 34.6b.
91. TMHT 209.4154.
92. E.g., see STSL 6.2a–3a, 40.5a–b.
93. STSL 27.17a–18a; CMMYL 48.12b–16b.
94. STSL 46.1b; MS 243.4a.

95. For Jen-tsung's suggestion, see JTSL 10.1a–b; MHY 33.4b. For Hsüan-tsung's innovation, see HTSL 46.6a; TMHT 209.4177.

96. HTSL 5.10a.

97. MS 161.6a–8b.

98. HTSL 93.7a–b.

99. HTSL 15.7a.

100. JTSL 4A.4b–5a.

101. HTSL 45.3a.

102. HTSL 48.2b.

103. *Ibid.*

104. HTSL 50.2a–b.

105. HTSL 54.9b–10a.

106. HTSL 79.4b.

107. For general data on Liu Kuan, see his biography in MS 151.11a–12b.

108. HTSL 44.10a.

109. For Ku's promotion, see HTSL 45.2b. For the order that he begin weeding out censors, see HTSL 45.3a–b.

110. For the first results, see HTSL 46.5a–b.

111. HTSL 47.8a–b.

112. HTSL 47.14b–15a.

113. *Ibid.*

114. HTSL 56.10b–11a.

115. The grand secretaries Yang Shih-ch'i and Yang Jung both apparently persuaded the emperor to deal leniently with Liu Kuan. See MS 151.12b.

116. MS 151.11a–12b.

117. Wang Shih-chen, *Yen-shan-t'ang Pieh-chi,* 23.2b–3a.

118. HTSL 56.10b–11a.

119. MS 151.12b.

120. Yeh, *Shui-tung Jih-chi,* 5.1a.

121. HTSL 46.5a–b. Cf. MHY 33.25a; Yeh, *Shui-tung Jih-chi,* 17.3b–4a.

122. HTSL 54.2b.

123. HTSL 56.7b, 70.8a. Cf. MS 158.3a.

124. HTSL 50.2a–b.

125. HTSL 51.13a–b, 61.3a–b. Cf. MS 158.4b.

126. HTSL 48.2b–3a.

127. HTSL 48.5a, 76.17b. Cf. Shen Te-fu, *Yeh-hu Pien,* 19.19a–21a.

128. HTSL 6.14a–b. Cf. MS 94.20a.

129. HTSL 42.10a.

130. HTSL 79.12a.

131. HTSL 83.8a–b.

132. HTSL 6.13a.

133. HTSL 113.14b.

134. HTSL 73.9a.

135. For Chang's restoration to office, see HTSL 79.4b. For his appointment as assistant censor-in-chief, see HTSL 113.5a.

136. HTSL 43.6b. Cf. MS 75.1b; Shen Te-fu, *Yeh-hu Pien,* 19.19a–21a.

137. HTSL 78.5a.

138. JTSL 1B.5b.

139. HTSL 19.4b.

140. HTSL 32.9b.

141. HTSL 64.15a.

142. HTSL 79.11a.

143. HTSL 74.5a.

144. HTSL 46.13a–b, 54.3a–b. Cf. Shen Te-fu, *Yeh-hu Pien,* 19.19a–21a.

145. HTSL 46.13a–b; Shen Te-fu, *Yeh-hu Pien,* 19.19a–21a.

146. JTSL 4A.8b.

147. HTSL 19.9b.

148. MHY 33.9b; CMMYL 48.9a–b. Cf. Ku Tso's biography in MS 158.2b–4b, and Yeh, *Shui-tung Jih-chi,* 2.12a–b, 6.4b.

149. HTSL 81.2b.

150. HTSL 84.16b–17a.

151. MS 158.2b–4b; *Ku-chin T'u-shu Chi-ch'eng, Kuan-ch'ang* section, 353.8a–9a.
152. See note 57 to Chapter 5.
153. STSL 26.1b.
154. STSL 30.29a–30b. Chao Nan-hsing also lamented that appointments as supervising secretaries were more valued than appointments as censors.
155. STSL 70.13b–14a, 78.3b.
156. STSL 39.8a, 52.21a; Hsü, *Hsiao-t'ien Chi-chuan,* 62.6a–7a.
157. STSL 23.1a, 57.7a–8a; MS 243.19b–21a.
158. See Chao Nan-hsing's biography in MS 243.1a–5b.
159. *Chung-cheng Piao-t'i,* by an unidentified compiler.
160. *Tung-lin Tang-jen Pang,* reproduced in many sources including Wen, *Hsien-po Chih-shih,* and Ch'en, *Tung-lin Lieh-chuan.*
161. *Tung-lin T'ung-chih Lu,* reproduced in Liu Jo-yü, *Cho-chung Chih Yü,* 1.24–29.
162. E.g., see KTSL 4.33a–34a; STSL 14.3b–4a, 19.29a–b, 27.27b–28a, 29.15a–b.
163. E.g., see KTSL 2.3a; STSL 5.24b–25a, 10.2a–3a, 12.1b, 22.5b–6a, 26.23b–24a, 39.4b–5a, 41.10b.
164. KTSL 1.8a.
165. STSL 61.23a–b.
166. STSL 43.13a.
167. KTSL 3.14b; STSL 5.33a, 77.20a.
168. STSL 5.29a, 9.18b.
169. STSL 12.8a, 13.18a, 15.4b–5a, 26.1a.
170. STSL 4.32b–33a, 5.7b, 24.22b–23a, 74.31a, 75.20b.
171. KTSL 1.36b–38a; STSL 2.8b–9b, 2.44a–45a, 2.52b, 38.10a, 40.2b, 48.5a, 58.10a–12a.
172. KTSL 4.28a–29a.
173. STSL 17.9b.
174. For the salary suspensions of Chang and Kao, see STSL 2.44a–45a. For that of Wang, see STSL 8.4b.
175. STSL 17.20b.
176. MS 241.3b–7a; STSL 74.11b–12a.
177. STSL 56.17b–18a, 59.10b–11a. Cf. K'ang P'ei-yang's biography in *Chi-nan-fu Chih* 52.27b–29a.
178. STSL 57.25b–26b, 63.16b; MS 231.4a; 243.3a–b, 5a; 306.25a–b.
179. STSL 55.38a, 58.18b–19a, 71.4a.
180. STSL 58.32a, 63.21a–22a, 72.4a.
181. STSL 66.13b–14a, 72.26b.
182. STSL 59.34a–35a, 72.17a–b, 73.25a.
183. STSL 69.4a, 76.2a.
184. STSL 54.1a, 54.12b–13a, 55.39a, 61.30a, 76.17b.
185. STSL 64.21a, 79.7a; *Chiang-nan T'ung-chih* 146.13b.
186. STSL 53.26b–27a, 61.17b, 79.35b.
187. STSL 58.18a–b, 65.31a–b, 81.7a.
188. STSL 47.3a. Cf. MS 243.4a–b.
189. STSL 53.16b, 59.13a, 70.24a, 82.21b–23a.
190. STSL 53.31b–33a, 60.18b, 76.32b. Cf. *Shun-t'ien-fu Chih* 107.20a.
191. Compilation of the blacklist of eunuch partisans, called *Ni An,* was

indeed a matter of great controversy. It is reproduced in Wen, *Hsien-po Chih-shih.*

192. MS 248.4b; STSL 57.3a–4a, 68.26a–b, 75.18a–b.

193. MS 275.1a–3b. Chang Shen-yen seems to have been very active as a censor in 1620, 1621, and 1622. After the sixth month of 1622, however, the *Shih-lu* makes no further mention of him. His MS biography, which is almost duplicated in *Shan-hsi T'ung-chih,* 131.19a–20a, gives no further information on him until the third month of 1625, when he apparently went home on leave. MS reports that he had previously offended Feng Ch'üan, who had become one of Wei Chung-hsien's protégés, and that Feng had friends impeach him for venality. In consequence, he was eventually sent to guard the frontier in modern Kansu, in the far northwest. Under Chuang-lieh-ti he was pardoned and resumed his career, finally becoming Nanking minister of personnel. I am unable to fill in any information on Chang's career in 1623 and 1624. Since Feng Ch'üan is generally considered responsible for mutilating the *Hsi-tsung Shih-lu* (see note 57 to Chapter 5), it is possible that he deleted from the records any references to this enemy after mid-1622.

194. MS 246.14a–16a; STSL 11.2a, 49.3a, 52.37b–38a, 66.7b, 74.11a–b.

195. STSL 6.4a–b, 15.4b–5a, 19.7b–8a, 19.37b–38a, 21.24a, 22.16a–b, 26.11a, 33.20a–22b, 52.33a–b, 55.42a, 73.27b.

196. MS 257.13a–15a; STSL 2.5a–b, 5.26b, 52.24a, 52.37b–38a, 60.8b, 65.1b.

197. STSL 56.4a–b, 59.31b, 64.15a–b. Cf. Fang Chen-ju's biography in MS 248.10b–13a.

198. STSL 52.37b–38a, 63.22b–23a.   199. Li Yen, *Tung-lin-tang,* p. 14.

200. STSL 61.33a; MS 245.20b–21a.   201. STSL 58.19a–b; MS 245.20b.

202. MS 244.23a–24b.

203. STSL 47.6b, 52.37b–38a, 56.17a. Cf. MS 244.1a–11a.

204. STSL 47.6b, 52.37b–38a, 56.17a. Cf. MS 244.11a–15a and Tso, *Nien-p'u.*

205. STSL 56.20a, 69.4a; MS 244.15b–19a.

206. MS 244.21b–23a.   207. MS 244.20a–21b.

208. STSL 63.35a–36a.   209. MS 245.1a–3a.

210. MS 245.3a–5a.

211. MS 245.5a–6b; Hucker, "Su-chou."

212. MS 243.15b–19b; STSL 65.20a–b.

213. MS 245.7b–11b; STSL 67.24b.

214. MS 245.15b–18b; STSL 68.13a.

215. Hummel, *Eminent Chinese,* I, 351–54.

216. Huang Tsung-hsi, *Ming-ju Hsüeh-an,* vol. 2 (section 12), p. 18.

217. MS 245.12a–15b; STSL 68.2a.

218. For the experiences of Yang Lien and Tso Kuang-tou in prison, see Tso, *Nien-p'u,* 2.5b ff.

219. *Ibid.,* 2.11b–12b, 2.17a–b.

220. *Ibid.,* 2.14a ff.

221. For the assessment of punitive damages, see STSL 65.20a.

222. Tso, *Nien-p'u,* 2.17a–b.

223. MS 244.11a.

Chapter seven

1. Ricci, *China in the 16th Century*, p. 49.
2. Medhurst, *China*, pp. 112–13.
3. Walker, "The Control System," pp. 12–14. Cf. Sun Yat-sen, *San Min Chu I*, pp. 356–57 (sixth lecture on the principle of people's democracy); and Wu Chih-fang, *Chinese Government*, p. 198.
4. Lin, *The Press and Public Opinion*, pp. 59–60.
5. Walker, "The Control System," pp. 19–20.
6. Williams, *The Middle Kingdom*, I, 431–33.
7. See Wright, *Chinese Conservatism*, p. 264.
8. Weber, *The Religion of China*, pp. 31, 48.
9. "Structure of the Chinese Government" (unsigned), p. 136. Williams, (*The Middle Kingdom*, I, 433) attributes these observations to E. C. Taintor.
10. Lin, *The Press and Public Opinion*, p. 62.
11. Finer, *Modern Government*, II, 863–64.
12. *Yüan-shih* 148.8b; cf. HTK ch. 54. Also cf. the judgment of a Swedish parliamentary committee in 1939 on the effectiveness of the public control officer called the Justitieombudsman (JO): "The less cause the JO has to intervene with his official authority the more surely is the objective of his office attained." See Chapman, *The Profession of Government*, p. 255.
13. Wittfogel's thesis, in its applications to China, is most succinctly stated in his article "Chinese Society," and is explained most fully in his book *Oriental Despotism*. The thesis has been criticized from different points of view by many scholars, including Mote in "Chinese Despotism," and Eisenstadt in "Oriental Despotisms."
14. Mote, "Chinese Despotism," pp. 18ff.
15. Ting, *T'e-wu Cheng-chih*.
16. On pp. 54–59 of his *Oriental Despotism*, where he discusses "the organization of quick locomotion and intelligence" in various "hydraulic" societies, and where he relates road systems and postal services to national intelligence services in some other societies, Wittfogel limits his comments about China to a discussion of the evolution and the workings of the postal-relay system.
17. Wittfogel, *Oriental Despotism*, p. 134.
18. *Ibid.*, pp. 135–36.
19. *Ibid.*, p. 136. My book *The Traditional Chinese State*, though not intentionally, seems to serve indirectly as a refutation of certain of Wittfogel's most emphasized theses.
20. Levenson, *Confucian China*, vol. 2 (*The Problem of Monarchical Decay*), especially Chapter V: "Confucianism and Monarchy: the Limits of Despotic Control."
21. *Ibid.*, p. 98.
22. *Ibid.*, p. 61.
23. *Ibid.*, p. 72.
24. Creel has persuasively argued that the traditional Chinese bureaucracy, in practice and in theory, did indeed measure up to Weber's criteria for a modern bureaucracy. See his article "Beginnings of Bureaucracy."

I agree with his principal thesis. However, the imperial bureaucracy in practice was by no means an apolitical administrative agent of the executive, as is commonly the case in modern states; it was an active political power in its own right.

25. Levenson, *Confucian China,* vol. 2, p. 62.

26. *Ibid.,* p. 73.

27. See the discussions of Hsiung T'ing-pi's career scattered through Chapter 5. Cf. his biography in MS 259.7a–24b.

28. STSL 15.24b.

29. See the discussions of the Tung-lin controversies in Chapter 5 and in my article "The Tung-lin Movement."

30. Chiang, *Tung-lin Shih-mo,* p. 33; MS 218.4a–9a (biography of Wang Hsi-chüeh).

31. Chiang, *Tung-lin Shih-mo,* p. 32; cf. MS 218.9a–14a (biography of Shen I-kuan).

32. Chiang, *Tung-lin Shih-mo,* p. 42; cf. MS 240.1a–9a (biography of Yeh Hsiang-kao).

33. MS 217.13b–15b (biography of Li T'ing-chi); cf. Chiang, *Tung-lin Shih-mo,* pp. 32–34.

34. MS 217.13b–15b.

35. Semedo, *The Monarchy of China,* p. 126.

36. *Ibid.,* p. 129.

37. E.g., see STSL 22.28b–29a, 23.8a–9a.

38. STSL 5.25b–26a.

39. STSL 35.40b.

40. STSL 2.34b–35a.

41. *Li-tai Chih-kuan Piao* I, 518–19.

42. Hucker, *The Traditional Chinese State,* p. 52.

Glossary and Bibliography

Glossary of Special Terms and Titles

Section I lists terms for which English
translations are given in the text
or Notes; Section II lists terms for which
only romanizations are given.

Section I, English

acting appointment, *shih-chih* 試職

administration commissioner, *pu-cheng shih* 布政使

administration vice commissioner, *ts'an-cheng* 參政

admonisher, *ssu-chien* 司諫

"annual provincial transfer," *nien-li wai-chuan* 年例外轉

Armory, *chün-ch'i chü* 軍器局

army-inspecting censor, *chien-chün yü-shih* 監軍御史

Army Inspecting Circuit, *chien-chün tao* 監軍道

assistant administration commissioner, *ts'an-i* 參議

assistant censor-in-chief, *ch'ien tu yü-shih* 僉都御史

assistant commissioner (of Regional Military Commission), *tu chih-hui ch'ien-shih* 都指揮僉事

assistant commissioner-in-chief, *tu-tu ch'ien-shih* 都督僉事

assistant county magistrate, *chu-pu* 主簿

assistant director (of Seal Office), *ssu-ch'eng* 司丞

assistant magistrate (subprefecture), *p'an-kuan* 判官

assistant minister (Court), *ssu-ch'eng* 寺丞

assistant prefect, *t'ung-p'an* 通判

assistant surveillance commissioner, *an-ch'a ch'ien-shih* 按察僉使

associate censor, *shih yü-shih* 侍御史

"avenues of criticism," *yen-lu* 言路

Battalion, *ch'ien-hu so* 千戶所

battalion commander, *cheng ch'ien-hu* 正千戶

battalion vice commander, *fu ch'ien-hu* 副千戶

branch Censorate, *hsing yü-shih t'ai* 行御史臺

branch Court of the Imperial Stud, *hsing t'ai-p'u ssu* 行太僕寺

branch Secretariat, *hsing chung-shu sheng* 行中書省

Bureau (in Ministry), *ch'ing-li ssu* 清吏司

Bureau of Appointments (Personnel), *wen-hsüan ch'ing-li ssu* 文選清吏司

Bureau of Ceremonies (Rites), *i-chih ch'ing-li ssu* 儀制清吏司

Bureau of Construction (Works), *ying-shan ch'ing-li ssu* 營膳清吏司

Bureau of Equipment (War), *ch'e-chia ch'ing-li ssu* 車駕清吏司

Bureau of Evaluations (Personnel), *k'ao-kung ch'ing-li ssu* 考功清吏司

Bureau of Forestry and Crafts (Works), *yü-heng ch'ing-li ssu* 虞衡清吏司

Bureau of Honors (Personnel), *yen-feng ch'ing-li ssu* 驗封清吏司

Bureau of Irrigation and Transportation (Works), *tu-shui ch'ing-li ssu* 都水清吏司

Bureau of Military Affairs, *shu-mi yüan* 樞密院

Bureau of Operations (War), *chih-fang ch'ing-li ssu* 職方清吏司

Bureau of Personnel (War), *wu-hsüan ch'ing-li ssu* 武選清吏司

Bureau of Provisions (Rites), *ching-shan ch'ing-li ssu* 精膳清吏司

Bureau of Provisions (War), *wu-k'u ch'ing-li ssu* 武庫清吏司

Bureau of Receptions (Rites), *chu-k'o ch'ing-li ssu* 主客清吏司

Bureau of Records (Personnel), *chi-hsün ch'ing-li ssu* 稽勳清吏司

Bureau of Remonstrance, *chien-yüan* 諫院

Bureau of Sacrifices (Rites), *tz'u-chi ch'ing-li ssu* 祠祭清吏司

Bureau of State Lands (Works), *t'un-t'ien ch'ing-li ssu* 屯田清吏司

"capital evaluation," *ching-ch'a* 京察

"case of the attack with the club," *ch'ih-t'ing an* 持梃案

"case of the red pills," *hung-wan an* 紅丸案

"case of the removal from the palace," *i-kung an* 移宮案

"case of the subversive book," *yao-shu an* 妖書案

censor, *yü-shih* 御史

censor-in-chief (pre-Ming), *yü-shih ta-fu* 御史大夫

censor-in-chief (Ming), *tu yü-shih* 都御史

Censorate (pre-Ming), *yü-shih t'ai* 御史臺 or *yü-shih fu* 御史府

Censorate (Ming), *tu ch'a-yüan* 都察院

Central Buddhist Registry, *seng-lu ssu* 僧錄司

Central Drafting Office, *chung-shu k'o* 中書科

Central Taoist Registry, *tao-lu ssu* 道錄司

ceremonial usher, *tsan-li lang* 贊禮郎

Chancellery, *men-hsia sheng* 門下省

chancellor of Hanlin Academy, *hsüeh-shih* 學士

chief clerk (Censorate), *tu-shih* 都事

chief clerk (Provincial Surveillance Office), *chih-shih* 知事

chief eunuch, *t'ai-chien* 太監

chief investigating censor, *chien-ch'a tu yü-shih* 監察都御史

Chief Military Commission, *tu-tu fu* 都督府

chief minister (Court), *ch'ing* 卿

chief supervising secretary, *tu chi-shih-chung* 都給事中

Chief Surveillance Office, *tu ch'a-yüan* 都察院

circuit, *tao* 道

circuit inspector (Han), *tz'u-shih* 刺史

circuit inspector (T'ang), *hsün-an yü-shih* 巡按御史

circuit intendant (Sung), *chien-ssu* 監司

circuit intendant (Ming), *tao-t'ai* 道臺

civil official, *wen-kuan* 文官

Coastal Patrol Circuit, *hsün-hai tao* 巡海道

collator, *chien-chiao* 檢校

College of Interpreters, *hui-t'ung kuan* 會同館

College of Translators, *ssu-i kuan* 四夷館

commission, *ch'ai-ch'ien* 差遣

commissioner-in-chief, *tu-tu* 都督

commissioner (Office of Transmission), *t'ung-cheng shih* 通政使

Company, *po-hu so* 百戶所

company commander, *po-hu* 百戶

"complied with," *chao-kuo* 照過

controller of the river, *ts'ao-chiang yü-shih* 操江御史

county, *hsien* 縣

county magistrate, *chih-hsien* 知縣

county vice magistrate, *hsien-ch'eng* 縣丞

court deliberation, *hui-i* 會議

Court of General Affairs, *t'ai-yüan* 臺院

Court of Imperial Entertainments, *kuang-lu ssu* 光祿寺

Court of Palace Affairs, *tien-yüan* 殿院

Court of Imperial Sacrifices, *t'ai-ch'ang ssu* 太常寺

Court of Surveillance, *ch'a-yüan* 察院

Court of State Ceremonial, *hung-lu ssu* 鴻臚寺

Court of the Imperial Stud, *t'ai-p'u ssu* 太僕寺

Defense Command, *liu-shou ssu* 留守司

Department of State Affairs, *shang-shu sheng* 尚書省

"delay," *chi-ch'ih* 稽遲

director (Ministry Bureau), *lang-chung* 郎中

director (Pasturage Office), *ch'ing* 卿

Directorate of Astronomy, *ch'in-t'ien chien* 欽天監

Directorate of Parks, *shang-lin-yüan chien* 上林苑監

district, *hsien* 縣

drafter, *chung-shu she-jen* 中書舍人

duke, *kung* 公

earl, *po* 伯

"ears and eyes of the emperor" *t'ien-tzu er-mu* 天子耳目

Eastern Depot, *tung-ch'ang* 東廠

education-intendant censor, *t'i-hsüeh yü-shih* 提學御史

Education Intendant Circuit, *t'i-tu hsüeh tao* 提督學道

Embroidered-uniform Guard, *chin-i wei* 錦衣衛

"error," *shih-ts'o* 失錯

erudite, *po-shih* 博士

eunuch, *huan-kuan* 宦官

"evasion," *mai-mo* 埋没

examiner, *chien-shih* 監試

fiscal intendant, *chuan-yün shih* 轉運使

functionary, *li* 吏

general, *chiang-chün* 將軍

General Accounts Section, *tu-chih k'o* 度支科

General Services Office, *ssu-wu t'ing* 司務廳

General Surveillance Circuit, *fen-hsün tao* 分巡道

generalissimo, *ta chiang-chün* 大將軍

granary-inspecting censor, *hsün-ts'ang yü-shih* 巡倉御史

Granary Section, *ts'ang k'o* 倉科

grand adjutant, *ts'an-tsan chi-wu* 參贊機務

grand commandant, *shou-pei* 守備

grand coordinator, *hsün-fu* 巡撫

grand councilor, *tsai-hsiang* 宰相

Grand Court of Revision, *ta-li ssu* 大理寺

grand guardian, *t'ai-pao* 太保

grand preceptor, *t'ai-shih* 太師

grand remonstrator, *chien-i ta-fu* 諫議大夫

Grand Secretariat, *nei-ko* 內閣

grand secretary, *ta hsüeh-shih* 大學士

grand supervisor of instruction, *chan-shih* 詹事

grand tutor, *t'ai-fu* 太傅

Guard, *wei* 衛

guard assistant commander, *chih-hui ch'ien-shih* 指揮僉事

guard commander, *chih-hui shih* 指揮使

guard judge, *chen-fu* 鎮撫

guard vice commander, *chih-hui t'ung-chih* 指揮同知

"guardians of the customs and fundamental laws," *feng-hsien kuan* 風憲官

Hanlin Academy, *han-lin yüan* 翰林院

Hanlin bachelor, *shu-chi-shih* 庶吉士

Imperial Academy of Medicine, *t'ai-i yüan* 太醫院

"in progress," *t'ung-chao* 通照

"inner court," *nei-t'ing* 內廷

intendant of transport and monopolies, *chih-chih fa-yün shih* 制置發運使

investigating censor, *chien-ch'a yü-shih* 監察御史

investigator (Ch'in), *chien-ch'a shih* 監察史

Irrigation Control Circuit, *shui-li tao* 水利道

judicial intendant, *t'i-tien hsing-yü* 提點刑獄

judicial review, *shen-lu* 審錄

judge (Grand Court of Revision), *p'ing-shih* 評事

judge (Provincial Administration Office), *li-wen* 理問

judge (Regional Military Commission), *tuan-shih* 斷事

judge (Guard), *chen-fu* 鎮撫

junior guardian, *shao-pao* 少保

junior preceptor, *shao-shih* 少師

junior supervisor of instruction, *shao chan-shih* 少詹事

junior tutor, *shao-fu* 少傅

junior tutor of the heir apparent, *t'ai-tzu shao-fu* 太子少傅

left supervising secretary, *tso chi-shih-chung* 左給事中

lesser functionary, *li* 吏

Literary Bureau, *nei-shu t'ang* 內書堂

loading expediter, *tsan-yün yü-shih* 儹運御史

magistrate (county), *chih-hsien* 知縣

magistrate (subprefecture), *chih-chou* 知州

marquis, *hou* 侯

mentor (Supervisorate of Imperial Instruction), *yü-te* 諭德

messenger, *hsing-jen* 行人

Messenger Office, *hsing-jen ssu* 行人司

metropolitan area, *ching-shih* 京師 or *chih-li* 直隸

Metropolitan Circuit, *ching-chi tao* 京畿道

Military Command, *shu-mi yüan* 樞密院

Military Defense Circuit, *ping-pei tao* 兵備道

military intendant, *an-fu shih* 安撫使

military officer, *wu-kuan* 武官

minister (Ministry), *shang-shu* 尚書

Ministry of Justice, *hsing-pu* 刑部

Ministry of Personnel, *li-pu* 吏部

Ministry of Revenue, *hu-pu* 戶部

Ministry of Rites, *li-pu* 禮部

Ministry of War, *ping-pu* 兵部

Ministry of Works, *kung-pu* 工部

Mint, *pao-yüan chü* 寶源局

monitor, *cheng-yen* 正言

Music and Dance Office, *shen-yüeh kuan* 神樂觀

National University, *kuo-tzu chien* 國子監

"nine chief ministers," *chiu ch'ing* 九卿

Northern Metropolitan Area, *pei chih-li* 北直隸

novice, *li-shih* 歷事 or *pan-shih* 辦事

Office for Surveillance, *an-ch'a ssu* 按察司

Office for the Rectification of Administration and for Surveillance, *su-cheng an-ch'a ssu* 肅政按察司

office manager, *ssu-wu* 司務

Office of Currency Supply, *ch'ao-chih chü* 抄紙局

Office of Music, *chiao-fang ssu* 教坊司

Office of Plate Engraving, *yin-ch'ao chü* 印鈔局

Office of Produce Levies, *ch'ou-fen chü* 抽分局

Office of Scrutiny, *k'o* 科

Office of Scrutiny for Justice, *hsing-k'o* 刑科

Office of Scrutiny for Personnel, *li-k'o* 吏科

Office of Scrutiny for Revenue, *hu-k'o* 戶科

Office of Scrutiny for Rites, *li-k'o* 禮科

Office of Scrutiny for War, *ping-k'o* 兵科

Office of Scrutiny for Works, *kung-k'o* 工科

Office of the Fundamental Law *hsien-ssu* 憲司

Office of Transmission, *t'ung-cheng ssu* 通政司

official, *kuan* 官

omissioner, *pu-ch'üeh* 補闕

"Outer Censorate," *wai-t'ai* 外臺

"outer court," *wai-t'ing* 外廷

"outer evaluation," *wai-ch'a* 外察

palace censor, *tien-chung shih yü-shih* 殿中侍御史

palace drafter, *chung-shu she-jen* 中書舍人

palace prison, *chen-fu ssu* 鎮撫司 (of the Embroidered-uniform Guard)

Pasturage Office, *yüan-ma ssu* 苑馬寺

Peking Branch Ministry, *pei-ching hsing-pu* 北京行部

Peking Gazette, *ti-ch'ao* 邸抄 or *ti-pao* 邸報

Police Office, *hsün-chien ssu* 巡檢司

Postal Service Circuit, *i-ch'uan tao* 驛傳道

prefect, *chih-fu* 知府

prefectural governor (of a capital prefecture), *fu-yin* 府尹

prefectural instructor, *chiao-shou* 教授

prefectural judge, *t'ui-kuan* 推官

prefecture, *fu* 府

prime minister, *tsai-hsiang* 宰相

prince, *wang* 王

Princely Establishment Administration Office, *wang-fu chang-shih ssu* 王府長史司

Princely Establishment administrator, *chang-shih* 長史

princess, *kung-chu* 公主

Prison Office, *ssu-yü ssu* 司獄司

prison superintendent, *ssu-yü* 司獄

probationary service, *li-cheng* 歷政

proctor, *sou-chien* 搜檢

province, *sheng* 省

provincial administration commissioner, *pu-cheng shih* 布政使

Provincial Administration Office, *ch'eng-hsüan pu-cheng ssu* 承宣布政司

provincial surveillance commissioner, *an-ch'a shih* 按察使

Provincial Surveillance Office, *t'i-hsing an-ch'a ssu* 提刑按察司

punishment regulator, *li hsing* 理刑

ration-expediting censor, *tu-hsiang yü-shih* 督餉御史

record-checking censor, *shua-chuan yü-shih* 刷卷御史

Record Checking Circuit, *shua-chuan tao* 刷卷道

record clerk, *chao-mo* 照磨

record clerk (in early Ming Censorate), *chao-mo kuan-kou* 照磨管勾

Record Office, *chao-mo so* 照磨所

"rectify administration," *su-cheng* 肅政

region (Yüan), *ch'u* 處 or *tao* 道

regional commander, *tsung-ping kuan* 總兵官

regional inspector, *hsün-an yü-shih* 巡按御史

Regional Military Commission, *tu chih-hui ssu* 都指揮司

regional military commissioner, *tu chih-hui shih* 都指揮使

regional military vice commissioner, *tu chih-hui t'ung-chih* 都指揮同知

regional vice commander, *fu tsung-ping kuan* 副總兵官

registrar, *ching-li* 經歷

Registry, *ching-li ssu* 經歷司

regulator of punishments, *li-hsing* 理刑

reminder, *shih-i* 拾遺

remonstrator, *chien-kuan* 諫官

right supervising secretary, *yu chi-shih-chung* 右給事中

river-control censor, *hsün-chiang yü-shih* 巡江御史

River Patrol Circuit, *kuan-ho tao* 管河道

"root of the state," *kou-pen* 國本

route (Yüan), *lu* 路

salt-control censor, *hsün-yen yü-shih* 巡鹽御史

Salt Control Circuit, *yen-fa tao* 鹽法道

Salt Distribution Commission, *tu chuan-yün yen shih-ssu* 都轉運鹽使司

Seal Office, *shang-pao ssu* 尚寶司

secretary (of Ministry Bureau), *chu-shih* 主事

secretarial censor, *chih-shu shih yü-shih* 治書侍御史

Secretariat, *chung-shu sheng* 中書省

Section (in Ministry Bureau), *k'o* 科

sentencer, *wen-hsing* 問刑

"seven chief ministers," *ch'i-ch'ing* 七卿

"source official," *yüan-shih* 源士

Southern Metropolitan Area, *nan chih-li* 南直隸

speaking censor, *yen-shih yü-shih* 言事御史

speaking official, *yen-kuan* 言官

Special Accounts Section, *chin-k'o* 金科

Statistics Section, *min-k'o* 民科

storehouse-inspecting censor, *hsün-k'u yü-shih* 巡庫御史

"straight-pointing commissioner," *chih-chih shih* 直指使

subprefecture, *chou* 州

substantive appointment, *shih-shou* 實授

Superintendency of Paper Currency, *pao-ch'ao t'i-chü ssu* 寶鈔提舉司

supervising secretary, *chi-shih-chung* 給事中

Supervisorate of Imperial Instruction, *chan-shih fu* 詹事府

supply-supervising censor, *tu-hsiang yü-shih* 督餉御史

supreme commander, *tsung-tu* 總督

supreme commander (Liaotung), *ching-lüeh* 經略

supreme duke, *shang-kung* 上公

surveillance commissioner, *an-ch'a shih* 按察使

surveillance commissioner (T'ang), *ts'ai-fang shih* 採訪使

surveillance commissioner (T'ang), *kuan-ch'a shih* 觀察使

Surveillance Office (Yüan), *t'i-hsing an-ch'a ssu* 提刑按察司

Surveillance Office (Yüan), *su-cheng lien-fang ssu* 肅政廉訪司

surveillance official, *ch'a-kuan* 察官

Surveillance Section (Sung), *ch'a-an* 察案

surveillance vice commissioner, *an-ch'a fu-shih* 按察副使

tael (Chinese ounce), *liang* 兩

"three great cases," *san ta-an* 三大案

"three judicial offices," *san fa-ssu* 三法司

"three provincial agencies," *san-ssu* 三司

touring commissioner (Sung), *hsün-shih* 巡使

training division, *ying* 營

translator (in early Ming Censorate), *i-shih* 譯事

transmission commissioner, *t'ung-cheng shih* 通政使

transport-control censor, *hsün-ho yü-shih* 巡河御史

Tribunal of Censors, *yü-shih t'ai* 御史臺 or *yü-shih fu* 御史府

troop purification, *ch'ing-chün* 清軍

Troop Purification Circuit, *ch'ing-chün tao* 清軍道

Tung-lin Academy, *tung-lin shu-yüan* 東林書院

Tung-lin Party, *tung-lin tang* 東林黨

usher (in early Ming Censorate), *yin-chin shih* 引進使

veto, *feng-po* 封駁

vice censor-in-chief (pre-Ming), *yü-shih chung-ch'eng* 御史中丞

vice censor-in-chief (Ming), *fu tu yü-shih* 副都御史

vice commissioner (Salt Distribution Commission), *t'ung-chih* 同知

vice commissioner-in-chief, *tu-tu t'ung-chih* 都督同知

vice commandant, *hsieh-t'ung shou-pei* 協同守備

vice director (of Ministry Bureau), *yüan-wai-lang* 員外郎

vice director (Seal Office), *shao-ch'ing* 少卿

vice minister (Court), *shao-ch'ing* 少卿

vice minister (Ministry), *shih-lang* 侍郎

vice prefect, *t'ung-chih* 同知

ward-inspecting censor, *hsün-ch'eng yü-shih* 巡城御史

Warden's Offices (in capital cities), *wu-ch'eng ping-ma ssu* 五城兵馬司

Western Depot, *hsi-ch'ang* 西廠

Section II, Chinese

ch'ao　超

chao-li　皂隸

chao-shua wen-chüan　照刷文卷

ch'ao-t'ing kang-chi　朝廷綱紀

ch'eng-fa　承發

cheng-fan ssu-tsui　正犯死罪

cheng-kuan　正官

cheng yü-shih　正御史

ch'ing-li chün-wu　清理軍務

chung　中

fang　房

feng-wen　風聞

hsiao　小

hsien-kang　憲綱

hsing　行

hsing-tsai　行在

hsün-an　巡按

hsün ch'a-ma yü-shih　巡茶馬御史

hsün-ch'ing　巡青

hsün ching-ying　巡京營

hsün-kuan yü-shih　巡關御史

hsün kuang-lu ssu yü-shih　巡光祿寺
御史

hsün-shih huang-ch'eng yü-shih　巡視
皇城御史

hsün-ts'ao yü-shih　巡操御史

jen-li　人吏

ju　儒

k'an-ho　勘合

kang-chi　綱紀

k'o-tao　科道

li　里

ling-shih　令史

men-tzu　門子

min　民

p'u-ping　舖兵

shen-ming　申明

shih　史

shih-lu　實錄

shou-ling-kuan　首領官

shu-li　書吏

shu-shou　書手

shua-chüan　刷卷

ssu-li　司吏

ssu-shou　司首

ta　大

t'ai-chien　臺諫

t'ai-sheng　臺省

t'ang-shang kuan　堂上官

teng　等

teng-wen ku　登聞鼓

t'ien-hsia　天下

tien-li　典吏

tsa-fan ssu-tsui　雜犯死罪

t'un-t'ien yü-shih　屯田御史

yin-ma yü-shih　印馬御史

yü　御

yü-tien　獄典

yüan　院

yün chuan　運甎

Bibliography

Works Cited Only by Alphabetical Abbreviations

CMMYL   Sun Ch'eng-tse 孫承澤. *Ch'un-ming Meng-yü Lu* 春明夢餘錄. Late Ch'ing blockprint edition.

CSPM   Ku Ying-t'ai 谷應泰. *Ming-shih Chi-shih Pen-mo* 明史紀事本末. *Wan-yu Wen-k'u* 萬有文庫 edition.

HTC   *Hsü T'ung-chih* 續通志. Reprint. Shanghai, 1936.

HTK   *Hsü Wen-hsien T'ung-k'ao* 續文獻通考. Reprint. Shanghai, 1936.

HTSL   *Hsüan-tsung Chang-huang-ti Shih-lu* 宣宗章皇帝實錄. Photolithographic reproduction, 1940.

HTT   *Hsü T'ung-tien* 續通典. Reprint. Shanghai, 1936.

JTSL   *Jen-tsung Chao-huang-ti Shih-lu* 仁宗昭皇帝實錄. Photolithographic reproduction, 1940.

KTSL   *Kuang-tsung Chen-huang-ti Shih-lu* 光宗眞皇帝實錄. Photolithographic reproduction, 1940.

MHY   Lung Wen-pin 龍文彬. *Ming Hui-yao* 明會要. Blockprint edition, 1887.

MS   *Ming-shih* 明史. Po-na edition, 1937.

MSHU   Fu Wei-lin 傅維鱗. *Ming-shu* 明書. *Kuo-hsüeh Chi-pen Ts'ung-shu* 國學基本叢書 edition.

MSK   Wang Hung-hsü 王鴻緒 et al. *Ming-shih Kao* 明史稿. Blockprint edition, 1723.

STSL   *Hsi-tsung Che-huang-ti Shih-lu* 熹宗哲皇帝實錄. Photolithographic reproduction, 1940.

TMHT   *(Ta) Ming Hui-tien* 大明會典. *Wan-yu Wen-k'u* 萬有文庫 edition.

TTSL   *T'ai-tsu Kao-huang-ti Shih-lu* 太祖高皇帝實錄. Photolithographic reproduction, 1940.

TWL   Ch'a Chi-tso 查繼佐. *Tsui-wei Lu* 罪惟錄. *Ssu-pu Ts'ung-k'an* 四部叢刊 edition.

WHTK   Ma Tuan-lin 馬端臨. *Wen-hsien T'ung-k'ao* 文獻通考. Reprint. Shanghai, 1936.

All Other Works Cited

Backhouse, E., and J. O. P. Bland. *Annals and Memoirs of the Court of Peking.* London, 1914.

Balazs, Etienne (trans.). *Le Traité juridique du "Souei-Chou."* Leiden, 1954.

Barnett, A. Doak. *Communist China: The Early Years, 1949-55.* New York, 1964.

Boxer, C. R. "Portuguese Military Expeditions in Aid of the Mings Against the Manchus, 1621-1647," *T'ien Hsia Monthly,* VII (1938), 24-36.

————. *South China in the Sixteenth Century.* London, 1953.

Brunnert, H. S., and V. V. Hagelstrom. *Present Day Political Organization of China.* Translated by A. Beltchenko and E. E. Moran. Shanghai, 1912.

Busch, Heinrich. "The Tung-lin Academy and Its Political and Philosophical Significance," *Monumenta Serica,* XIV (1949-50), 1-163.

Castonnet des Fosses, H. *La Chine sous les Ming.* Extrait des *Annales de l'Extrême-Orient et de l'Afrique.* Paris, 1887.

Chang Hsüan 張萱. *Hsi-yüan Wen-chien Lu* 西園聞見錄. Reprint of a Ming manuscript. Peking, 1940.

Chang T'ien-tse. *Sino-Portuguese Trade from 1514 to 1644.* Leiden, 1934.

Chapman, Brian. *The Profession of Government.* London, 1959.

Chavannes, Edouard (trans.). *Les Memoires historiques de Se-ma Ts'ien.* 5 volumes. Paris, 1895-1905.

Chen Chih-mai. "Impeachments of the Control Yüan: A Preliminary Survey," *Chinese Social and Political Science Review,* XIX (1935-36), 331-66 and 515-42.

Ch'en Ting 陳鼎. *Tung-lin Lieh-chuan* 東林列傳. Blockprint edition, 1711.

Chi-nan-fu Chih 濟南府志. Blockprint edition, 1850.

Chiang-nan T'ung-chih 江南通志. Blockprint edition, 1736.

Chiang P'ing-chieh 蔣平階. *Tung-lin Shih-mo* 東林始末. *Chung-kuo Li-shih Yen-chiu Tzu-liao Ts'ung-shu* 中國歷史研究資料叢書 edition.

Ch'ien Mu 錢穆. *Chung-kuo Li-tai Cheng-chih Te-shih* 中國歷代政治得失. Hong Kong, 1952.

————. *Kuo-shih Ta-kang* 國史大綱. Reprint edition, 2 volumes in 1. Shanghai, 1947.

Ch'ien Tuan-sheng. *The Government and Politics of China.* Cambridge, Mass., 1950.

Chin Jih-sheng 金日升. *Sung-t'ien Lü-pi* 頌天臚筆. Blockprint edition, 163-?

China Yearbook 1957-58. Taipei, 1958.

Ching-kuan K'ao-ch'a 京官考察. 2-volume manuscript, 1623 ?

Ch'ing-shih Kao 清史稿. Peking, 1928.

Chrimes, S. B. *An Introduction to the Administrative History of Mediæval England.* Oxford, 1952.

Chu Tung-jun 朱東潤. *Chang Chü-cheng Ta-chuan* 張居正大傳. Shanghai, 1947.

Chung-cheng Piao-t'i 衆正標題. Included in volume 4 of Ming dynasty manuscript collectanea entitled *Pi-ts'e Ts'ung-shuo* 秘冊叢說.

Crawford, Robert B. "Eunuch Power in the Ming Dynasty," *T'oung Pao,* XLIX (1961), 115-48.

Creel, H. G. "The Beginnings of Bureaucracy in China: The Origin of the *Hsien,*" *Journal of Asian Studies,* XXIII (1964-65), 155-84.

——. *The Birth of China.* New York, 1937.

——. *Confucius, the Man and the Myth.* New York, 1949.

de Bary, W. T. "Chinese Despotism and the Confucian Ideal," in *Chinese Thought and Institutions* (edited by J. K. Fairbank; Chicago, 1957,) pp. 163-203.

Dunne, George H. *Generation of Giants: The Story of the Jesuits in China in the Last Decades of the Ming Dynasty.* Notre Dame, Ind., 1962.

Duyvendak, J. J. L. "The True Dates of the Chinese Maritime Expeditions in the Early Fifteenth Century," *T'oung Pao,* XXXIV (1938), 341-412.

Eisenstadt, S. N. "The Study of Oriental Despotisms as Systems of Total Power," *Journal of Asian Studies,* XVII (1957-58), 435-46.

Fairbank, J. K., and S. Y. Teng. "On the Transmission of Ch'ing Documents," *Harvard Journal of Asiatic Studies,* IV (1939), 12-46.

——. "On the Types and Uses of Ch'ing Documents," *Harvard Journal of Asiatic Studies,* V (1940), 1-71.

Feifel, Eugene. *Po Chü-i as a Censor.* The Hague, 1961.

Finer, Herman. *The Theory and Practice of Modern Government.* 2 volumes. London, 1932.

Franke, Wolfgang. "Preliminary Notes on the Important Chinese Literary Sources for the History of the Ming Dynasty (1368-1644)," *Studia Serica Monographs,* series A, number 2. Chengtu, 1948.

———. "Yü Ch'ien, Staatsmann und Kriegsminister, 1398-1457," *Monumenta Serica,* XI (1946), 87-122.

Ginsburgs, George, and Arthur Stahnke. "The Genesis of the People's Procuratorate in Communist China, 1949-1951," *The China Quarterly,* no. 20 (October-December 1964), pp. 1-37.

Grimm, Tilemann. "Das Neiko der Ming-Zeit, von den Anfängen bis 1506," *Oriens Extremus,* I (1954), 139-77.

———. *Erziehung und Politik im Konfuzianischen China der Ming-Zeit.* Hamburg, 1960.

Han Fei Tzu 韓非子. *Han Fei Tzu Chi-chieh* 韓非子集解 edition. Shanghai, 1897.

Han Yü-shan. *Elements of Chinese Historiography.* Hollywood, 1955.

Ho Ping-ti. *The Ladder of Success in Imperial China.* New York, 1962.

Howorth, H. H. *History of the Mongols, from the 9th to the 19th Century.* 4 volumes. London, 1876-1927.

Hsiao I-shan 蕭一山. *Ch'ing-tai T'ung-shih* 清代通史. Volume I. Shanghai, 1927.

Hsieh Kuo-chen 謝國楨. *Ming Ch'ing Chih Chi Tang-she Yün-tung K'ao* 明清之際黨社運動考. Reprint. Shanghai, 1935.

Hsieh Pao Chao. *The Government of China, 1644-1911.* Baltimore, 1925.

Hsü Tzu 徐鼒. *Hsiao-t'ien Chi-chuan* 小腆紀傳. Late Ch'ing blockprint edition.

———. *Hsiao-t'ien Chi-nien* 小腆紀年. Late Ch'ing blockprint edition.

Huang Chang-chien 黃彰健 (editor). *Ming Shih-lu Chiao-k'an Chi* 明實錄校勘記. Volume 4. Taipei, 196-?.

Huang, Ray. *The Grand Canal During the Ming Dynasty.* Unpublished Ph.D. dissertation, University of Michigan, 1964.

Huang Ta-hua 黃大華. "Ming Ch'i-ching K'ao-lüeh" 明七卿考略, in *Er-shih-wu-shih Pu-pien* 二十五史補編, volume VI (Shanghai, 1936), pp. 8571-78.

Huang Tsung-hsi 黃宗羲. *Ming-ju Hsüeh-an* 明儒學案. *Kuo-hsüeh Chi-pen Ts'ung-shu* 國學基本叢書 edition.

Hucker, C. O. "Confucianism and the Chinese Censorial System," in *Confucianism in Action* (edited by D. S. Nivison and A. F. Wright; Stanford, 1959), pp. 182-208.

——. "Governmental Organization of the Ming Dynasty," *Harvard Journal of Asiatic Studies,* XXI (1958), 1-66.

——. "Su-chou and the Agents of Wei Chung-hsien," in *Silver Jubilee Volume of the Zinbun-Kagaku-Kenkyusyo,* Kyoto University (Kyoto, 1954), pp. 224-56.

——. "The Traditional Chinese Censorate and the New Peking Regime," *The American Political Science Review,* XLV (1951), 1041-57.

——. *The Traditional Chinese State in Ming Times (1368-1644).* Tucson, 1961.

——. "The Tung-lin Movement of the Late Ming Period," in *Chinese Thought and Institutions* (edited by J. K. Fairbank; Chicago, 1957), pp. 132-62.

——. "The Yüan Contribution to Censorial History," *Bulletin of the Institute of History and Philology,* Academia Sinica, extra volume number 4 (1960), 219-27.

Hummel, A. W. (editor). *Eminent Chinese of the Ch'ing Period.* 2 volumes. Washington, 1943-44.

Hung Mai 洪邁. *Jung-chai Sui-pi* 容齋隨筆. *Ssu-pu Ts'ung-k'an* 四部叢刊 edition.

Hung, William. *Tu Fu, China's Greatest Poet.* Cambridge, Mass., 1952.

Kao I-han 高一涵. *Chung-kuo Yü-shih Chih-tu Ti Yen-ko* 中國御史制度的沿革. Reprint. Shanghai, 1933.

Ko Shao-min 柯劭忞. *Hsin Yüan-shih* 新元史. Tientsin, 1922.

Kracke, E. A., Jr. "The Chinese and the Art of Government," in *The Legacy of China* (edited by R. Dawson; Oxford, 1964), pp. 309-39.

——. *Civil Service in Early Sung China, 960-1067.* Cambridge, Mass., 1953.

Ku Chieh-kang. "A Study of Literary Persecution During the Ming," translated by L. C. Goodrich, *Harvard Journal of Asiatic Studies,* III(1938), 254-311.

Ku-chin T'u-shu Chi-ch'eng 古今圖書集成. Photolithographic reproduction, 1934.

Ku Ling 顧苓. *San-ch'ao Ta-i Lu* 三朝大議錄. *Kuo-hsüeh Wen-k'u* 國學文庫 edition.

Ku Yen-wu 顧炎武. *Jih-chih Lu* 日知錄. *Kuo-hsüeh Chi-pen Ts'ung-shu* 國學基本叢書 edition.

Lan-t'ai Fa-chien Lu 蘭臺法鑑錄. Blockprint edition of the Wan-li period, reproduced as item 563 in the Library of Congress microfilm series entitled "Rare Books National Library Peking."

Latourette, Kenneth Scott. *The Chinese, Their History and Culture.* Third edition revised. New York, 1946.

Legge, James (trans.). *The Li-Ki.* Included in *Sacred Books of the East* (edited by Max Müller), volume XXVIII. Oxford, 1895.

———. *The Works of Mencius.* Included in his *The Chinese Classics,* second edition, volume II. Oxford, 1895.

Levenson, Joseph R. *Confucian China and Its Modern Fate.* Volume 2: *The Problem of Monarchical Decay.* Berkeley, 1964.

Li Chi 禮記. *Sung-pen Shih-san-ching Chu-shu* 宋本十三經注疏 edition, 1887.

Li Ch'ih 李燾. *Huang Sung Shih-ch'ao Kang-yao* 皇宋十朝綱要. Typeprint edition, n.d.

Li Hsiung-fei. *Les Censeurs sous la Dynastie Mandchoue (1616-1911) en Chine.* Paris, 1936.

Li-k'o Chi-shih-chung Shih-chi 禮科給事中仕籍. Blockprint edition of the period 1522-66, reproduced as item 1176 in the Library of Congress microfilm series entitled "Rare Books National Library Peking."

Li Kuang-t'ao 李光濤. "Chi Ming-chi Ping-ying Chih Chi-pi" 記明季兵營之積弊, *Ta-lu Tsa-chih* 大陸雜志, Vol. VI, no. 12 (June 1953), pp. 15-19.

———. "Mao Wen-lung Niang-luan Tung-chiang Pen-mo" 毛文龍釀亂東江本末, *Bulletin of the Institute of History and Philology,* Academia Sinica, XIX (1948), 367-488.

Li-tai Chih-kuan Piao 歷代職官表. *Kuo-hsüeh Chi-pen Ts'ung-shu* 國學基本叢書 edition. Shanghai, 1937.

Li Tao 李燾. *Hsü Tzu-chih T'ung-chien Ch'ang-pien* 續資治通鑑長編. Blockprint edition, 1819.

Li Wen-chih 李文治. *Wan Ming Min-pien* 晚明民變. Shanghai, 1948.

Li Yen 李棪. *Tung-lin-tang Chi-k'ao* 東林黨籍考. Peking, 1957.

Liang Fang-chung. *The Single-whip Method of Taxation in China.* Translated by Wang Yü-ch'üan. Cambridge, Mass., 1956.

Liao, W. K. (trans.). *The Complete Works of Han Fei Tzu.* Volume I. London, 1939.

Lin Yutang. *A History of the Press and Public Opinion in China.* Chicago, 1936.

———. *The Gay Genius: The Life and Times of Su Tungpo.* New York, 1947.

Linebarger, Paul M. A. *The China of Chiang K'ai-shek: A Political Study.* Boston, 1941.

———, Djang Chu, and Ardath W. Burks. *Far Eastern Governments and Politics: China and Japan.* Second edition. New York, 1956.

Ling-hsien Chih 陵縣志. Revised blockprint edition, 1875.

Liu Hsin-hsüeh 劉心學. *Ssu-ch'ao Ta-cheng Lu* 四朝大政錄. *Kuo-hsüeh Wen-k'u* 國學文庫 edition.

Liu Jo-yü 劉若愚. *Cho-chung Chih Yü* 酌中志餘. *Cheng-chiao-lou Ts'ung-k'o* 正覺樓叢刻 edition.

Lü K'un 呂坤. *Shih-cheng Lu* 實政錄. *Ch'ü-wei-chai Ch'üan-chi* 去偽齋全集 edition.

Mano Senryo 間野潛龍, "Kobucho no Tosatsuin ni tsuite" 洪武朝の都察院について, *Otani Daigaku Kenkyu Nempo* 大谷大學研究年報, XIII (1960), 209-36.

———. "Mindai Tosatsuin no Seiritsu ni tsuite" 明代都察院の成立について, *Shirin* 史林, XLIII (1960), 194-216.

Mayers, William Frederick. *The Chinese Government.* Shanghai, 1897.

Medhurst, W. H. *China: Its State and Prospects.* Boston, 1838.

Meng Sen 孟森. *Ming-tai Shih* 明代史. Taipei, 1957.

Michael, Franz. *The Origin of Manchu Rule in China.* Baltimore, 1942.

Mote, F. W. "Confucian Eremitism in the Yüan Period," in *The Confucian Persuasion* (edited by A. F. Wright; Stanford, 1960), pp. 202-40.

———. "The Growth of Chinese Despotism," *Oriens Extremus*, VIII (1961), 1-41.

———. *The Poet Kao Ch'i.* Princeton, 1962.

Naito Torajiro 内藤虎次郎. *Shina Shigakushi* 支那史學史. Tokyo, 1953.

Nieh Ch'ung-ch'i 聶崇岐. "Chung-kuo Chien-ch'a Chih-tu Chih Yen-pien" 中國監察制度之演變, in *I-shih Pao* 益世報 (Tientsin), October 14, 1947.

Pao Ch'eng 包拯. *Pao Hsiao-su Kung Tsou-i* 包孝肅公奏議. Blockprint edition, 1863.

Pulleyblank, E. G. *The Background of the Rebellion of An Lu-shan.* London, 1955.

Ratchnevsky, Paul. *Un Code des Yuan*. Paris, 1937.

Ricci, Matthew. *China in the 16th Century, the Journals of* . . . . Translated by Louis J. Gallagher. New York, 1953.

Rotours, Robert des (trans.). *Le Traité des examens, traduit de la nouvelle histoire des T'ang (Chap. XLIV-XLV)*. Paris, 1932.

———. "Les Grands fonctionnaires des provinces en Chine sous la dynastie des T'ang," *T'oung Pao*, XXV (1927), 219-332.

———. (trans.). *Traité des fonctionnaires et traité de l'armée, traduits de la nouvelle histoire des T'ang (Chap. XLVI-L)*. 2 volumes. Leiden, 1947-48.

Sah Mong-wu. "The Impact of Hanfeism on the Earlier Han Censorial System," *Chinese Culture*, I (1957), 75-111.

Semedo, C. Alvarez. *The History of That Great and Renowned Monarchy of China*. Translated from the Italian "by a person of quality." London, 1655.

Shan-hsi T'ung-chih 山西通志. Blockprint edition, 1892.

Shen Pang 沈榜. *Wan-shu Tsa-chi* 宛署雜記. Reprint. Peking, 1961.

Shen Te-fu 沈德符. *Yeh-hu Pien* 野獲編. Reprinted blockprint edition, 1869.

Sheng Lang-hsi 盛朗西. *Chung-kuo Shu-yüan Chih-tu* 中國書院制度. Shanghai, 1934.

Shun-t'ien-fu Chih 順天府志. Blockprint edition, 1876-78.

Siu Qui. *Le Pouvoir de Contrôle en Chine*. Nancy, 1937.

"Structure of the Chinese Government" (unsigned article), *The Chinese Repository*, IV (1835), 136.

Su Shih 蘇軾. *Tung-p'o Tsou-i* 東坡奏議, in *Su Tung-p'o Ch'uan-chi* 蘇東坡全集 (blockprint edition, 1908).

Sun, E-tu Zen (trans.). *Ch'ing Administrative Terms*. Cambridge, Mass., 1961.

Sun Feng-chi 孫逢吉. *Chih-kuan Fen-chi* 職官分紀. *Ssu-k'u Ch'uan-shu Chen-pen Ch'u-chi* 四庫全書珍本初集 edition.

Sun Yat-sen. *San Min Chu I: The Three Principles of the People*. Translated by F. W. Price. Edited by L. T. Chen. Shanghai, 1929.

Sung Hui-yao Kao 宋會要槁. Photolithographic reproduction, 1936.

Sung-shih 宋史. Po-na edition.

Ta Ming Lü Chi-chiai Fu-li 大明律集解附例. Reprinted blockprint edition, 1908.

Tang, Edgar Cha. "The Censorial Institution in China, 1644-1911," in Harvard University Graduate School of Arts and Sciences, *Summaries of Theses* . . . 1932 (Cambridge, Mass., 1933), pp. 155-58.

T'ao I-shih 陶以詩. *Kiangsi Fu-i Ch'uan-shu* 江西賦役全書. Fragmentary blockprint edition of the Wan-li period, reproduced in the Library of Congress microfilm series entitled "Rare Books National Library Peking."

T'ien-pien Ti-ch'ao 天變邸抄. *Chieh-yüeh Shan-fang Hui-ch'ao* 借月山房彙鈔 edition.

Ting I 丁易. *Ming-tai T'e-wu Cheng-chih* 明代特務政治. Peking, 1950.

Tout, T. F. *The Collected Papers of Thomas Frederick Tout.* Volume III. Manchester, 1934.

Tsao, W. Y. *The Constitutional Structure of Modern China.* Melbourne, 1947.

Tso Tsai 左宰. *Tso Chung-i Kung Nien-p'u* 左忠毅公年譜, appended to *Tso Chung-i Kung Wen-chi* 左忠毅公文集 (blockprint edition of the Ch'ing dynasty).

Tsou I 鄒漪. *Ch'i Chen Yeh-sheng* 啓禎野乘. Reprint. Peking, 1936.

Tung Tso-pin. *An Interpretation of the Ancient Chinese Civilization.* Taipei, 1952.

Tung, William L. *The Political Institutions of Modern China.* The Hague, 1964.

Tung-lin Shu-yüan Chih 東林書院志. Revised edition, 1881.

Van der Sprenkel, O. B. "High Officials of the Ming," *Bulletin of the School of Oriental and African Studies,* University of London, XIV (1952), 87-114.

————. "Population Statistics of Ming China," in *Bulletin of the School of Oriental and African Studies,* University of London, XIV, no. 2 (1953), 289-326.

Waley, Arthur (trans.). *The Analects of Confucius.* London, 1938.

————. *The Life and Times of Po Chü-i.* New York, 1949.

Walker, Richard L. "The Control System of the Chinese Government," *The Far Eastern Quarterly,* VII (1947-48), 2-21.

Wang Shih-chen 王世貞. *Yen-chou Shih-liao* 弇州史料. Blockprint edition of the Wan-li period.

————. *Yen-shan-t'ang Pieh-chi* 弇山堂別集. Blockprint edition, 1590.

Wang Te-chao 王德昭. *Ming-chi Chih Cheng-chih Yü She-hui* 明季之政治與社會. Chungking, 1942.

Wang Yi-t'ung. *Official Relations Between China and Japan, 1368-1549.* Cambridge, Mass., 1953.

Wang Yü-ch'üan. "An Outline of the Central Government of the Former Han Dynasty," *Harvard Journal of Asiatic Studies,* XII (1949), 134-87.

Watson, Burton. *Ssu-ma Ch'ien, Grand Historian of China.* New York, 1958.

Weber, Max. *The Religion of China.* Translated and edited by Hans H. Gerth. Glencoe, Ill., 1951.

Wen Ping 文秉. *Hsien-po Chih-shih* 先撥志始. *Chung-kuo Li-shih Yen-chiu Tzu-liao Ts'ung-shu* 中國歷史研究資料叢書 edition.

Williams, Samuel Wells. *The Middle Kingdom.* Revised edition, 2 volumes. New York, 1883.

Wist, Hans. *Das Chinesische Zensorat.* Hamburg, 1932.

Wittfogel, Karl A. "Chinese Society: An Historical Survey," *Journal of Asian Studies,* XVI (1956-57), 343-64.

————. *Oriental Despotism : A Comparative Study of Total Power.* New Haven, 1957.

Wright, Mary Clabaugh. *The Last Stand of Chinese Conservatism.* Stanford, 1957.

Wu Chao-ts'ui 吳兆莘. *Chung-kuo Shui-chih Shih* 中國稅制史. Shanghai, 1937.

Wu Chi-hua 吳緝華. *Ming-tai Hai-yün Chi Yün-ho Ti Yen-chiu* 明代海運及運河的研究. Taipei, 1961.

Wu Chih-fang. *Chinese Government and Politics.* Shanghai, 1934.

Wu Han 吳晗. *Chu Yüan-chang Chuan* 朱元璋傳. Shanghai, 1949.

Wu Ying-chi 吳應箕. *Tung-lin Pen-mo* 東林本末. *Kuei-ch'ih Hsien-che I-shu* 貴池先哲遺書 edition.

Yang Lien 楊漣. *Yang Ta-hung Chi* 楊大洪集. *Ts'ung-shu Chi-ch'eng* 叢書集成 edition.

Yeh Sheng 葉盛. *Shui-tung Jih-chi* 水東日記. Blockprint edition, 1680.

Ying Chia 應檟 et al. *Shen-lu Shu-lüeh* 審錄疏畧. Ming manuscript, reproduced as item 272 in the Library of Congress microfilm series entitled "Rare Books National Library Peking."

Yü Teng 于登. "Ming-tai Chien-ch'a Chih-tu Kai-shu" 明代監察制度概述, *Chin-ling Hsüeh-pao* 金陵學報, VI (1936), 213-29.

Yüan-shih 元史. Po-na edition.

Yüan Tien-chang 元典章. Reprinted blockprint edition, 1908.

Index

Index

Abahai, 157
Academies, 163, 214–15. *See also* Tunglin Academy; Hanlin Academy
Admonishers, 52
An Jan, 328
An Pang-yen, 157
An Shen, 209
Annam, 110, 128f, 140, 150, 267, 329
"Annual provincial transfers," 62, 269
Army-inspecting censors, 78, 250
Army Inspecting Circuit, 72
Assistant censors-in-chief, 49–51 *passim*
Assistant surveillance commissioners, 54, 70–73. *See also* Provincial Surveillance Offices
Associate censors, 12, 26, 47–48
"Attack with the club, case of," 164, 186, 231

Battalions, 33
Branch Censorates, 26–27, 52, 330–32
Branch Secretariats, 25–26
Buddhism, 130, 135, 188, 248–49
Bureau of Military Affairs, 6, 25
Bureau of Remonstrance, 18, 52ff, 325–26. *See also* Remonstrators
Bureaus (in Ministries), 39–40

Capital evaluations, 97, 163f, 167–68, 178, 195, 214
"Case of the attack with the club," 164, 186, 231
"Case of the red pills," 166–67, 185
"Case of the removal from the palace," 167, 185, 198, 206–7, 215–16, 274, 359
Censorate, Ming, 9, 47–52, 55–62 pas-
sim, 66, 164, 328; role in judicial administration, 100, 237–50. *See also particular censorial titles*; Branch Censorate; Nanking Censorate
Censorate, pre-Ming, 12–28 *passim*, 50, 56, 325–26. *See also* Branch Censorate *and particular censorial titles*
Censorship, *see* Censorial system
Censorial officials: use of terms explained, 9n; prestige and influence of, 20–22, 175–76, 297–300; magisterial powers of, 23, 27, 87, 124, 237–54; appointments, tenure, and promotions of, 57–62, 235, 256–58, 335–38 *passim*; career patterns of, 62–65, 339–40; independence of, 20–22, 54–55, 74, 326; punishments of, 13, 22, 179–80, 185, 254–86, 317–18, 325. *See also* Surveillance officials; Speaking officials; *and titles of particular censorial officials, especially* Investigating censors *and* Supervising secretaries
Censorial system: use of terms explained, 9n; early history of, 9–29; Ming organization of, 47–57; evaluations of, 287–301. *See also* Surveillance officials; Speaking officials; Remonstrators; *and titles of particular censorial agencies and offices, especially* Censorate; Offices of Scrutiny; Investigating censors; Supervising secretaries
Censors, 9n, 132, 322–23. *See also particular censors' titles* (Investigating censors, etc.); Censorate; Surveillance

Provincial governors, *see* Grand coordinators

Provincial Surveillance Offices: organization and functions of, 9, 38, 53–58 *passim*, 62, 70–73, 81, 88, 180–81, 250–53 *passim*; precursors of, 13–16; judicial role of, 98–99, 237–50 *passim*; declining censorial role of, 29, 57, 62, 249, 339

Punishments, 223, 232, 238, 275, 284; commutation of, 114, 143–46; of censorial officials, 13, 22, 179–80, 254–86, 317–18, 325; by censorial officials, 27, 87, 124, 244–45. *See also* Judicial administration

Ration-expediting censors, 81

Recommendations, censorial, *see* Proposals

Record checking, *see* Document control

Record-checking censors, 91, 104–7, 349

Record Checking Circuits, 71, 105

Record clerk, 47, 50, 54

Record Offices, 50, 51, 54

"Red pills, case of," 166–67, 185

Regional inspectors, 52, 70, 86–94, 164, 342, 345f; activities and powers of, 78, 84–85, 98–99, 105, 175, 228–29, 236, 238f, 244–46, 251–53 *passim*; disciplining of, 179–80, 256f

Regional Military Commissions, 33, 38, 54, 248

Registrars, 47, 50, 54

Registries, 50, 51, 54

Reminders, 17, 23, 52, 330, 333. *See also* Remonstrators; Speaking officials; Omissioners

Remonstrance, censorial, 6–8, 12–13, 16–20, 27–28, 131, 132–34, 205, 206–13. *See also* Remonstrators; Speaking officials

Remonstrators, 17–20, 22, 255, 325. *See also* Remonstrance; Speaking officials; Grand remonstrators; Omissioners; Reminders; Bureau of Remonstrance

"Removal from the palace, case of," *see under* "Case"

Revenues, *see* Taxes; Ministry of Revenue

Ricci, Matteo, 2–3, 86, 96–97, 229, 245, 287

Right supervising secretaries, 53

River-patrol censors, 82

River Patrol Circuits, 72

Salt-control censors, 83

Salt Control Circuits, 72

San-ch'ao Yao-tien, 217

Schools, 36–37, 137, 226, 245; censorial surveillance over, 71, 84–85; censorial proposals about, 138, 207

Secretarial censors, 26, 47f

Secretariat, 6, 12, 17–18, 25, 40, 46, 48f

Semedo, C. Alvarez, 86, 298–99, 343

"Seven chief ministers," 69

Shang dynasty, 10

Shao Ch'i, 263

Shao Fu-chung, 278

She Ch'ung-ming, 157

Shen Ch'un, 138

Shen Hsün, 231

Shen I-kuan, 298

Shen Ting, 125

Shen Ts'ui, 198, 360; censorial denunciations of, 275, 279–83 *passim*

Shen-tsung, Ming emperor, 43, 45, 83, 153, 155, 158–59, 161–65 *passim*, 356

Shen Wei-ping, 187

Shih-lu: general nature of, 118–19, 122; controversies over, 215–16; incompleteness of, 268–69, 350, 355–56

Shih San-wei, 192, 214, 217, 276

Shih-tsung, Ming emperor, 43, 45

Shih Yu-hsiang, 212

Shou-ling-kuan, 332

Shu Chi, 245

Soldiers, *see* Military service

Source officials, 53

Speaking officials, 9n, 13, 17f, 27–28, 52–53, 55, 132, 175–76, 236, 322–24. *See also* Censorial officials; Remonstrators; Supervising secretaries; Bureau of Remonstrance

Straight-pointing commissioner, 330

Su Shih, 325–26

Su Shu, 214

Subprefectures, 38

Sui dynasty, 323–24

Sun Ch'eng-tsung, 157, 230

Sun Chieh, 129, 187, 201; memorials of, 186, 190, 223, 228, 274, 360

Sun Shao-t'ung, 223

Sun Shen-hsing, 201, 360

Sun Wei, 64–65

Sun Yat-sen, 287

Sun Yu-ju, 209–10

Sung Chung, 247–48

Sung dynasty, 11–24 *passim*

Sung Shih-hsiang, 198, 211

DATE DUE

6/23			
JAN 30 1975			
GAYLORD			PRINTED IN U.S.A.